Consumer Credit

Law and Practice

Second Edition
by Alexander Hill-Smith

Practical Finance and Banking Guides

Consumer Credit: Law and Practice
Second Edition
by Alexander Hill-Smith
(2015)

Consumer Credit

Law and Practice

Second Edition

Alexander Hill-Smith
Barrister, New Square Chambers

informa law
from Routledge

Second edition published 2015
by Informa Law from Routledge
2 Park Square, Milton Park, Abingdon, Oxon OX14 4RN

and by Informa Law from Routledge
711 Third Avenue, New York, NY 10017

Informa Law from Routledge is an imprint of the Taylor & Francis Group, an informa business

First edition published by Sweet & Maxwell 1985

British Library Cataloguing in Publication Data
A catalogue record for this book is available from the British Library

Library of Congress Cataloging in Publication Data
A catalog record for this book has been requested

ISBN: 978-1-138-01991-1
eISBN: 978-1-315-77862-4

Typeset in Plantin
by Florence Production Ltd, Stoodleigh, Devon, UK

For Isobel, Edmund, Robert and Toby

For Isobel, Edmund, Peter and Toby

Outline contents

	Table of cases	xxi
	Table of statutes	xxv
	Table of statutory instruments	xxxvii
	Table of decisions, directives, regulations, treaties and conversions	xlvi
	Table of the Provisions of the FCA Handbook	xlvii
1	Key concepts in consumer credit law	1
2	The regulatory framework	35
3	Regulated activities and exempt agreements	44
4	Authorisation and the failure to obtain it	64
5	Continuing regulatory powers and obligations after authorisation	86
6	Advertisement and financial promotion	96
7	Pre-contract requirements	113
8	Requirements governing entry into agreements	128
9	Withdrawal and cancellation	155
10	Rights of the borrower and hirer	184
11	Rights and duties of the lender and owner	216
12	The provision and regulation of security	251

13 Regulated mortgage contracts: the Mortgages and Home Finance: Conduct of Business Sourcebook 271

14 The conduct of particular types of credit activity 304

15 Operation of ancillary credit activities 329

16 Powers of the court: the Financial Ombudsman Service 345

Index 367

Contents

Table of cases xxi
Table of statutes xxv
Table of statutory instruments xxxvii
Table of decisions, directives, regulations, treaties and conversions xlvi
Table of the Provisions of the FCA Handbook xlvii

1 **Key concepts in consumer credit law** 1
Credit 1
Consumer credit agreement 3
The definition of 'creditor' 4
The borrower 5
Running account and fixed sum agreements 6
Financial ceilings 8
Restricted and unrestricted use credit 9
Borrower-lender and borrower-lender-supplier agreements 11
Consumer hire agreements 14
Hire agreement and credit agreement 16
Financial limit 16
Small agreements 17
Multiple agreements 18
Linked transactions 20
Exceptions 22
Non-commercial agreements 22
Total charge for credit 24
The 1980 TCC Regulations and CONC Appendix 1.1 26
The APR 29
Assumptions to be made in calculating the APR 30
Land-related agreements 32
The 2010 TCC Regulations and FCA Handbook CONC Appendix 1.2 32

The charges to be taken into account 32
Assumptions 33

2 The regulatory framework **35**
The regulatory history of consumer credit and consumer hire 35
Director General of Fair Trading 35
Office of Fair Trading 36
Financial Services Authority 36
Consumer Credit Act 2006 37
Financial Conduct Authority 37
The Prudential Regulation Authority 38
The Competition and Markets Authority 38
Powers of the FCA 38
The structure and interpretation of the Handbook 40
Block 1: high level standards 41
Block 2: prudential standards 42
Block 3: business standards 42
Block 4: regulatory processes 42
Block 5: redress 43
Block 6: specialist sourcebooks 43
Tailored handbooks 43
Other guides 43

3 Regulated activities and exempt agreements **44**
Regulated activities 44
Regulated and exempt agreements for the purpose of the Consumer Credit Act 1974 and the RAO 46
Regulated Activities Order 47
Regulated mortgage contracts 47
Home reversion plans, home purchase plans and sale and rent back agreements 49
Regulated and exempt credit agreements for the purpose of the Regulated Activities Order 50
Credit for more than £25,000 for business purposes 51
Financing foreign transactions 51
The purchase of land on mortgage for non-residential purposes 52
Secured loans in relation to specific lenders 52
Low number of payments exemption 53
Exemption relating to the total charge for credit 55
Exemption relating to high net worth borrower 55

Hire agreement where payments exceed £25,000 56
Gas, electricity and water meters 56
Hire agreement entered into by high net worth hirers 56
Credit broking 57
The canvassing exception 59
Debt counselling, debt adjusting, debt collecting, debt administration 59
Debt counselling 60
Debt adjusting 60
Debt collecting 61
Debt administration 61
Electronic system in relation to lending 61
Credit reference agency 62

4 **Authorisation and the failure to obtain it** **64**
Application for authorisation 64
Consideration of the application 64
The threshold conditions 65
Procedure for determination of the application 67
Controlled functions 68
Failure to obtain approval 70
Interim permission and transitional arrangements 71
Interim permission 72
Appointed representatives 73
Exemption for professionals 75
Reference to the tribunal 77
Criminal liability for acting without authorisation 78
Civil consequences for breach of the authorisation requirements 80
Entry into agreements with unauthorised persons 80
Entry into agreements with persons with insufficient authorisation 80
Agreements made through unauthorised persons 81
Consequences of unenforceability 82
Discretionary enforcement by the court 83
Discretionary enforcement by the FCA 84

5 **Continuing regulatory powers and obligations after authorisation** **86**
Cancellation or variation of authorisation by the FCA 86
Prohibition order 88
Disciplinary action against an authorised person 89

Duties and disciplining of approved persons 91
Reporting 92
Notification of change in control 94

6 Advertisement and financial promotion **96**
Advertisements and other forms of financial promotion 96
General provisions 97
Advertisement of regulated credit agreements not secured on land 98
Promotion of credit agreements secured on land 99
Promotions by credit brokers 100
Unfair practices by lenders 100
Financial promotion of debt adjusting and debt counselling 101
Promotions not in writing 101
Quotations 101
Canvassing borrower-lender and ancillary credit agreements off trade premises 102
Circulars to minors 104
Unlawful financial promotions 106
Controlled activities and controlled investments 108
Types of controlled activities and controlled investments 108
Exempted communications 110
Consequences of unlawful financial promotion 111
Criminal sanctions 112
Misleading statements 112

7 Pre-contract requirements **113**
Disclosure of pre-contract information 113
Applicability of the Disclosure of Information Regulations 2004 113
Information that must be provided under the Disclosure of Information Regulations 2004 114
Sanctions for non-compliance 115
Distance contracts and distance marketing 115
Disclosure of Information Regulations 2010 117
The pre-contract information 118
Telephone contracts 118
Other types of distance contract 120
Pawn agreements 120
Authorised non-business overdraft agreement 120
Financial Services (Distance Marketing) Regulations 2004: disclosure of information 121

Disclosure of information with hire contracts 122
Information requirements 123
Pre-contract explanations 123
Copy of prospective agreement 125
Creditworthiness assessment 126

8 Requirements governing entry into agreements 128
Agreements outside the formalities requirements 128
Waiver 130
Operation of the Agreements Regulations 130
The Agreements Regulations 2010 132
The 1983 Agreements Regulations 133
Failure to comply with the Agreements Regulations 134
Duty to supply a copy of the executed agreement 134
Authorised business and non-business overdrafts 135
The supply of copies: the original requirements 137
The form of copies to be supplied 138
Consequences 141
Formalities involving agreements secured on land 141
To what agreements the procedures apply 141
Pre-contract requirements 142
The formalities of entering into an agreement 143
Following the agreement 146
Modifying agreements and variation 146
Variation 146
Varying the interest rate 148
Section 82(1) variations 149
Modifying agreements 150
Service under the Consumer Credit Act 1974 151
Manner of service 152
Timing of service 153

9 Withdrawal and cancellation 155
Common law right of withdrawal 155
Withdrawal under the Consumer Credit Act 156
Upon whom may notice of withdrawal be served? 156
The effect on linked transactions 157
Financial consequences of withdrawal 159
Withdrawal from a concluded agreement 159
Withdrawal from a modifying agreement 161
The right of cancellation under the Consumer Credit Act 1974 161

What is a cancellable agreement? 161
The modifying agreement 164
The formalities required with a cancellable agreement 164
One copy 165
Exemption from the second cancellation notice 166
Contractual cancellation rights 167
Failure to comply with cancellation formalities 167
Method of cancellation 169
The consequences of cancellation and withdrawal under the Consumer Credit Act 1974 171
The effect on the main agreement 171
The effect on linked transactions 172
Money paid by the borrower or hirer or relative prior to cancellation 173
Money paid to the borrower by the lender prior to cancellation 174
Goods received by the borrower or hirer or relative prior to cancellation 177
Goods given by the borrower in part exchange 179
The effects of cancellation on security provided 180
Cancellation rights under the Financial Services (Distance Marketing) Regulations 2004 181
Cancellation under the Consumer Contracts (Information, Cancellation and Additional Charges) Regulations 2013 182

10 Rights of the borrower and hirer **184**
The borrower's right to information 184
The statement of information 185
The copy agreement 186
Consequences of failure to comply 186
The duty to provide statements of account 187
Running account agreements 187
Content of statements of account 187
When must statements be provided? 188
Dispensing notices 189
Sanctions with running account agreements 189
Statements of account with fixed sum agreements 190
Content of fixed sum annual statements 190
Consequences of failure to comply 191
Fixed sum instalment statements 191
The right to terminate a hire purchase or conditional sale agreement 192

Exercising the right of termination 192
Consequences of termination 193
Return of the goods 193
Financial consequences 194
Worked example 195
Comparison with early settlement 196
The hirer's right to terminate a hire agreement 197
Termination of open-end credit agreements 198
Liability of the lender for the conduct of the negotiator 199
The requirements that goods must be sold or proposed to be sold by the credit broker to the creditor 201
Section 56(1)(c) 202
No deemed agency with lease agreements 202
Serving notice of rescission 203
Liability of the lender for breach of the supply contract 204
Agreements to which section 75 applies 204
The statutory indemnity 205
Extent of a lender's liabilities 206
Rights against goods 207
Extra-territorial effect 208
Cash price in excess of £30,000 208
The interrelation between sections 56 and 75 208
Challenging unfair contract terms: the unfair terms in Consumer Contracts Regulations 1999 209
When the regulations apply 210
When does the unfairness test apply? 210
The core exclusion 211
Applying the unfairness test 212
The list of illustrative terms 213
An individual challenge to fairness 214
Regulatory challenge 214

11 Rights and duties of the lender and owner 216
Collecting arrears 216
Disputed debts 218
Collecting payments following assignment 218
Sending out arrears notices 219
When an arrears notice is needed with a fixed sum credit agreement 219
An arrears notice with a running account agreement 220
The contents of the arrears notices 221
Contents of fixed sum credit agreement arrears notices 222

Content of a running account arrears notice 222
Failure to serve a required arrears notice 223
Time order 223
Default sum notice 223
Contents of a default sum notice 224
Consequences of failure to serve a default sum notice 224
Interest on a default sum 224
Using continuous payment authorities 225
Operating the continuous payments authority 226
Cancellation 227
Requirement for a default notice 227
When a default notice is needed 227
General form and contents of default notices 228
Specific information to be included in a default notice 229
Default information sheet 231
Service of a default notice 231
Errors in the default notice 232
Actions of the borrower following service of a default notice 233
Effects of an invalid notice 234
Enforcement and termination notices 236
Form and contents of enforcement and termination notices 237
Recovery of goods under hire purchase, conditional sale and hire agreements 238
Contravention of section 92 239
Protected goods 240
When goods become protected 241
Addition of goods 242
Consent by the borrower 243
Termination by the borrower 244
Consequences of wrongful repossession of goods 245
Procedure on an application to recover goods 245
Enforcement following the death of the borrower or hirer 246
Handling complaints 247

12 The provision and regulation of security **251**
Security 251
Types of security 252
Surety and security instrument 253
Formalities connected with the security instrument 253
Formalities in connection with security to be provided by the borrower or hirer 255

The continuing rights of the surety 255
The right to withdraw 255
The right to receive further copies of the agreement and further copies of the security instrument: the right to a statement of information 255
Extent of liability of a surety 257
Improper execution of a security instrument and of the regulated credit or hire agreement 258
Ineffective security 259
Transfer of land charges 260
Exercise of a power of sale in the case of ineffective mortgage security 262
Negotiable instruments as security 263
Taking payment, taking security and negotiating a cheque 265
Exceptions to section 123 266
Consequences of non-compliance with section 123 267
Third party rights in a negotiable instrument 268
Anomalies 269

13 Regulated mortgage contracts: the Mortgages and Home Finance: Conduct of Business Sourcebook **271**
Scope of the Mortgages and Home Finance: Conduct of Business Sourcebook 271
General principles of conduct of business 272
Financial promotion of regulated mortgage contracts 273
Exempt transactions 274
Non-real time financial promotions 275
Real time financial promotions 277
Initial disclosure by the firm to the customer on initial contact 277
Assessing the suitability of the regulated mortgage contract 279
Execution-only transactions 281
Procedure for an execution-only sale 282
Policy and record keeping 283
Providing the customer with an illustration 284
The mortgage offer 285
Information to be given following entry into the regulated mortgage contract 286
Annual mortgage statements 287
Notification of changes in terms 288
Further advances 288
Rate switches and removal of a party 289
Alteration in payment amounts 289

Further advances with a business loan, or loan to a high net worth individual 290
Calculation of APR 291
Responsible lending 291
Assessment of affordability 292
Income 292
Outgoings 293
Policy 294
Loans solely for business purposes and for high net worth individuals 294
Interest-only mortgages 295
Interest roll-up mortgages 296
Bridging loan 297
Regulating the level of charges imposed on the borrower 297
Excessive charges 298
Early repayment charges 298
Payment shortfall charges 299
Recovery of arrears 299
Dealing with customers in arrears 299
Record keeping 301
Provision of information in relation to arrears 301
Repossession proceedings 302

14 The conduct of particular types of credit activity **304**
The conduct of credit token agreements 304
Misuse of credit tokens 306
Overdraft agreements 308
Authorised business overdraft 309
Authorised non-business overdraft 310
Non-business overdraft agreements where the overdraft may be repaid more than three months later 310
Disclosure of pre-contract information 311
Pre-contract explanations 312
Creditworthiness assessment 312
Entry into the agreement 312
Signature of the agreement 313
Copy of the agreement 313
Withdrawal 314
Subsequent variation of interest rates 314
Tacit agreement to allow an overdraft 315
Termination of an overdraft agreement 315

High-cost short-term credit 316
HCSTC agreements and continuous payment authorities 317
Rolling over HCSTC agreements 319
APR cap 320
Taking a pawn 320
Entering into the pawn agreement: the regulatory requirements 321
Record keeping 323
Borrower's right to redeem 323
Consequences of a failure to redeem 324
Realisation of the pawn 326
Default notice? 327
Application for a time order 328

15 Operation of ancillary credit activities **329**
Conduct of credit brokers 329
Fees and commissions 331
Return of brokerage fees 331
Regulation of credit reference agencies 333
Obligations of the lender and credit broker 333
Obligations of the credit reference agency under the Data Protection Act 1998 335
Obligations of the credit reference agency under section 158 of the Consumer Credit Act 1974 336
The right of the consumer to seek correction of an entry 337
Debt advice and debt management agreement 339
Requirements prior to contract 339
The debt management agreement 340
The financial statement 340
The debt solution proposed 341
Operating the debt management agreement 341
Operating an electronic lending platform 342
Pre-contract information and explanations 342
The right of withdrawal from a P2P agreement 343
Arrears notice obligations 344
High-cost short-term credit agreements 344

16 Powers of the court: the Financial Ombudsman Service **345**
The power of the court to make an enforcement order 345
When an enforcement order is needed 345
Irredeemable unenforceability 346

Approach of the court of an application for an enforcement order 347
Procedure 348
Power of the court to make a time order 348
When a time order can be sought 348
The powers of the court on a time order 349
The effect of a time order 350
Procedure 351
Powers of the court in relation to recovery of goods 352
Return orders 352
Transfer order 353
Example 355
Procedure 355
Powers of the court in respect of unfair relationships 356
The extent of the jurisdiction 356
The matters to which the court will have regard 357
Unfairness 359
Procedure 361
Financial Ombudsman Service 362
Referring a complaint to the Financial Ombudsman Service 362
Procedure of the Financial Ombudsman Service 364
The award of the Ombudsman 365

Index 367

Table of cases

Advanced Industrial Technology Corporation Ltd *v.* Bond Street Jewellers Ltd 2006 EWCA Civ 923 320
Attorney-General for Belize *v.* Belize Telecom 2009 1 WLR 1988 10

Bank of Scotland *v.* Euclidian (No 1) 2007 CTLC 151; 2007 EWHC 1732 .... 168, 251
Bentinck Ltd *v.* Cromwell Engineering Ltd 1971 1 QB 324 244
Black Horse Ltd *v.* Langford 2007 RTR 38; 2007 EWHC 907 (QB) 201
Brandon *v.* American Express Services Europe Ltd 2011 CTLC 177; 2011 EWCA Civ 1187 237
Branwhite *v.* Worcester Works Finance Ltd [1969] 1 AC 552 .... 180, 200
Brierly *v.* Kendall 1852 17 QB 937 .... 235, 327
Brown and others *v.* Innovatorone Ltd 2012 EWHC (Comm) 1321 82
Brown *v.* Sheen and Richmond Car Sales Ltd 1950 1 All ER 1102 202
Byrne & Co *v.* Leon van Tienhoven 1850 5 CPD 344 155

Calladine-Smith *v.* Saveorder Ltd 2011 3 EGLR 55; 2011 EWHC 2501 .... 154, 231
Can *v.* James Broderick & Co 1942 2 KB 275 240
Capital Finance Ltd *v.* Bray 1964 1 WLR 323 193
Carey *v.* HSBC Bank plc 2010 CTLC 121; 2009 EWHC 3417 186
Carr *v.* James Broderick & Co Ltd [1942] 2 KB 275 245
CF Asset Finance Ltd *v.* Okonji 2014 EWCA Civ 870 156
Chartbrook Ltd *v.* Persimmon Homes Ltd 2009 AC 1101 11
Cityland and Property (Holdings) Ltd *v.* Dabrah 1968 Ch 166 298
Clark *v.* In Focus Asset Management and Tax Solutions 2014 1 WLR 2502 365
Conlon *v.* Black Horse Ltd 2013 EWCA Civ 1658 359–60
Consolidated Finance *v.* Collins 2013 CTLC 121; 2013 EWCA Civ 475 11
Consolidated Finance *v.* McCluskey 2012 CTLC 133; 2012 EWCA Civ 1325 10
Cuckmere Brick Co *v.* Mutual Finance Ltd 1971 Ch 949 302

Deutsche Bank (Suisse) SA *v.* Khan 2013 EWHC 482 (Comm) 359
Dimond *v.* Lovell 2000 1 QB 216 (Court of Appeal); 2002 1 AC 384 (House of Lords) 1, 2, 16, 346
Director General of Fair Trading *v.* First National Bank plc 2002 1 AC 481 .... 211, 212, 213, 359
Durkin *v.* DSG Retail Ltd 2014 1 WLR 1148; 2014 UKSC 21 ..... 206, 207, 333

Edginton *v.* Fitzmaurice 1885 29 ChD 459 163
Egan *v.* Langham Investments Ltd [1938] 1 KB 667 131
Eshun *v.* Moorgate Mercantile Ltd 1971 1 WLR 722 235

Faith Panton Property Ltd *v.* Hodgetts 1981 1 WLR 927 353
F.C. Finance Ltd *v.* Francis 1970 114 SJ 568 244
Fileman *v.* British Railway Traffic and Electric Company Ltd 1945 171 LT 407 240
Financings Ltd *v.* Stimson 1962 1 WLR 1184 155
First National Bank Ltd *v.* Syed 1990 2 All ER 250 349
Fitzwilliam *v.* Richall Holding Services Ltd 2013 1 P & CR 19 261
Forthright Finance *v.* Ingate 1997 4 All ER 99 201

George Mitchell (Chesterhall) *v.* Finney Lock Seeks Ltd 1983 2 AC 803 359
Goldsmiths Co *v.* West Metropolitan Railway Co [1904] 1 KB 1 138
Goshawk Dedicated (No 2) Ltd *v.* Bank of Scotland 2006 2 All ER 610 .... 6, 7, 8, 22, 139, 168, 173, 346
Governor and Company of the Bank of Scotland *v.* Euclidian (No 1) Ltd 2007 EWHC 1732 (Comm) 168, 251

Hanyet Securities Ltd *v.* Mallett [1968] 1 WLR 1265 131
Harris *v.* Lombard New Zealand Ltd 1974 2 NZLR 161 240
Harrison *v.* Black Horse Ltd 2012 Lloyds' Rep IR 521; 2011 EWCA Civ 1128 .... 359, 359–60
Hector Whaling Ltd 1936 1 Ch 208, Re 231
Helden *v.* Strathmore Ltd 2011 Bus LR 1592; 2011 EWCA Civ 542 .... 23, 45, 83
Humberclyde Finance Ltd *v.* Thompson 1997 CCLR 23 27

J P Morgan Chase Bank NA *v.* Northern Rock (Asset Management) plc 2014 1 WLR 2197 191
Jarrett *v.* Barclays Bank plc 1999 QB 1 208
Joblin *v.* Watkins and Roseveare Motors Ltd [1949] 1 All ER 47 321
Johnson *v.* Agnew 1979 1 All ER 883 203
Jones (R.E.) Ltd *v.* Waring and Gillow Ltd [1926] AC 670 267
Jones *v.* Link Financial Ltd 2013 1 WLR 693 .... 4, 260
Julian Hodge Bank *v.* Hall 1998 CCLR 14 241

Ketley *v.* Gilbert 2001 RTR 327 54
Kiriri Cotton Co *v.* Dewani 1960 AC 192 234

Lagden *v.* O'Connor 2003 QB 36 15
Lombard Tricity Finance Ltd *v.* Paton 1989 1 All ER 918 147
London North Securities Ltd *v.* Meadows 2005 EWCA Civ 956 28
London Scottish Finance Ltd, Re, 2013 EWHC 4047; 2014 Bus LR 424 .... 260, 358

Malory Enterprise Ltd *v.* Cheshire Homes (UK) Ltd 2002 Ch 216 261
Maple Leaf Volatility Master Fund *v.* Rouvroy 2009 CCLR 9; 2009 EWHC 257 (Comm) 2, 359
McGinn *v.* Grangewood Securities Ltd 2002 EWCA Civ 552 26
McGuffick *v.* The Royal Bank of Scotland plc 2010 1 All ER 634; 2009 EWHC 2386 (Comm) 82, 187
McMillan Williams *v.* Range 2004 1 WLR 1858 .... 1, 2
Mercantile Credit Ltd *v.* Cross 1965 QB 205 .... 239, 244
Modern Light Cars Ltd *v.* Seals 1934 1 KB 32 264
Moody *v.* Godstone 1966 1 WLR 1085 154
Morris *v.* Brown & Co 1918 AC 1 147
Multiservice Bookbinding Ltd *v.* Marden 1979 Ch 84 298

Nash and Staunton *v.* Paragon Finance plc 2001 EWCA Civ 1466; 2002 1 WLR 685 .... 31, 147, 148, 357
National Westminster Bank *v.* Story, Pallister 1999 CCLR 70 10
Nejad *v.* City Index Ltd 2000 CCLR 7; 2001 GCCR 2461 2
Nissan Finance *v.* Lockhart 1993 CCLR 39 347

Office of Fair Trading *v.* Abbey National Bank plc 2010 1 AC 696 212
Office of Fair Trading *v.* Ashbourne Management Services 2011 CTLC 237; 2011 EWHC 1237 (Ch) 212
Office of Fair Trading *v.* Foxtons Ltd 2010 1 WLR 663 215
Office of Fair Trading *v.* Lloyds TSB plc 2006 2 All ER 821; 2007 1 QB 1 13
Office of Fair Trading *v.* Lloyds TSB plc 2008 1 All ER 205; 2003 1 AC 316 208
Oscar Chess Ltd *v.* Williams [1957] 1 WLR 370 131

Palk *v.* Mortgage Service Funding plc 1993 Ch 330 303
Paragon Mortgages Ltd *v.* McEwan-Peters 2011 EWHC 2491 (Comm) 359
Parker-Tweedale *v.* Dunbar Bank plc 1991 Ch 12 303
Patel *v.* Patel 2009 EWHC 3264 358
Plevin *v.* Paragon Personal Finance Ltd 2013 EWCA Civ 1658 .... 358, 359–60
Plevin *v.* Paragon Personal Finance Ltd 2014 1 WLR 4222; 2014 UKSC 61 .... 358, 360
Porter *v.* General Guarantee Corporation Ltd 1982 RTR 384 204
Price *v.* Romilly 1960 1 WLR 1360 233
Prohotovot' s.r.o. *v.* Kor Kovska C76/10 211
Purnell Secretarial Services Ltd *v.* Lease Management Services Ltd 1994 CCLR 127 201–2

R (Heather Moor & Edgecomb Ltd) *v.* Financial Ombudsman Service 2009 1 All ER 328; 2008 EWCA Civ 642 .... 364, 365
R *v.* Carr-Briant 1943 2 All ER 156; 1943 KB 607 .... 105, 325
R *v.* County of London Quarter Sessions Appeal Committee 1956 1 QB 682 154
Rahman *v.* HSBC Bank plc 2012 EWHC 11 (Ch) 359
Rahman *v.* Sterling Credit 2001 1 WLR 496 357
Rankline *v.* American Express Services Europe Ltd 2009 CCLR 3 187
Reading Trust Ltd *v.* Spero 1930 1 KB 492 .... 168, 233
Regina (Davies) *v.* Financial Services Authority 2004 1 WLR 185 77

Savva *v.* Hussein 1996 2 EGLR 65 230
Schnabel *v.* Allard 1967 1 QB 627 231
Scotland *v.* British Credit Trust 2014 EWCA Civ 290 358
Silvester *v.* Ostrowska 1959 1 WLR 1060 233
Singer Manufacturing Company *v.* Clark 1880 61 LTR 591 320
Smeaton *v.* Equifax plc 2013 2 All ER 959; 2013 EWCA Civ 108 333
Southern and District Finance plc *v.* Barnes 1996 1 FCR 679 .... 349, 350
Southern Pacific Mortgages Ltd *v.* Heath 2010 Ch 254; 2010 2 WLR 1081 .... 18, 19, 20
Southern Pacific Personal Loans Ltd 2013 EWHC 2485 335
Southern Personal Loans Ltd *v.* Walker 2010 4 All ER 277; 2010 1 WLR 1819 3
Stena Line *v.* Merchant Navy Ratings Pension Fund Trustees 2011 Pens LR 223; 2011 EWCA Civ 543 10

Temperance Loan Fund Ltd *v.* Rose 1932 2 KB 522 .... 168, 233
Thew *v.* Cole 2004 RTR 25 54
TRM Copy Centre (UK) Ltd *v.* Lanwall Services Ltd 2009 1 WLR 1375 .. 14, 15

Underwood Ltd *v.* Martins Bank Ltd 1924 1 KB 775 266
United Dominion Trust Ltd *v.* Bycroft 1954 1 WLR 345 264
United Dominion Trust Ltd *v.* Ennis [1968] 1 QB 54 .... 193, 245
United Dominion Trust Ltd *v.* Taylor 1980 SLT 28 206
Unity Finance Ltd *v.* Woodcock 1963 1 WLR 455 .... 251, 252

Watchtower Investments Ltd *v.* Payne 2001 GCCR 3055; 2001 EWCA Civ 1159 .... 3, 26
West Bromwich Building Society *v.* Wilkinson 2005 1 WLR 2303 303
Wilson *v.* First County Trust Ltd 2001 QB 407 322
Wilson *v.* First County Trust Ltd (No 2) 2004 1 AC 816 .... 168, 346
Wilson *v.* Robertsons (London) Ltd 2006 EWCA Civ 1088 325
Woodchester Services Ltd *v.* Swain & Co. 1999 1 WLR 263 232

Yeoman Credit Ltd *v.* Latter 1961 1 WLR 828 257
Yeoman Credit Ltd *v.* Waragowski 1961 1 WLR 1124 245
Yorkshire Bank plc *v.* Hall 1999 1 WLR 1713 302

Zoan *v.* Rouamba 2000 1 All ER 1509; 2000 2 All ER 620 54

Table of statutes

Administration of Justice Act 1970
s 40 .... 61, 217
s 40(1)(c) 217
s 40(3)(a) 217
s 40(3A) 217
s 40(5) 217
Agricultural Credits Act 1928 .... 228, 252

Betting and Loans (Infants) Act 1892 104
Bills of Exchange Act 1882
s 29 268
s 29(1) 264
s 29(2) 263
s 38 263
s 73 265
Bills of Sale Acts 1878–1883 207

Consumer Credit Act 1974 ..... 45, 89, 151–154, 183
s 1 35
s 1(1)(d) 35
s 2(2) 35
s 4(a) 12
s 4(b) 12
s 4(c) 12
s 8(1) 3
s 8(3) 46
s 8(4) 5
s 9(1) 1
s 9(3) 2–3
s 9(4) 3, 24, 26
s 10 5
s 10(2) 7
s 10(3) 8
s 10(3)(b)(iii) 9
s 11 .... 9, 10
s 11(1)(a) 9, 12
s 11(1)(b) 10, 12
s 11(1)(c) 10
s 11(2) 11, 232
s 11(3) 10
s 11(4) 10
s 12 .... 11, 12
s 12(a) 12, 177, 180, 200
s 12(b) 12, 173, 177, 180, 202, 204, 206, 207
s 12(c) 204, 206, 207
s 13 .... 11, 12, 14
s 13(b) 11, 14
s 14(3) 7
s 15 14
s 15(2) 46
s 16 46
s 16(6)(C) 36
s 16A 46
s 16B 46, 51
s 16C 46, 52
s 17 17
s 17(1) 17, 129
s 17(1)(b) 17
s 17(2) 17
s 17(3) 17–18
s 17(4) 17–18
s 18 .... 10, 18
s 18(1) 18, 19
s 18(1)(a) 19, 20
s 18(1)(b) 18, 19, 20
s 18(2) 18, 19, 20, 28
s 18(3) 18, 19, 20
s 18(5) 7

s 19 .... 11, 20
s 19(1) 252
s 19(1)(a) 21
s 19(1)(b) 21, 173–174
s 19(1)(c) 21, 22
s 19(2) 22
s 19(3) 21, 157, 158
s 20 .... 3, 24
s 20(1) 24
s 33A 72
s 36 92
s 36A 92
s 39 79
s 40 80
s 40(1A)(b) 81
s 40(2) 84
s 41 35
s 45 98
s 48(1) 102
s 48(2) 102
s 49 .... 11, 102
s 49(1) 103
s 49(2) 103
s 49(3) 103
s 49(5) 103
s 50 104
s 50(1) 105
s 52 .... 101, 102
s 55 .... 113, 117, 123
s 55(2) 115, 117
ss 55–73 309
ss 55–74 126
s 55A 124
s 55B 126
s 55C 125, 135, 314
s 55C(2) 125
s 55C(3) 125
s 55C(4) 125, 314
s 55C(5) 125
s 56 .... 24, 131, 157, 202, 203, 208–209, 310, 334, 358
s 56(1) 162, 199, 200
s 56(1)(a) 200
s 56(1)(b) 200, 202
s 56(1)(c) 202
s 56(2) 199, 200, 201
s 56(3) 200
s 56(4) 157
s 57 .... 156, 157, 159
s 57(1) 156, 157, 159, 171
s 57(2) 156
s 57(3)(a) 157, 158
s 57(3)(b) 157
s 57(4) 159
s 58 .... 114, 117, 130–131, 141, 142, 145, 146, 162
s 58(1) 144
s 58(2) 142
s 60 310
s 60(3) 129, 130
s 60(5) 130
s 61 .... 141, 145
s 61(1) 134
s 61(1)(a) 132, 133, 134
s 61(1)(b) 131, 132
s 61(1)(c) 131
s 61(2) 144
s 61(2)(b) 145
s 61(2)(c) 144
s 61(3) 141
s 61(4) 131
s 61A 134, 135, 137, 145, 151, 310, 314, 322
s 61A(1) 135
s 61A(3) 135
s 61A(4) 135
s 61A(5) 135
s 61A(6) 137, 314
s 61A(6)(a) 135
s 61A(6)(b) 135
s 61A(8) 57
s 61B 135, 136, 151, 310
s 61B(1) 313
s 61B(2) 136
s 61B(2)(a) 313
s 61B(2)(b) 136, 314
s 61B(2)(c) 136, 314
s 61B(3) 314
s 62 .... 137, 140
s 62(1) 137, 138
s 62(2) 138, 145, 146, 152, 165
s 62(3) 152
s 63 .... 137, 140
s 63(1) 137, 165
s 63(2) 138, 146, 164, 170
s 63(2)(b) 138, 146
s 63(3) 138, 164

s 63(4) 138, 164
s 63(5) 141
s 64(1) 152, 164, 165, 167, 168, 346
s 64(1)(b) 140, 165, 167, 170
s 64(2) 165
s 64(4) 166
s 64(4)(a) 170
s 64(4)(b) 166
s 65(1) 134, 258, 345
s 66 306
s 66A 21, 119, 135, 141, 151, 154, 159, 161, 171, 310, 314, 322
s 66A(2) 160
s 66A(3) 160
s 66A(5) 154
s 66A(5)(a) 160
s 66A(6) 154
s 66A(6)(b) 160
s 66A(7) 160
s 66A(7)(b) 21
s 66A(8) 160
s 66A(9)(a) 160
s 66A(9)(b) 160
s 66A(10) 160
s 66A(11) 160
s 66A(12) 160
s 66A(13) 21, 160
s 66A(14) 141, 159, 181
s 67 .... 140, 161
s 67(1)(a) 141, 162
s 67(1)(b) 163
s 67(2) 161
s 68 152
s 68(a) 169
s 68(b) 170
s 69 22
s 69(1) 21, 152, 169, 333
s 69(1)(i) 172
s 69(1)(ii) 173
s 69(2) 171, 172, 173, 179, 333
s 69(4) 171, 173
s 69(5) 173
s 69(6) 169
s 69(7) 170
ss 69–73 171
s 70 173
s 70(1) 173
s 70(1)(b) 171
s 70(1)(c) 173, 177
s 70(2) 178
s 70(3) 173, 174
s 70(4) 174
s 70(5) 174
s 70(6) 174
s 70(7) 174
s 70(8) 173
s 71 .... 174, 177, 181, 260
s 71(1) 174, 175, 176
s 71(2)(a) 175
s 71(2)(b) 175
s 71(3) 159, 174, 176, 177
s 71(4) 175
s 72 .... 177, 181, 260
s 72(2)(b) 178
s 72(3) 177
s 72(5) 178
s 72(6) 178
s 72(6)(a) 179
s 72(6)(b) 179
s 72(7) 179
s 72(8) 178
s 72(9) 179
s 72(9)(c) 172
s 72(9)(d) 172
s 72(10) 178
s 72(11) 177, 181
s 73 .... 178, 179
s 73(2) 180
s 73(4) 180
s 73(5) 178, 180
s 73(6) 180
s 73(7) 179
s 74 .... 126, 142, 156, 157, 162
s 74(1) 23
s 74(1A) 24
s 74(1)(a) 126, 142
s 74(1B) 126, 136, 310
s 74(1)(b) 126, 142, 309, 315
s 74(1C) 128, 136, 310
s 74(1)(c) 129
s 74(1D) 129, 310
s 74(1)(d) 129
s 74(1E) 309
s 74(2) 17
s 74(2A) 129

s 74(3) 129
s 74(4) 129
s 75 .... 11, 23, 202, 204, 205, 206, 207, 208–209
s 75(1) 204, 205, 206
s 75(2) 205, 207
s 75(3) 23, 204
s 75(3)(c) 205
s 75(4) 205
s 75(5) 206
s 75A 208
s 75A(2) 208
s 75A(3) 208
s 75A(5) 208
s 75A(7) 208
s 75A(8) 208
s 76 .... 234, 236, 237, 239, 256, 349
s 76(1) 328
s 76(2)(a) 237
s 76(4) 236
s 76(6) 236
s 77 .... 184, 186, 255–256
s 77(1) 185
s 77(2) 185
s 77(3)(a) 185
s 77(3)(b) 185
s 77(4) 187
s 77(4)(a) 186
s 77(5) 23, 184
s 77A 8, 190
s 77A(1E) 190
s 77A(3) 190
s 77A(6) 191
s 77A(7) 191
s 77A(8) 23, 190
s 77B 24, 191, 192
s 77B(5) 192
s 77B(6) 192
s 77B(8) 192
s 77B(9) 191
s 78 .... 8, 152, 184, 186, 189, 255–256
s 78(1) 185
s 78(2) 185
s 78(3)(a) 185
s 78(4) 187, 189, 221, 256
s 78(5) 256
s 78(6) 187, 315
s 78(6)(a) 186
s 78(7) 17, 23, 184, 187
s 78A 148, 149, 192, 214, 314, 315
s 78A(1) 148
s 78A(2) 149, 315
s 78A(3) 148
s 78A(4) 149, 315
s 78A(5) 149, 314
s 78A(6) 148, 149
s 79 .... 184, 186, 255–256
s 79(1) 185
s 79(2)(a) 185
s 79(2)(b) 185
s 79(3) 187
s 79(3)(a) 186
s 79(4) 23, 184
s 80(1) 238
s 80(2) 238
s 81 .... 241, 243
s 82 .... 146, 148, 149
s 82(1) 147, 149–150, 186
s 82(1A) 148
s 82(1B) 149
s 82(1C) 149
s 82(1D) 149
s 82(1E) 149
s 82(2) 147, 161, 164
s 82(2A) 150
s 82(3) 147, 150, 151
s 82(5) 151, 164
s 82(5A) 151, 164
s 82(6) 164
s 82(6A) 151, 161
s 82(6B) 161
s 82(7) 23
s 82(8) 150
s 83(1) 306
s 83(2) 24
s 83(3A) 306
s 83(3C) 306
s 84 307
s 84(1) 307, 308
s 84(2) 307, 308
s 84(3) 308
s 84(5) 308
s 84(6) 308
s 84(8) 308
s 85(1) 306

s 85(2) 306
s 85(3) 17
s 86 246–247
s 86(1) 245, 247
s 86(2) 245, 247
s 86(3) 245
s 86(4) 247
s 86(6) 247
s 86A 221, 231
s 86B 256, 349
s 86B(1) 219
s 86B(2)(a) 220
s 86B(3) 220
s 86B(5) 220
s 86B(6) 221
s 86B(7) 219
s 86B(9) 220
s 86B(10) 220
s 86B(12A) 24, 219
s 86C 256, 349
s 86C(1) 220
s 86C(4) 221
s 86C(5) 219
s 86C(7) 24, 219
s 86D(3) 223
s 86D(4) 223
s 86D(6)(b)(i) 223
s 86D(6)(b)(ii) 223
s 86D(6)(c) 223
s 86D(8) 24
s 86E(4) 224
s 86E(6) 223
s 86E(8) 223
s 86F 224
s 87 .... 152, 199, 227, 228, 231, 234, 236, 237, 327–328, 349
s 87(1) 228, 350
s 87(1)(c) 328
s 87(1)(e) 236, 328
s 87(2) 227
s 87(3) 228
s 87(5) 199, 228
s 87(7) 149
s 88 229
s 88(1)(c) 230
s 88(2) 230, 231, 233
s 88(3) 229
s 89 233
s 90 259
s 90(1) 241
s 90(1)(a) 241
s 90(1)(b) 241
s 90(1)(c) 242
s 90(2) 241
s 90(3) 242
s 90(4) 242
s 90(5) 244
s 90(6) 242
s 90(7) 240
s 91 .... 238, 259
s 91(a) 245
s 91(b) 245
s 92 .... 234, 238, 239, 241
s 92(1) 239, 241
s 92(3) 239
s 94 196
s 94(2) 196
s 94(3) 324
s 96(1) 21
s 98 .... 234, 236, 237, 238, 256, 349
s 98(1) 236
s 98(2)(a) 237
s 98(6) 236
s 98A 198, 213, 237, 315
s 98A(1) 199, 316
s 98A(2) 199
s 98A(3) 199, 316
s 98A(4) 199, 228
s 98A(6) 199
s 98A(7) 199
s 98A(8) 316
s 99 .... 152, 192, 193, 194, 244
s 99(1) 192, 196
s 99(2) 194
s 99(3) 193
s 99(4) 193, 196
s 100 .... 192, 193, 195, 244, 245
s 100(1) 194, 195
s 100(2) 194
s 100(3) 194, 195
s 100(4) 194, 196
s 100(5) 194
s 101 .... 197, 198
s 101(1) 197
s 101(2) 198
s 101(3) 197

s 101(4) 197
s 101(5) 197
s 101(7)(a) 197
s 101(7)(b) 197
s 101(7)(c) 198
s 101(8) 198
s 101(8A) 198
s 101(9) 197
s 102 ..... 203, 204
s 103(4) 24
s 105(1) 253
s 105(2) 253, 254
s 105(4) 254
s 105(4)(a) 254
s 105(4)(b) 254
s 105(5) 254
s 105(5)(a) 254
s 105(5)(b) 254
s 105(6) 253
s 105(7) 258
s 105(8) 259
s 106 ..... 180, 181, 260, 262, 267
s 106(a) 258, 260, 263
s 106(b) 260
s 106(c) 260
s 106(d) 260
s 107 ..... 255, 256
s 107(5) 23
s 108 ..... 255, 256
s 108(5) 23
s 109 ..... 255, 256
s 109(5) 23
s 110 ..... 184, 186, 256
s 110(1) 256
s 110(2) 24, 256
s 110(2)(b) 185
s 110(2)(c) 185
s 110(3) 256
s 110(3)(a) 186
s 111(1) 232, 256
s 111(2) 257
s 113(1) 257, 258
s 113(2) 259, 267
s 113(3) 259
s 113(3)(a) 180
s 113(3)(c) 259
s 113(3)(d) 258
s 113(5) 181, 260
s 113(6) 180, 255, 259
s 113(7) 257
s 113(8) 257
s 114(1) 322
s 114(2) 321
s 114(3) 24, 323
s 114(3)(a) 321
s 116 321
s 116(1) 323
s 116(2) 323
s 116(3) 323
s 116(4) 323
s 117 324
s 117(1) 323, 325
s 117(2) 325
ss 117–122 321
s 118 323
s 118(1)(b) 324
s 118(2) 324
s 119(1) 325
s 119(2) 325
s 120 326
s 120(1)(a) 323, 324, 328
s 120(1)(b) 328
s 120(2) 328
s 121 326
s 121(1) 326
s 121(3) 326, 327
s 121(4) 326
s 121(5) 326
s 121(6) 327
s 121(7) 327
s 123 ..... 264, 265, 266–267, 268
s 123(1) 265, 266, 268, 269
s 123(2) 265, 268, 269, 270
s 123(3) 265, 266, 268, 269
s 123(5) 24, 266
s 123(6) 266
s 124(1) 267
s 124(2) 267
s 124(3) 267
s 125 ..... 264, 269
s 125(1) 267
s 125(2) 268, 269
s 125(4) 268
s 126 47
s 126(2) 47, 51, 348
s 127 ..... 117, 167, 168, 169, 232, 314, 349
s 127(1) 258

s 127(1)(a) 258, 345
s 127(1)(b) 258, 345
s 127(1)(c) 232
s 127(1)(d) 267, 346
s 127(1)(za) 115, 345
s 127(1)(zb) 314, 346
s 127(2) 258, 347, 350
s 127(3) 132, 346, 347
s 127(4) 167, 168, 346, 347
s 127(4)(a) 168, 346
s 127(4)(b) 167, 346
s 128 247
s 129 350
s 129(1) 348, 349
s 129(1)(a) 347
s 129(1)(ba) 223
s 129(2) 233, 349
s 129(2)(a) 258, 327, 349
s 129(2)(b) 350
s 129A(1) 223
s 129A(2) 223, 349
s 130(1) 351
s 130(2) 349, 352
s 130(3) 327
s 130(4) 351
s 130(5)(a) 350
s 130(5)(b) 350
s 130(5)(c) 350
s 130(6) 352
s 131 .... 246, 353, 356
s 131(3)(b) 245
s 132 352
s 133 352
s 133(1)(b)(i) 352
s 133(1)(b)(ii) 354
s 133(2) 354
s 133(3) 354
s 133(4) 353
s 133(5) 353
s 133(6) 353, 354
s 133(7) 354
s 135 .... 347, 350, 352
s 135(1)(b) 245, 356
s 135(2) 352
s 135(4) 348, 353
s 136 .... 347, 350, 352
s 138(1) 356
s 140(1)(a) 357
s 140(1)(b) 357
s 140A 360–361
s 140A(1)(c) 358
s 140A(2) 359
s 140A(4) 357
s 140A(5) 297, 356
ss 140A–140D 356
s 140B(1)(d) 361
s 140B(2)(a) 361
s 140B(2)(b) 361
s 140B(2)(c) 361
s 140B(4) 361
s 140B(8) 361
s 140B(9) 359
s 140C(1) 356
s 140D 356
s 141(1) 348, 355
s 141(2) 348
s 141(3A) 348
s 141(4) 348
s 141(5) 258, 348
s 142 259
s 142(1) 258, 259, 347
s 142(2) 170, 245
s 145 57
s 145(1) 103
s 145(8) 62, 333
s 146 59
s 149 82
s 152 .... 101, 102
s 153(2) 104
s 154 103
s 155 .... 331, 332, 333
s 155(1) 332, 333
s 155(2A) 332
s 155(2)(b) 332
s 155(2)(c) 332
s 155(4) 332
s 157 200
s 157(1) 114, 334
s 157(2) 334
s 157(2A) 335
s 157(3) 335
s 157(4) 334
s 157(A1) 334
s 158 .... 335, 336–337, 337, 338
s 158(1) 336
s 158(1)(c) 336
s 158(2) 337
s 158(4) 336

s 158(5) ... 337
s 159 ... 336
s 159(1) ... 337
s 159(2) ... 338
s 159(3) ... 338
s 159(5) ... 338
s 159(8) ... 338
s 160 ... 338
s 160(1) ... 337
s 160(3) ... 337
s 160(5) ... 338
s 160A ... 57
s 161 ... 35
s 167(2) ... 97
s 168(1) ... 104, 106
s 169(1) ... 106
s 170(1) ... 190
s 170(3) ... 190
s 171(4)(a) ... 306
s 171(4)(b) ... 308
s 171(5) ... 105
s 172 ... 185
s 172(1) ... 256
s 172(3) ... 186
s 173 ... 192
s 173(1) ... 198, 204, 205, 224
s 173(3) ... 239, 243, 257
s 175 ... 157, 158, 203
s 176(1) ... 152
s 176(2) ... 152, 156, 231
s 176(3) ... 153
s 176(4) ... 153
s 176(5) ... 153, 232
s 176(6) ... 153, 232, 247
s 176(7) ... 153
s 176(8) ... 152, 231
s 176A ... 145, 152, 164, 231
s 176A(1) ... 153
s 176A(1)(a) ... 153
s 176A(2) ... 154
s 177(1) ... 261, 262
s 177(2) ... 263
s 177(3) ... 261
s 177(4) ... 262
s 180 ... 138
s 180(3) ... 140
s 183 ... 103
s 184 ... 13, 18, 22, 198
s 184(1) ... 12, 171, 173, 177, 178
s 184(5) ... 20, 171, 173, 177, 178
s 185 ... 5
s 185(1) ... 185
s 185(1)(a) ... 5, 227
s 185(2) ... 189, 190
s 185(2A) ... 189
s 185(2B) ... 189
s 185(2C) ... 189
s 185(2D) ... 189
s 185(5) ... 5
s 187 ... 12, 13
s 187(1) ... 12
s 187(2) ... 12
s 187(3) ... 13
s 187(3A) ... 13
s 187(5) ... 13
s 187A ... 224
s 189 ... 4, 198
s 189(1) ... 2, 5, 21, 23, 24, 46, 103, 120, 126, 136, 145, 149, 152, 157, 161, 169, 200, 204, 210, 231, 232, 251, 252, 253, 255, 309, 310, 314, 320, 321, 334, 337, 342, 356
s 189(2) ... 23
s 189(2A) ... 136, 310
s 189(5) ... 259
s 189B ... 5
s 189B(1) ... 5
s 189B(2)(b) ... 5
Sch 1 ... 103, 104
Sch 2 ... 19
example 2 ... 200
example 3 ... 202
example 16 ... 10
example 18 ... 20
Sch 4 ... 224
Part 9 ... 47
Part III ... 35
Part IV ... 96
Part V ... 126, 142, 309, 310, 315
Consumer Credit Act 2006 ... 3, 4, 5, 6, 132, 151, 223, 346, 362
s 2(2) ... 16
s 15 ... 167, 168, 347
ss 38–43 ... 37

s 56 37
s 86C(7) 219
Sch 3
para 1(2) 357
para 11 .... 167, 347
para 14 357
para 15 357

Data Protection Act 1998 185
s 7 .... 335, 336
s 7(1)(c) 335
s 7(2) 335
s 7(10) 335
s 9 336
s 9(2) 336
s 9(3) 336

Energy Act 2011
s 1 .... 6, 51
Enterprise Act 2002 .... 190, 210
s 2(1) 36
s 211 .... 36, 38
s 212 38
s 213(1) 36
Sch 13
para 5 36
para 9C 36
Part 8 36
Enterprise Act 2012
s 212 215
Enterprise and Regulatory Reform Act 2013 38

Factors Act 1889
s 1(4) 321
Finance Act 1976
Sch 4 30
Financial Service Act 2012 37
s 89 112
s 92 112
Financial Services (Banking Reform) Act 2013
s 30 91
s 131 320
s 131(3) 320
Financial Services and Markets Act 2000 .... 25, 38–39, 42, 113, 271
s 1A(1) 37
s 1A(6) 38
s 1B(2) 37
s 1B(3) 37
s 1C(1) 37
s 2A(1) 38
s 19 .... 44, 73, 78
s 19(1) 80
s 20(1) 79
s 20(2)(a) 79
s 21 .... 106, 108, 109, 110, 112
s 21(3) 107
s 21(4) 107
s 21(8) 107, 108
s 21(13) 107
s 22 45
s 22(1) 44, 45, 47
s 22(1A) 44, 45
s 22(4) 47
s 22(5) 45
s 23(1) 79
s 23(1A) 79
s 23(1)(b) 44
s 23(1B) 79
s 23(1C) 79
s 23(2) 79
s 24 79
s 25 112
s 26 259
s 26(1) 80
s 26(2) 82
s 26(3) 80
s 26A 80, 259
s 26A(2) 82
s 26A(4) 81
s 26A(5) 81
s 27 .... 81, 259
s 27(1)(d) 81
s 28 83
s 28(2) 82
s 28(3)(a) 83
s 28(3)(b) 83
s 28(5) 83, 84
s 28(6) 84
s 28A 259
s 28A(2)(b) 84
s 28A(3) 84
s 28A(4)(a) 84

s 28A(4)(b) 84
s 28A(9) 84
s 28B 85
s 28B(3) 85
s 30 106
s 30(6) 112
s 30(7) 112
s 31 78
s 39(1) 73, 74
s 39(1)(a) 73
s 39(1)(b) 74
s 39(1C) 74
s 39(1)(C)(b) 74
s 39(1D) 74
s 39(3) 74
s 39(6) 74
s 55B 65
s 55C 65
s 55E(4) 64
s 55E(5) 67
s 55J(1) 86
s 55J(12) 86
s 55L 86
s 55N 87
s 55N(4) 87
s 55R 64
s 55U 84
s 55U(1) 64
s 55U(4) 39
s 55V(1) 67
s 55V(2) 67
s 55X(1) 67
s 55X(2) 67
s 55X(4) 68
s 55Y(2) 87
s 55Y(3) 87
s 55Y(4) 87
s 55Y(5) 87
s 55Z(1) 87
s 55Z(2) 87
s 55Z3(1) 68
s 55Z3(2) 88
s 56(1) 88
s 56(2) 88
s 56(4) 88
s 56(5) 88
s 57(1) 88
s 57(4) 88
s 57(5) 88
s 58(1) 89
s 58(3) 89
s 58(4) 89
s 58(5) 89
s 59(1) 68
s 59(2) 68
s 59(3)(a) 39
s 59(5) 68
s 59(7A) 69
s 59(7B) 69
s 59(10) 68
s 60 69
s 60(2) 64, 69
s 60(4) 64
s 61(1) 64, 69
s 61(4) 69
s 63A 70
s 63A(1) 70
s 63A(4) 70
s 63A(5) 70
s 63B(2) 70
s 63B(5) 71
s 63C 71
s 64 .... 39, 91, 92
s 64(6) 39
s 66 92
s 66(1) 92
s 66(3A) 92
s 66(3D) 92
s 66(4) 92
s 67(1) 92
s 68 92
s 132 77
s 133(5) 77
s 133(6) 77
s 133(6A) 77
s 137A 39
s 137C 39
s 137C(1A) 39
s 137C(6) 39
s 137D(1) 40
s 137D(2) 40
s 137O 39, 65
s 138C 39
s 138D 39, 40, 97
s 139A 39
s 140B(3) 362
s 178 94
s 179 94

s 181 94
s 182 94
s 185 94
s 186 94
s 189 94
s 189(1) 96
s 191D 94
s 191F 95
s 204A 89
s 205 89
s 206 89
s 206A 90
s 206A(1A) 90
s 207 90
s 208 91
s 209 89
s 210 89
s 226A 362
s 229(9) 366
s 230(3) 366
s 230A 366
s 231 365
s 231(5) 365
s 232 365
s 299(4) 366
s 326(1) 76
s 327(3) 76
s 327(4) 76
s 327(7) 76
s 328 77
s 347 89
s 387 70
s 387(1) 90
s 387(2) 67, 90
s 388 .... 68, 91
s 388(1) 67
s 389 91
s 391 (1A) 68
s 391(1A) 91
s 391(1ZA) 68, 90
s 391(5) 88
s 392 88
s 394 88
s 394(1)(a) 87, 90
s 394(1)(b) 87, 91
s 394(4) 87, 91
s 395 .... 67, 90
s 397 112
s 401 79

Sch 2
- para 1 45
- para 10 45
- para 23 .... 36, 39
- para 23(2) 45
- para 23A 45
- Part I 45
- Part II 45
- Part IIA 45

Sch 5 40
Sch 6 39
- para 2B 66
- para 2C 66
- para 2D 66
- para 2D(3A) 67
- para 2E 67
- para 2F 67
- para 2F(3) 67
- para 2G 65, 250
- para 2G(1)(a) 65, 66
- para 2G(1)(d) 65
- para 2G(1)(da) 65
- para 2G(1)(e) 65
- para 2G(2) 66
- para 2G(3) 65
- para 2G(4) 66
- para 2G(5) 66
- para 2G(6) 66
- para 26(1)(b)(i) 65

Sch 17
- para 16 366

Part 4A 71, 72, 78, 81

Hire Purchase Act 1965 192, 235, 240, 353
- s 33(1) 241

Housing Subsidies Act 1967 30
Human Rights Act 1998 .... 168, 346

Interpretation Act 1976 160
Interpretation Act 1978 42
- s 6 229
- s 7 .... 153, 231

Land Registration Act 2002
- s 29 262–263
- s 30 .... 261, 262
- Sch 4 .... 261, 263

Law of Property (Miscellaneous Provisions) Act 1989
s 2(1) 145
Law of Property Act 1925
s 101(1) 262
s 104(2) 263

Moneylenders Act 1927 233
s 6 .... 131, 168

Regulation of Financial Services (Land Transactions) Act 2005 45

Statute of Frauds 1677 252
Statutory Declarations Act 1835 323–324
s 18 324

Tribunals Courts and Enforcement Act 2007
s 13 78

Unfair Contract Terms Act 1977 210

Table of statutory instruments

Agreements Regulations 1983
see Consumer Credit (Agreements) Regulations 1983, SI 1983/1553
Agreements Regulations 2010
see Consumer Credit (Agreements) Regulations 2010, SI 2010/1014

Cancellation of Contracts in a Consumer's Home Regulations 2008, SI 2008/1816 129
Civil Procedure Rules 1998, SI 1998/3132
Part 7, PD 7B
para 3.1(5) 361
para 4.1 .... 245, 355
para 4.2 246
para 4.3 351
para 5.2 361
para 6B 348
para 7.1 351
para 7.3 351
para 7.3(11) 351
para 7.4(2) 348
para 8 356
para 8.1 351
para 10.2 361
para 10.3 361
Part 55, Part 55A
para 7 352
Consumer Contracts (Information, Cancellation and Additional Charges) Regulations 2013, SI 2013/3134 .... 5, 116, 123, 124, 129, 152, 182–183
Reg 2 116
Reg 6(b) 116, 182
Reg 14(1) 182
Reg 14(2) 182
Reg 29(1) 182
Reg 29(2) 182
Reg 32(1) 182
Reg 32(5) 182
Reg 32(6) 182
Reg 35 182
Reg 38 21
Reg 38(1) 183
Reg 38(2) 183
Reg 38(3) 183
Reg 38(4) 183
Sch 3
Part B 182
Consumer Credit Act (Commencement No 4 and Transitional Provisions) Order 2008 .... SI 2008/831
Sch 1 4
Sch 2 4
Sch 3 4
Consumer Credit (Advertisement) Regulations 2004, SI 2004/1484 .... 96, 97, 99
Consumer Credit (Advertisement) Regulations 2010, SI 2010/1970 .... 96, 97, 99
Consumer Credit (Agreements) Regulations 1983, SI 1983/1553 .... 130, 133–134, 139, 345
Reg 2(4) 133
Reg 2(5) 134

Reg 2(6) 133
Reg 2(7) 134
Reg 5 134
Reg 6(3) 134
Reg 8(1A) 130, 144
Sch 1
para 20 255
Sch 2
Part I 145
Sch 5 134
Sch 6 134
Sch 7 133

Consumer Credit (Agreements) Regulations 2010, SI 2010/1014 .... 25, 114, 130–131, 132–133, 139, 312–313, 345
Reg 2(1) 313
Reg 2(1A) 131, 144
Reg 2(2) 313
Reg 2(3) 313
Reg 2(4) 132, 312, 313
Reg 3(1) 132
Reg 3(2) 132
Reg 3(3) 132
Reg 3(5) 133
Reg 3(6) 133
Reg 3(7) 133
Reg 4(3) 133
Reg 6 .... 313, 322
Reg 7(1) 132
Reg 7(2) 132
Reg 7(4) 133
Reg 8 .... 133, 313
Reg 10(3) 313
Sch 1
para 3 132
para 4 132
para 13 132
para 23 255
paras 12–14 129
Sch 2
para 6 132
Sch 3
para 9 255
Sch 4 132

Consumer Credit (Amendment) Regulations 2010, SI 2010/1969 148

Consumer Credit (Cancellation Notices and Copies of Documents) Regulations 1983, SI 1983/1557 345
Reg 2 138
Reg 2(1) 164
Reg 2(2) 138
Reg 2(2)(b) 139
Reg 3(1) 135
Reg 3(2) 186
Reg 3(2)(b) 254
Reg 3(2)(c) 254
Reg 4 144
Reg 5(3) 165
Reg 5(4) 139, 167
Reg 6 165
Reg 6B 166
Reg 10 256
Reg 11 135
Reg 11 .... 144, 254
Reg 11(h) 145
Schedule 139, 164–165, 169
Part I 144
Part V 165
Part VI 165

Consumer Credit (Cancellation Notices and Copies of Documents) (Amendment) Regulations 1984, SI 1984/1108
Reg 2(b) 139
Reg 3(1) 140
Reg 3(2) 140
Reg 11 140–141

Consumer Credit (Content of Quotations) and Consumer Credit (Advertisement) Regulations 1999, SI 1999/2725 102

Consumer Credit (Credit Reference Agency) Regulations 2000, SI 2000/290 336
Reg 3 .... 334, 336
Reg 5 339
Sch 2 337
Sch 3 337

Consumer Credit (Credit Tokens Agreements) Regulations 1983, SI 1983/1555 307

Consumer Credit (Disclosure of Information) Regulations 2004, SI 2004/1481 .... 113–115, 122, 123, 135, 311–312, 345
Reg 2(1) 117, 143
Reg 2(1)(a) 114
Reg 2(1)(b) 113
Reg 2(1)(c) 113
Reg 2(2) 114
Reg 2(3)(a) 114
Reg 2(3)(b) 114
Reg 2(3)(c) 114, 312
Reg 3(1) 114
Reg 3(1A) 114
Reg 4(d)(i) 115
Reg 4(d)(ii) 115
Reg 4(d)(iii) 115
Reg 7(6) 116
Consumer Credit (Disclosure of Information) Regulations 2010, SI 2010/1013 .... 25, 113, 117–121, 135, 312, 314, 322, 343, 345
Reg 1(6) 120, 321
Reg 2(2) 117, 130, 143
Reg 2(3) 117, 130, 311
Reg 2(4) 312
Reg 2(5) 117, 121
Reg 2(6) 117
Reg 3 .... 118, 119, 120
Reg 3(1) 119
Reg 3(1)(c) 120
Reg 3(2) 118
Reg 4 116
Reg 4(2) 119
Reg 4(2)(a) 119
Reg 4(2)(b) 119
Reg 4(2)(c) 119
Reg 4(2)(e) 119
Reg 4(2)(f) 119
Reg 4(3) 119
Reg 4(4) 119
Reg 5 .... 116, 120
Reg 6 .... 116, 119
Reg 6(2) 118, 120
Reg 6(3) 120
Reg 7(2) 118, 119
Reg 7(6) 121
Reg 8 .... 118, 119, 120
Reg 8(4) 118
Reg 9(2) 120, 321
Reg 10 .... 122, 311
Reg 10(2) 121, 311
Reg 10(3) 120, 121, 136, 311
Reg 10(5) 121, 136, 313
Reg 10(5A) 121
Reg 10(5)(e) 121
Reg 10(6) 121
Reg 10(8) 121, 136, 313
Reg 10(9) 121
Reg 11 .... 120–121, 311
Sch 1 321
Sch 3 .... 121, 311
Consumer Credit (Early Settlement) Regulations 2004/SI 2004/1483 .... 196, 238
Reg 2(3) 194
Consumer Credit (Enforcement, Default and Termination Notices) Regulations 1983, SI 1983/1561 .... 236, 327
Reg 2(4) 229
Reg 2(4A) 228
Reg 2(5) 228
Reg 2(6) 228
Reg 2(7) 228
Reg 2(8) 237
Reg 2(9) 23, 237
Sch 1
para 3 237
para 4 238
para 4(c) 238
para 5 238
Sch 2 228
para 3(a) 229
para 3(b) 229
para 3(c) 229–230
para 3(d) 230
para 4 230
para 6(f) 229, 231
para 8A 192
para 9 229
para 10 229
para 10A 231
Sch 3
para 3 237
para 4(b) 238

para 5 238
Consumer Credit (EU Directive) Regulations 2010, SI 2010/1010 113
Consumer Credit (Further Increase of Monetary Amounts) Order 1998, SI 1998/997 184
Consumer Credit (Guarantees and Indemnities) Regulations 1983, SI 1983/1556 254
Schedule, Part III 255
Consumer Credit (Increase of Monetary Amounts) Order 1983, SI 1983/1571 307
Consumer Credit (Increase of Monetary Limits) Order 1983, SI 1983/1878 205
Consumer Credit (Increase of Monetary Limits) Order 1998, SI 1998/996 .... 3, 17
Consumer Credit (Information Requirements and Duration of Licences and Charges) Regulations 2007, SI 2007/1167
Reg 12(1) 191
Reg 19 221
Reg 19(2)(a) 222
Reg 19(2)(b) 222
Reg 19(4) 222
Reg 20 222
Reg 24 221
Reg 29 224
Reg 41 .... 190, 221
Reg 42 71
Sch 1
para 3 190
Part 2 190
Part 3 191
Sch 2
para 1 188
para 4 188
Sch 3
para 17 220
Part 4 222
Consumer Credit Licensing (Appeals) Regulations 1998, SI 1998/1203
Reg 3(1) 71
Consumer Credit (Linked Transactions) (Exemptions) Regulations 1983, SI 1983/1560 .... 22, 173, 252
Reg 1(2) 158
Reg 1(2A) 158
Consumer Credit (Loss of Pawn Receipt) Regulations 1983, SI 1983/1576 324
Consumer Credit (Negotiable Instruments) (Exemption) Order 1984, SI 1984/435 266–267
Consumer Credit (Notice of Cancellation Rights) (Exemptions) Regulations 1983, SI 1983/1558 166
Consumer Credit (Notice of Variation of Agreements) Regulations 1977, SI 1977/328
Reg 2 150
Reg 3(2)(a) 150
Reg 3(2)(b) 150
Reg 4 150
Consumer Credit (Pawn Receipts) Regulations 1983, SI 1983/1566 322
Consumer Credit (Payments Arising on Death) Regulations 1983, SI 1983/1554 129
Consumer Credit (Prescribed Periods for Giving Information) Regulations 1983, SI 1983/1569 .... 185, 256
Consumer Credit (Quotations) Regulations 1989, SI 1989/1126 101
Consumer Credit (Quotations) (Revocation) Regulations 1997, SI 1997/211 101
Consumer Credit (Realisation of Pawn) Regulations 1983, SI 1983/1568
Reg 2(2) 327
Reg 3 326
Reg 76(5) 327
Reg 87(4) 327
Reg 98(5) 327

Sch 1 326
Sch 2 327
Consumer Credit (Rebate on Early Settlement) Regulations 1983, SI 1983/1562 298
Consumer Credit (Repayment of Credit on Cancellation) Regulations 1983, SI 1983/1559 175
Sch 2 159
Consumer Credit (Running Account Credit Information) Regulations 1983, SI 1983/1570 187
Reg 2(3) 188
Reg 3(2) 188
Reg 3(2)(a) 189
Reg 3(2)(b) 189
Reg 3(3) 189
Schedule
para 1A 188
para 5 188
para 6 188
para 7 188
Consumer Credit (Total Charge for Credit) Regulations 1980, SI 1980/51 .... 24–25, 26–32, 144, 252, 291
Reg 1(2) 27, 31, 32
Reg 1A 25
Reg 2(1)(a) 30
Reg 2(1)(b) 30
Reg 2(1)(c) 30
Reg 2(1)(d) 31, 32
Reg 2(1)(e) 32
Reg 2(2)(a)(i) 30
Reg 2(2)(a)(ii) 30
Reg 2(2)(b) 31
Reg 2(3) 30
Reg 3 26
Reg 4 .... 26, 27, 28
Reg 4(1)(c) 29
Reg 4(b) 27
Reg 5 .... 26, 28
Reg 5(1)(a) 28
Reg 5(1)(b) 28
Reg 5(1)(c) 28, 33
Reg 5(1)(d) 29
Reg 5(1)(e) 29
Reg 5(1)(f) 29
Reg 5(1)(g) 29
Reg 5(1)(h) 29
Reg 5(1)(j) 29
Reg 5(2) 29
Reg 6 29
Reg 6A 30
Reg 7 30
Reg 13 30
Reg 14 30
Reg 15 31
Reg 15A(2) 32
Reg 15A(3) 32
Reg 15A(4) 32
Reg 16 31
Reg 17 30
Reg 18 31
Consumer Credit (Total Charge for Credit) Regulations 2010, SI 2010/1011 .... 24–25, 252
Reg 3 25
Reg 4(2) 32
Reg 4(3) 33
Reg 4(4) 33
Reg 4(5)(a) 33
Reg 4(5)(b) 33
Reg 4(6) 33
Reg 5 32
Consumer Credit (Total Charge for Credit) (Amendment) Regulations 2012 SI 2012/1745
Reg 2(c) 34
Reg 6 33
Reg 6(a) 33
Reg 6(e) 33
Reg 6(f) 33
Reg 6(g) 33
Reg 6(h) 33
Reg 6(i) 34
Reg 6(j) 34
Reg 6(k) 34
Reg 6(l) 34
Reg 6(m)(i) 34
Consumer Protection (Distance Selling) Regulations 2000, SI 2000/2334 115
Reg 3(1) 116
Reg 5 116
Sch 1 116

Consumer Protection from Unfair Trading Regulations 2008, SI 2008/1277 .... 36, 217

Electronic Money Regulations 2011, SI 2011/99 90
Enterprise Act 2002 (Part 8 Domestic Infringements) Order 2003, SI 2003/1593 36

Financial Services Act 2012 (Misleading Statements and Impressions) Order 2013, SI 2013/637 112
Financial Services and Markets Act 2000 (Appointed Representatives) Regulations 2000, SI 2001/1217
- Art 2 73
- Art 3 74

Financial Services and Markets Act 2000 (Appointed Representatives) (Amendment) Regulations 2014, SI 2014/206 74
Financial Services and Markets Act 2000 (Carrying on Regulated Activities by Way of Business) Order, SI 2001/1177 44
Financial Services and Markets Act 2000 (Consumer Credit) (Designated Activities) Order 2014, SI 2014/334 .... 79, 80–81
Financial Services and Markets Act 2000 (Consumer Credit) (Miscellaneous Provisions) Order 2014 84
Financial Services and Markets Act 2000 (Controllers) (Exemption) Order 2009, SI 2009/774
- Art 6A 94

Financial Services and Markets Act 2000 (Financial Promotions) Order (FPO) 2001, SI 2001/1335 .... 107, 111
Financial Services and Markets Act 2000 (Financial Promotions) Order (FPO) 2005, SI 2005/1529 277
- Art 4C 110
- Art 17 110
- Art 18 110
- Art 27 110
- Art 28 274
- Art 28A 274–275
- Art 28B 110, 275
- Art 46 109
- Art 46A 110
- Art 48 110
- Art 50 110
- Sch 1
  - para 4B 110
  - para 4C(5) 110
  - para 4C(6) 110
  - para 5A 110
  - para 5B 110
  - para 10 109
  - para 10A 109
  - para 10B 109
  - para 10BA 108–109
  - para 10BB 109
  - para 10C–10K 109
  - para 28 109
  - Part 2 112

Financial Services and Markets Act 2000 (Professions) (Non-Exempt Activities) Order 2001, SI 2001/1227, inserted by, SI 2006/2383 and, SI 2009/1342
- Art 6A(3) 76
- Arts 6A–6H 76
- Art 6C(3) 76
- Art 6E(3) 76
- Art 6G(3) 76

Financial Services and Markets Act 2000 (Regulated Activities) Order (RAO) 2001, SI 2001/544 .... 1, 45, 210
- Art 25A 47, 48, 73
- Art 25B 49, 73
- Art 25C 49, 73
- Art 25E 49
- Art 27 49
- Art 28A 49
- Art 29 49
- Art 29A 48
- Art 29D 73

Art 36A 57, 73, 110
Art 36A(1)(a) 59
Art 36A(1)(a)–(c) 57
Art 36A(1)(c) 59
Art 36A(2) 57, 58
Art 36A(3) 58
Art 36A(4) 58
Art 36B 59
Art 36B(1)(b) 59
Art 36B(2) 59
Art 36B(3)(b) 59
Art 36B(4) 59
Art 36C 57
Art 36D 58
Art 36E 58
Art 36F 58
Art 36H 61, 62, 63, 110, 342
Art 36H(1) 62
Art 36H(2) 62
Art 36H(2A) 62
Art 36H(2B) 62
Art 36H(2C) 62
Art 36H(3) 62
Art 36H(5) 62
Art 36H(6) 62
Art 36H(8) 62
Art 36I 62
Art 39A 73
Art 39D 60
Art 39E 60, 73
Art 39F 61, 73, 79
Art 39F(1) 81
Art 39F(3) 61
Art 39G 61, 73
Art 39H 61
Art 39J 60
Art 39K(1)(a) 59
Art 39K(1)(b) 60
Art 53A 49, 73
Art 53B 49, 73
Art 53C 49, 73
Art 53D 49
Art 60B 50, 73, 79, 81, 109
Art 60B(3) 46, 50, 142
Art 60C 58, 97
Art 60C(2) 47, 50, 52, 142
Art 60C(3) 9, 51, 142
Art 60C(4) 51
Art 60C(5) 51, 130, 208
Art 60C(6) 51, 130, 208
Art 60C(7) 51
Art 60C(8) 51
Arts 60C–60H 46, 47, 50
Art 60D 52, 58, 142
Art 60D(3) 52
Art 60D(3)(a) 52
Art 60E 52, 53, 58, 142
Art 60E(3) 52
Art 60E(5) 53
Art 60E(7) 52
Art 60E(8) 53
Art 60F 25
Art 60F(2) 53
Art 60F(3) 54
Art 60F(4) 53
Art 60F(5) 54
Art 60F(6) 54
Art 60F(7) 53
Art 60G 25, 55, 58
Art 60G(3) 55
Art 60G(4) 55
Art 60G(6) 55
Art 60G(7) 55
Art 60H 9, 25, 55, 56, 58
Art 60H(f) 56
Art 60L 11, 57
Art 60L(1) 11
Art 60L(2) 11
Art 60M 3, 25
Art 60N 14, 73
Art 60N(2) 14
Art 60N(3) 47
Art 60O 16, 56, 58, 109
Art 60O(2) 16
Art 60O(3) 15, 16
Arts 60O–60Q 47
Art 60P 56
Art 60Q 56, 58, 109
Art 61 .... 36, 47, 50, 109, 271, 332
Art 61(2) 48
Art 61(3) 47
Art 61(3)(a)(i) 48
Art 61(3)(b) 48
Art 61(4)(b) 48
Art 62 48
Art 63 48

Art 63B 49, 50
Art 63F 47, 49, 50
Art 63F(3) 50
Art 63J 49, 50
Art 64 73
Art 89A 73
Art 89A(6) 63
Art 89B, 62 333
Art 89B(1) 63
Art 89B(2) 63
Art 89B(3) 63
Art 89C 63
Part 2
Chapter 14A 46, 332
Chapter 14B 46

Financial Services and Markets Act 2000 (Regulated Activities) Amendment (No 2) Order 2013, SI 2013/1881 .... 46, 94, 102, 108
Art 31(2) 71
Art 31(3) 71
Art 31(8) 71
Art 32(2) 71
Art 56(1) 72
Art 56(4) 72
Art 56(9)(a) 72
Art 56(9)(b) 72
Art 56(10) 72
Art 56(11) 72
Art 58(1)(a) 72
Art 58(1)(b) 73
Art 58(1)(c) 73
Art 58(4) 73
Art 59(4) 73
Financial Services and Markets Act 2000 (Threshold Conditions) Order 2013, SI 2013/555 65
Financial Services and Markets Tribunal (Legal Assistance) Regulations 2001, SI 2001/2632
Reg 6 78
Reg 8 78
Financial Services and Markets Tribunal (Legal Assistance Scheme – Costs) Regulations 2001/3633
Reg 12 78
Financial Services (Consumer Credit) Order 2013, SI 2013/1882
Art 3 89
Art 3(3) 92
Art 4 89
Financial Services (Distance Marketing) Regulations 2004, SI 2004/2095 .... 116, 119, 121–122, 124, 152, 154, 181–182
Part 2 123
Reg 4 123
Reg 5 123
Reg 7(2) 122
Reg 7(3) 122
Reg 7(4) 122
Reg 7(7) 122
Reg 9 182
Reg 9(3) 123
Reg 9(4) 154
Reg 10 182
Reg 10(5) 123, 311
Reg 10(5A) 311
Reg 10(5)(e) 311
Reg 10(6) 311
Reg 10(8) 311
Reg 10(9) 311
Reg 11(1)(d) 181
Reg 11(1)(g) 181
Reg 11(1)(h) 181
Reg 13 .... 123, 182
Reg 13(1)(b) 123
Reg 13(6) 123
Sch 1 123
Sch 2 .... 122, 123
Sch 3 311

Payment Services Regulations 2009, SI 2009/209 90
Privacy and Electronic Communications (EC Directive) Regulations 2003, SI 2003/2426
Reg 25 330
Reg 26 330

The Consumer Credit (Exempt Agreements) Order 1989, SI 1989/869 .... 46, 54
Transfer of Tribunal Functions Order 2010, SI 2010/22 77
Tribunal Procedure (Upper Tribunal) Rules 2008, SI 2008/2698
Reg 10 77
Reg 10(3)(d) 78
Reg 10(3)(e) 78
Tribunal Procedure (Upper Tribunal) (Amendment) Rules 2010, SI 2010/47 as amended by Tribunal Procedure (Amendment No 2) Rules 2013, SI 2013/606 77

Unfair Terms in Consumer Contracts Regulations 1999, SI 1999/2083 (UTCCR, replacing Regulations SI 1994/3159) 36, 209–215, 297–298
Reg 3(1) 210
Reg 4(1) 210
Reg 5(1) 210, 212
Reg 5(2) 210
Reg 5(3) 211
Reg 5(4) 210
Reg 6 211
Reg 6(1) 213
Reg 6(2) 211, 212, 298
Reg 7(1) 211
Reg 7(2) 212
Reg 8 298
Reg 8(1) 214
Reg 8(2) 214
Reg 10 .... 214, 215
Reg 10(4) 215
Reg 11 215
Sch 2
para 1 214
para 1(g) 213
para 1(j) 213
para 2(a) 213
para 2(b) 213
para 2(d) 214

Table of decisions, directives, regulations, treaties and conversions

Consumer Credit Directive (Directive 2008/48/EC of 23 April 2008 on credit agreements for consumers and repealing Council Directive 87/102/EEC) 21, 25, 117, 130, 309, 310
Consumer Credit Directive (Directive 2008/48/EC on credit agreements for consumers and repealing Council Directive 87/102/EEC) 159

Distance Selling Directive (Directive 97/7/EC of 20 May 1997 on the protection of consumers in respect of distance contracts) 115

Unfair Business Practices Directive (Directive 2005/29/EC of 11 May 2005 on unfair business practices in the European Union) 36
Unfair Terms Directive (Council Directive 93/12/EEC of 5 April 1993 on unfair terms in consumer contracts) 36, 209

Table of the Provisions of the FCA Handbook

Consumer Credit Sourcebook (CONC) 40, 42, 96
CONC 1.4
CONC 1.4.1(3) R 56
CONC 1.4.3(2) R 56
CONC 1.4.4 R 56
CONC 1.4.8 R 51
CONC 2
Annex 1 R 122
Annex 2 R 122
CONC 2.4
CONC 2.4.2 R 334
CONC 2.5
CONC 2.5.3(1) R 329
CONC 2.5.3(2) R 330
CONC 2.5.3(3) R 329
CONC 2.5.3(5) R 330
CONC 2.5.3(6) R 330
CONC 2.5.4 G 330
CONC 2.5.5 R 334
CONC 2.5.6 R 334
CONC 2.5.8 330
CONC 2.5.8 R 330
CONC 2.5.8(2) R 330
CONC 2.5.8(6) R 330
CONC 2.5.8(7) R 330
CONC 2.5.8(9) R 330
CONC 2.5.8(14) R 331
CONC 2.7 121
CONC 2.7.2(3) R 121
CONC 2.7.3 R 122
CONC 2.7.4 R 122
CONC 2.7.9 R 122
CONC 2.7.11 R 122
CONC 2.9 304
CONC 3 .... 97, 142
CONC 3.3
CONC 3.3.1 R 97
CONC 3.3.2 R 97
CONC 3.3.3 R 98
CONC 3.3.4 G 98
CONC 3.3.5 G 97
CONC 3.3.9 G 98
CONC 3.3.11 G 98
CONC 3.4
CONC 3.4.1 R 316
CONC 3.4.1(2) 317
CONC 3.5
CONC 3.5.2 R 98
CONC 3.5.3(1) R 98
CONC 3.5.3(3) R 98
CONC 3.5.4 G 98
CONC 3.5.5 R 98
CONC 3.5.6 G 98
CONC 3.5.7 R 98
CONC 3.5.9 R 99
CONC 3.5.12 R 99
CONC 3.5.13 R 99
CONC 3.6
CONC 3.6.5 R 100
CONC 3.6.5(2)(c) R 100
CONC 3.6.5(4) R 100
CONC 3.6.5(5) R 99
CONC 3.6.6 R 99
CONC 3.6.8 R 99
CONC 3.6.10 R 99
CONC 3.7
CONC 3.7.3 R 100
CONC 3.7.4 G 100
CONC 3.8 100
CONC 3.8.2(1) 100
CONC 3.8.2(2) 100

CONC 3.8.2(3) 100
CONC 3.8.3(2) 100
CONC 3.9
CONC 3.9.3 R 101
CONC 3.9.3(3) R 101
CONC 3.9.3(6) R 101
CONC 3.9.3(9) R 101
CONC 3.9.3(14) 101
CONC 3.9.4 R 101
CONC 3.9.5(1) R 101
CONC 3.9.5(4) R 101
CONC 3.9.10 R 101
CONC 3.9.11 R 101
CONC 4.1 102
CONC 4.1.3 R 102
CONC 4.1.4(1) R 102, 329
CONC 4.1.4(2) R 102, 329
CONC 4.1.5(2)(D) R 102
CONC 4.2 .... 143, 317, 322, 343
CONC 4.2.1 R 124
CONC 4.2.1(3) R 312
CONC 4.2.1(4) R 312
CONC 4.2.1(5) R 312
CONC 4.2.2 G 124
CONC 4.2.5 312
CONC 4.2.5(1) R 124
CONC 4.2.5(2) 124
CONC 4.2.5(2) R 124
CONC 4.2.5(3) R 125
CONC 4.2.5(4) R 125
CONC 4.2.5(5) 124
CONC 4.2.5(6) R 322
CONC 4.2.8 R 317
CONC 4.2.9 R 125
CONC 4.2.10 R 125
CONC 4.2.11 R 124
CONC 4.2.12 R 124
CONC 4.2.15 R 304
CONC 4.8.2 R 124
CONC 4.3 343
CONC 4.3.2(2) R 342
CONC 4.3.2(3) R 342
CONC 4.3.3 G 342
CONC 4.3.4(1) R 342
CONC 4.3.4(1) (borrower) R 343
CONC 4.3.4(2)(e) R 343
CONC 4.3.5 R 343
CONC 4.3.6 R 343
CONC 4.4
CONC 4.4.2(1) R 331
CONC 4.4.2(2) R 331
CONC 4.4.2(3) R 331
CONC 4.4.4(4) R 331
CONC 4.5
CONC 4.5.3 R 331
CONC 4.5.4 R 331
CONC 4.6
CONC 4.6.2 R 225
CONC 4.6.2(a) R 317
CONC 4.6.2(b) R 317
CONC 4.6.2(j) R 317
CONC 4.6.3 R 225
CONC 4.6.4 R 225
CONC 4.7
CONC 4.7.2 R 315
CONC 5.2
CONC 5.1.1 R 126
CONC 5.2.1 .... 126, 312
CONC 5.2.1(2) 126
CONC 5.2.1(3) 126
CONC 5.2.1(4) R 322
CONC 5.2.1(6) 126, 312
CONC 5.2.2 R 126, 143, 312
CONC 5.2.3 127
CONC 5.2.4(4) G 127
CONC 5.3
CONC 5.3.1 G 126
CONC 5.3.1(2) G 127
CONC 5.3.1(6) G 127
CONC 5.3.2 R 127
CONC 5.3.4 R 127, 322
CONC 5.4
CONC 5.4.2(2) R 330
CONC 5.4.3 R 329
CONC 5A 320
CONC 5A.4 344
CONC 5A.5 .... 320, 344
CONC 6.2
CONC 6.2.1 R 127
CONC 6.3
CONC 6.3.4 R 315
CONC 6.3.4(3) R 315
CONC 6.4 241
CONC 6.4.2(1) R 243
CONC 6.4.2(2) R 243

CONC 6.5
CONC 6.5.2 R 218
CONC 6.6 323
CONC 6.6.3 R 323
CONC 6.6.6 R 323
CONC 6.6.7 R to
CONC 6.6.9 R 323
CONC 6.7
CONC 6.7.2(4) R 319
CONC 6.7.4 R 304
CONC 6.7.5 R 305
CONC 6.7.5(2) R 305
CONC 6.7.6 R 305
CONC 6.7.7 R 305
CONC 6.7.8 R 305
CONC 6.7.9 R 305
CONC 6.7.10 R 305
CONC 6.7.12 R 305
CONC 6.7.13 R 305
CONC 6.7.14 R 148, 305
CONC 6.7.15 G 148, 305
CONC 6.7.16 R 148, 305
CONC 6.7.17 R 318
CONC 6.7.20 R 319
CONC 6.7.22 R 319
CONC 6.7.23 319
CONC 6.7.24 R 226
CONC 6.8
CONC 6.8.2 G 329
CONC 6.8.4 R 332
CONC 6.8.5(1) G 332
CONC 6.8.5(3) G 332
CONC 6.8.3(5) 333
CONC 7.10
CONC 7.10.1 R 216
CONC 7.10.3 G 216
CONC 7.12
CONC 7.12.2 R 218
CONC 7.12.2(4) R 217
CONC 7.12.2(6) R 218
CONC 7.12.3(3)(b) G 217
CONC 7.13
CONC 7.13.1 R 218
CONC 7.14
CONC 7.14.3 R 218
CONC 7.14.5 R 218
CONC 7.14.8 R 218
CONC 7.14.10 R 218
CONC 7.15
CONC 7.15.4 R 218
CONC 7.15.8 R 218
CONC 7.17
CONC 7.17 R 344
CONC 7.17.2(1) R 344
CONC 7.17.3(5) 344
CONC 7.17.4 R 344
CONC 7.17.5(4) R 344
CONC 7.18
CONC 7.18 R 344
CONC 7.18.2(4) R 344
CONC 7.19
CONC 7.19 R 344
CONC 7.2
CONC 7.2.1 R 216
CONC 7.2.1(2) R 216
CONG 7.2.1 R 216
CONC 7.3
CONC 7.3.4 R 216
CONC 7.3.9 R 217
CONC 7.3.10 R 216
CONC 7.3.11 R 217
CONC 7.3.12 G 217
CONC 7.3.14(1) 216
CONC 7.4
CONC 7.4.1 R 218
CONC 7.5
CONC 7.5.1 G 218, 219
CONC 7.6
CONC 7.6.1(1) R 226
CONC 7.6.1(2) R 226
CONC 7.6.2(3) G 226
CONC 7.6.3 R 226
CONC 7.6.5(2) G 226
CONC 7.6.6 G 226
CONC 7.6.7 R 226
CONC 7.6.9 G 226
CONC 7.6.12(1) R 318
CONC 7.6.12(2) R 318
CONC 7.6.12(3) R 318
CONC 7.6.12(5) R 318
CONC 7.6.13(1) 318
CONC 7.6.13(1) R 319
CONC 7.6.13(2) 318
CONC 7.6.14(1) R 319
CONC 7.6.14(2) R 319
CONC 7.6.15(3) G 317, 318
CONC 7.6.16 R 227

CONC 7.7
CONC 7.7.5 216–7
CONC 7.9
CONC 7.9.1 217
CONC 7.9.6 216
CONC 7.9.7 216
CONC 7.9.12(2) R 217
CONC 7.9.14 217
CONC 8.2
CONC 8.2.4 R 339
CONC 8.3
CONC 8.3.1 R 339
CONC 8.3.1(3) R 339
CONC 8.3.4 R 339
CONC 8.3.4(2) R 339
CONC 8.3.7(2) 339
CONC 8.3.7(3) 339
CONC 8.4
CONC 8.4.1 R 340
CONC 8.4.3 R 340
CONC 8.5
CONC 8.5.1 R 340
CONC 8.5.1(3) R 340
CONC 8.6
CONC 8.6.1 R 341
CONC 8.6.4 G 341
CONC 8.6.5 R 341
CONC 8.7
CONC 8.7.2(1) R 340
CONC 8.7.3(1) G 340
CONC 8.7.4(1) R 339
CONC 8.7.4(2) R 340, 341
CONC 8.7.4(3) 341
CONC 8.7.6(3) R 340
CONC 8.7.6(6) 340
CONC 8.8
CONC 8.8.1(2) R 341
CONC 8.8.1(3) R 341
CONC 8.8.1(4) R 341
CONC 8.8.1(5) R 341
CONC 8.8.1(6) R 341
CONC 8.8.1(8) R 341
CONC 9.2
CONC 9.2.2(2) R 338
CONC 9.2.3 R 338
CONC 11.2
CONC 11.2.2 R 343
CONC 11.2.3 R 343
CONC 11.2.3(4) R 343
CONC 11.2.4 R 343
CONC 13.1
CONC 13.1.2 G 186
CONC 13.1.3 G 185
CONC 13.1.3(2) G 185
CONC 13.1.4(2) G 186
CONC 13.1.4(6) G 186
CONC 13.1.6(2) G 186
CONC 14.1
CONC 14.1.2(2) R 74
CONC 14.1.4(1) R 75
CONC 14.1.4(2) R 75
CONC 15.1
CONC 15.1.3 R 142
CONC 15.1.5(1) R 143
CONC 15.1.5(2) R 143
CONC 15.1.5(3) R 143
CONC 15.1.5(6) R 143
CONC 15.1.8(2) R 143
CONC 15.1.8(3) R 143
CONC 15.1.9 G 143
CONC 15.1.10(2) G 143
CONC 15.1.10(3) G 143
CONC 15.1.11 R 143
CONC 15.1.12(2) R 146
CONC 15.1.13(1) R 146
CONC 15.1.13(3) R 146
CONC 15.1.15 R 146
CONC App 1 25
CONC App 1.1 291
CONC App 1.1 R 25
CONC App 1.1.3(1)(a) R 30
CONC App 1.1.3(1)(b) R 30
CONC App 1.1.3(1)(c) R 30
CONC App 1.1.3(1)(d) R 31
CONC App 1.1.3(1)(e) R 32
CONC App 1.1.3(2)(a) R 30
CONC App 1.1.3(2)(b) R 31
CONC App 1.1.3(3) R 30
CONC App 1.1.4 R 26
CONC App 1.1.5 R .. 26, 27, 28
CONC App 1.1.6 R 26, 28
CONC App 1.1.6(1)(a) R 28
CONC App 1.1.6(1)(b) R 28
CONC App 1.1.6(1)(c) R 28
CONC App 1.1.6(1)(d) R 29
CONC App 1.1.6(1)(e) R 29
CONC App 1.1.6(1)(f) R 29
CONC App 1.1.6(1)(g) R 29

CONC App 1.1.6(1)(h) R 29
CONC App 1.1.6(1)(i) R 29
CONC App 1.1.6(2) 29
CONC App 1.1.7 R 29
CONC App 1.1.8 R 29
CONC App 1.1.8(b) R 30
CONC App 1.1.9 R 30
CONC App 1.1.12 R 30
CONC App 1.1.13 R 30
CONC App 1.1.14 R 31
CONC App 1.1.15(2) R 32
CONC App 1.1.15(3) R 32
CONC App 1.1.15(4) R 32
CONC App 1.1.16 R 31
CONC App 1.1.17 R 30
CONC App 1.1.18(b) R 31
CONC App 1.2 R 25
CONC App 1.2.2 R 32
CONC App 1.2.3(2) R 32
CONC App 1.2.3(3) R 33
CONC App 1.2.3(4) R 33
CONC App 1.2.3(5)(a) R 33
CONC App 1.2.3(5)(b) R 33
CONC App 1.2.3(6) R 33
CONC App 1.2.5 R 33
CONC App 1.2.5(a) R 33
CONC App 1.2.5(b) R 33
CONC App 1.2.5(e) R 33
CONC App 1.2.5(f) R 33
CONC App 1.2.5(g) R 33
CONC App 1.2.5(h) R 33
CONC App 1.2.5(i) R 34
CONC App 1.2.5(j) R 34
CONC App 1.2.5(k) R 34
CONC App 1.2.5(l) R 34
CONC App 1.2.5(m) R 34
CONC App 1.2.6 R 32
CONC App 1.3 52
CONC App 1.4
CONC App 1.4.2 R 55
CONC App 1.4.6 R 55, 56
CONC App 1.4.7 R 55, 56
CONC App 1.4.8 R 56
Credit Unions sourcebook (CREDs) 43

Decision Procedure and Penalties Manual (DEPP) 43, 89
DEPP 2 .... 87, 88, 90, 91
DEPP 2.2
DEPP 2.2.1 90
DEPP 2.5
DEPP 2.5.3 67
DEPP 2.5.4 68
DEPP 2.5.5 68
DEPP 2.5.7 88
DEPP 2.5.8 88
DEPP 3.2
DEPP 3.2.16 .... 68, 90
DEPP 6.2
DEPP 6.2.1 90
DEPP 6.2.1 G 71
DEPP 6.2.9A G 71
DEPP 6.2.9A(5) 71
DEPP 6.2.9A(6) 71
DEPP 6.6 90
DEPP 6.7 90
DEPP 6.7.3(3) G 90
Dispute Resolution: Complaints (DISP) 43
Chapter 6A 92
D 1 Annex 1A 250
D 1 Annex 1B 250
DISP 1.10
DISP 1.10 4 R 250
DISP 1.10.1(2) R 249
DISP 1.10.4 249
DISP 1.10.4A R 249
DISP 1.10.6A R 249
DISP 1.10A.1 R 250
DISP 1.10A.1(1A) R 250
DISP 1.10A.4 R 250
DISP 1.10A.7 G 250
DISP 1.2
DISP 1.2.1 R 248
DISP 1.3
DISP 1.3.1 R 248
DISP 1.3.3 R 248
DISP 1.3.7 R 248
DISP 1.4
DISP 1.4.1 R 248
DISP 1.4.1(3) R 248
DISP 1.4.1(4) 248
DISP 1.4.1(5) R 249
DISP 1.4.4 R 364
DISP 1.5
DISP 1.5.1 R 249

DISP 1.6
DISP 1.6.1 R 248
DISP 1.6.2 R 248
DISP 1.6.2(1) R 363
DISP 1.6.2(2) R 249
DISP 2.8.2(2) R 363
DISP 1.7
DISP 1.7.1 R 249
DISP 1.7.2 R 249
DISP 1.8
DISP 1.8.1 R 248
DISP 1.9
DISP 1.9 R 249
DISP 2.3
DISP 2.3.1 R 362
DISP 2.3.1(3) R 362
DISP 2.3.1(4) R 362
DISP 2.3.2-A G 362
DISP 2.7
DISP 2.7.1 R 362
DISP 2.7.2 R 363
DISP 2.7.3 R 362
DISP 2.7.3(1) R 362
DISP 2.8
DISP 2.8.1(2) R 363
DISP 2.8.2(1) R 363
DISP 2.8.2(3) R 363
DISP 2.8.2(5) R 363
DISP 2.8.3 G 363
DISP 2.8.4 G 363
DISP 3.2
DISP 3.2.2 R 363
DISP 3.3
DISP 3.3.3(17) R 364
DISP 3.3.4 R 364
DISP 3.3.4(8) R 364
DISP 3.3.4(9) R 364
DISP 3.3.4(10) R 364
DISP 3.3.5 R 364
DISP 3.5
DISP 3.5.1 R 364
DISP 3.5.4(1) R 364
DISP 3.5.4(2) R 365
DISP 3.5.5 R 364
DISP 3.6
DISP 3.6.4 R 365
DISP 3.6.6 R 365
DISP 3.6.6(1) R 365
DISP 3.6.6(4A) R 365
DISP 3.7
DISP 3.7.2 R 365
DISP 3.7.4 R 366
DISP 3.7.5 G 366
DISP 3.7.7 R 366
DISP 3.7.8 R 366
DISP 3.7.9 R 366
DISP 3.7.10 E 366
DISP 6.2
DISP 6.2.4 – 6.2.9 G 92
DISP 6.2.9 G 92

Enforcement Guide (EG)
EG 12.2 79

Fit and Proper Test for Approved Persons (FIT) 42

General Provisions (GEN)
GEN 2
GEN 2.1.10 G 40
GEN 2.2.1 R 41
GEN 2.2.2 G 41
GEN 2.2.7 41
GEN 2.2.7 R 42
GEN 2.2.11 R 42

Insurance Conduct of Business Rules (ICOB) 360

Mortgages and Home Finance: Conduct of Business Sourcebook (MCOB) 40, 42, 97, 99
MCOB 1.2
MCOB 1.2.1(1) R 271
MCOB 1.2.3(1) 272
MCOB 1.2.3(2)(b) 272
MCOB 1.2.3A R 272
MCOB 1.2.9C R 272
MCOB 1.2.9D R 272
MCOB 1.2.9E R 272
MCOB 1.2.10 R 272
MCOB 1.3
MCOB 1.3.3B R 272
MCOB 2.2
MCOB 2.2.6 R 272
MCOB 2.2.8 G 272

MCOB 2.3
- MCOB 2.3.2 R 273
- MCOB 2.3.5 G 273

MCOB 2.5
- MCOB 2.5A.1 273

MCOB 2.6
- MCOB 2.6.2 273
- MCOB 2.6.2 R 273
- MCOB 2.6.3 R 273
- MCOB 2.6.27 R 276
- MCOB 2.6A.1 273

MCOB 3 273

MCOB 3.10
- MCOB 3.10.1 R 277
- MCOB 3.10.3 G 277

MCOB 3.11
- MCOB 3.11.1(2) G 273
- MCOB 3.11.2 R 277

MCOB 3.2
- MCOB 3.2.3 R 273
- MCOB 3.2.4 R 275
- MCOB 3.2.4(3) R 277
- MCOB 3.2.5(2) R 275
- MCOB 3.2.5(3) R 274

MCOB 3.5
- MCOB 3.5.5 R 274

MCOB 3.6
- MCOB 3.6.3 R 275
- MCOB 3.6.3(1) R 275
- MCOB 3.6.3(g) R 275
- MCOB 3.6.8(1) R 276
- MCOB 3.6.8(2) R 276
- MCOB 3.6.9 R 276
- MCOB 3.6.13 R 276
- MCOB 3.6.16 G 276
- MCOB 3.6.17 R 276
- MCOB 3.6.17(3) R 276
- MCOB 3.6.23 R 276
- MCOB 3.6.24 G 276
- MCOB 3.6.25 R 276

MCOB 3.7
- MCOB 3.7.1 R 274
- MCOB 3.7.1(4) R 274
- MCOB 3.7.3 R 277

MCOB 3.8 277
- MCOB 3.8.2 R 277

MCOB 4.1
- MCOB 4.1.2 R 281
- MCOB 4.1.2C G 282
- MCOB 4.1.2D G 282

MCOB 4.4
- MCOB 4.4A.1 R 278
- MCOB 4.4A.2(1) R 278
- MCOB 4.4A.4(1) R 278
- MCOB 4.4A.4(2) R 278
- MCOB 4.4A.5G 278
- MCOB 4.4A.8 R 278
- MCOB 4.4A.9 R 278
- MCOB 4.4A.13 G 278
- MCOB 4.4A.17 R 278
- MCOB 4.4A.18 R 279
- MCOB 4.4A.21 279

MCOB 4.7
- MCOB 4.7A 280, 281, 282
- MCOB 4.7A.2 R 279
- MCOB 4.7A.3 R 279
- MCOB 4.7A.3(2) R 279
- MCOB 4.7A.4(1) E 280
- MCOB 4.7A.5(1) R 279
- MCOB 4.7A.5(3) R 280
- MCOB 4.7A.6 R 280
- MCOB 4.7A.9 R 280
- MCOB 4.7A.10 G 280
- MCOB 4.7A.12 R 280
- MCOB 4.7A.13 R 280
- MCOB 4.7A.15 R 281
- MCOB 4.7A.19 R 281
- MCOB 4.7A.23 G 281
- MCOB 4.7A.25 R 281
- MCOB 4.7A.25(2) R 281

MCOB 4.8
- MCOB 4.8A.2 G 282
- MCOB 4.8A.3 G 282
- MCOB 4.8A.4 G 281
- MCOB 4.8A.5 R 281
- MCOB 4.8A.7 282
- MCOB 4.8A.10 R 282
- MCOB 4.8A.11(1) G 282
- MCOB 4.8A.14(1) R 282
- MCOB 4.8A.14(2) R 283
- MCOB 4.8A.14(4)(a) R 283
- MCOB 4.8A.14(4)(b) R 283
- MCOB 4.8A.14(5) 283
- MCOB 4.8A.15 R 282
- MCOB 4.8A.17 R 283
- MCOB 4.8A.18(1) R 284
- MCOB 4.8A.18(2) R 284
- MCOB 4.8A.18(3) R 283

MCOB 5 .... 285, 289, 290
MCOB 5 Annex 1 R 284
MCOB 5.3
MCOB 5.3.1 R 284
MCOB 5.3.2 G 284
MCOB 5.4
MCOB 5.4.1 R 284
MCOB 5.4.10 R 284
MCOB 5.5
MCOB 5.5.1 R 284
MCOB 5.5.1(2)(a) R 284
MCOB 5.5.11 R 285
MCOB 5.5.15 R 284
MCOB 5.6
MCOB 5.6 R 284
MCOB 5.6.5 R 284
MCOB 5.6.6 R 285
MCOB 5.6.7 G 285
MCOB 5.7
MCOB 5.7 R 285
MCOB 5.7.2(6) R 285
MCOB 5.7.2(7) R 285
MCOB 6.3
MCOB 6.3.2 R 285
MCOB 6.4
MCOB 6.4.1 R 285
MCOB 6.4.1(2) R 285
MCOB 6.4.3 R 286
MCOB 6.4.4 R 285
MCOB 6.4.4(4)(b) R 286
MCOB 6.4.4(5) R 285
MCOB 6.4.4(5)(b) R 286
MCOB 6.4.4(7A) R 286
MCOB 6.4.5 G 286
MCOB 6.4.9 R 285
MCOB 6.4.11(1) R 286
MCOB 6.4.11(6) R 286
MCOB 6.4.11A R 286
MCOB 6.4.13 R 286
MCOB 6.7
MCOB 6.7.1 R 286
MCOB 7 290
MCOB 7.4
MCOB 7.4.1 R 286
MCOB 7.4.1(9) R 287
MCOB 7.4.2 R 287
MCOB 7.4.4 R 287
MCOB 7.5
MCOB 7.5.1 R 287
MCOB 7.5.1(2) R 287
MCOB 7.5.3(1)(a) R 287
MCOB 7.5.3(1)(b)(ii) R 288
MCOB 7.5.3(2)(a) 288
MCOB 7.5.3(2)(customer) R 288
MCOB 7.5.3(3) R 288
MCOB 7.5.3(4) (firm) R 288
MCOB 7.5.3(4) R 288
MCOB 7.5.3A R 288
MCOB 7.6.1 R 288
MCOB 7.6.2 R 288
MCOB 7.6
MCOB 7.6.7 R 289
MCOB 7.6.9(1) R 289
MCOB 7.6.9(2) R 289
MCOB 7.6.10 G 289
MCOB 7.6.14 R 289
MCOB 7.6.18 R 289
MCOB 7.6.22 R 289
MCOB 7.6.28 R 289
MCOB 7.6.28A R 290
MCOB 7.6.28A(2) R 290
MCOB 7.6.31 R 290
MCOB 7.7
MCOB 7.7.1(2) R 290
MCOB 7.7.1A G 290
MCOB 7.7.2 R 290
MCOB 7.7.3 R 290
MCOB 10 .... 276, 291
MCOB 10.2
MCOB 10.2.1 G 291
MCOB 10.3
MCOB 10.3.2 G 291
MCOB 10.4
MCOB 10.4.3 G 291
MCOB 11 .... 279, 291
MCOB 11.6
MCOB 11.6.2(1) R 291
MCOB 11.60(3) R 296
MCOB 11.6.4 E 291–2
MCOB 11.6.5(1) R 292
MCOB 11.6.5(2)(a) R 292
MCOB 11.6.5(2)(b) R 292
MCOB 11.6.6 R 292
MCOB 11.6.7 G 292
MCOB 11.6.8(2) G 292
MCOB 11.6.9(6) G 293
MCOB 11.6.10(2) 293

MCOB 11.6.11 G 293
MCOB 11.6.11(1) G 293
MCOB 11.6.13(3) G 293
MCOB 11.6.14 R 293
MCOB 11.6.15(3) G 293
MCOB 11.6.16(2) R 294
MCOB 11.6.18 R 293
MCOB 11.6.18(2) R ... 293, 294
MCOB 11.6.18(3) R 293
MCOB 11.6.20 R 294, 295
MCOB 11.6.22 R 294
MCOB 11.6.23 G 294
MCOB 11.6.24 R 294
MCOB 11.6.26 R 294
MCOB 11.6.26(1) 295
MCOB 11.6.26(2) 295
MCOB 11.6.30 G 295
MCOB 11.6.32(1) 295
MCOB 11.6.32(1) R 295
MCOB 11.6.32(3) 295
MCOB 11.6.34 R 294
MCOB 11.6.34(1) R 295
MCOB 11.6.34(2) R 295
MCOB 11.6.39(1) R 295
MCOB 11.6.39(3) R 295
MCOB 11.6.40 G to
MCOB 11.6.52 G 296
MCOB 11.6.41 R 295, 297
MCOB 11.6.42 G 295
MCOB 11.6.45 G 295
MCOB 11.6.46 E 295
MCOB 11.6.48 R 296
MCOB 11.6.49 R 296
MCOB 11.6.50 R 296
MCOB 11.6.53 E 297
MCOB 11.6.54(2) G 297
MCOB 11.6.55(1) R 297
MCOB 11.6.55(2) R 297
MCOB 11.6.57 R 296
MCOB 11.6.58 R 296
MCOB 11.6.59 G 296
MCOB 11.6.60 R 294
MCOB 11.6.60(2) R 294
MCOB 12 297
MCOB 12.1
MCOB 12.1.4 R 298
MCOB 12.3
MCOB 12.3.2 G 298
MCOB 12.3.4 R 299
MCOB 12.4
MCOB 12.4.1 299
MCOB 12.4.2 G 299
MCOB 12.4.4(1) 299
MCOB 12.4.4(3) R 299
MCOB 12.4.6(3) G 299
MCOB 12.4.8 R 299
MCOB 12.5
MCOB 12.5.1 R 298
MCOB 12.5.3 G 298
MCOB 13.3
MCOB 13.3.1 R 299
MCOB 13.3.1(2) R 299
MCOB 13.3.1A R 300
MCOB 13.3.1A(2) R 300
MCOB 13.3.1A(2)
(customer) R 300
MCOB 13.3.2A R 300
MCOB 13.3.2A(4) R 300
MCOB 13.3.2A(5) R 301
MCOB 13.3.2A(6) R 300
MCOB 13.3.3 G 299
MCOB 13.3.3A R 300
MCOB 13.3.4A(1) R 300
MCOB 13.3.4AA R 300
MCOB 13.3.4B R 301
MCOB 13.3.4D G 301
MCOB 13.3.6 G 300
MCOB 13.3.9(1) R 301
MCOB 13.3.9(2) R 301
MCOB 13.3.10 G 301
MCOB 13.4.1 R 301
MCOB 13.4.1(1) R 301
MCOB 13.4.4 R 301
MCOB 13.5
MCOB 13.5.1 R 302
MCOB 13.5.2 G 302
MCOB 13.5.3 R 299
MCOB 13.5.4 R 299
MCOB 13.6 302
MCOB 13.6.1 303
MCOB 13.6.1(2) R 302
MCOB 13.6.1(a) R 302
MCOB 13.6.2 G 302
MCOB 13.6.4(2) 303
MCOB 13.6.6 R 303
MCOB 13.7
MCOB 13.7 R 302

Perimeter Guidance Manual (PERG) 43, 47
PERG 8 107
PERG 8.17
PERG 8.17.3 109
PERG 8.4 97
PERG 8.6 96
Principles for Businesses (PRIN) 41, 43
Professional Firms (PROF) 43, 75
PROF 3
PROF 3 Annex 1 77
PROF 3 Annex 2 77
PROF 4.1
PROF 4.1.2 R 77
PROF 4.1.3 R 77
Prudential Sourcebook for Mortgage and Home Finance Firms, and Insurance Intermediaries (MIPRU)
MIPRU 42
MIPRU 4.1.4 R 42

Senior Management Arrangements, Systems and Controls (SYSC)
SYSC 4.1.1 R 41
Statements of Principle and Code of Practice for Approved Persons (APER) 42
APER 2.1
APER 2.1A.3 P 91
CHAPTER 4 91
Supervision (SUP)
Chapter 10A 69
SUP 7.2
SUP 7.2.5 87
SUP 7.3
SUP 7.3.2 86
SUP 7.3.4 87
SUP 10A
Annex 4 69
SUP 10A.4.4 R 69
SUP 10A.6 69
SUP 10A.7.1 69
SUP 10A.8 70
SUP 10A.9 70
SUP 11 94
SUP 11.4
SUP 11.4.2A R 95
SUP 12.2
SUP 12.2.3 G 73
SUP 12.4
SUP 12.4.2(2) R 75
SUP 12.4.2(3) R 75
SUP 12.4.5B R 75
SUP 12.5 74
SUP 12.5.5(3) R 74
SUP 12.5.6A(b) R 74
SUP 12.5.6A(c) R 74
SUP 12.5.6A(d) R 74
SUP 12.5.6A(e) R 74
SUP 12.6
SUP 12.6.1 R 75
SUP 12.6.6 R 75
SUP 12.6.8 G 75
SUP 12.6.9 G 75
SUP 12.7
SUP 12.7(3) R 75
SUP 12.7(4) R 75
SUP 12.8
SUP 12.8.1 R 75
SUP 12.8.3 R 75
SUP 16
Annex 21 R 93
SUP 16.11
SUP 16.11.1 R 93
SUP 16.11.5 93
SUP 16.12
SUP 16.12.29 C 93
SUP 16.12.29B R 93
SUP 16.2 250

Threshold Conditions (COND) 42, 65

Unfair Contract Terms Regulatory Guide (UNFCOG)
UNFCOG 1.1
UNFCOG 1.1.2 G 215
UNFCOG 1.3
UNFCOG 1.3.1(3) G 211
UNFCOG 1.3.4(1) G 215
UNFCOG 1.3.4(2) G 215

1 Key concepts in consumer credit law

Credit

1. The key concept underlying the whole law of consumer credit is of course that of credit. It is not so much defined but elucidated in section 9(1) of the Consumer Credit Act 1974 as including 'a cash loan and any other form of financial accommodation'.

2. A credit agreement is one under which the lender agrees to provide credit to the borrower. The Consumer Credit Act 1974 describes the parties to the credit agreement as creditor and debtor but the Financial Services and Markets Act 2000 (Regulated Activities) Order 2001,[1] the RAO, refers to the parties as borrower and lender. This is the preferred modern terminology that will be utilised here. Whether any particular agreement is to be classified as a credit agreement is a question to be decided by reference to the circumstances at the date of the agreement.[2] Moreover, the court, in deciding whether an agreement involves the provision of credit, will not be confined to the literal wording of the agreement but will consider its essential nature.[3]

3. Central to the concept is the entitlement to deferment of payment that would otherwise fall due. This was explained by the Court of Appeal in *Dimond v Lovell*,[4] where Lord Justice Scott said at [54]: 'If payment for goods of services or land is deferred after the time when, if nothing about payments had been agreed, the payment would be due, the payer is being given credit.'

4. Moreover, the deferment must be a matter of contractual entitlement, not mere forbearance on the part of the lender. This was a point made by Professor Goode in his *Consumer Credit Legislation* in a passage approved by Lord Justice Scott.[5]

1 SI 2001/544.
2 *McMillan Williams v Range* 2004 1 WLR 1858 at [16].
3 *McMillan supra* at [23].
4 2000 1 QB 216.
5 At [56], [57].

5. In the *Dimond* case, the hire company supplied cars on hire to victims following a road traffic accident, but under the relevant agreement, payment for the hire did not become due until finalisation of the accident claim. The relevant agreement was found to be a credit agreement as well as a hire agreement. Lord Hoffman, in the House of Lords, said: 'The only obligation of the [hire company] under the agreement was to provide the vehicle. In the absence of credit, it would have been entitled to payment during or at the end of the hire. All the provisions about pursuit of the claim were express or implied conditions and therefore constituted the granting of credit.'[6]

6. Deferment will not always be easy to ascertain; Lord Hobhouse, in *Dimond v Lovell*, said that the test would not 'always be a satisfactory one to apply'.[7]

7. Where the operation of the agreement may or may not give rise to a debit balance, the court is unlikely to find that it gives rise to the provision of credit. In *Nejad v City Index Ltd*,[8] Mr Nejad was a customer of City Index with whom he had a credit account. Mr Nejad was entitled to bet on movements of various financial indices and could continue to do so up to the time when his financial exposure as a result of the bets undertaken was up to the limit set on what was described as his credit account. The court rejected an argument on behalf of Mr Nejad that this was a credit agreement as the financial position of Mr Nejad could not be ascertained until the closing of the individual bets, at which time there might or might not be a balance owning by Mr Nejad. Put shortly, the agreement did not give rise to any deferment of an existing liability. The significance of the credit account was that Mr Nejad was not required to put up financial security to cover his financial position but this in itself was not the grant of credit.

8. Likewise, an *advance payment* for services to be performed in the future is not the grant of credit in that it does not involve the deferment of an obligation to pay. So payment of advance commission was held not to be credit in the employment case of *McMillan Williams v Range*.[9] However, it was an important factor in that case that the parties hoped and believed that the amount advanced would be covered by the commission to be earned in due course. It might have been different if the amount of the advance was in excess of what the parties could reasonably have expected the employee to earn in due course.

9. Section 9(3) caters for the case of a hire purchase transaction. The amount of credit is the total price of the goods (i.e. the total amount payable under the agreement including the option to purchase)[10] less the deposit

6 2002 1 AC 384 at 395.

7 At page 405.

8 2001 GCCR 2461.

9 2004 1 WLR 1858; also *Maple Leaf Volatility Master Fund v Rouvroy* 2009 CCLR 9.

10 Section 189(1) definition of 'total price'.

and the other items entering into the total charge for credit. Doubtless this provision is intended to prevent an argument that because a hire purchase agreement is framed as a hire agreement it could not be a credit agreement.

10. Section 9(4) reflects the fundamental concept that credit involves financial assistance to the debtor, not the charges and expenses he or she incurs for the credit.[11] It provides that: 'For the purposes of this Act, an item entering into the total charge for credit shall not be treated as credit even though time is allowed for its payment.' In relation to any particular credit agreement, it is necessary to consider the total charge for credit rules made by the FCA under Article 60M of the RAO[12] in order to differentiate between an item that forms part of the credit or conversely is part of the total charge for credit. Merely because the credit agreement provides for interest to be charged on an item does not mean that the item forms part of the credit.[13]

11. In deciding whether a particular item is part of the credit, the terms of the agreement, although relevant, are not determinative: 'The Court must consider all the circumstances including the documents relating to the agreement and may well have to ascertain objectively the purpose of the borrowing.'[14]

12. Credit provided in a currency other than sterling is to be treated as provided in sterling of an equivalent amount.[15]

Consumer credit agreement

13. A consumer credit agreement is an agreement concluded between a lender and the borrower, being an *individual* for the provision of credit of any amount.[16] It embraces both regulated agreements and exempt agreements for the purposes of the Regulated Activities Order. The 1974 Act uses the terms 'creditor' and 'debtor', and not 'lender' and 'borrower', but the Regulated Activities Order uses the latter terminology so those terms will be used here.

14. At the time of the coming into force of the Consumer Credit Act 2006, the definition of 'consumer credit agreement' limited such agreements to those in which the amount of credit did not exceed £25,000.[17]

11 *Watchtower Investments Ltd v Payne* 2001 GCCR 3055, quoting Professor Goode.

12 These follow the Total Charge for Credit Regulations made under section 20 of the Consumer Credit Act 1974.

13 *Southern Personal Loans Ltd v Walker* 2010 1 WLR 1819.

14 *Watchtower Investments* at [52] per Peter Gibson LJ.

15 Section 9(2).

16 Section 8(1).

17 At the time of the 1974 Act, the limit was £5,000, later increased to £15,000 as from 20 May 1985. The limit was then increased to £25,000 by the Consumer Credit (Increase of Monetary Limits) Order 1998 SI 1998/996 with effect from 1 May 1998.

However, this definition led to difficulties as the calculation of the amount of credit was not always straightforward, depending in some circumstances on whether an item did or did not form part of the total charge for credit, and whether or not an agreement was or was not a multiple agreement. The removal of the financial ceiling by the 2006 Act thankfully largely removed this area of controversy. The financial ceiling was lifted from credit agreements concluded after 6 April 2008.[18] However, an exception was made for a certain category of 'relevant agreements' as defined in the relevant Commencement Order where the applicable date was 31 October 2008.[19] A relevant agreement is one secured by land mortgage on overseas property, or one secured on property in the United Kingdom where less than 40 per cent of the land is used in connection with a dwelling.[20]

The definition of 'creditor'

15. The lender with whom the consumer credit agreement is concluded can of course be either an individual or body corporate; in fact, the latter is more common. By virtue of section 189 of the Act, the term also includes an assignee of the lender. The definition provides that 'unless the context otherwise requires, "creditor" means the person, providing credit under a consumer credit agreement or the person to whom his rights and duties under the agreement have passed by assignment or operation of law, and in relation to a prospective consumer credit agreement, includes the prospective creditor'.

16. In *Jones v Link Financial Ltd*,[21] the original lender had assigned the benefit of a debt accruing under a loan agreement to Link Financial, who duly gave notice of the assignment of the debt to the borrower. Link Financial then took proceedings on the debt. In defence, the borrower contended that Link Financial was not a creditor for the purposes of this definition since, it was argued, Link Financial had not taken an assignment of any *duties* owed by the lender under the loan agreement. Therefore, it was said, Link Financial could not recover the debt from the borrower. This argument was rejected since Link Financial had taken on the obligations necessary to be fulfilled in connection with recovery of the debt (for instance, service of a default notice) and was therefore a creditor for the purposes of the definition.

18 Schedule 2, Consumer Credit Act (Commencement No 4 and Transitional Provisions) Order SI 2008/831.

19 Schedule 3, Consumer Credit Act (Commencement No 4 and Transitional Provisions) Order SI 2008/831.

20 Schedule 1, Consumer Credit Act (Commencement No 4 and Transitional Provisions) Order SI 2008/831.

21 2013 1 WLR 693.

The borrower

17. The borrower under a consumer credit agreement must be an *individual.* Credit agreements concluded with borrowers who are not individuals are entirely outside the ambit of the Act.

18. The natural meaning of the term 'individual' is that of a natural person but it has an extended meaning under the Consumer Credit Act 1974. It can of course include an agreement concluded with more than one individual and this situation is catered for by section 185 of the Act.

19. The term 'individual' is defined by section 189(1) to include a partnership of two or three persons, provided that not all of the partners are bodies corporate. It can also include an unincorporated association provided that not all of the members of the unincorporated association are bodies corporate. This definition was introduced by the Consumer Credit Act 2006 and is the same definition as is found in the RAO.

20. An agreement entered into with an individual and a body corporate is a consumer credit agreement and the body corporate is treated as an individual for the purposes of the Act.[22] Where an agreement is entered into with more than one individual, anything to be done in relation to an individual has to be done in relation to each of them.[23]

21. What is important for the purpose of the definition of consumer credit agreement is the legal nature of the borrower. It is irrelevant whether or not the borrower is entering into the loan for the purposes of its business, although this may be relevant as to whether the agreement is an *exempt* agreement. The position is to be contrasted with the definition of 'consumer' in the Consumer Contracts (Information, Cancellation and Additional Charges) Regulations 2013,[24] which defines an 'individual' as someone acting for purposes outside his or her trade or profession.

22. The Act continues to apply if the agreement is assigned by the borrower, whether or not to an individual, including by operation of law (e.g. to a trustee in bankruptcy).[25]

23. By an amendment having effect from 28 February 2014, a green deal plan is not a consumer credit agreement unless the requirements of section 189B are satisfied.[26] An agreement satisfying these requirements is known as a 'green deal consumer credit agreement'. The property in question must either be a dwelling or the person making the arrangement must be an individual.[27] The amount of credit is taken to be the amount of the

22 Section 185(5).
23 Section 185(1)(a).
24 SI 2013/3134.
25 See the definition of 'debtor' in section 189(1).
26 Section 8(4).
27 Section 189B(1).

improvement costs.[28] A green deal plan is one as specified by section 1 of the Energy Act 2011.[29]

24. The Act distinguishes between various types of consumer credit agreements, distinctions important in a variety of different contexts. Specifically, the Act distinguishes between:

(a) fixed sum and running account agreements;
(b) restricted use and unrestricted use credit agreements; and
(c) borrower-lender and borrower-lender-supplier agreements.

25. A very important distinction is between regulated and exempt agreements.

26. Other different categories of importance in different contexts are credit token agreements, pawn agreements, non-commercial agreements, small agreements and multiple agreements. These differing categories will be explained hereafter.

Running account and fixed sum agreements

27. Section 10 of the Consumer Credit Act 1974 draws a distinction between running account and fixed sum credit agreements. The Act proceeds by defining running account credit and then providing that any credit that is not running account credit is a fixed sum agreement. It makes clear that credit received by instalments is still fixed sum credit.

28. By an amendment to the definition made by the Consumer Credit Act 2006, running account credit must be provided under a consumer credit agreement.[30] This means that the agreement must be with an individual as defined by the Act.

29. Running account credit is defined as 'a facility under a consumer credit agreement whereby the debtor is enabled to receive from time to time (whether in his own person or by another person) from the creditor or a third party cash, goods and services (or any of them) to an amount or value such that, taking into account payments made by or to the credit of the debtor, the credit limit (if any) is not at any time exceeded'.

30. Professor Goode has referred to running account agreements as being in essence 'revolving credit' with payments being made in and out throughout the duration of the agreement.[31]

28 Section 189B(2)(b).
29 Section 189(1).
30 The original definition referred to credit being provided under a 'personal credit agreement'. There is now no difference between a personal credit agreement and a consumer credit agreement in the light of the abolition of a credit ceiling in the definition of consumer credit agreement.
31 Consumer Credit Law and Practice, cited with approval in *Goshawk Dedicated (No 2) Ltd v Bank of Scotland* 2006 2 All ER 610 at [94].

31. Accordingly, central to the concept is the credit limit. This is, normally speaking, the extent of credit that the individual is allowed under the terms of the agreement. The term 'credit limit' is defined[32] as 'as respects any period, the maximum debit balance which, under the agreement, is allowed to stand on the account during that period, disregarding any term of the agreement allowing that maximum to be exceeded merely temporarily'.

32. The amount of credit provided under a running account credit agreement is equal to the credit limit. There is a distinction between running account being *provided* and its being *drawn down*. Credit is provided at the outset when the agreement is entered into but it is utilised only when the credit is drawn down subsequently. The distinction is illustrated by section 14(3) in relation to credit token agreements.

33. If in the case of a running account agreement, there is a term in the agreement to allowing the credit limit to be exceeded merely temporarily, this does not amount to a separate agreement for fixed sum credit, or amount to any change in the credit limit.[33]

34. Examples of running account agreements are store card agreements, credit card agreements and overdraft facilities.

35. Although Professor Goode has referred to running account agreements as involving what he refers to as 'revolving credit' with payments going in and out of the credit facility over time, this definition is incomplete. Fixed sum credit, by contrast, can arise when an amount is earmarked in some way for some specific purpose. However, difficult situations can arise.

36. The distinction between the two types of credit was extensively discussed by Sir Francis Ferris in *Goshawk Dedicated (No 2) Ltd v Governor and Company of the Bank of Scotland.* At issue, there was a complicated arrangement whereby the bank provided funding to individuals for the funding of accident claims through the courts. It was a term of the credit arrangements that the bank would finance future disbursements connected with the litigation (court fees, photocopying costs and so forth). It was also a requirement that a legal expenses insurance policy should be taken out to fund an adverse costs order in the event that the claim was unsuccessful. The premium on this insurance policy was known prior to the credit being advanced and was funded by the credit but this was not a requirement of the scheme.

37. There was no dispute that the obligation to fund future disbursements was running account credit as the amounts were not known in advance. In issue was whether the amount used to fund the insurance premium was fixed sum credit on the basis that this was an amount that was known at the time. It was held that it was not.

32 Section 10(2).
33 Section 18(5), Example 23 Schedule 2.

38. Sir Francis Ferris discussed the position in relation to both a credit card and store card agreements. Plainly, these were running account agreements. But what of the situation when an initial balance is transferred from another card agreement at the time that the agreement is entered into? Or an initial purchase is put on to the store card at the time it was taken out? Are the initial balance and the initial store purchase fixed sum transactions on the basis that the amounts were known about and fixed at the time the agreements were entered into? The judge accepted the arguments advanced by both Professor Goode and Professor Guest[34] that these initial transactions formed part of the running account agreement and were not to be considered fixed sum agreements notwithstanding that the amount of the payments was known prior to the agreement being entered into.[35]

39. The judge found the position in *Goshawk* to be analogous to this situation; the payment of the insurance premium was running account credit notwithstanding that the amount of the premium was known in advance. The judge attached importance to the fact that the credit agreement did not require that the insurance policy premium should be funded out of the credit. Probably this fact was not critical to the legal analysis.

40. The distinction between running account and fixed sum agreements is important in a number of contexts, for instance in the rules applying to the supply of statements during the course of the agreement under sections 78 and 77A.

Financial ceilings

41. At the time that the Act was originally enacted, the Act did not regulate agreements where the amount of credit exceeded £5,000, later increased to £15,000 and then £25,000. In the case of the Act, this prima facie meant that a running account agreement would not be a regulated agreement if the credit limit exceeded £5,000 (later increased). The Act was alive to the possibility that an agreement might impose an artificially high credit limit that did not reflect the reality of the situation, perhaps with a view to avoiding the application of the Act. This was countered by section 10(3), which provides that for the purposes of any provision in the Act that specifies a credit ceiling, the amount of credit provided shall not be taken to exceed that ceiling if the credit limit does not exceed that ceiling or, in other cases, whether or not there is a credit limit, if:

(a) the borrower is not able to draw at any one time an amount of credit that exceeds that ceiling, excluding for this purpose any charges that enter into the calculation of the total charge for credit; or

34 In his Encyclopaedia of Consumer Credit Law.
35 *Goshawk* at [103].

(b) if there is an increase in charges when the debit balance on the account rises about a given amount, not being an amount above the relevant ceiling; or

(c) if, at the time that the agreement is made, 'it is probable, having regard to the terms of the agreement and other relevant consideration, the debit balance will not any time rise above the specified amount'.[36] This last test may be difficult to apply in practice and will or may depend on the personal circumstances of the borrower.

42. Although the most significant financial ceiling has been abolished, there are still provisions in the Act that are subject to certain financial ceilings.

43. Thus, a credit agreement is an exempt agreement if the loan is made predominantly for business purposes and the credit exceeds £25,000.[37] Another exemption exempts loans to individuals in an amount in excess of £60,260.[38]

Restricted and unrestricted use credit

44. A fundamental distinction is that between restricted and unrestricted use credit.[39] The definition is important, for instance, for the purpose of distinguishing between a borrower-lender and a borrower-lender-supplier agreement. Broadly, the distinction is that between credit advanced for a specific contractual purpose (restricted use) and credit advanced where the borrower is free to use the money advanced as he or she wishes (unrestricted use).

45. The Act refers to three specific types of restricted use credit. The definition only applies to regulated agreements.

46. The type of restricted use credit referred to in section 11(1)(a) is that 'to finance a transaction between the debtor and creditor whether forming part of that agreement or not'. This includes a shop account and, more subtly, a hire purchase, conditional sale or credit sale agreement. In all of these cases, the lender is financing the underlying transaction between himself or herself and the borrower.

47. The next type of restricted use credit within section 11(1)(b) is to 'finance a transaction between a debtor and a person ("the supplier") other than the creditor'.

48. Any agreement that in fact leaves the borrower free as a matter of practice to utilise the credit as he or she wishes cannot be restricted use,

36 Section 10(3)(b)(iii).
37 Art 60C(3) RAO.
38 Art 60H RAO.
39 Section 11.

even if the credit agreement itself limits its application to one or more specific purposes.[40] Any agreement therefore that actually provides the borrower with cash in hand cannot be restricted use since the borrower could spend it as he or she wishes.

49. It is not a requirement of this provision that the identity of the supplier be known at the time of the agreement.[41] Thus, a credit card agreement comes within section 11(1)(b) insofar as it allows access to good or services.[42] The identity of the suppliers with whom transactions will be concluded will not be known at the date the credit card agreement is entered into but this does not matter by virtue of section 11(4).

50. The final type of restricted use credit agreement (within section 11(1)(c)) is that 'to refinance any existing indebtedness of the debtor's whether to the creditor or another person'. A bank, for example, may open a loan account in order to allow the borrower to discharge the arrears off the mortgage. In order for such an agreement to be 'restricted use', it is again necessary that the borrower should not have free access to the credit advanced.[43]

51. In respect of all of these categories, in order for there to be a restricted use agreement, it must be a contractual term, express or implied, of the credit agreement that the monies lent be utilised for the restricted purpose.[44] The reasons for this requirement were expressed by Lord Justice Auld as follows: 'The distinction that Mr Gilman has sought to draw between an implied contractual term and a common purpose or intention short of such a term is, as he put it, "very fine". It is nevertheless a distinction which the courts may have to make, and one which in my view, is important in setting the proper limits of the working of sections 18 and 11. To allow a drift into non-contractual common purpose of intention as a test of operation of these provisions would introduce a dangerously vague element into an already overcomplicated and somewhat uncertain statutory control.'

52. This reasoning was followed by the Court of Appeal in *Consolidated Finance v McCluskey*,[45] where the Court of Appeal considered whether a term could be implied into the particular credit agreement to restrict the credit to a particular purpose (within section 11(1)(b)). In considering whether to imply a term to use credit for a particular purpose, the court will apply the normal tests for the implication of a term in the law of contract, as explained in *Attorney-General for Belize v Belize Telecom*[46] and subsequent cases.[47]

40 Section 11(3).
41 Section 11(4).
42 Schedule 2 Example 16.
43 Section 11(3).
44 *National Westminster Bank v Story, Pallister* 1999 CCLR 70.
45 2012 EWCA Civ 1325.
46 2009 1 WLR 1988.
47 In particular, *Stena Line v Merchant Navy Ratings* 2011 EWCA Civ 543.

53. Furthermore, in considering the meaning of the contract to see whether there is an expressed or implied contractual purpose, the court will need to examine the factual background known to the parties to see what the contractual intention was, again applying standard contractual principles of construction[48] as developed after *Chartbrook Ltd v Persimmon Homes Ltd.*[49]

54. These are the three categories of 'restricted use' credit. Where a credit agreement does not fall into one of these three, it is 'unrestricted use'.[50]

55. The RAO also uses the terms 'restricted use' and 'unrestricted use', and the definitions are the same.[51]

Borrower-lender and borrower-lender-supplier agreements

56. In relation to the Consumer Credit Act 1974, all regulated consumer credit agreements are either borrower-lender-supplier or borrower-lender agreements.[52] The distinction is important in a number of contexts, in the definition of linked transactions,[53] in the provision making the canvassing of borrower-lender agreements a criminal offence,[54] and also in the provision rendering the lender liable for breaches of contract by the supplier in the case of borrower-lender-supplier agreements.[55]

57. The same terminology is used in the Regulated Activities Order but the agreements are there referred to as borrower-lender and borrower-lender-supplier agreements.[56] Given that the RAO terminology has been used hitherto, agreements will be referred to in this way hereafter.

58. The paradigm borrower-lender agreement is the loan. The lender will normally not know how the money is to be spent; if the lender does know, the lender must, generally speaking, have no business interest in it being spent in that particular way. A borrower-lender-supplier agreement involves obtaining credit for a specific purpose. This will almost invariably involve obtaining credit for goods (including cash) or services. An agreement to refinance existing indebtedness, however, is automatically a borrower-lender agreement.[57] Moreover, the mere use of credit for a defined ancillary purpose will not of itself render the agreement a 'borrower-lender-supplier'

48 *Consolidated Finance Ltd v Collins* 2013 EWCA Civ 475.
49 2009 AC 1101.
50 Section 11(2).
51 Art 60L(1) and (2) RAO.
52 Sections 12, 13.
53 Section 19.
54 Section 49 Consumer Credit Act 1974.
55 Section 75.
56 Reg 60L.
57 Section 13(b).

agreement. There must be some business link-up between creditor and supplier for the definition to apply. This business link-up is of course especially close where the creditor and supplier are one and the same!

59. It is now appropriate to look at the actual terms of the definitions as set out in sections 12 and 13. There are three types of borrower-lender-supplier agreements as defined in section 12.

60. Section 12(a) covers restricted use agreements falling within section 11(1)(a). This covers where credit is used to finance a transaction between the debtor and creditor. Examples of such transactions are hire purchase, conditional sale and credit sale agreements where the finance company both supplies the goods and provides the credit. Another example is the account opened by a customer with a department store. In such a situation, the store both provides the credit and supplies the goods.

61. Section 12(b) comprises restricted use credit agreements falling within section 11(l)(b) (i.e. where the credit is to be used to finance a transaction with a third party, not the creditor and is made under pre-existing arrangements or in contemplation of future arrangements between the creditor and the third party) (the supplier).

62. This type of borrower-lender-supplier agreement must be 'restricted use' so that the debtor must not be free to use the money as he or she wishes. There must also be some business link-up either planned or already existing between the creditor and the supplier. The 'arrangements' referred to in the section will often, in practice, mean a regular arrangement in which a supplier steers a potential customer towards a particular creditor (finance company). The finance company may or may not pay commission to the supplier for the introduction.

63. The meaning of 'arrangements' in the Act is amplified by section 187.

64. Section 187(1) provides in relation to pre-existing arrangements that: 'A consumer credit agreement shall be treated as entered into under pre-existing arrangements between a creditor and supplier if it is entered into in accordance with, or in furtherance of, arrangements previously made between previously made between persons mentioned in subsection 4(a), (b), (c).' The persons mentioned in subsection 4(a), (b) and (c) are the creditor and supplier and their respective associates.[58]

65. Future arrangements are considered in section 187(2), which provides that: 'A consumer credit agreement shall be treated as entered into under future arrangements between a creditor and supplier if it is entered into in the expectation that arrangements will be subsequently made between persons mentioned in subsection 4(a), (b), (c) for the supply of cash, goods or services (or any of them) to be financed by the consumer credit agreement.'

58 As defined by section 184(1).

66. There are specific exclusions from the scope of arrangements. Payment arrangements made by a lender to a supplier are excluded if they are arrangements that the lender holds itself out as willing to make with suppliers generally.[59] Also excluded are arrangements made with a bank for electronic transfer of funds out of a current account.[60]

67. Section 187 was intended to expand the scope of what is meant by 'arrangements'.[61] The term 'arrangements' is a broad one and covers both direct and indirect arrangements. It was deliberately chosen by parliament 'with a view to embracing a wide range of different commercial structures having substantially the same effect'.[62]

68. The classic instance of a borrower-lender-supplier agreement within section 12(b) is the credit card agreement insofar as it can be used for the acquisition of goods and services.[63] In *Office of Fair Trading v Lloyds TSB*,[64] arrangements were held to exist between a card issuer and a supplier in the case of a credit card even though there was no direct contractual relationship between them, the contract in each case being with a merchant acquirer.

69. Where creditor and supplier are, however, 'associated' (as defined in section 184), there is a rebuttable presumption that pre-existing arrangements exist between them.[65] An example of this will be where lender and supplier are both subsidiaries of the same parent company. The law assumes until the contrary is proved that there existed a tie-up, 'pre-existing arrangements' between the two at the time credit was advanced. In many cases, however, this would, in any event, be obvious.

70. Also included in this context are agreements allowing for the provision of cash by third parties in a case where the necessary 'arrangements' are in existence. Where cash is obtained in this way, it is provided under a borrower-lender-supplier agreement.

71. The final category of agreements within section 12(c) involves unrestricted use agreements (i.e. where the debtor will be free in fact to apply the moneys credited as he or she wishes). Such credit agreements will, however, only be borrower-lender-supplier if the lender knows that the money is to be used to finance a transaction with a particular supplier and if there exist 'pre-existing arrangements' between that lender and the supplier. It will not in this final category render an agreement borrower-lender-supplier simply because the creditor is hopeful that *future* arrangements may flow out of the transaction. The arrangements must be pre-existing.

59 Section 187(3).
60 Section 187(3A).
61 *Office of Fair Trading v Lloyds TSB plc* 2006 2 All ER 821 at [65], Court of Appeal, point not considered in the House of Lords.
62 *Office of Fair Trading v Lloyds TSB plc* at [64].
63 Schedule 2 Example 16.
64 2006 2 All ER 821, Court of Appeal.
65 Section 187(5).

72. This final category of borrower-lender-supplier agreements will be relatively unusual. Normally, when creditor and supplier have some business arrangement between themselves, the lender ensures that the supplier actually receives the money by paying the supplier directly. This, however, will render the agreement 'restricted use' and so falls into the second category described above. Only where the lender actually allows the borrower unrestricted access to the money will this final category be relevant.

73. A loan from the bank will not (normally) be borrower-lender-supplier even if it is for a specific project such as the building of an extension by a specific builder. This is because the bank is unlikely to have existing arrangements with that builder relevant to the loan.

74. This being the definition of borrower-lender-supplier agreements, it is unnecessary to scrutinise section 13 with care, the section that defines borrower-lender agreements. This is because these two types of agreement are mutually exclusive and it is only necessary to decide whether or not an agreement falls in one category for it to be excluded from the other and vice versa. It is not correct, however, to say that the definition of a borrower-lender agreement in section 13 is unnecessary. Section 13(b) specifies that refinancing agreements are always borrower-lender agreements. If this was not expressly stipulated, there are circumstances when such agreements could fall within the categories of borrower-lender-supplier agreements described above. Section 13(b) specifically removes this possibility.

Consumer hire agreements

75. Entry into a regulated consumer hire agreement as owner is a regulated activity by virtue of Article 60N of the Regulated Activities Order, as is exercise of the owner's rights and duties under such an agreement.[66]

76. A consumer hire agreement is also a regulated agreement for the purposes of the Consumer Credit Act 1974[67] and the definitions are the same. The reason that consumer hire was included within the ambit of the Consumer Credit Act 1974 is that hire is, in many instances, in essence, a form of finance. This was explained by Baroness Hale of Richmond in the following terms in *TRM Copy Centre (UK) Ltd v Lanwall Services Ltd*:[68] 'If a chattel such as a television set or a car is rented out for a long period, perhaps for most of its expected life, then the effect is much as a hire purchase or conditional sale agreement. The capital cost is spread out over the term and repaid by the consumer in the form of rental payments at the end of which there will be little if any value left in the item. The hirer who

66 Article 60N(2).
67 Section 15 Consumer Credit Act 1974.
68 2009 1 WLR 1375.

gets no ownership at the end of the term is even worse off than the hirer who at least becomes the owner when all the instalments are paid.'

77. A consumer hire agreement is one entered into by the owner[69] with a hirer who is an individual,[70] the agreement not being a hire purchase agreement and in respect of which the period of hiring is capable of subsisting for more than three months.

78. Three months must be the upper limit to the period of bailment in order for it not to be a consumer hire agreement; it is irrelevant in these circumstances that payments may extend over a period of greater than three months.[71] If a hire agreement being otherwise less than three months contains an option available to the hirer that, if exercised, could extend the period of the hire agreement beyond three months, it is capable of subsisting for more than three months and is therefore a consumer hire agreement.

79. At the heart of a consumer hire agreement is an agreement 'for the bailment or (in Scotland) the hiring of goods to the hirer'. What constitutes a sufficient bailment to give rise to a consumer hire agreement for this purpose has been the subject of controversy.

80. The House of Lords case of *TRM Copy Centre (UK) Ltd v Lanwall Services Ltd*[72] involved the provision (to use a neutral word) of a photocopier to an individual retailer under the terms of a Location Agreement. The Location Agreement allowed the owner of the photocopier to place the photocopier in a specific location in retail premises. The expectation (and reality) was that members of the public would pay for photocopies on the machine and the owner would make money by virtue of being entitled to these payments, less a commission due to the retailer. The retailer had to pay nothing by way of rental for the positioning of the photocopier in his shop beyond accounting for the monies obtained from use of the photocopier by members of the public.

81. It was held that although the arrangement as between owner and retailer could be described as bailment, it was not hire for the purposes of the Consumer Credit Act. Whether or not the agreement constituted an agreement for hire had to be considered by reference to its commercial purpose. The purpose of the arrangement was not to seek payments from the retailer, but to maximise the return to the owner from use of the photocopier. This was not an arrangement whereby the photocopier was being hired to the retailer as there were no rental payments.

69 The owner is defined as someone who bails goods under a consumer hire agreement: Article 60O(3).

70 Or 'relevant recipient of credit' (i.e. a partnership of two or three persons not all of whom are bodies corporate or an unincorporated association not all of whose members are a body corporate).

71 *Lagden v O'Connor* 2003 QB 36.

72 2009 1 WLR 1375 at 1383 at [22].

Hire agreement and credit agreement

82. It is possible for an agreement to be both a hire agreement and a credit agreement as was demonstrated by the case of *Dimond v Lovell*.[73] In this case, a specialist hire company hired replacement vehicles to motor accident victims pending resolution of the accident claim involving their original vehicle. The company hired a vehicle on the basis that no rental was payable for the vehicle until the accident claim had been resolved. The obligation to pay rental was therefore deferred and this deferment had the characteristics of credit. In the Court of Appeal, it was argued that a hire agreement and a credit agreement could not subsist and were mutually incompatible. This argument, which was not renewed in the House of Lords, was rejected.[74]

Financial limit

83. For agreements concluded prior to 6 April 2008, hire agreements were not consumer hire agreement if the total amount of hire payments payable under the agreement exceeded £25,000. This limit was abolished by the Consumer Credit Act 2006 for agreements concluded after 6 April 2008.[75]

84. Accordingly, the subject of financial limits is of little continuing importance although there are doubtless still a number of hire agreements still in operation concluded before 6 April 2008.

85. There is, however, one exemption that contains a financial limit, namely if the hirer is required by the agreement to make payments of more than £25,000 and the agreement is entered into wholly or predominantly for the purposes of a business carried on or intended to be carried by the hirer. The agreement will be presumed to be made predominantly for business purposes if the agreement includes a declaration made by the hirer that provides that the agreement is made predominantly for the purposes of a business carried on or intended to be carried on by the hirer. FCA Rules must also be complied with in this connection.[76] However, the exemption in Article 60O will not apply if any of the owners (if there is more than one) or any person who has acted on behalf of any of the owners in entering into the agreement knows or has reasonable cause to suspect that the agreement is not entered into for the purposes of a business carried on or intended to be carried on by the hirer.[77]

73 2000 QB 216 (Court of Appeal); 2002 1 AC 384 (House of Lords).
74 2000 QB 216 at [64] to [67].
75 Section 2(2) Consumer Credit Act 2006.
76 Art 60O(2) RAO.
77 Art 60O(3) RAO.

Small agreements

86. Small agreements are elaborately defined in section 17 of the Act.

87. A small agreement is, as its name suggests, one in which the payments required of a borrower or hirer are small. In fact, a small consumer credit agreement is one where, as from 1 January 1984, the credit advanced is less than £50 (see Consumer Credit (Increase of Monetary Unit) Order 1983).[78] A small running account credit agreement is one where the credit limit falls below this figure.[79] All hire purchase and credit sale agreements fall outside the definition (section 17(1)).

88. A small consumer hire agreement is one where the total hire payments required of a hirer are less than £50.[80] This figure is the contractual minimum that the hirer must be required to pay (the possibility that he or she may exercise an option to terminate should be taken into account). Of course, the *actual* payments made by a hirer under a small agreement may be more than £50.

89. No agreement that is secured may be a small agreement save where the security given is a guarantee or indemnity.[81] In particular, this means that no pawn transaction is ever a small agreement.

90. The significance of a small agreement is as follows:

(a) 'Small borrower-lender-supplier agreements for restricted use credit' are not governed by those parts of the Act that dictate the form of an agreement and the copies to be supplied; nor are such agreements cancellable (section 74(2)). But this category of small agreements is, in effect, confined to: (1) small credit sales; (2) small credit token agreements (but the credit limit would have to be below £50, which must be highly unusual); and (3) small connected lending transactions where the money advanced is paid directly to the supplier.
(b) With a small credit token agreement, there is no need to supply a fresh copy of the agreement every time a credit token other than the first is supplied (section 85(3)). This provision is complementary to that contained in section 74(2), which removes the duty to supply a copy of the agreement when the agreement is first concluded.
(c) There is no need to provide periodic statements of account in the case of small running account agreements (section 78(7)).

91. Finally, section 17(3) and (4) contains anti-avoidance provisions to meet the possibility that a lender may artificially enter into a number of

78 SI 1983/1878.
79 Section 17(2).
80 Section 17(1)(b).
81 Section 17(1).

agreements all of which are 'small' when he or she would more naturally enter into a single agreement not having this status. Section 17(3) provides that where a lender acts in this way by entering into a number of agreements and it 'appears probable' that he or she did so in order to avoid the provisions of the Act, then the agreements lose their status as 'small' agreements and are to be treated as if fully regulated. This anti-avoidance provision applies equally whether the series of allegedly 'small' agreements is entered into between the lender and the same party or between the lender and associated parties (as defined in section 184).[82]

Multiple agreements

92. The definition of 'multiple agreement' contained in section 18(1) is as follows: 'The section applies to an agreement (a multiple agreement) if its terms are such as – (a) to place a part of it within one category of agreement mentioned in this Act, and another part of it within a different category of agreement so mentioned, or within a category of agreement not so mentioned, or (b) to place it, or a part of it, within two or more categories of agreement so mentioned.'

93. By virtue of section 18(2), 'where a part of an agreement falls within subsection (1), that part shall be treated for the purposes of this Act as a separate agreement'.

94. Section 18(3) provides that 'where an agreement falls within subsection (1)(b), it shall be treated as an agreement in each of the categories in question, and this Act shall apply accordingly'.

95. The construction of these provisions has proved problematic and has been a source of academic contention between Professor Goode and the draftsman of the Act, Mr Francis Bennion.

96. However, the correct interpretation of section 18 has been settled by the decision of the Court of Appeal in *Southern Pacific Mortgages v Heath*,[83] such that it is no longer necessary to look at earlier case law. That case concerned a remortgage transaction involving a loan of about £29,000. Of that loan, £19,000 went to redeem the previous mortgage and the balance went to the borrower for his own purposes. Accordingly, in relation to the loan, the sum of £19,000 credit was restricted use credit and the balance of about £10,000 was unrestricted use credit. The issue was whether this was a multiple agreement with the consequence that these two elements of the agreement, the restricted use and unrestricted use credit, were to be treated as *separate agreements*. If they were to be treated as separate agreements, then they were both regulated agreements as they were both below the financial ceiling then applicable of £25,000.

82 Section 17(4).
83 2010 2 WLR 1081.

97. The Court of Appeal held that the agreement was not a multiple agreement. It reasoned as follows.

98. The meaning of 'categories of agreement' must be the same in both subsections 18(1)(a) and (b). Section 18(1) must, moreover, be referring to the situation where agreements had characteristics that put the agreement or part of the agreement within one or more *disparate categories* as provided for by the Act.

99. Such disparate categories might be: restricted and unrestricted use, debtor-creditor and debtor-creditor-supplier, fixed sum and running account credit, credit and hire. The Court of Appeal recognised that there might be other categories as well.[84] The Court of Appeal then held that section 18(1) (a) and (b) were mutually exclusive and referred to two different situations.[85]

100. Section 18(1)(a) referred to an agreement that was in parts. If the agreement is in parts, then the question is whether the parts are in different categories. If they are, then by virtue of section 18(2), they are to be treated as separate agreements.

101. Section 18(1)(b), however, is where there is what Professor Goode has referred to as a *unitary* agreement (i.e. one not divisible into parts) that has characteristics that place it into distinct categories. In such a case, however, by virtue of section 18(3), it is not to be treated as separate agreements but is to be treated as a single agreement with the characteristics of the various categories into which it falls.

102. On this basis, the remortgage transaction under consideration in *South Pacific Mortgages* was a unitary agreement because it could not be divided into parts. It therefore fell within section 18(1)(b) and section 18(3) and was not to be treated as separate agreements. Accordingly, it was unregulated as the lender contended.

103. This analysis, however, does not fit easily with the examples of multiple agreement given at Schedule 2 of the Act, as the Court of Appeal recognised.

104. Example 16 set out in Schedule 2 to the Act gives an illustration of a credit token agreement where the credit token can be used both to acquire goods and obtain cash. Insofar as it can be used to acquire goods, it is a debtor-creditor-supplier agreement. Insofar as it can be used to obtain cash, it is a debtor-creditor agreement. The analysis of the position set out in the Act was as follows: 'In that the whole of the agreement falls within several categories of agreement mentioned in this Act, it is, by section 18(3), to be treated as an agreement in each of those categories. So far as it is a debtor-creditor-supplier agreement, providing restricted use credit, it is by section

84 [31].
85 [42].

18(2) to be treated as a separate agreement; and similarly so far as it is a debtor-creditor-supplier agreement providing unrestricted use credit.'

105. The Court of Appeal held that the first of the two sentences quoted above was correct. The Court of Appeal held that the credit token agreement was a unitary agreement and so fell within section 18(1)(b) so that section 18(3) applied to it. The second sentence, however, was wrong. The credit token agreement was not to be considered as two separate agreements.[86]

106. The Court of Appeal also analysed Example 18 contained in Schedule 2 to the Act, which gives an analysis of the position of a current account coupled with an overdraft facility. As far as the overdraft facilities are concerned, it is a regulated consumer credit agreement for unrestricted use running account credit. The analysis forming part of Example 18 says: 'It is also a multiple agreement, part of which (i.e. the part not dealing with the overdraft), as referred to in section 18(1)(a), falls within a category of agreement not mentioned in the Act.'

107. The Court of Appeal accepted this analysis of Example 18 as correct (contrary to the views of Professor Goode) on the basis that the overdraft and current account facilities could be seen as separate parts of the agreement as they could each function independently and had different terms. On this basis, it would be correct to describe the agreement as a multiple agreement within section 18(1)(a).[87]

108. The decision in *Southern Pacific Mortgages* is welcome in that it minimises the artificiality inherent in section 18 of treating a single agreement as a number of separate agreements. Moreover, the significance of the classification has been reduced by the reforms of the Consumer Credit Act 2006, which abolished the financial ceiling on consumer credit agreements and ended irredeemable unenforceability.

Linked transactions

109. Section 19 of the Consumer Credit Act 1974 introduces the concept of 'linked transactions'. The term is also used in the same sense in regulation 60E of the RAO in connection with the definition of exempt transactions secured on land.

110. The definition of such transactions is technical. The essence of the definition is that it relates to a side agreement that is connected with a regulated consumer credit or consumer hire agreement, which can conveniently be referred to as the principal agreement. The side agreement may be made with the debtor or hirer but may also be entered into with a relative of the debtor or hirer as defined by section 184(5).

86 [50].
87 [51].

111. A security agreement cannot be a linked transaction. 'Security' is defined in section 189(1) as a 'mortgage, charge, pledge, bond, debenture, indemnity, guarantee, bill, note or other right . . . to secure the carrying out of the obligations of the [borrower] or hirer under the agreement'. An insurance policy is not within the definition of security.

112. The definition is important because of the rule that linked transactions do not take effect until the principal agreement is concluded.[88] Also, if the principal agreement is cancelled, so is a linked transaction.[89] Likewise if a borrower is discharged before the time provided for under the agreement by virtue of section 96(1).

113. However, the concept of 'linked transactions' is not to be found in provisions that derive from the EU Consumer Credit Directive. That uses the alternative concepts of 'ancillary service' or 'ancillary contract'. So where a party withdraws from a credit agreement under the right of withdrawal conferred by section 66A, the withdrawal also has the effect of giving rise to a withdrawal from any contract for an ancillary service,[90] defined as a service that relates to the provision of credit.[91] Under regulation 38 of the Consumer Contracts (Information, Cancellation and Additional Charges) Regulations 2013,[92] an ancillary contract is one whereby the consumer acquires goods and services 'related' to the principal agreement, including from a third party on the basis of arrangements between the third party and the trader.

114. There are three categories of linked transaction identified in section 19(1).

115. The first is where the side agreement is entered into as a consequence of a contractual *term* in the principal agreement.[93] The borrower or hirer must be contractually obligated to conclude the transaction.

116. The second type of linked transaction is a supply contract financed by a borrower-lender-supply agreement.[94] An example here would be a motor vehicle insurance policy sold alongside a hire purchase agreement for a motor vehicle.

117. The third category[95] itself encompasses a range of transaction types depending on the *purpose* of the transaction and where the *party* entering into the transaction must be within a number of categories.

88 Section 19(3).
89 Section 69(1).
90 Section 66A(7)(b).
91 Section 66A(13).
92 SI 2013/3134.
93 Section 19(1)(a).
94 Section 19(1)(b).
95 Section 19(1)(c).

118. The purpose of the transaction must be either to induce entry into the principal agreement, or for a purpose 'related' to the principal agreement, or, in the case of a restricted use credit agreement, for a purpose related to the transaction financed or to be financed by the principal agreement.[96]

119. The persons entering into the agreement entered into for one of these purposes must be:[97]

(a) the creditor or owner or associate;[98]
(b) someone who has been represented by someone who is a negotiator in a borrower-lender-supplier agreement;[99] or
(c) someone who knows that the principal agreement will be made or contemplates that it *might* be.

120. Category (c) is potentially wide and it is difficult to see how someone could fall within category (b) and not also fall within category (c).

Exceptions

121. There are a number of linked transactions that continue to have effect notwithstanding the fact that the principal agreement is not entered into, or cancelled under section 69, or subject to early termination under section 96. These are specified by the Consumer Credit (Linked Transactions) (Exemptions) Regulations 1983.[100] These are insurance contracts, contracts of guarantee of goods and deposit and current accounts opened pursuant to the agreement.

122. In *Goshawk Dedicated (No 2) Ltd v Governor and Company of the Bank of Scotland*,[101] the court considered the classification of a funding arrangement under which monies were advanced to fund the conduct of litigation and also the premium on a legal expenses insurance policy. The legal expenses insurance policy was held to be a linked transaction coming within the Consumer Credit (Linked Transactions) (Exemptions) Regulations and so surviving cancellation of the loan agreement.

Non-commercial agreements

123. Of greater significance is that category of agreement known as 'non-commercial agreements'. A 'non-commercial agreement' is defined in

96 Section 19(1)(c).
97 Section 19(2).
98 As defined by section 184.
99 For instance, a motor car dealer that introduces a borrower to a source of hire purchase finance may also represent an insurer in selling motor vehicle insurance.
100 SI 1983/1560.
101 2006 2 All ER 610.

section 189(1) as a 'consumer credit or a consumer hire agreement not made by the lender or owner in the course of a business carried on by him'.

124. A 'business' includes a 'profession or trade'.[102] It is suggested that the term 'business' in this context is to be given a broad meaning – that it refers not only to profit-making activities, but to all occupations or duties other than those entered into purely for pleasure or domestic reasons. In particular, the business does not have to be related to the provision of credit or hire in any way.

125. So if neither the lender nor owner is engaged in business, the agreement will be 'non-commercial'. Most domestic and social arrangements will fall into this category.

126. By section 189(2), it is provided that 'a person is not to be treated as carrying on a particular type of business merely because he enters into a transactions belonging to a business of that type'. Section 189(2) is not primarily directed at the definition of non-commercial agreement since the definition does not depend upon the type of business in which the relevant lender or owner is engaged. It does, however, emphasise that it needs more than occasional transactions to constitute a business.

127. It is for the court to assess whether a loan was entered into in the course of a business or not. Provided that the first instance judge looks at all the relevant factors for and against the existence of a business, the Court of Appeal will be reluctant to interfere.[103]

128. Non-commercial agreements are released from many of the provisions of the Act:

(a) such agreements do not have to be in any particular form; the copies and cancellations provisions do not apply, nor do the disclosure of information requirements (section 74(1));
(b) the lender is not liable for breaches of contract committed by the supplier under section 75 in the case of a non-commercial agreement (section 75(3));
(c) there is no need to serve a default, termination or enforcement notice with a non-commercial agreement save where security has been provided (Enforcement, Default and Termination Notice Regulations, regulation 2(9));
(d) the lender or owner of goods has no duty to give the borrower or hirer or surety either information about, or a copy of, the agreement in the case of a non-commercial agreement (sections 77(5), 77A(8), 78(7), 79(4), 107(5), 108(5) and 109(5));
(e) the rules governing modifying agreements and the procedures for varying the terms of an agreement do not apply to a non-commercial agreement (section 82(7));

102 Section 189(1).
103 *Helden v Strathmore* 2011 Bus LR 1592.

(f) the borrowers are not protected from the consequences of misuse of a credit facility in the case of a non-commercial agreement (section 83(2));
(g) there is no requirement to serve an arrears notice (section 86B(12A), 86C(7) and 86D(8));
(h) the borrower or hirer in a non-commercial agreement has no right to a termination statement (section 103(4));
(i) the borrower or hirer has no right to receive a copy of a security instrument in the case of a non-commercial agreement (section 110(2));
(j) provisions in relation to the taking of pledges do not apply with non-commercial agreements (section 114(3)); and
(k) a lender or owner is free to take a negotiable instrument whether as security or payment in the case of a non-commercial agreement (section 123(5)).

129. In fact, the list of exemptions is so long that it would be easier to state what provisions of the Act *did* extend to non-commercial agreements. The provisions dealing with the death of a borrower or hirer, the termination of a hiring agreement, the form of a guarantee or indemnity, and the extent of the liability of a surety all apply. The deemed agency created by section 56 applies.[104] Likewise does the provision requiring the obligation to provide a statement on request in connection with a fixed sum agreement.[105] Non-commercial agreements may also be reopened as unfair relationships. Other provisions generally do not apply or apply to only a very restricted extent.

Total charge for credit

130. The total charge of credit is as its name implies, the cost to the borrower of obtaining credit from the lender. It is defined as the sum calculated in accordance with Regulations made under section 20.[106] The purpose of the Regulations is to establish the true cost of credit to the borrower.[107] It is a fundamental feature of the Act that an item entering into the total charge for credit is not to be treated as part of the credit notwithstanding that time is allowed for its payment.[108]

131. Consumer Credit (Total Charge for Credit) Regulations, made under section 20 of the Consumer Credit Act 1974, set out to provide answers to two questions:

104 Section 74(1A).
105 Under section 77B.
106 Section 189(1).
107 Section 20(1).
108 Section 9(4).

(a) What items of expenditure are to be included in the total charge for credit?
(b) Given these items, what is the overall rate of total charge for credit (the APR)?

132. The first question is not only important because the answer to it is a necessary prerequisite to answering the second, but it is essential in order to determine the *total credit advanced* under an agreement.

133. This can be an important exercise in a number of contexts. Certain activities are exempt activities only when the total credit exceeds a particular figure.[109] A further exemption applies only when the total charge for credit is below a certain figure.[110] Moreover, the total credit and the APR have to be disclosed in the text of credit agreements in accordance with Agreements Regulations. An incorrect statement will render the agreement improperly executed and so unenforceable save on application to the court.

134. There were two sets of TCC Regulations, the 1980[111] and 2010[112] Regulations. The 2010 Regulations were introduced to comply with the requirements of the EU Directive 2008/48 whereupon the 2010 Regulations became the principal Regulations. The application of the 1980 Regulations was confined to agreements (and prospective agreements) to be secured on land.[113] All other regulated credit agreements became subject to the 2010 Regulations. Furthermore, even within the categories of agreement to which the 1980 Regulations applied, the 2010 Regulations also applied to agreements in which the lender had given disclosure of information in purported compliance with the Disclosure of Information Regulations 2010.[114]

135. Both sets of Regulations have now been repealed but they continue to apply in the same circumstances for the purpose of the new regulatory regime introduced by the Financial Services and Markets Act 2000. Article 60M of the RAO allows the FCA to make rules specifying how the total charge for credit to the borrower is be determined. The FCA has made Rules that are now to be found in FCA Handbook CONC Appendix 1. These Rules reproduce both the 2010 Regulations and the 1980 Regulations. The 1980 Regulations are to be found at CONC App 1.1 R and the 2010 Regulations at CONC App 1.2 R.

136. The case law applicable to the construction of the 1980 and 2010 Regulations will continue to have relevance to the new Rules contained in CONC Appendix 1. Under the 1980 and 2010 Regulations, disputes arose

109 Art 60F (£25,000), 60H (£60,260).
110 Art 60G RAO.
111 SI 1980/51.
112 SI 2010/1011.
113 Reg 1A TCC 1980.
114 Reg 3 TCC 2010.

whether any particular item falls within the total charge for credit. In construing the Regulations and now Appendix 1, it is essential to bear in mind the fundamental point that an item entering into the total charge for credit shall not be treated as part of the credit.[115] The converse is also true in that a transaction that is part of the credit should not be considered a charge for the purposes of the total charge for credit.[116]

137. In *Watchtower Investments Ltd v Payne*,[117] the borrower remortgaged his house and part of the advance was used to discharge the arrears on the first mortgage, the lender making the payment direct to the first mortgagee. The question arose whether the amount of the payment to the first mortgagee should have entered into the total charge for credit. The Court of Appeal held that it should not, on the basis that, by its nature, the payment was part of the credit and therefore not of the nature of a charge that could form part of the total charge for credit. A critical part of the reasoning of the Court of Appeal was that discharge of arrears was part of the purpose of the loan.

138. In deciding whether a particular item is part of the credit, the terms of the agreement, although relevant, are not determinative. The Court of Appeal said: 'The Court must consider all the circumstances including the documents relating to the agreement and may well have to ascertain objectively the purpose of the borrowing.'[118]

139. A different result was arrived at in *McGinn v Grangewood Securities Ltd*,[119] where the arrears were only for one month and the borrower did not even realise he was in arrears. The agreement provided for arrears to be discharged out of the credit advanced but the court held that on the facts there, it was no part of the purpose of the loan to discharge the small amount of arrears that had accrued. Accordingly, the repayment of arrears did not form part of the credit and the repayment amount formed part of the total charge for credit.

140. Furthermore, the total charge for credit is to be fixed by reference to the date of the agreement; subsequent events, such as the movement of indexed base rates for example, are not relevant.[120]

The 1980 TCC Regulations and CONC Appendix 1.1

141. Those charges to be taken into account are those falling within regulation 4 and CONC App 1.1.5 R. It is then necessary to see if any of the exclusions in regulation 5 and CONC 1.1.6 R apply.

115 Section 9(4) Consumer Credit Act 1974.
116 *Watchtower Investments Ltd v Payne* 2001 EWCA Civ 1159.
117 2001 EWCA Civ 1159.
118 *Watchtower Investments* at [52] per Peter Gibson LJ.
119 2002 EWCA Civ 552.
120 Reg 3 TCC 1980; CONC App 1.1.4 R.

142. Charges caught by regulation 4 and CONC App 1.1.5 R are either:

(a) interest payments provided for under the agreement;
(b) 'other charges at any time payable under the transaction by or on behalf of the borrower or a relative of his whether to the lender or any other person . . . notwithstanding that the whole or any part of the charge may be repayable at any time or that the consideration therefore may be repayable at any time or that the consideration therefore may include matters not within the transaction or subsisting at a time not within the duration of the agreement'; or
(c) insurance premiums required by the lender as a condition of entering into the agreement and the sole purpose of which is to provide for repayment of credit in the event of death, invalidity, illness or unemployment of the borrower.[121]

143. The reference to 'other charges' in (b) relates to sums 'payable' under the 'transaction'. 'Payable' can include an optional payment; it is not a requirement of regulation 4(b) that payment is obligatory under the terms of the agreement.[122] 'Transaction' is defined in regulation 1(2)[123] and largely determines the scope of regulation 4.[124] It has a restricted meaning and refers, in addition to the agreement itself, to:

(a) Linked transactions falling within section 19(1)(a) (i.e. transactions required as a term of the credit agreement) (e.g. the insurance of goods let on hire purchase). It follows, therefore, that not every linked transaction is included in the computation of the total charge for credit.
(b) Any contract for the provision of security under the agreement. An example here would be a survey and valuation carried out as a pre-condition for the lender taking the security of a second mortgage.
(c) Any credit brokerage contract relating to the agreement.[125]
(d) A contract that the lender 'requires to be entered into or continued' by the borrower or a relative of his or hers as a condition for entering into the agreement. An example here is a requirement of a lender selling a freezer on credit that the borrower must buy a freezer-load of food before the lender will enter into the credit agreement. Another example will be the life insurance policy that a lender may demand to secure the repayment of moneys owing in the event of the death of the borrower during the currency of the agreement.

121 This category (c) was added with effect from 14 April 2000.
122 *Humberclyde Finance Ltd v Thompson* 1997 CCLR 23.
123 Now defined in the FCA Handbook Glossary.
124 It is also clear that the word 'charges' does not extend to items that form part of the credit.
125 This part of the definition was added with effect from 30 June 1989.

144. Regulation 4[126] makes it clear that it is irrelevant that the duration of a transaction (e.g. of a life insurance policy) may extend beyond the duration of the credit agreement. It is also irrelevant that the borrower may become eligible to a refund in respect of certain of the charges imposed. The use of the phrase 'payable' in regulation 4 indicates that it is not a requirement for a head of charge to be *compulsory* before it enters into the total charge for credit. Thus, the option fee on a hire purchase agreement should therefore enter into the calculation of total charge for credit even though this is a sum that the borrower is not contractually bound to pay.

145. Once the particular charges have been scrutinised to see if they fall within the above categories, it is then necessary to see if they are removed by one of the 11 categories set out in regulation 5.[127] If they are removed, the charges will not form part of the total charge for credit.

146. The following categories of charge are exempted:

(a) Charges stipulated as arising on default of the borrower.[128] For example, the agreement may provide that a higher rate of interest is payable on sums that are overdue under the agreement. The existence of this higher rate is ignored.
(b) Default charges that may become payable by a lender to a third party and subsequently recoverable from the borrower under the terms of the agreement are also to be left out of account.[129]
(c) Charges equally payable by a cash and credit purchaser are to be left out of account.[130] A comparison has to be made with a hypothetical cash transaction to see if it is an ancillary charge to the credit transaction.[131] For example, both cash and credit purchasers of cookers may have to pay an installation charge. The installation charge will therefore be left out of account. However, the charge must be payable under an ancillary transaction. If the agreement in respect of which the charge is payable is part of a multiple agreement and therefore to be considered as an independent agreement by section 18(2) of the Consumer Credit Act 1974, this exemption will not apply as the charge can no longer be considered an ancillary charge.[132]
(d) Incidental charges, other than a fee charged to a credit broker, entered into by the borrower prior to the credit agreement, which provide benefits to the borrower additional to the right of access to credit and

126 CONC App 1.1.5 R.
127 CONC App 1.1.6 R.
128 Reg 5(1)(a) TCC 1980; CONC App 1.1.6(1)(a) R.
129 Reg 5(1)(b) TCC 1980; CONC App 1.1.6(1)(b) R.
130 Reg 5(1)(c) TCC 1980; CONC App 1.1.6(1)(c) R.
131 *London North Securities v Meadows* 2005 EWCA Civ 956 at [53].
132 *London North Securities v Meadows* at [55].

where it is not a term of the incidental transaction that a credit agreement is entered into.[133] The classic example of such a charge is the club membership subscription in a case where membership of the club provides access to special credit facilities. The Automobile Association is an example of such a club. Were it not for this exemption, the AA annual membership fee would have to be taken into account in calculating the total charge for credit of a credit agreement entered into as a result of AA membership.

(e) Charges for the care, maintenance, protection and care of goods but only if incurred in circumstances when the land or goods is in immediate danger of not being capable of being reasonably enjoyed or used, or where comparable arrangements are available from elsewhere and where the arrangements are made with a person to be selected by the borrower and where, if the lender's approval is required, it cannot be reasonably withheld.[134]

(f) Charges for money transmission services in respect of a current account whereby the borrower can procure payments to him or herself.[135]

(g) Guarantee charges other than those required as a condition of the agreement, the purpose of which is to ensure complete or partial repayment in the event of death, invalidity, illness or unemployment of the borrower.[136]

(h) Charges for the transfer of funds or for opening an account are to be left out of account except if the borrower does not have reasonable freedom of choice in the matter and the charges are abnormally high; charges for collection of payments do, however, form part of the total charge for credit.[137]

(i) Insurance premiums other than those falling within regulation 4(1)(c).[138]

The APR

147. The rate of total charge is to be expressed as an annual percentage rate,[139] the APR. The APR is to be expressed to one decimal place.[140] There will be rounding up where the second decimal place exceeds 5, so a calculation giving a figure of 22.89 per cent, will be expressed as an APR

133 Reg 5(1)(d) TCC 1980; CONC App 1.1.6(1)(d) R.
134 Reg 5(1)(e), reg 5(2) TCC 1980; CONC App 1.1.6(1)(e) R; CONC App 1.1.6(2) R.
135 Reg 5(1)(f) TCC 1980; CONC App 1.1.6(1)(f) R.
136 Reg 5(1)(g) TCC 1980; CONC App 1.1.6(1)(g) R.
137 Reg 5(1)(h) TCC 1980; CONC App 1.1.6(1)(h) R.
138 Reg 5(1)(j) TCC 1980; CONC App 1.1.6(1)(i) R.
139 Reg 6 TCC 1980; CONC App 1.1.7 R.
140 CONC App 1.1.8 R.

of 22.9 per cent, not 22.8 per cent. Where the second decimal place is less than 5, then the second decimal place will be disregarded.[141]

148. The Regulations provide a precise formula to enable the calculation of APR to be done.[142] A computer is needed to solve the equation.

Assumptions to be made in calculating the APR

149. Certain assumptions need to be made to enable the APR to be calculated.

150. *Tax relief*: Any tax relief to which the borrower may be entitled should be ignored in calculating the total charge for credit, except certain life insurance relief under Schedule 4 Finance Act 1976.[143] The existence of any housing grants should also be ignored[144] but any subsidy received under the option mortgage scheme established by the Housing Subsidies Act 1967 should be taken into account (regulation 2(3), CONC App 1.1.3(3) R).

151. *Timing of provision of credit*: Credit is deemed to be provided at the earliest permissible date under the agreement.[145] Thus, if credit is to be provided by no later than a certain date, it is deemed to be provided at that date.[146] If it is not possible to ascertain the earliest date of provision of credit, it is assumed to be provided on the date of the agreement.[147]

152. *Amount of credit*: The amount of credit will often be stipulated in the agreement. If it is not, then in the case of running account credit, the amount of credit is deemed to be the credit limit; in other circumstances, it is assumed to be £100.[148]

153. *Timing of repayment of credit*: If credit is to be repaid by a certain date, it shall be assumed to be repaid on that date.[149] In such circumstances, any right in the creditor to demand earlier repayment is ignored.[150]

154. If at the date of the agreement, the period for which credit is to be provided is uncertain, it is to be assumed that credit will be provided for one year.[151]

155. A special rule applies to running account agreements and fixed sum agreements where a period rate of charge is charged. This is defined as a rate of charge for a specified period encompassing all charges entering into

141 Reg 6A TCC 1980; CONC App 1.1.8(b) R.
142 Reg 7 TCC 1980; CONC App 1.1.9 R.
143 Reg 2(1)(a); CONC App 1.1.3(1)(a) R.
144 Reg 2(1)(b); CONC App 1.1.3(1)(b) R.
145 Reg 2(2)(a)(i); CONC App 1.1.3(2)(a) R.
146 Reg 2(2)(a)(ii); CONC App 1.1.3(2)(a) R.
147 Reg 17; CONC App 1.1.17 R.
148 Reg 13; CONC App 1.1.12 R.
149 Reg 2(2)(a)(ii); CONC App 1.1.3(2)(a) R.
150 Reg 2(1)(c); CONC App 1.1.3(1)(c) R.
151 Reg 14; CONC App 1.1.13 R.

the total charge for credit.[152] The credit is assumed to be provided immediately after the start of the period, and to remain outstanding throughout the period and repaid immediately after the end of the period.[153]

156. *Amount of charges*: Where the amount of a charge is to be fixed by reference to an index, the total charge for credit is calculated on the assumption that the level of the index remains constant at the level prevailing at the date of the agreement.[154]

157. If the period for which credit is to be provided cannot be precisely ascertained at the date of the agreement but the agreement provides for a charge to increase within a period of one year from the date of the agreement, then it is assumed that the amount of the charge is the highest amount provided for.[155]

158. *Repayment of charges*: If there is uncertainty about the date when a charge is to be paid, it is to be assumed that it is to be paid at the date of the agreement or where this cannot be reasonably be expected, it is to be assumed that the charge will be repaid at the earliest date when repayment can be expected. If the agreement provides for payment of a number of charges, it will be assumed that the first is repayable at the date of the agreement, the last is repayable on the last date of the agreement and the remainder at equal intervals throughout the agreement.[156]

159. *Uncertain events*: The amount of certain charges may vary depending on the timing or occurrence of a future event. If the timing or the occurrence of the event is uncertain, it is assumed that the event will never take place.[157] This assumption will operate, for example, in the case of a loan to an employee where one of the terms of the loan provides for an increase in interest charges in the event of an employee leaving his or her employment. This contingency is assumed never to arise for the purposes of calculating the total charge for credit. Another application of this assumption arises where the lender has the unilateral right under a credit agreement to vary the charges imposed, as with many credit card agreements. It is assumed that the lender will not exercise this power for the purposes of calculating the total charge for credit – an assumption that may frequently be unrealistic in practice.[158] However, the assumption does not apply where the event is certain to occur and where the earliest date of its occurrence can be ascertained at the date of the agreement.[159] The event is then assumed to happen on this earliest date.

152 Reg 1(2); FCA Handbook Glossary.
153 Reg 2(2)(b); CONC App 1.1.3(2)(b) R.
154 Reg 15; CONC App 1.1.14 R.
155 Reg 16; CONC App 1.1.16 R.
156 Reg 18; CONC App 1.1.18(b) R.
157 Reg 2(1)(d): CONC App 1.1.3(1)(d) R.
158 *Nash and Staunton v Paragon Finance plc* 2001 EWCA Civ 1466 at [64].
159 Reg 2(1)(d): CONC App 1.1.3(1)(d) R.

Land-related agreements

160. Specific requirements were introduced in respect of land-related agreements as from 14 April 2000. A land-related agreement is one that is intended to finance the purchase or retention of land or 'the renovation or improvement of a building'.[160]

161. If an agreement provides for the possibility of a variation to an interest rate in an eventuality that must occur, it is assumed that the variation will take place.[161] This is contrary to the assumption that would otherwise be made by regulation 2(1)(d). The rate of interest to be assumed will be fixed by reference to what is referred to as the 'initial standard variable rate'. This is defined as the rate that would be charged by the lender as at the date of the agreement, or if this cannot be ascertained, the rate that the lender has charged on other land-related agreements.[162] Where a future rate cannot be ascertained, it is assumed to be the initial standard variable rate.[163]

The 2010 TCC Regulations and FCA Handbook CONC Appendix 1.2

162. Compared to the 1980 Regulations, the 2010 Regulations, as now reproduced in CONC Handbook Appendix 1.2 R, are a model both of simplicity and clarity. They apply to all regulated agreements other than those secured on land and even in the case of such agreements, the 2010 Regulations apply if the lender has opted in by complying with the 2010 Disclosure of Information Regulations.[164] It is perhaps a shame that the 1980 Regulations, as now enshrined in CONC Appendix 1.1 R, were kept in force at all.

163. The APR is to be calculated in accordance with a Schedule to the 2010 Regulations, now CONC Appendix 1.2.6 R.[165]

The charges to be taken into account

164. The charges to be taken into account include the cost of maintaining the credit account and the cost of making, handling and processing payments and drawdowns.[166] But these costs need not be included if the opening of an account is optional and the costs of so doing have been clearly

160 Reg 1(2); FCA Handbook Glossary.
161 Reg 2(1)(e); CONC App 1.1.3(1)(e) R.
162 Reg 15A(2); CONC App 1.1.15(2) R.
163 Reg 15A(3), (4); CONC App 1.1.15(3), (4) R.
164 CONC App 1.2.2 R.
165 Reg 5.
166 Reg 4(2); CONC 1.2.3(2) R.

spelt out in the initial agreement or if the costs do not relate to the provision of the overdraft facility.[167]

165. The cost of an ancillary service must be included in the cost of credit if it was compulsory for the borrower to take up the ancillary service.[168] Ancillary services are those that relate to the provision of credit and include, in particular, insurance and payment protection policies.[169]

166. Excluded are charges that may be payable on a default.[170]

167. Also excluded are charges that would be payable if the transaction were for cash.[171]

Assumptions

168. In calculating the APR, a number of assumptions may need to be made and these are specified in regulation 6 as substituted by the Consumer Credit (Total Charge for Credit) Amendment Regulations 2012.[172] These are now to be found in CONC App 1.2.5 R.

169. *No premature determination*: It is assumed that there will be no premature determination of the agreement.[173]

170. *Variable charges*: As with the 1980 Regulations, it is assumed that these indexed amounts, if they cannot be calculated, remain constant and at the same level as at the commencement of the agreement.[174]

171. *Initial fixed rate followed by a variable rate*: If the variable rate is to be fixed by reference to an index, the amount of the variable rate is fixed by reference to the index amount at the date of the agreement.[175]

172. *Drawdown*: Where a borrower is given freedom of drawdown, the borrower is assumed to exercise this right immediately and to its maximum extent.[176] If the credit agreement confers a number of different drawdown options, the borrower is assumed to select the most common option and the highest rate of interest and charge is then applied to it.[177] The lender is to determine the most common option by looking at the transactions during the previous 12-month period. In the case of a new product, the lender will have to ascertain what is expected to be the most common product.[178]

167 Reg 4(3); CONC 1.2.3(3) R.
168 Reg 4(4); CONC 1.2.3(4) R.
169 Reg 4(6;) CONC 1.2.3(6) R.
170 Reg 4(5)(a); CONC 1.2.3(5)(a) R.
171 Reg 4(5)(b); CONC 1.2.3(5)(b) R; this is the equivalent exclusion contained at reg 5(1)(c) of the 1980 Regulations.
172 SI 2012/1745.
173 Reg 6(a); CONC 1.2.5(a) R.
174 CONC App 1.2.5(b) R.
175 Reg 6(e); CONC App 1.2.5(e) R.
176 Reg 6(f); CONC App 1.2.5(f) R.
177 Reg 6(g); CONC App 1.2.5(g) R.
178 Reg 6(h); CONC App 1.2.5(h) R.

173. *Overdraft*: This is assumed to be drawn down immediately and to remain fully drawn down through the duration of the facility.[179] If no period has been fixed, the duration of the facility is assumed to be three months.[180]

174. *Open end consumer credit agreement other than an overdraft*: With an open end consumer credit agreement (i.e. one of revolving credit of no fixed duration),[181] the credit is assumed to be drawn down for a period of one year.[182] The final repayment is assumed to repay all capital and charges. The capital is assumed to be repaid in equal monthly amounts starting one month from the initial drawdown. If only one capital repayment is permitted, this is assumed to take place at the end of a year.[183]

175. *Repayment of capital*: If this cannot be ascertained, it shall be assumed to be at the earliest date and lowest amount permissible.[184] There are a number of default assumptions that apply if other assumptions have not come into play; for instance, a non-interest charge is assumed to be payable at the date of the agreement.[185]

176. *Running account agreement*: Where the credit limit is not specified, it shall be assumed to be £1,200.

179 Reg 6(i); CONC App 1.2.5(j) R.
180 Reg 6(j); CONC App 1.2.5(i) R.
181 Reg 2(c); FCA Handbook Glossary.
182 Reg 6(k); CONC App 1.2.5(k) R.
183 Reg 6(l); CONC App 1.2.5(l) R.
184 Reg 6(m)(i); CONC App 1.2.5(m), (i) R.
185 Reg 6(l); CONC App 1.2.5(l) R.

2 The regulatory framework

The regulatory history of consumer credit and consumer hire

Director General of Fair Trading

1. The Consumer Credit Act 1974 appointed the Director General of Fair Trading as the regulatory authority for the purposes of that Act. Section 1 of the Consumer Credit Act 1974, as originally enacted, provided for the Director General 'to superintend the working and enforcement of the Act and regulations made under it'. He was also directed, when expedient, to enforce the Act.[1]

2. The Director General was responsible for the licensing regime under Part III of the Act.

3. The Secretary of State[2] was given a general supervisory role. He was entitled to give 'general directions indicating considerations to which the Director should have particular regard in carrying out his functions under this Act, and may give specific directions on any matter connected with the carrying out by the Director of those functions'.[3] Persons aggrieved by the licensing decisions of the Director General were given a right to appeal to the Secretary of State.[4]

4. The duty to enforce the Act was shared between the Director General and the local weights and measures authorities, with the local weights and measures authorities[5] reporting to the Director General any prosecutions brought under the Act.[6]

1 Section 1(1)(d).

2 As a matter of constitutional law, all of the Secretaries of State are one, so no particular Secretary of State was identified in the legislation. In fact, the Secretary of State for Trade and Industry took responsibility for consumer affairs.

3 Section 2(2).

4 Section 41 Consumer Credit Act 1974.

5 Department of Commerce for Northern Ireland.

6 Section 161.

Office of Fair Trading

5. The functions and property of the Director General were transferred to the Office of Fair Trading by the Enterprise Act 2002.[7] Part 8 of that Act also conferred, with effect from 20 June 2003, extended enforcement powers on the Office of Fair Trading to uphold certain domestic and community legislation by means of application to the court for an enforcement order.

6. The enforcement powers in respect of domestic legislation conferred by section 211 of the Enterprise Act 2002 apply to the Consumer Credit Act 1974 by Enterprise Act 2002 (Part 8 Domestic Infringements) Order 2003.[8]

7. The enforcement powers in respect of community legislation have been extended to the Unfair Terms in Consumer Contracts Regulations 1999[9] and Consumer Protection Unfair Trading Regulations 2008[10] by virtue, respectively, of paragraphs 5 and 9C of Schedule 13 of the Enterprise Act 2002.

8. The local weights and measures authorities and the Department of Enterprise can also act as enforcers under this legislation.[11]

Financial Services Authority

9. A major change occurred following the Financial Services and Markets Act 2000. This Act ushered in regulation by the Financial Services Authority under the 2000 Act of credit agreements secured on land. Schedule 2 paragraph 23 of the Act referred to entry into such agreements as potential regulated activities.

10. The Financial Services and Markets Act 2000 (Regulated Activities) Order 2001 included within the categories of activities regulated by the 2000 Act, the entry into or administration of 'regulated mortgage contracts'.[12] Contracts of this type are mortgages secured by a first charge over a dwelling house for the borrower.[13] Such transactions are, of course, of enormous economic significance in that they include virtually every domestic property purchase.

11. At the same time, the Consumer Credit Act 1974 was amended[14] so as to make regulated mortgage contracts exempt agreements for the

7 Section 2(1) Enterprise Act 2002.
8 SI 2003/1593.
9 SI 1999; implementing the Unfair Terms Directive, Council Directive 93/12/EEC of 5 April 1993.
10 SI 2008/1277; implementing the Unfair Business Practices Directive, 2005/29/EC of 11 May 2005.
11 Section 213(1) Enterprise Act 2002.
12 Article 61 RAO.
13 Specifically, 40 per cent or more of the relevant land has to be intended for use as a dwelling house by the borrower.
14 By adding section 16(6C) Consumer Credit Act 1974.

purposes of that Act, thereby taking them outside the regulation of the 1974 Act for almost every purpose (except for the extortionate credit bargain provisions).

12. These provisions took effect on 31 October 2004 and the Financial Services Authority thereby became the responsible regulator for a large category of secured lending.

Consumer Credit Act 2006

13. The Consumer Credit Act 2006 strengthened the role of the Office of Fair Trade in connection with licensing giving new powers to the OFT.[15] In 2006, the power of the Secretary of State to hear licensing appeals was transferred to a newly created independent Consumer Credit Appeals Tribunal.[16]

Financial Conduct Authority

14. The regulatory landscape has fundamentally changed from 1 April 2014.

15. The Financial Services and Markets Act 2012 created two new regulators, the Financial Conduct Authority, 'the FCA', and the Prudential Regulatory Authority, 'the PRA', to replace the Financial Services Authority, 'the FSA'. (The FCA is the successor to the FSA.)[17]

16. The FCA has both strategic and operational objectives. The strategic objective is to see that the relevant markets function well.[18]

17. The operational objectives of the FCA are:[19]

(a) the consumer protection objective (i.e. securing an appropriate degree of protection for consumers);[20]
(b) the integrity objective; and
(c) the competition objective.

18. Both the strategic objective and these operational objectives are very relevant for the consumer credit industry, and the FCA will, as from 1 April 2014, be the relevant regulator for almost every purpose.

19. The FCA has a number of *general functions* that must be discharged in such a way as to promote these objectives, comprising the making of rules, issuing codes of practice, giving guidance under the Act and

15 Sections 38 to 43 Consumer Credit Act 2006.
16 Section 56 Consumer Credit Act 2006.
17 Section 1A(1) Financial Services and Markets Act 2000.
18 Section 1B(2) Financial Services and Markets Act 2000.
19 Section 1B(3).
20 Section 1C(1).

determining general policy and principles.[21] The FCA has and will continue to use these general functions to regulate the consumer credit industry.

The Prudential Regulation Authority

20. The Prudential Regulation Authority is a body corporate[22] and a division of the Bank of England. Its objective is to promote the safety and soundness of PRA-authorised persons. The activities regulated by it are deposit taking and the entry into contracts of insurance. It has relevance to the way credit unions and debt management organisations handle client monies. But these legal requirements are outside the scope of this book. The relevant regulator for all matters for which this book is concerned is the FCA subject to a residual continuing role for the Office of Fair Trading.

The Competition and Markets Authority

21. From 1 April 2014, the Office of Fair Trading has ceased to exist as its functions have been divided between the Financial Conduct Authority and the Competition and Markets Authority. The Competition and Markets Authority now becomes the principal enforcer for the purposes of sections 211 and 212 of the Enterprise Act 2002 pursuant to the Enterprise and Regulatory Reform Act 2013. Local weights and measures authorities will continue to act in tandem with both the Competition and Markets Authority under that Act and the FCA in connection with the enforcement of the provisions of the Consumer Credit Act 1974.

Powers of the FCA

22. The Consumer Credit Act regulatory regime, as far as the OFT was concerned, was primarily focused on licensing. The Secretary of State had the power to make regulations governing the conduct of credit and ancillary credit business but these were little used, save in the field of credit advertising.

23. By contrast, the FCA has more extensive powers to regulate the credit and ancillary credit market going beyond authorisation.[23]

24. The Financial Services and Markets Act 2000 as amended requires the relevant regulator to promulgate and publish various rules, guidance, codes of practice and statements of principle, including:

21 Section 1A(6).

22 Section 2A(1).

23 The authorisation process is also more extensive in that there is need to obtain authorisation not only to carry on regulated activities, but also to exercise controlled functions.

(a) the pronouncement of Statements of Principle;[24]
(b) the promulgation of accompanying Codes of Practice;[25]
(c) the making of Rules[26] applicable to authorised persons with respect to the carrying on of both regulated and unregulated activities as appear to be expedient for the FCA carrying on the operational objectives;
(d) the making of evidential rules, not binding in their own right but always relating to another rule;[27]
(e) the making of rules of specific types, such as product intervention rules,[28] the making of rules specifying what functions are to be treated as controlled functions for the purpose of obtaining approval to those carrying them out;[29]
(f) the giving of guidance about the operation of the Act and the Rules;[30]
(g) the publication of a Threshold Code amplifying the Threshold Conditions laid down in Schedule 6 of the Financial Services and Markets Act 2000;[31] and
(h) the giving of directions as to how various steps are to be undertaken with regard to the FCA (e.g. in relation to applying for authorisation).[32]

25. The rule-making powers are particularly wide ranging in the context of credit related regulated activities. The FCA has particular rule-making powers that allow the FCA to prohibit entry into certain specified types of regulated credit agreements,[33] including agreements that contain:

(a) charges of a prohibited type or of excessive amounts; and
(b) charges of prohibited duration.

26. The particular rules that may be made by the FCA potentially extend to all types of credit agreement except agreements secured on land.[34] By section 137C(1A), the FCA must make rules in respect of agreements involving high-cost short-term credit with a view to protecting consumers against excessive credit charges.

24 Section 64 Financial Services and Markets Act 2000.
25 Section 64(6) Financial Services and Markets Act 2000.
26 Section 137A Financial Services and Markets Act 2000.
27 Section 138C.
28 Section 138D.
29 Section 59(3)(a).
30 Section 139A.
31 Section 137O.
32 Section 55U(4).
33 Section 137C.
34 Section 137C(6). The subsection refers to the definition of credit agreement in paragraph 23 of Schedule 2 of the Financial Services and Markets Act 2000. This defines credit agreement as one where one person provides another person with credit and defines credit as any cash loan or other financial accommodation.

27. There is an analogous but more limited power in the FCA to make product intervention rules prohibiting an authorised person from entering into specified agreements with specified persons, or not entering into agreements unless specific requirements are met, or doing things that might result in persons entering into agreements of a specified type.[35] The rules may regulate the terms and conditions that can be included in agreements so specified or impose requirements on the invitations and inducements that may be offered.[36]

28. All of these different rules, statements, codes and guidance are gathered together and published in what is known as the Handbook. The FCA and PRA each have separate Handbooks but only the FCA Handbook CONC is directly relevant to the conduct of regulated consumer credit activities. The Handbook MCOB regulates regulated mortgage contracts and home purchase plans.

The structure and interpretation of the Handbook

29. The Handbook is of vast importance in laying the framework for the ongoing regulatory regime established by the Financial Services and Markets Act 2000. It is available both in electronic form and in hard copy. It can be daunting to those unfamiliar with it and the terminology employed; the FCA publishes a Reader's Guide, which provides useful guidance on what the Handbook contains and how to navigate around the Handbook.[37]

30. The Handbook is divided into what are referred to as *blocks*. There are seven blocks and their content is summarised below, except Block 7, containing listing, prospectus and disclosure rules, which is of no relevance to a book on consumer credit.

31. Each block is, in turn, divided into *modules*. Modules are identified by means of acronyms written in capitals. Each module is broken up into *chapters*. Each chapter contains individual *paragraphs*. Schedules appear at the end of some modules and these follow a standard pattern. So, for instance, Schedule 5 sets out which of the provisions in a module potentially give rise to a right to damages under section 138D and under what circumstances and to whom.

32. Not every provision in the Handbook has the same status; some are rules, some contain guidance, some are directions. There is an icon against each paragraph that signifies the status of that provision. So, for instance, the icon 'R' stands for rule, 'G' stands for guidance, 'E' stands for evidential provision, 'D' stands for directions and so forth.

33. There are two types of modules within each block, either *sourcebooks* or *manuals*. Sourcebooks contain binding obligations in the form of rules.

35 Section 137D(1).
36 Section 137D(2).
37 GEN 2.1.10 G.

Alongside the rules will be guidance. Manuals contain technical matters governing the relationship of the regulator with the authorised person; so, for example, the fees to be paid on making an authorisation application are to be found in the manual. Guides solely consist of guidance on various aspects of the regulatory regime.

34. There is also a Glossary containing definitions. Terms defined in the Glossary are shown printed in italics in the Handbook.[38] There are many such terms and it will not be possible to understand the Handbook without reference to the Glossary.

Block 1: high level standards

35. Block 1 is concerned with what are known as 'high level standards', setting out the basic regulatory principles as they apply to authorised persons.

36. The first module is entitled 'PRIN' (standing for principles for businesses), setting out 11 core principles. Thus, the first provides that a firm must conduct its business with integrity. The second that a firm must conduct its business with due skill and diligence. The third that a firm must take reasonable care to organise and control its affairs responsibly and effectively, with adequate management systems. The sixth, headed 'Customer's interests', is that a firm must pay due regard to the interests of its customers and treat them fairly. The seventh concerns itself with communicating with clients and provides that a firm must pay due regard to the information needs of its clients and communicate information to them in a way that is clear, fair and not misleading.

37. The second module within Block 1 is SYSC, standing for 'senior management arrangements, systems and controls', focusing on the responsibilities of directors and senior management. For instance, it is provided that a firm must have robust governance arrangements that include a clear organisational structure with well-defined, transparent and consistent lines of responsibility and must put into effect processes to identify, manage and monitor the risks it might be exposed to.[39]

38. An important module within Block 1 is entitled GEN (standing for 'general'). GEN2 sets out certain principles to be applied in the interpretation of the Handbook. Thus, GEN 2.2.1 R provides that 'every provision in the Handbook must be interpreted in the light of its purpose'. An understanding of the purpose of a particular provision may be assisted by guidance given in the Handbook but that guidance should not be treated as a complete or definitive explanation of the purpose of a provision.[40]

38 GEN 2.2.7.
39 SYSC 4.1.1. R.
40 GEN 2.2.2 G.

39. Insofar as terms are defined in the Glossary, those terms are to be given the meaning there assigned to them; otherwise, terms are to be given their natural meaning.[41]

40. GEN also provides that the Interpretation Act 1978 applies to the interpretation of the Handbook.[42] For example, words in the singular include the plural and vice versa.

41. Other important modules in this block are COND, which sets out the minimum threshold conditions for authorisation, and APER, which sets out the Statements of Principle and Code of Practice for Approved Persons. The module FIT expands on the fit and proper test for approved persons.

Block 2: prudential standards

42. Block 2 is concerned with prudential standards and is of less direct relevance to the consideration of the law of consumer credit. The module known as MIPRU contains the prudential requirements for mortgage and home finance firms. The rules impose capital requirements but do not apply to banks or friendly societies that have their own prudential requirements.[43]

Block 3: business standards

43. This is an important block in that it sets out the various standards to be adopted by businesses regulated by the Financial Services and Markets Act 2000. Its effect is obviously far wider than the control of regulated consumer credit businesses.

44. However, one module in the consumer credit context is MCOB, standing for 'mortgages and home finance: conduct of business', which will be examined independently. Mortgage and home reversion brokers have their own tailored handbook containing the Handbook content most relevant to these activities.

45. There is a Consumer Credit Handbook, known as CONC, governing the conduct of consumer credit business. This is of central importance.

Block 4: regulatory processes

46. Block 4 is concerned with regulatory processes, including disciplinary functions.

47. A wide-ranging module in this block is SUP (supervision), which covers such matters as the waiver and modification of rules, the controlled functions of approved persons and qualifying for authorisation.

41 GEN 2.2.7 R.
42 GEN 2.2.11 R.
43 MIPRU 4.1.4 R.

48. Another important module in this block is DEPP (decision procedure and penalties), which sets out the decision-making procedure of the FCA and gives guidance as to the imposition of disciplinary measures.

Block 5: redress

49. Block 5 concerns redress. The first chapter is labelled DISP and sets out details of the complaints procedure that a firm must put in place. This is of relevance to regulated consumer credit businesses.

Block 6: specialist sourcebooks

50. Block 6 contains specialist sourcebooks. There is one for credit unions labelled CREDs. There is also one explaining the exemption from authorisation for professional firms labelled PROF.

Tailored handbooks

51. There are a number of tailored handbooks. These are bespoke rulebooks that provide the most relevant information for each industry segment. They are targeted at smaller firms. Of relevance to the credit industry, there is a tailored guide for mortgage and home reversion brokers. If a firm reasonably relies on a tailored handbook, the FCA will not take disciplinary action in respect of any matter omitted from such a handbook.

Other guides

52. There has already been made mention of the reader's guide. There is an enforcement guide (EG), describing the approach of the FCA to its main enforcement powers. There is also what is known as the perimeter guidance manual (PERG), which gives guidance on the circumstances in which authorisation is required.

3 Regulated activities and exempt agreements

Regulated activities

1. The concept of regulated activities is central to the regulatory regime of the Financial Services and Markets Act 2000. It is no exaggeration to say the Act only applies to regulated activities. No person may carry on a regulated activity in the United Kingdom unless that person is an authorised person or an exempt person;[1] this prohibition is referred to in the Act as the 'general prohibition'. Breach of the general prohibition is a criminal offence, which, if tried on indictment, carries a maximum prison sentence of two years.[2]

2. Regulated activities must be of certain types as specified in the Regulated Activities Order. But there is an initial requirement that before any activity can be a regulated activity, it must be 'carried on in the course of business'.[3] The phrase is not defined by the Act and can sometimes raise difficulties.

3. In fact, it is also provided that with certain types of regulated activity, in order for someone to engage in a regulated activity, the relevant agreement must not only be entered into when that person was acting in the course of business, that person must 'carry on the business of engaging in that activity'.[4] The distinction is a fine one between entering into an arrangement in the course of business and between having a business of engaging in activities of that type, but the distinction will be important when an agreement is entered into in the course of carrying on a different business other than that of entering the agreement in question.

4. The question of whether a person carries on an activity in the course of business, or, if appropriate, whether the person carries on the business of engaging in that activity, is a matter of secondary fact or inference that

1 Section 19 Financial Services and Markets Act 2000.
2 Section 23(1)(b) Financial Services and Markets Act 2000.
3 Section 22(1), 22(1A) Financial Services and Markets Act 2000.
4 Financial Services and Markets Act 2000 (Carrying on Regulated Activities by Way of Business) Order 2001 SI 2001/1177 as amended.

is a matter of assessment for the trial judge with which the appeal court will not interfere if the appropriate factors have been considered.[5]

5. The activities that qualified as regulated are to be specified by the Treasury.[6] The Act imposes some limit on the type of activities that may be specified.

6. Section 22 of the Act provides that regulated activities must relate to an *investment* of a specified kind, or must be of a type of *activity* that is specified in relation to property of any kind (not just investments).[7] In addition, as from 24 January 2013, the activity can relate to the business of gathering information about a person's financial standing, or the setting of a specified benchmark (such as LIBOR).[8] The former category, gathering information about a person's financial standing, encompasses the activities of credit reference agencies. A person need not, of course, be an individual to engage in the relevant activity.

7. Schedule 2 to the Act supplements section 22, although in terms that make it clear that Schedule 2, surprisingly, has little independent substantive effect. It does not in itself limit or prescribe the range of activities that the Treasury may specify as regulated activities. Thus, paragraph 1 of Schedule 2 provides that Part I to the Schedule describes, in general terms, those activities for which provision *may*, not must, be specified by the Treasury under section 22 as regulated activities. Likewise, paragraph 10 of Schedule 2 makes it clear that Part II of Schedule 2 sets out in general terms those types of investments that the Treasury *may* specify under section 22.

8. Schedule 2 as originally enacted included the following at paragraph 23 as the only category that was related to the provision of credit: '(1) Rights under any contract of sale which – (a) one person provides another with credit, and (b) the obligation of the borrower is secured on land.' As from 24 January 2013, paragraph 23 is amended to 'rights under any contract under which one person provides another with credit'.

9. Credit was defined to include any cash loan or other financial accommodation, the same definition as found in the Consumer Credit Act 1974.[9]

10. Then, as from 19 February 2006, there was added a further paragraph 23A pursuant to the Regulation of Financial Services (Land Transactions) Act 2005. As from 24 April 2013, paragraph 23B extends to contracts of hire.

11. Now, as from 24 January 2013, there is added at Part 2A certain types of information-gathering activities.

12. The Treasury has duly specified regulated activities by means of the Regulated Activities Order 2001[10] as frequently amended and for present

5 *Helden v Strathmore Ltd* 2011 EWCA Civ 542 at para 39.
6 Section 22(5) Financial Services and Markets Act 2000.
7 Section 22(1) Financial Services and Markets Act 2000.
8 Section 22(1A) Financial Services and Markets Act 2000.
9 Schedule 2 paragraph 23(2) Financial Services and Markets Act 2000.
10 Financial Services and Markets Act 2000 (Regulated Activities) Order SI 2001/544.

purposes most substantively by the Financial Services and Market Act 2000 (Regulated Activities) Amendment (No 2) Order 2013,[11] which take effect on 1 April 2014. These new regulated activities relate to many activities connected to the provision of credit and to the conclusion of hire agreements. The relevant activities will be described hereafter.

Regulated and exempt agreements for the purpose of the Consumer Credit Act 1974 and the RAO

13. A regulated agreement for the purposes of the 1974 Act is divided between regulated credit and regulated consumer hire agreements, as defined by section 8(3) and section 15(2), respectively.[12]

14. Subsections 8(3) and 15(2) have been amended by the Financial Services and Markets Act 2000 (Regulated Activities) (Amendment) (No 2) Order 2013[13] with effect from 1 April 2014 so that now, section 8(3) provides that: 'A consumer credit agreement is a regulated agreement within the meaning of the Act [i.e. the Consumer Credit Act 1974] if it is a regulated credit agreement for the purposes of Chapter 14A of Part 2 of the Regulated Activities Order.'

15. Section 15(2) adopts a similar definition for a regulated consumer hire agreement as follows: 'A consumer hire agreement is a regulated agreement within the meaning of the Act if it is a regulated consumer hire agreement for the purposes of Chapter 14B of Part 2 of the RAO.' Note that the RAO talks about a regulated credit agreement (omitting the word 'consumer') but about a regulated *consumer* hire agreement.

16. Thus, regulated credit agreements and regulated consumer hire agreements are precisely aligned for the purposes of the 1974 Act and the RAO.

17. Prior to these amendments, the Consumer Credit Act 1974 had different categories of exempt agreement contained at sections 16, 16A, 16B and 16C of the Act and the Consumer Credit (Exempt Agreements) Order 1989 as amended. These sections and the Exempt Agreements Order have all been repealed by the Regulated Activities (No 2) Order 2013[14] so no further consideration will be given to the categories of exempt agreement previously contained in the Consumer Credit Act 1974. Some, but not all, of these exemptions are now replicated in the exemptions to be found at Articles 60C–60H of the Regulated Activities Order.

18. A regulated credit agreement is defined under the RAO as a credit agreement with an individual other than an exempt agreement.[15] Those

11 SI 2013/1881.
12 Section 189(1); the definition was substituted with effect from 26 July 2013.
13 SI 2013/1881.
14 SI 2013/1881.
15 Art 60B(3).

exemptions are at Articles 60C–60H of the RAO. An important point to note is that regulated mortgage contracts and home purchase plans are also exempt agreements[16] notwithstanding that entry into agreements of this type are regulated activities[17] and subject to regulation by the 2000 Act. These types of agreement are therefore unaffected by the provisions of the Consumer Credit Act 1974, subject only to the effect of section 126 of the 1974 Act.[18]

19. A regulated consumer hire agreement is one that is a hire agreement concluded with an individual other than a hire agreement exempt by virtue of Articles 60O–60Q.[19]

Regulated Activities Order

20. The Financial Services and Markets Act 2000 provides that the categories of regulated activity are to be specified by the Treasury, subject to the requirements that a regulated activity must relate to an *investment*[20] specified by the Treasury or relate to a specified activity 'carried on in relation to property of any kind'.[21]

21. These investments and activities are specified in the Regulated Activities Order 2001[22] as amended many times. The FCA has published guidance on the provisions of the Regulaties Activities Order known as the Perimeter Guidance or PERG.

22. Certain regulated activities comprise activities of relevance to the provision of credit or hire.

Regulated mortgage contracts

23. From the commencement of the Regulated Activities Order on 1 December 2001, it was provided that the entry into, or administration of, regulated mortgage contracts was a regulated activity.[23]

24. The expression 'regulated mortgage contract' has a very specific meaning.[24]

16 Art 60C(2).
17 Art 61 and 63F RAO.
18 However, by section 126(2) Consumer Credit Act 1974, such agreements are treated as regulated agreements for the purposes of section 126 and Part 9 of the Act.
19 Art 60N(3).
20 A term not defined in the Act save that it may relate to an asset, right or interest of any kind: Section 22(4) Financial Services and Markets Act 2000.
21 Section 22(1) Financial Services and Markets Act 2000.
22 Financial Services and Markets Act 2000 (Regulated Activities) Order SI 2000/544.
23 Art 61.
24 Art 61(3).

25. It applies where the lender grants credit to the borrower secured by means of a first legal mortgage on land (other than a timeshare) in the United Kingdom.[25] (A second charge does not qualify.) Moreover, at least 40 per cent of the land charged must be intended to be used as, or in connection with, a dwelling by the borrower. (It is also a regulated activity if money is borrowed by trustees to be charged on a house at least 40 per cent used as a dwelling by a beneficiary or a related person.)

26. The borrower must be an individual or trustees for an individual.[26] Thus, a loan to a corporation cannot be a regulated mortgage contract. However, it is no bar to a loan being a regulated mortgage contract that it was entered into for business purposes provided that it was charged on the place of residence of the individual.

27. Where there are two or more storeys, the relevant percentage is to be calculated by reference to the aggregate of the floor areas of the stories.[27]

28. It is also a regulated activity to *administer* a regulated mortgage contract.[28] Administration in this context entails the activity of notifying the borrower of various contractual matters such as changes in interest rates or other matters, or collecting monies due under the agreement; it does not, however, entail enforcement action.[29] However, it is not administration if an unauthorised person gets an authorised person to carry out the administration provided the unauthorised person does not administer the regulated mortgage contract him or herself for more than a month after any such arrangement comes to an end.[30]

29. It is also not a regulated activity for an unauthorised person to carry out administration pursuant to an agreement with a person authorised to carry out administration of a regulated mortgage contract.[31]

30. A further regulated activity was added in 2004 to cover broking in respect of a regulated mortgage contract (i.e. making arrangements for a person to enter a regulated mortgage contract with another party, or making arrangements for a variation in the terms of a regulated mortgage contract so as to vary the borrower's obligations).[32]

31. However, the making of arrangements, without more, to enable the parties to a proposed regulated mortgage contract to communicate with one another, is not a regulated activity.[33] Nor is it a regulated activity to draw

25 Art 61(3)(a)(ii).
26 Art 61(3)(a)(i).
27 Art 61(4)(b).
28 Art 61(2) RAO.
29 Art 61(3)(b) RAO.
30 Art 62 RAO.
31 Art 63 RAO.
32 Art 25A RAO.
33 Art 27 RAO.

up or arrange for the drawing up of a contract or formal agreement or variation thereof.[34]

32. Nor is it a regulated activity for an unauthorised person to make arrangements if it is intended that the transaction be entered into with an authorised person on the basis of advice from an authorised person, or in circumstances where no advice has been sought from the unauthorised person, or in circumstances, if advice has been sought from the unauthorised person, the unauthorised person has declined to give it but has instead recommended that advice be sought from an authorised person.[35]

33. Furthermore, as from October 2004, it also became a regulated activity to *advise* someone on the merits of entering a particular regulated mortgage contract, or of entering into a variation of a particular mortgage contract.[36]

Home reversion plans, home purchase plans and sale and rent back agreements

34. As from 6 April 2007, a number of similar but distinct activities also became regulated, which comprised:

(a) entering into or administering regulated home reversion plans;[37] and
(b) entering into or administering regulated home purchase plans.[38]

35. In addition, in June 2010, entering into or administering sale and rent back agreements[39] became a regulated activity.

36. Just as with regulated mortgage contracts, brokerage in respect of each of these activities (i.e. comprising the making of arrangements in respect of transactions to be entered into by others) also constitute regulated activities.[40] The same exceptions as to what qualifies as arranging apply. Likewise, it is a regulated activity to give advice on the merits of entering a particular home reversion plan, home purchase plan or sale and rent back agreement.[41]

37. The terms 'home reversion plans', 'home purchase plans' and 'sale and rent back agreements' all have their own specific definitions.

34 Art 28A RAO.
35 Art 29 RAO.
36 Art 53A RAO.
37 Art 63B RAO.
38 Art 63F RAO.
39 Art 63J RAO.
40 Art 25B, 25C, 25E RAO.
41 Art 53B, 53C, 53D.

38. A home reversion plan is one where:[42]

(a) the person to be authorised purchases an interest in a property belonging to the client;
(b) under the arrangement, the person selling the interest, or a relative, must be entitled to reside in at least 40 per cent of the property as a dwelling and must intend to do so; and
(c) that person's residency entitlement must come to an end with a terminating event, being either death or admission to a care home or a period of 20 years or more.

39. This is not a credit agreement; it involves the sale of an asset.

40. A sale and rent back agreement is the same as a home reversion plan without the requirement for the specific sale event that constitutes part of the definition of a home reversion plan.[43] Instead, the seller of the property will have an obligation to pay rent to the purchaser of the property. This is not a credit agreement.

41. A home purchase plan, on the other hand, is a credit agreement. It provides for the seller of the home[44] to continue to reside at the property[45] and to be obliged to repurchase it over the course of a specified period.[46] Such an arrangement provides for monies to be advanced on the security of the home; it is therefore a credit agreement.

Regulated and exempt credit agreements for the purpose of the Regulated Activities Order

42. Article 60B lays down the fundamental starting point that entry into a credit agreement with an individual is a regulated activity. There are exceptions made for certain categories of exempt agreement. An exempt agreement for the purposes of the RAO is defined as one defined as exempt coming within Articles 60C–60H.[47]

43. Regulated mortgage contracts and home purchase plans both involve the provision of credit but they are separately regulated, under Articles 61 and 63F, respectively. It would not be appropriate for these activities to be regulated activities under Article 60B as well, so these activities are therefore exempt agreements for the purpose of Article 60B.[48] The effect of this

42 Art 63B RAO.
43 Art 63J RAO.
44 Which may include trustees for an individual.
45 Or the beneficiary behind the trust.
46 Art 63F(3).
47 Art 60B(3).
48 Art 60C(2).

exemption is that regulated mortgage contracts and home purchase plans are almost entirely unaffected by the Consumer Credit Act 1974. An exception to this are the provisions in that Act relating to judicial control, including the grant of time orders and the making of suspended orders, which provisions apply to regulated mortgage contracts.[49]

Credit for more than £25,000 for business purposes

44. An agreement is an exempt agreement if the credit advanced exceeds £25,000 and the loan is made wholly or predominantly for business purposes.[50] The amount of credit is to be determined by excluding any sums entering into the total charge for credit. This exemption mirrors that previously found in section 16B of the Consumer Credit Act 1974. For a loan to qualify for exemption, the borrower may make a declaration in the required format that the loan is being entered into predominantly for business purposes. This has the effect of raising a presumption that the loan is made for this purpose, but it is not an absolute requirement for exemption that a declaration should be made. The form of the declaration must comply with CONC 1.4.8 R. It must be signed by the borrower and must contain a statement that the borrower agrees to forego the protection of the Consumer Credit Act 1974.

45. But if the loan is for a green deal plan,[51] then the agreement is exempt even if the credit is less than £25,000,[52] but in this case the loan must be wholly for the purposes of the green deal plan and not just predominantly.[53]

46. When a borrower makes a declaration that an agreement has been entered into predominantly for business purposes, there is a presumption to this effect unless the lender,[54] or anyone acting on the lender's behalf, has reasonable cause to believe that this is not the case.[55]

Financing foreign transactions

47. Credit is exempt if the agreement is made in connection with trade in goods and services to take place overseas and between the United Kingdom and another country.[56]

49 Section 126(2) Consumer Credit Act 1974.
50 Art 60C(3).
51 Within section 1 Energy Act 2011.
52 Art 60C(4).
53 Art 60C(7).
54 Or if there is more than one lender, any of the lenders.
55 Art 60C(5), (6).
56 Art 60C(8).

The purchase of land on mortgage for non-residential purposes

48. An exemption provides that a loan secured on land for the purchase of that land for non-residential purposes is exempt provided that no more than 40 per cent of the land is used or is intended to be used for the purpose of providing a home for the purchaser or a relative of the purchaser.[57] Where the property is a building that comprises two or more floors, the floor areas of each of the storeys must be aggregated.[58] The transaction is also exempt if the loan is to trustees and no more than 40 per cent of the land is to be used as a home by a beneficiary of the trust or a relative of that beneficiary.

49. 'Relative' has a particular meaning in this context. It includes a person who is a spouse or civil partner, or someone with whom the borrower is in a relationship that has the characteristics of a relationship of husband or wife (including someone of the same sex). The definition of relative also includes the parent, brother, sister, child, grandparent or grandchild.[59]

50. This exemption mirrors that formerly in section 16C of the Consumer Credit Act 1974.

Secured loans in relation to specific lenders

51. An agreement is exempt if the loan is what is called a 'relevant credit agreement', which is secured on the land and is entered into with certain specified lenders considered to be reputable.[60] All local authorities come within this category. Other lenders considered sufficiently reputable are specified in FCA Handbook CONC App 1.3.[61] (Housing authorities are considered below.)

52. To be eligible for exemption, the relevant credit agreement must fall within one of three categories.[62] The definition is complicated.

53. The first type of a relevant credit agreement is a borrower-lender-supplier agreement financing either the purchase of land or the provision of dwellings on the land. Moreover, the loan must be secured on that land. Note, however, that agreements for the purchase of land in respect of which at least 40 per cent will be used as a dwelling for the borrower or a relative, which might otherwise come within this exemption, is in any event exempted as a regulated mortgage contract by virtue of Article 60C(2).

54. The second type is a borrower-lender agreement; an agreement is of this type if: (a) the borrower is given unrestricted use of the credit; (b) the

57 Art 60D.
58 Art 60D(3)(a); this seems to apply only to buildings in existence at the time of purchase.
59 Art 60D(3).
60 Art 60E.
61 Art 60E(3).
62 See the definition in Art 60E(7).

purpose is to refinance existing indebtness; or (c) the loan is for a specific purpose, if there is no tie-up, existing or contemplated, between the lender and the intended recipient of funds. The borrower-lender agreement must be secured on land. It does not matter that the land is unconnected with the purpose of the loan.

55. The third type is a borrower-lender-supplier agreement to finance certain specific types of linked transaction that must conform to a number of specific requirements.[63] To be a linked transaction in this context, the agreement must not form part of the credit agreement itself or be security. Moreover, entry into the linked transaction must be required as a term of the credit agreement, or the linked transaction must be financed by the credit agreement, or the lender or an associate of the lender must have initiated the transaction and the transaction in addition must either be related to the credit agreement or have been entered into in order to induce the lender to enter into the credit agreement. The types of linked transaction that can be potentially exempt are contracts of insurance, contracts that amount to a guarantee of goods and contracts for the operation of a current account.

56. Another category of exempt agreement is an agreement entered into with a housing association. The loan must be intended for use in connection with a dwelling and the loan must be secured on that land.[64]

Low number of payments exemption

57. There is an exemption that is specific to borrow-lender-supplier agreements (i.e. one where the credit is tied to a particular supplier) where there are a small number of repayments made over a limited period of time.[65] Such an agreement is exempt if it is for fixed sum credit and the borrower is required to make no more than four repayments over a period of no more than 12 months. Moreover, there must be no interest or other significant charges; alternatively, the credit must be secured on land.[66] This exemption is suitable for retailers that wish to offer interest-free credit. It does not apply to agreements for the financing of the purchase of land, hire purchase or conditional sale agreements or pawn agreements.[67]

58. A further type of exempt agreement is a borrower-lender-supplier agreement to finance the purchase of land to be repaid in no more than four repayments, which is either secured on land or is interest free.[68] There is no requirement here, unlike the previous exemption, that the repayments be made over a 12-month period.

63 Article 60E(8) RAO.
64 Art 60E(5).
65 Art 60E.
66 Art 60F(2).
67 Art 60F(7).
68 Art 60F(4).

59. It is likewise exempt if the borrower-lender-supplier agreement is an agreement for running account credit to be repaid in only one repayment at the end of specified intervals that must not exceed three months (save in the case of an agreement secured on land when the three-month time limit does not apply).[69] There must be no credit charges unless the agreement is secured on land. This exemption is utilised in respect of charge cards such as American Express when it is a term of the agreement that the credit must be repaid in full at the end of each period.

60. There is also an exemption in the case of credit to pay the premium on a contract of insurance connected with the land or anything on the land. The lender must have made a loan secured on a legal mortgage. If the loan for the insurance premium is also secured on land, then the interest rate payable under the insurance premium loan must not exceed that payable under the principal agreement. If the agreement is not secured on land, the credit must be provided without charge. The number of payments must be limited to 12 but there is no maximum repayment period stipulated.[70]

61. Another exemption applies, in like circumstances, to agreements to fund the premium not of insurance connected with the land, but for life insurance that provides for payment of a sum that does not exceed the amount of credit. With this exemption, it is also necessary that the lender be a lender under a credit agreement secured on land.[71]

62. The low number of payments exemption has been considered by the courts on a number of occasions, principally in relation to the requirement that the four repayments must be repaid within a period of no more than 12 months. The leading case in the Court of Appeal is *Zoan v Rouamba*.[72] In that case, the court had to consider the construction of a credit hire agreement and held that on its true construction, as a result doubtless of a drafting error on the part of the owner, the hirer was entitled to make the last payment one day after the end of the 12-month period from the date of the agreement, so that, as a consequence, the requirements of the low number of payments exemption were not met. The obvious intention of the owner that the agreement should be exempt was thereby frustrated. However, it was held that the agreement could not be construed in the light of the Consumer Credit (Exempt Agreements) Order as it was unrealistic to expect that the hirer would have had any knowledge of these legal requirements. It would have been different if both parties to the transaction had been aware of the exemption regime. The result of this case seems unjust. Similar exercises in construction were carried out, with the same result, in *Ketley v Gilbert*[73] and, with the opposite result, in *Thew v Cole*.[74]

69 Art 60F(3).
70 Art 60F(5).
71 Art 60F(6).
72 2000 2 All ER 620.
73 2001 RTR 327.
74 2004 RTR 25.

Exemption relating to the total charge for credit

63. Unlike the previous exemption, this exemption applies only to borrower-lender agreements;[75] the 'small number of payments' and 'low cost of credit' exemptions are therefore mutually exclusive.

64. To qualify for this exemption, the loan must be offered to only a particular class of individuals and not to the public generally. The loan must either provide that the only charge in the total charge for credit is interest and the interest must not exceed 1 per cent above the highest of the base rates published by the banks listed in Article 60G(7), or the loan terms must not permit of any increase of any item in the total charge for credit and the total charge for credit must not exceed 1 per cent above the highest base rate of the specified banks.[76]

65. Furthermore, one of the following must apply: the agreement must be secured on land, or it must be offered by an employer to an employee as an incident of employment, or it must meet the 'general interest rate test', or the total amount payable under the agreement must not vary according to a formula having effect by reference to movements in the level of any index or other factor.

66. The general interest test means that it is offered under a statute with a general interest purpose (i.e. for the purpose of advancing the public good generally) and the terms on which it is offered is lower than that available on the prevailing market.[77]

Exemption relating to high net worth borrower

67. This exemption applies when a qualifying loan is made to a high net worth individual.[78] To qualify under this exemption, the loan must either be secured on land or the credit must be for more than £60,260; the borrower must be a high net worth individual (i.e. someone with a net income of more than £150,000 a year[79] or free assets of at least £500,000 throughout the year).[80] In calculating a person's free assets value, the value of a person's primary residence and any borrowing secured upon it is to be ignored, as is any entitlement that may be received in the future on termination of service or retirement. The borrower must make a declaration in the form set out at CONC App 1.4.6 R agreeing to forego the protection of the Act. It must be set out in the credit agreement no less prominently than other information in the agreement and must be signed by the borrower unless the agreement is signed.[81]

75 Art 60G.
76 Art 60G(3), (4).
77 Art 60G(6).
78 Art 60H.
79 I.e. less tax and national insurance.
80 App 1.4.7 R.
81 CONC App 1.4.2 R.

68. The borrower must make a statement of assets and income in the prescribed form. It must have been prepared in the period of one year leading up to the conclusion of the agreement.[82] This must be signed by either the lender[83] or an accountant belonging to one of the established accountancy bodies.[84] Further, the statement must have been provided to the borrower before the agreement is entered into.[85]

Hire agreement where payments exceed £25,000

69. This is similar to the exemption exempting certain business loan agreements where the credit exceeds £25,000 except that hire agreements are exempt where the hirer is required under the terms of the agreement to make total payments exceeding £25,000 and the hiring is entered into predominantly for business purposes.[86] The same requirements apply, including the effect of a declaration made by the hirer that provides that the hiring is predominantly for business purposes. The declaration must comply with CONC App 1.4.8 R and be signed by the hirer unless the agreement itself is signed, in which case the declaration must be set out predominantly in the agreement.

Gas, electricity and water meters

70. The hiring of these is exempt where the supply is by a statutory body authorised to supply gas, electricity or water.[87]

Hire agreement entered into by high net worth hirers

71. This exemption is analogous to the exemption relating to credit agreements at Article 60H save that there is no requirement that the hire agreement be secured on land or as to the total payments payable under the hire agreement.[88] Otherwise, the same conditions apply, including as to the provision of a declaration made by the hirer and a statement of income and assets. The declaration made by the hire must be in the form set out at CONC App 1.4.6 R. The declaration of high net worth must comply with CONC App 1.4.7 R as with the high net worth credit exemption, and must in the same way be signed by an accountant. 'High net worth' has the

82 CONC App 1.4.1(3) R.
83 However, a lender is only qualified if authorised to accept deposits; CONC App 1.4.4 R.
84 CONC App 1.4.3(2) R.
85 Art 60H(f).
86 Art 60O.
87 Art 60P.
88 Art 60Q.

same meaning (i.e. a net income of at least £150,000 per annum or free assets of at least £500,000).

Credit broking

72. Credit broking is a regulated activity by virtue of Article 36A of the RAO. The relevant definition refers to no less than six types of activity that constitute credit broking. The phrase credit broking is misleading to the extent that it also extends, in respect of the second type of activity, to making introductions to those offering to enter into hire agreements. The phrase 'hire broking' might have been used, but it was not.

73. The Consumer Credit Act 1974 rather confusingly refers not to credit broking, but to *credit brokerage*, which is defined in section 145 of the Consumer Credit Act 1974 as meaning 'the carrying on of an activity of the kind specified by article 36A(1)(a) to (c) of the Regulated Activities Order, disregarding the effect of paragraph (2) of that Article'.

74. In the different terminology of the Consumer Credit Act 1974, those carrying out activities (d)–(f) are referred to as *credit intermediaries*, terminology inserted into the 1974 Act initially at section 160A, and now at section 61A(8).

75. Perhaps unusually, there is no requirement that a credit broker must be acting in the course of business but it is not credit brokerage if no fee is charged; fee in this context includes pecuniary consideration or other form of financial consideration.[89]

76. The first three types of activity are concerned with the effecting of introductions of an individual or relevant recipient of credit to someone acting as lender in respect of a credit agreement, or owner in respect of a hire agreement, or someone acting as credit broker in respect of an agreement of these types (i.e. so that it is credit brokerage to introduce an individual to a relevant credit broker). However, the eventual person to whom the introduction is being made, be it lender or owner, must be acting in the course of business.

77. Furthermore, it must be an individual or 'the relevant recipient of credit' that is introduced. A relevant recipient of credit is a partnership of two or three persons (not more), not all of whom are bodies corporate or an unincorporated body of person, not comprising solely bodies corporate and not comprising a partnership.[90] This is the same as the definition of 'individual' in the Consumer Credit Act 1974.

78. The fourth category of activity that constitutes credit broking is presenting or offering a prospective regulated credit agreement. However, it is not credit broking if the person presenting or offering the regulated

89 Art 36C RAO.
90 Art 60L RAO.

credit agreement is intending to enter into it as lender or owner.[91] A lender is not credit broker to itself.

79. The fifth category is undertaking preparatory work with a view to an individual or relevant recipient of credit entering into a credit agreement. But if the intention is that the person undertaking the preparatory work is to act as lender or owner, again that is not credit broking.[92]

80. The sixth category is entering into a credit agreement on behalf of a lender. This envisages that the credit broker should make a practice of entering an agreement as agent for the true lender.

81. In respect of these typs of credit broking activities, the agreement contemplated by the activity must be regulated, *except* that most of the exemptions set out in the Regulated Activities Order do not apply. Thus, it is still credit broking if the introduction relates to an anticipated credit agreement that is an exempt falling within articles 60C, 60D, 60E, 60G and 60H.[93] Accordingly, it is credit broking to introduce someone with a view to that person entering into a regulated mortgage contract.[94] In the case of an anticipated hire agreement, it is still credit broking if the anticipated hire agreement is an exempt agreement falling within articles 60O and 60Q.

82. However, the operation of an electronic lending platform, 'peer to peer', is specifically excluded from credit broking as that forms a discrete regulated activity.[95] Nor does it matter if the relevant law of the proposed credit or hire agreement is intended to be governed by the law of a country outside the United Kingdom.[96]

83. Nor is it credit broking to introduce an individual[97] with a view to that person entering into a regulated mortgage contract if the person making the introduction has authorisation to enter into regulated mortgage contracts (regardless whether in this particular case there is any intention on the part of the introducer to enter into the particular regulated mortgage contract in respect of which the introduction is made). It is also not credit brokerage to introduce someone, with a view to that person entering into a regulated mortgage contract, to someone who has credit brokerage authorisation to make introductions to those authorised to enter into regulated mortgage contracts.[98]

84. A barrister acting in that capacity or a solicitor acting in contentious business is specifically excluding from acting as a credit broker.[99] A solicitor

91 Art 36D RAO.
92 Art 36D RAO.
93 Art 36A(4).
94 Which is exempt under Art 60C.
95 Art 36A(2).
96 Art 36A(3) RAO.
97 Including a relevant recipient of credit as defined.
98 Art 36E.
99 Art 36F RAO.

introducing clients to sources of mortgage finance during the course of conveyancing work is not excluded from the definition of credit broker.

The canvassing exception

85. A person engaged in door-to-door canvassing off trade premises is not engaged in credit broking when trying to introduce people to sales on credit or to enter into consumer hire agreements, provided the criteria below are satisfied.[100] This must be their sole credit broking activity to qualify for the exemption.[101] This exemption follows a similarly worded exemption that was previously contained in section 146 of the Consumer Credit Act 1974.

86. In more detail, it is not credit broking for someone to canvass entry by a prospective borrower into restricted use credit agreements to finance a prospective transaction between the prospective borrower and the lender.[102] Nor is it credit broking to canvass off trade premises the entry by a prospective hirer into regulated consumer hire agreements off trade premises.[103] But for this exception, these canvassing activities would be credit broking within categories Article 36A(1)(a) and (c) above.

87. The visit must be for the purpose of making oral representations.[104] The exclusion does not cease to apply if a leaflet is handed over at the same time for the prospective customer to consider.

88. 'Off trade premises' means any place other than where the following are conducting business:[105] the canvasser, the employer or principal[106] of the canvasser, the trade premises of the prospective borrower, the trade premises of the intended supplier of the goods or serves intended to be financed.[107]

Debt counselling, debt adjusting, debt collecting, debt administration

89. Debt counselling, debt adjusting, debt collecting and debt administration apply equally to consumer credit and consumer hire agreements.

90. Barristers and advocates are specifically exempted from all these activities when acting in that capacity.[108] Solicitors are exempted if their

100 Art 36B RAO.
101 Art 36B(2).
102 Or associate of the lender.
103 Article 36B(1)(b).
104 Art 36B(3)(b).
105 Including temporarily.
106 If the canvasser is an agent.
107 Art 36B(4).
108 Art 39K(1)(a) RAO.

advice is given solely in the context of contentious work[109] (i.e. if confined to situations where legal proceedings have begun before a court or arbitrator).[110]

91. All of these activities are also excluded when they relate to regulated mortgage contracts.[111] Regulated mortgage contracts are subject to their own regime.

Debt counselling

92. *Debt counselling* is the most passive of the four types of regulated activity under consideration here. As its name implies, it consists of the business of giving advice in relation to the 'liquidation' of debts (i.e. in relation to their discharge by payment or otherwise).[112] All those who regularly give advice on consumer affairs participate in debt counselling: money advice centres, law centres, citizens advice bureaux and bank managers are all debt counsellors.

Debt adjusting

93. *Debt adjusting* is a regulated activity that involves:[113]

(a) Participating in negotiations with the lender or owner for a rescheduling or rearrangement of the debts owing.
(b) Taking over the obligations of the borrower to the lender in exchange for payments from the borrower. Here, the debt adjuster will pay off the debt to the lender or owner and seek recovery from the borrower or hirer in turn. The debt will probably be rescheduled over a longer period and the debt adjuster will normally charge the borrower for the service. The rescheduling agreement will in itself probably be a credit agreement and subject to regulation. Banks typically participate in this species of debt adjusting activity.
(c) 'Any similar activity concerned with the liquidation of a debt'. Probably, it is debt adjusting under this final category to introduce a borrower or hirer to a third party who may agree to reschedule the borrower or hirer's indebtedness, although the activity could also be classified as credit broking.

109 Art 39K(1)(b) RAO.
110 It does not seem sufficient that proceedings are only contemplated, although once proceedings are in fact begun, steps taken beforehand will doubtless be covered.
111 Art 39J.
112 Art 39E.
113 Art 39D.

Debt collecting

94. *Debt collecting* is a regulated activity involving taking steps to obtain payment of debts due from borrowers or hirers under consumer credit or consumer hire agreements.[114] Various methods can be employed for obtaining payment; written or verbal demands may suffice. Taking legal proceedings may be necessary; house calls may take place (but it is to be noted that it is an offence under section 40 of the Administration of Justice Act 1970 unlawfully to harass borrowers into making payment by making demands that are likely to alarm, distress or humiliate the borrower or his or her family). Participation in such activities amounts to debt collection.

95. However, it is not debt collecting if the actions are done in the course of operating a peer-to-peer lending platform.[115] This constitutes a regulated activity under Article 39H.

Debt administration

96. It is the regulated activity of *debt administration*[116] to:

(a) Perform duties for a lender or owner under a credit or hire agreement. An example of such a duty might be sending out of statutory arrears notices on behalf of the lender or owner.
(b) Exercise or enforce the rights of the owner or hirer under the agreement. This will not presumably include activities that include debt collecting as this is covered by Article 39F, but it would include the recovery of goods in respect of hire purchase or hire agreements in the event of termination.

97. This does not include activities within the operation of a peer-to-peer lending platform.

Electronic system in relation to lending

98. This category of activity, at Article 36H of the RAO, regulates the activity of operating an electronic platform enabling the matching of buyers and lenders; the article uses the undefined phrase 'electronic system'. This activity is sometimes known as 'peer-to-peer lending' or 'P2P' and was introduced as a discrete regulated activity following the consultation paper in March 2013, FSA 13/07. The operator of such a system will need to be authorised.

114 Art 39F.
115 Art 39F(3).
116 Art 39G.

99. For this activity to be regulated, the system must be capable of determining which agreement should be made available to the borrower and lender in each case. This may, not must, be as a result of the application of general instructions provided by the borrower or lender.[117]

100. Further, in order for the operator to require authorisation, two further conditions must be satisfied.

101. First, the operator must collect the repayments of capital and interest from the borrower and account to these to the lender (less any deduction or retention).[118] The second condition is that the operator of the platform must arrange to collect payments from the borrower or must act for the lender in enforcing the lender's rights against the borrower.[119] These conditions are still satisfied if the operator performs them through the intervention of an appointed third party.[120]

102. The activity will only be a regulated activity in relation to what are called '36H agreements'.[121] This means that either the lender is an individual,[122] or that the amount of the loan must be equal to or less than £25,000 and the borrower must not enter into the loan predominantly for the reasons of his or her business.[123] There is no requirement that the lender is carrying on a regulated activity,[124] so an electronic system may be a regulated activity even if the lenders only make one-off loans.

103. There are a number of activities ancillary to the enabling activity that are also regulated in the context of operating an electronic system, including:[125] the presentation of agreements to the lender and borrower, providing financial information to enable the lender to decide whether to enter into a loan agreement, taking steps to collect or enforce a debt due under a relevant agreement, and dealing with credit reference agencies and the information obtained from such.

104. Information society services are excluded from this provision.[126]

Credit reference agency

105. A credit reference agency is an organisation that carries on by way of business the regulated activity specified by Article 89B of the RAO.[127]

117 Art 36H(2).
118 Art 36H(2A).
119 Art 36H(2C).
120 Art 36H(2B).
121 Article 36H(1) RAO.
122 Or relevant person as defined as a partnership consisting of two or three persons not all of whom are bodies corporate or an incorporated body not all of whose members are bodies corporate.
123 Art 36H(5), (6).
124 Art 36H(8).
125 Article 36H(3).
126 Article 36I.
127 Section 145(8) Consumer Credit Act 1974.

106. The activity involves:

(a) collecting information about the financial standing of individual or relevant recipients of credit; and
(b) furnishing that information.[128]

107. The activity does not qualify if these activities are not primary activities.[129] Nor does the activity apply to peer-to-peer lending falling within Article 36H,[130] or to solicitors or barristers acting in the course of contentious business.[131]

108. A credit reference agency must not be confused with a credit information agency. A credit information agency is a much wider term and while it includes a credit reference agency, it also includes a person who carries on credit broking or debt adjusting, debt counselling, debt collecting, debt administration, entry into regulated consumer credit or hire agreements.[132]

128 Art 89B(1).
129 Art 89B(2).
130 Art 89B(3).
131 Art 89C.
132 Art 89A(6).

4 Authorisation and the failure to obtain it

Application for authorisation

1. If a firm intends to carry on a regulated activity, it must apply for authorisation. In order to apply for authorisation, a person must apply to the appropriate regulator, which, in respect of credit-related regulated activities, is the FCA. If the person seeking authorisation is a member of a group that contains a PRA-authorised entity, then the FCA must consult the PRA before deciding the matter.[1]

2. The application must be made as directed by the FCA.[2] Obviously, it must contain a statement of the regulated activities for which permission is sought.[3] In practice, the application is made directly via the FCA website. A fee is payable. The information that will have to be produced will depend significantly on whether the proposed activities are classified as high risk or low risk.

Consideration of the application

3. The Regulator will only grant the application for authorisation if satisfied that the applicant is a fit and proper person.[4] The Regulator may consider a wide variety of matters in reaching its decision. The Regulator may seek further information from the applicant if the Regulator reasonably thinks this is necessary to consider the application.[5] The FCA may also take into accounts any known associate of the applicant (i.e. to 'have regard to any person appearing to be, or likely to be, in a relationship with the applicant or a person given permission which is relevant').[6]

1 Section 55E(4).
2 Section 60(2).
3 Section 55U(1).
4 Section 61(1) Financial Services and Markets Act 2000.
5 Section 60(4) Financial Services and Markets Act 2000.
6 Section 55R.

The threshold conditions

4. In order to qualify for authorisation, a firm must, as a minimum, satisfy and continue to satisfy certain basic minimum conditions known as the threshold conditions.[7]

5. The threshold conditions are set in Schedule 6 of the Financial Services and Markets Act 2000 supplemented by the Threshold Code.[8] The FCA is given power to amend Schedule 6,[9] a power it has recently used with effect from 1 April 2013.[10] The threshold conditions are set out in a module of the Handbook known as COND, which does not add much to the requirements set out in Schedule 6 as amended.

6. In the field of consumer credit at least, the FCA adopts a risk-based approach in that different threshold conditions apply, in many instances, to higher risk and lower risk firms. The distinction is a very important one as it defines the initial regulatory approach adopted by the FCA. A lower risk firm will be subjected to light touch, or at least lighter touch, regulation. A lower risk firm carries on what is referred to as a 'relevant credit activity', as defined at paragraph 2G of Schedule 6.

7. A relevant credit activity is one where the activities of the firm are confined to the following:

(a) those who supply goods or services on credit other than on hire purchase or conditional sale and who make no charge for the credit;[11] it is also low risk if such persons carry on debt adjusting;
(b) loan agreements where the local authority is the lender;[12]
(c) those who let goods on consumer hire;[13] it is also low risk if such persons carry on debt adjusting;
(d) those who are suppliers of goods or services and who engage in credit brokerage in connection with the intended supply, save that those who supply goods while on the domestic premises of the customer (other than occasionally) are excluded; this applies, for instance, to car dealers who will direct potential purchasers to a source of credit finance;[14] it is also low risk if such a supplier/credit broker also carries on debt adjusting;[15] and

7 Section 55B Financial Services and Markets Act 2000.
8 Made under section 137O Financial Services and Markets Act 2000.
9 Section 55C Financial Services and Markets Act 2000.
10 Financial Services and Markets Act 2000 (Threshold Conditions) Order 2013 SI 2013/555.
11 Schedule 6 paragraph 2G(1)(d).
12 Schedule 6 paragraph 2G(1)(da).
13 Schedule 6 paragraph 2G(1)(e).
14 Schedule 6 paragraph 2G(1)(a), (3).
15 Schedule 6 paragraph 26(1)(b)(i).

(e) those who engage in credit brokerage for a green deal plan or in respect of consumer hire of vehicles.[16]

8. However, if the activities are secured in land, then the activity will not qualify as a relevant credit activity, unless the lender is a not-for-profit body.[17]

9. Moreover, the business of debt adjuster and debt counsellor is also low risk if done by a not-for-profit organisation. 'Not-for-profit', however, has a specific meaning in this context; the organisation must not be allowed to make a profit under its constitution in that any surplus must be required to be paid to charitable and public purposes and not distributed among its members.[18] The mere fact that the organisation decides not to charge for its services is not enough to make it not-for-profit.

10. The threshold conditions that a non-PRA regulated firm must satisfy in order to obtain authorisation are less onerous for a 'low risk' firm (i.e. those engaged in a 'relevant credit activity') and are as follows:

(a) *Legal status*. This is to ensure that the firm exists as a corporate entity. In the case of a higher risk firm[19] only, the FCA will check with companies' house and review the appropriateness of the company name.
(b) *Location of offices*. In the case of both higher risk and lower risk firms, in the case of a body corporate, the head office where the central management is based should be in the UK.[20] If the firm is not a body corporate but has a head office here, then the firm must carry on business here.
(c) *Effective supervision*. A firm must be capable of being effectively supervised by the FCA[21] and should have a structure that enables this to be done. In the case of relevant credit activities, the FCA will not be concerned with the nature of the regulated activities or their complexity. In the case of a higher risk firm, the FCA will review the model and structure chart of the firm, including the owners and business controllers. In the case of a lower risk firm, automated checks will be carried out on key controllers only, although complex structures may be investigated.
(d) *Appropriate resources*. A firm must have appropriate financial and other resources for the business that it intends to carry on.[22] However, in the case of firms carrying on only relevant credit activities, the require-

16 Schedule 6 paragraph 2G(1)(a), (4), (5).
17 Schedule 6 paragraph 2G(2).
18 Schedule 6 paragraph 2G(6).
19 I.e. one not engaged in a relevant credit activity.
20 Schedule 6 paragraph 2B.
21 Schedule 6 paragraph 2C.
22 Schedule 6 paragraph 2D Financial Services and Markets Act 2000.

ment is satisfied if the firm should be capable of meeting its debts as they fall due.[23] With lower risk firms, the FCA, having reviewed basic financial information provided, will rely in the first instance on self-certification.

(e) *Suitability.* A firm must be fit and proper having regard to all the circumstances.[24] This applies to a firm that carries on a relevant credit activity, as well as other firms. With a higher risk firm, the FCA will review criminal records and perhaps consult trading standards. Lesser checks on a sample basis will be conducted with a lower risk firm.

(f) *Business model.* A higher risk firm will have to submit a detailed business plan so that the FCA can assess whether its business strategy is suitable.[25] This will not apply to a low risk firm.[26] In practice, this is considered by many firms seeking authorisation to be the most onerous part of the application process.

Procedure for determination of the application

11. The FCA must determine a complete application within six months.[27] If an application is incomplete, the relevant time limit is 12 months.[28] Of course, in giving permission, the FCA is not bound to give permission in the same terms as sought. It can refuse part of the application or impose limitations or even give permission for a regulated activity not included in the permission.[29]

12. If the FCA proposes to refuse permission, or attach limitations or requirements, then the FCA must serve a warning notice on the authorised person.[30] This must be in writing and state the action that the FCA intends to take and the reasons for it.[31] The FCA staff acting under executive procedures may take the decision to serve a warning notice.[32]

13. The warning notice will point out the right of the recipient to make representations, including oral representations. The notice will stipulate the time in which written representations must be made, which must not be less than 14 days.[33] The recipient may apply for an extension of time,

23 Schedule 6 paragraph 2D(3A) Financial Services and Markets Act 2000.
24 Schedule 6 paragraph 2E.
25 Schedule 6 paragraph 2F.
26 Schedule 6 paragraph 2F(3).
27 Section 55V(1) Financial Services and Markets Act 2000.
28 Section 55V(2) Financial Services and Markets Act 2000.
29 Section 55E(5) Financial Services and Markets Act 2000.
30 Section 55X(1), (2) Financial Services and Markets Act 2000.
31 Section 388(1) Financial Services and Markets Act 2000.
32 DEPP2.5.3 in accordance with a procedure laid down to comply with section 395 Financial Services and Markets Act 2000.
33 Section 387(2) Financial Services and Markets Act 2000.

normally within seven days of receipt of the warning notice, and any request for an extension will be considered by the Chairman or Deputy Chairman of the Regulatory Decisions Committee.[34] Neither the FCA nor the person receiving the warning notice may publish it or any details concerning it.[35]

14. Once a decision is reached, a decision notice will be given.[36] If no representations have been made, the decision notice will be issued by default.[37] If representations are made, the decision will be taken by the Regulatory Decisions Committee of the FCA,[38] which sits as a panel of at least three. The decision notice must be in writing and state reasons.[39] It must also draw attention to the right of the authorised person to refer the matter to the tribunal. A person to whom a decision notice is given may not publish the notice or any details concerning it unless and until the FCA has published details of the notice.[40]

15. If an applicant is aggrieved at the outcome of an application, the applicant can refer the matter to the tribunal.[41]

Controlled functions

16. It is not sufficient that a firm obtain authorisation to carry on a regulated activity; it is also necessary to obtain the approval of the FCA in respect of those persons intended to perform what are referred to as 'controlled functions'.[42] This regulatory requirement did not have any equivalent in the regulatory regime under the Consumer Credit Act 1974 and comprises an additional layer of regulation.

17. Arrangements requiring approval coming within the scope of this requirement include employment contracts, partnerships and appointment to an office.[43] Furthermore, if an approved person engages a contractor to carry on a performed function, the approved person must take reasonable care to ensure that the regulator approves the performance of the controlled function.[44]

18. Where the FCA is the appropriate regulator, controlled functions can be of two types:[45]

34 DEPP 3.2.16.
35 Section 391(1ZA) Financial Services and Markets Act 2000.
36 Section 55X(4) Financial Services and Markets Act 2000.
37 DEPP 2.5.4.
38 DEPP 2.5.5.
39 Section 388 Financial Services and Markets Act 2000.
40 Section 391(1A) Financial Services and Markets Act 2000.
41 Section 55Z3(1) Financial Services and Markets Act 2000.
42 Section 59(1) Financial Services and Markets Act 2000.
43 Section 59(10) Financial Services and Markets Act 2000.
44 Section 59(2) Financial Services and Markets Act 2000.
45 Section 59(5).

(a) a significance influence function; and
(b) a customer dealing function.

19. A person may be considered to exercise a significance influence function if that person's position gives that person significance influence over the authorised person's affairs.[46] A person may be considered to exercise a customer dealing function if that person has dealings with customers or their property.[47] Within these constraints, it is for the FCA to specify, by making rules, what controlled functions there are.

20. It is for the authorised person, or the person seeking authorisation, to seek the necessary approval for a person to carry out an approved function.[48] The application must be made as directed by the FCA.[49] The FCA will only give its consent if it considers that the candidate for the performance of a controlled function is a fit and proper person.[50]

21. The FCA has three months to consider an application (although if the application is made as part of an application for authorisation to carry on regulated activities, the FCA can, if later, wait until that application is determined before giving its decision). The three-month period can be extended if the FCA seeks further information.[51] If the FCA is considering not giving approval, it must serve a warning notice.

22. The rules made in this connection are contained in Block 4 of the Handbook, in the module labelled SUP (standing for supervision), Chapter 10A. These have been amended to apply a special regime for consumer credit firms.

23. These rules apply a much-diminished regime for limited permission firms and not-for-profit debt advice bodies, as well as for sole traders.

24. The relevant significant influence functions are:

(a) *The governing functions.*[52] These apply to those directing a firm's affairs. The FCA has provided that appointment as a director, including non-executive director, or chief executive or partner or significant management or customer function all qualify as significant influence functions.[53]
(b) *The apportionment and oversight function.*[54] Here, the FCA examines to see that responsibilities are properly divided among the directors and

46 Section 59(7B).
47 Section 59(7A).
48 Section 60 Financial Services and Markets Act 2000.
49 Section 60(2); the application form, form A, is at SUP 10A Annex 4.
50 Section 61(1).
51 Section 61(4).
52 Defined at SUP 10A.6.
53 SUP 10A.4.4 R.
54 SUP 10A.7.1.

senior managers and to ensure that systems and controls are properly maintained. This is the one significant influence function for which firms with limited permission require approval.

(c) *Compliance oversight function.* Here, the FCA ensures that someone has oversight of regulatory compliance. This applies only to debt management and credit repair firms.

(d) *Systems and controls function.*[55] Here, the FCA is concerned to see that someone is reporting on how the firm is complying with internal systems and controls. This does not apply to limited permission firms. This position can be filled by someone also performing a governing function role.

(e) *Significant management functions.*[56] This will only apply in a large organisation to a senior manager with significant independent responsibilities. It does not apply to firms with limited permission.

(f) *Protecting clients' money and assets.* This applies only to a large debt management firm and a large not-for-profit debt advice firm holding at least £1 million.

25. The customer function does not apply to credit regulated firms.

Failure to obtain approval

26. Penalties can be imposed by the FCA on a person who performs controlled functions without approval.[57] An alternative is public censure. In order to consider imposing a penalty, the FCA must be satisfied that the relevant person has performed a controlled function without obtaining the necessary approval and that he or she knew or could be expected to have known that he or she was performing a controlled function without the required approval.[58]

27. A three-year limitation period applies from the time that the FCA knew that the person had performed a controlled function without authorisation, or had knowledge from which that could be reasonably inferred.[59] The right of the FCA to impose a penalty lapses if a warning notice has not been served on the person within that time.

28. The warning notice must state the penalty intended to be imposed.[60] It also must give reasons for the decision[61] and must specify a reasonable

55 SUP 10A.8.
56 SUP 10A.9.
57 Section 63A Financial Services and Markets Act 2000.
58 Section 63A(1) Financial Services and Markets Act 2000.
59 Section 63 A (4), (5).
60 Section 63B(2) Financial Services and Markets Act 2000.
61 Section 387 Financial Services and Markets Act 2000.

period, not less than 14 days, to enable the recipient to make representations to the FCA.

29. The FCA may then follow the warning notice with a decision notice specifying the penalty. Thereafter, the person may, if dissatisfied with the penalty, appeal to the tribunal.[62]

30. In accordance with section 63C of the Financial Services and Markets Act 2000, the FCA has published a Statement of Policy setting out its approach to the imposition of penalties; this is to be found at Chapter 6 of the module headed DEPP (see, in particular, DEPP 6.2.1 G and DEPP 6.2.9A G). The FCA will consider the appropriateness of taking action against the person instead of or in addition to taking action against the authorised person.[63] The FCA will also consider the seniority of the person; the more senior the person, the more seriously the FCA is likely to consider the matter.[64]

Interim permission and transitional arrangements

31. The length of a standard consumer credit licence has been five years from 6 April 2008;[65] it was longer before then. No more consumer credit licenses are being issued from 1 April 2014.

32. If an application for a standard licence has been made prior to this date but not been determined by the OFT, then it is treated as if an application had been made for Part 4A permission to the FCA.[66] This is so even if the OFT has issued a notice saying it is minded to refuse a licence.[67] For the purposes of the requirements of the Financial Services and Markets Act 2000 for determining the application, the application is treated as made to the FCA on 1 April 2014.[68]

33. However, if the OFT has refused a licence, and the appeal period of 28 days[69] has not expired by 1 April 2014, then the decision is treated as a refusal of Part 4A permission by the FCA.[70] The applicant will be able

62 Section 63B(5) Financial Services and Markets Act 2000.

63 DEPP 6.2.9A(5).

64 DEPP 6.2.9A(6).

65 Regulation 42 Consumer Credit (Information Requirements and Duration of Licences and Charges) Regulations 2007 SI 2007/1167.

66 Article 31(3) Financial Services and Markets Act 2000 (Regulated Activities) Amendment No 2 Order SI 2013/1881.

67 Article 31(2) Financial Services and Markets Act 2000 (Regulated Activities) Amendment No 2 Order 2013 SI 2013/1881.

68 Article 31(8) Financial Services and Markets Act 2000 (Regulated Activities) Amendment No 2 Order SI 2013/1881.

69 By virtue of regulation 3(1) Consumer Credit Licensing (Appeals) Regulations 1998 SI 1998/1203.

70 Article 32(2) Financial Services and Markets Act 2000 (Regulated Activities) Amendment No 2 Order SI 2013/1881.

to appeal to the tribunal in the same way as with any other authorisation refusal. However, the appeal period will be measured from the time of refusal by the OFT. If in fact an appeal was lodged prior to 1 April 2014, the appeal will be heard but it will be treated as an appeal from refusal of a Part 4A authorisation.

Interim permission

34. In circumstances where a consumer credit licence was current at 1 April 2014, the licensed person needed to obtain an interim permission from the FCA. This was obtainable as of right provided it is sought between 2 September 2013 and 31 March 2014 and the correct fee paid.[71]

35. Application for an interim possession should be made via the FCA website (www.fca.org.uk/clicked). The fee payable is £150 for a sole trader and £350 for others. It is possible to claim a rebate in respect of the amount paid to the OFT in respect of the unexpired period of a consumer credit licence as at 1 April 2014. The FCA is administering the rebate scheme.

36. An interim permission is to be treated as an authorisation under Part 4A of the Financial Services and Markets Act 2000.[72] If the holder of the consumer credit licence was already authorised under FSMA before 1 April 2014, then interim permission is to be treated as a variation of the existing authorisation.[73] The interim permission gives permission in respect of those activities covered by the consumer credit licence[74] and it is the effect of the licence that matters, not any description applied to it.[75] Furthermore, any licence condition imposed by the OFT under section 33A Consumer Credit Act 1974 is now to be treated as imposed by the FCA.[76]

37. An interim permission will not last indefinitely. The FCA, in due course, will make a direction requiring application for a full Part 4A permission to be made by a certain date;[77] such a direction may differ as between different classes of person and activities and is subject to amend-

71 Article 56(4) Financial Services and Markets Act 2000 (Regulated Activities) Amendment No 2 Order SI 2013/1881.

72 Article 56(9)(b) Financial Services and Markets Act 2000 (Regulated Activities) Amendment No 2 Order SI 2013/1881.

73 Article 56(9)(a) Financial Services and Markets Act 2000 (Regulated Activities) Amendment No 2 Order SI 2013/1881.

74 Article 56(1) Financial Services and Markets Act 2000 (Regulated Activities) Amendment No 2 Order SI 2013/1881.

75 Article 56(11) Financial Services and Markets Act 2000 (Regulated Activities) Amendment No 2 Order SI 2013/1881.

76 Article 56(10) Financial Services and Markets Act 2000 (Regulated Activities) Amendment No 2 Order SI 2013/1881.

77 Article 58(1)(a) Financial Services and Markets Act 2000 (Regulated Activities) Amendment No 2 Order SI 2013/1881.

ment by the FCA.[78] It will then be for the applicant to make an application by such a date and the interim permission will last until the application is determined. If no application is made by the required date, then the interim permission lapses on the date specified by the FCA.[79] If the FCA does not give a direction in any particular instance, then the interim permission will lapse on 1 April 2016.[80]

38. A person with interim permission may not appoint an appointed representative.[81]

Appointed representatives

39. An authorised person is entitled in certain circumstances to conduct regulated business by means of an appointed representative without that appointed representative being authorised. The person appointing the representative is known as the 'principal'; the principal must be authorised.[82]

40. A duly appointed representative is exempt from the general prohibition contained in section 19 of the 2000 Act that only authorised persons can undertake regulated activities.[83] This is obviously beneficial for both the appointed representative and his or her or its principal in that there is no requirement for such a representative to obtain authorisation under the 2000 Act. There is no requirement that a representative be an individual as opposed to a partnership or limited company or some other form of entity.[84]

41. Such appointed representatives can only operate in certain specific types of regulated activity specified by the Financial Services and Markets Act 2000 (Appointed Representatives) Regulations 2000[85] as amended by the Financial Services and Markets (Regulated Activities) (Amendment No 2) Order 2013.[86] The activities are identified by reference to the various categories of regulated activity referred to in the Regulated Activities Order and include all regulated consumer credit, hire and ancillary activities.[87]

78 Article 58(4) Financial Services and Markets Act 2000 (Regulated Activities) Amendment No 2 Order SI 2013/1881.

79 Article 58(1)(b) Financial Services and Markets Act 2000 (Regulated Activities) Amendment No 2 Order SI 2013/1881.

80 Article 58(1)(c) Financial Services and Markets Act 2000 (Regulated Activities) Amendment No 2 Order SI 2013/1881.

81 Article 59(4) Financial Services and Markets Act 2000 (Regulated Activities) Amendment No 2 Order SI 2013/1881.

82 Section 39(1)(a) Financial Services and Markets Act 2000.

83 Section 39(1) Financial Services and Markets Act 2000.

84 SUP 12.2.3 G.

85 Article 2, SI 2001/1217.

86 SI 2013/1881.

87 Article 2 of SI 2001/1217 as amended specifies the activities at Articles 25A, 25B, 25C, 36A, 39A, 29D, 39E, 39F, 39G, 53A, 53B, 53C, 60B, 6.0N, 64, 89A, 36H.

42. Prior to the Financial Services Act 2012, there was an absolute requirement that a representative must not be authorised.[88] This rule has now been modified in that if[89] someone is authorised in respect of a *qualifying activity*, that person may also act as a representative in respect of a *relevant additional activity*. What constitutes a qualifying activity and a relevant additional activity are prescribed by the Treasury by the Appointed Representative Amendment Regulations 2014 SI 2014/206.

43. In order for someone to be appointed a representative for these purposes, there must be a formal contract between the principal and the representative that complies with the requirements of the Appointed Representative Regulations[90] and of SUP 12.5.

44. In the context of many types of regulated credit activity, the contract must allow the principal to control or prohibit the appointed representative from representing counter parties.[91] If the contract permits the appointed representative to have other principals, then the contract must require the representative to notify each principal of the identity of any other principals and the business carried on for them.[92]

45. Furthermore, the principal must accept responsibility in writing for the activities of the representative in carrying on those activites.[93]

46. The effect of appointing someone as representative is that the principal becomes responsible 'to the same extent as if he had expressly permitted it' for anything done or not done by the representative 'in carrying on the business for which he has accepted responsibility'.[94] This is a form of statutory deemed agency that makes the principal liable for the acts and omissions of the representative.

47. However, the knowledge and intentions of the representative are not to be attributed to the principal for the purpose of attaching criminal liability 'unless it is reasonable for them to be attributed to him'.[95]

48. In general, an appointed representative can have more than one principal but an appointed representative carrying on mortgage related activities can have only one principal in that field of activity;[96] likewise with activities related to lifetime mortgages, reversion activities and home purchase activities.[97] This is now also the case in respect of all credit-related regulated activities (i.e. lending and debt collection).[98] In a case where an

88 Section 39(1) Financial Services and Markets Act 2000.
89 Section 39(1C), (1D) Financial Services and Markets Act 2000.
90 Section 39(1)(b), 39(1)(C)(b) Financial Services and Markets Act 2000.
91 Article 3 of SI 2001/1217.
92 SUP 12.5.5(3) R.
93 Section 39(1).
94 Section 39(3) Financial Services and Markets Act 2000.
95 Section 39(6) Financial Services and Markets Act 2000.
96 SUP 12.5.6A(b) R.
97 SUP 12.5.6A(c), (d), (e) R.
98 CONC 14.1.2(2) R.

appointed representative has more than one principal, each of the principals should enter an agreement with the other principals covering such matters as the scope of each appointment and the sharing of information.[99]

49. Before appointing someone, the principal must ensure that the proposed representative is suitable and solvent and does not have close links that preclude effective supervision by the principal.[100] The principal must also set up suitable controls for the purpose of monitoring the regulated activities of the representative.[101]

50. Having appointed a representative, the principal must notify the FCA on the form specified.[102] The firm must establish, implement and maintain adequate policies and procedures to ensure compliance by the agent with the firm's obligations under the regulatory system.[103] Moreover, the firm must take all reasonable steps to prevent any conflicts of interest arising between the agent and the client of the firm.[104]

51. Once having appointed a representative, if the principal considers that the appointed representative is no longer solvent or suitable, or has acquired close links that render the representative incapable of being effectively supervised, then the principal must either see the position is remedied or terminate the appointment.[105] The principal must also ensure that the representative does not carry on unauthorised activities.[106]

52. If an authorised representative carries on a controlled function for the principal, then it will be necessary to obtain approval for that person to carry on the controlled function.[107]

53. The FCA must be notified by the principal on termination of the appointment of a representative, whether that termination is the act of the representative or the principal.[108] Clients must be informed of the position.[109] The principal must keep, for a period of three years following termination, a record of the appointment of the representative.

Exemption for professionals

54. Certain professional firms are exempt from the need to obtain authorisation in respect of certain categories of regulated business activity. Guidance is given in that module of the Handbook entitled PROF.

99 SUP 12.4.5B R.
100 SUP 12.4.2(2) R.
101 SUP 12.4.2(3) R.
102 SUP 12.7(3), (4) R.
103 CONC 14.1.4(1) R.
104 CONC 14.1.4(2) R.
105 SUP 12.6.1 R.
106 SUP 12.6.6 R.
107 SUP 12.6.8 G, SUP 12.6.9 G.
108 SUP 12.8.1 R.
109 SUP 12.8.3 R.

55. For the exemption to apply, the professional firm must be a member of a designated professional body[110] and subject to regulation by that body. The designated professional bodies are:

(a) the Law Societies of England and Wales, Scotland or Northern Ireland;
(b) the Institutes of Chartered Accountants;
(c) the Association of Certified Accountants;
(d) the Institute of Actuaries;
(e) the Council of Licensed Conveyancers; and
(f) the Royal Institution of Chartered Surveyors.

56. There are certain categories of activity excluded from this exemption as set out in the Financial Services and Markets Act 2000 (Professions) (Non-Exempt Activities) Order 2001,[111] some of which are credit-related. These non-exempt credit-related activities are:[112] advising in relation to regulated mortgage contracts, home reversion plans, home purchase plans or sale and rent back, or entering into such arrangements.

57. However, giving advice in relation to such transactions remains within the exemption if the advice does no more than endorse the advice given by an authorised person.[113] Obviously, a professional firm should only give such an endorsement if this is appropriate advice for the client.

58. Other types of regulated credit activity engaged in by an exempt professional firm are potentially exempt from the need for authorisation subject to a number of conditions.

59. Thus, it is also a requirement that the regulated activity be only incidental to the professional services provided by the firm in respect of which the firm is regulated by its professional body.[114]

60. It is also a requirement that the exempt professional firm should not, without accounting for the same to the client, receive any payment in connection with these activities from any third party other than the client.[115]

61. It is also a requirement that the exempt professional firm should be regulated by its own professional body in respect of such activities and should not carry on any other regulated activities other than as an appointed representative (in respect of which the exempt professional firm will of course be exempt from authorisation).[116]

110 Section 326(1) Financial Services and Markets Act 2000.
111 SI 2001/1227 as amended.
112 Articles 6A to 6H Financial Services and Markets Act 2000 (Professions) (Non-Exempt Activities) Order 2001 inserted by SI 2006/2383 and SI 2009/1342.
113 Art 6A(3), 6C(3), 6E(3), 6G(3) Financial Services and Markets Act 2000 (Professions) (Non-Exempt) Activities Order 2001.
114 Section 327(4) Financial Services and Markets Act 2000.
115 Section 327(3) Financial Services and Markets Act 2000.
116 Section 327(7) Financial Services and Markets Act 2000.

62. An exempt professional firm must not claim to have authorisation under the Act or the FCA[117] and must make it clear that it does not have such authorisation before conducting any such activity.[118]

63. The FCA has the power, after following the statutory procedure, to issue a direction excluding persons or classes of business from the exemption.[119] But no such direction has yet been issued.[120]

Reference to the tribunal

64. The Financial Services and Markets Act 2000 sets up a comprehensive statutory scheme enabling persons against whom decisions are made to take the matter to a specialist tribunal with a right of appeal on points of law direct to the Court of Appeal.

65. The tribunal was initially known as the Financial Services and Markets Tribunal.[121] However, the functions of that Tribunal were transferred to the Upper Tribunal as from 6 April 2010 by the Transfer of Tribunal Functions Order.[122]

66. Judicial review is not precluded by the statutory scheme, but will only be appropriate in exceptional circumstances. It is not an exceptional circumstance that the only point raised is a point of law as that can be properly dealt with by the tribunal.[123] There is also power for a judicial review case to be transferred to the Upper Tribunal.

67. Procedure before the Upper Tribunal is governed by Schedule 3 of the Tribunal Procedure (Upper Tribunal) Rules 2008 added by the Tribunal Procedure (Upper Tribunal) (Amendment) Rules 2010.[124]

68. In a disciplinary reference, the tribunal must decide what action to take and must then remit the matter to the decision-maker to give effect to its determination.[125] In other instances, the tribunal must remit the matter to the decision-maker having made appropriate findings of fact and law, matters to be taken into account and procedural steps to be taken.[126]

69. The jurisdiction of the tribunal to make a costs order in proceedings before it is governed by regulation 10 of the Tribunal Procedure (Upper Tribunal) Rules 2008.[127] In a financial services case, the tribunal may not

117 PROF 4.1.2 R.
118 PROF 4.1.3 R.
119 Section 328 Financial Services and Markets Act 2000.
120 PROF 3 Annex 1, 2.
121 Section 132 Financial Services and Markets Act 2000.
122 SI 2010/22.
123 *Regina (Davies) v Financial Services Authority* 2004 1 WLR 185.
124 SI 2010/747 as amended by Tribunal Procedure (Amendment No 2) Rules 2013 SI 2013/606.
125 Section 133(5) Financial Services and Markets Act 2000.
126 Section 133(6), (6A) Financial Services and Markets Act 2000.
127 SI 2008/2698.

make a costs order unless the original decision that led to the reference was unreasonable[128] or if the Upper Tribunal considers that one of the parties has acted unreasonably in bringing, defending or conducting the proceedings.[129]

70. Appeal from the Upper Tribunal lies on point of law to the Court of Appeal from the Upper Tribunal with the permission of either the Upper Tribunal or the Court of Appeal.[130]

71. In some circumstances, following the making of an application, the Upper Tribunal may make financial assistance available to meet the cost of an appearance before the tribunal in connection with a hearing under the Financial Services and Markets Act 2000. If it decides to grant financial assistance, the tribunal will make a legal assistance order specifying any financial contribution that may be payable under it.[131] A financial assistance order will only be made if it is in the interests of justice to make an order and if the financial resources of the applicant are such that he or she needs assistance with the costs likely to be incurred in relation to proceedings before the tribunal.[132]

72. If an applicant receives a financial assistance order, any solicitor and advocate instructed will have to apply to the Senior Courts Costs Office for payment in line with guidance contained at section 30 of the Senior Court Costs Office Guide. The application for payment will have to be made within three months of the conclusion of proceedings.[133]

Criminal liability for acting without authorisation

73. Section 19 of the Financial Services and Markets Act 2000 sets out the 'general prohibition', defined as carrying on a regulated activity without being an authorised person or an exempt person. An authorised person is, by virtue of section 31 of the Act, someone who has authorisation under Part 4A of the Act to carry on a regulated activity. It is not a breach of the general prohibition for a person with authorisation in respect of certain regulated activities to carry on further activities for which authorisation ought to have been, but has not been, obtained. (That is not to say that such conduct does not give rise to the possibility of disciplinary action and, in

128 Rule 10(3)(e) Tribunal Procedure (Upper Tribunal) Rules 2008.
129 Rule 10(3)(d) Tribunal Procedure (Upper Tribunal) Rules 2008.
130 Section 13 Tribunals Courts and Enforcement Act 2007.
131 Regulation 6 Financial Services and Markets Tribunal (Legal Assistance) Regulations 2001 SI 2001/2632.
132 Regulation 8 Financial Services and Markets Tribunal (Legal Assistance) Regulations 2001 SI 2001/2632.
133 Regulation 12 Financial Services and Markets Tribunal (Legal Assistance Scheme – Costs) Regulations 2001/3633.

the instance to be discussed below, may give rise to criminal liability in the case of credit-related activities.)

74. It is a criminal offence for person to act in breach of the general prohibition, punishable either summarily or on indictment.[134] This offence is termed by the Act an 'authorisation offence'.[135]

75. The Act creates an additional category of authorisation offence where an authorised person carries on a 'credit-related regulated activity' without the necessary authorisation.[136] A credit-related regulated activity is one designated by the Treasury by order subject to certain restrictions.[137] Credit-related regulated activities have now been specified[138] as lending under regulated agreements[139] and debt collection.[140] This echoes the position under the Consumer Credit Act 1974, which made it a criminal offence to engage in any activities for which a licence was required when not a licensee under a licence covering those activities.[141]

76. However, save in this instance of a credit-related regulated activity, it is not a criminal offence for an authorised person to carry on unauthorised activity,[142] although such conduct is of course in breach of the requirements of the Act[143] and does of course lay the person open to disciplinary action from the regulator. It is also a separate criminal offence to claim falsely to be authorised or to claim falsely to be exempt from authorisation.[144] In proceedings for this offence, it is a defence to show that all reasonable steps were taken to avoid committing the offence.

77. Criminal proceedings for any offence under the Act can be brought only by the FCA or the Secretary of State or with the consent of the Director of Public Prosecutions.[145] In respect of the attitude of the FCA to prosecution, the Enforcement Guide ('EG') states unhelpfully at 12.2 that 'the FCA's general policy is to pursue through the criminal justice system all those cases where criminal prosecution is appropriate'. The Guide also states that the FCA will adhere to the basic principles set out in the Code for Crown Prosecutors.

134 Section 23(1) FSMA.
135 Section 23(2).
136 Section 23(1A).
137 Section 23(1B) and (1C).
138 Financial Services and Markets Act 2000 (Consumer Credit) (Designated Activities) Order 2014 SI 2014/334.
139 Within Article 60B RAO.
140 Within Article 39F RAO.
141 Section 39 Consumer Credit Act 1974.
142 Section 20(2)(a).
143 Section 20(1).
144 Section 24.
145 Section 401.

Civil consequences for breach of the authorisation requirements

Entry into agreements with unauthorised persons

78. The Financial Services and Markets Act 2000 confers certain civil remedies on those who enter into an agreement in respect of a regulated activity with a person who ought to be authorised under Part 4A of the Act but is not. A person, other than an exempt person, who does not have authorisation, is in breach of what the Act calls the 'general prohibition'.[146] The general prohibition applies to all regulated activities covered by the Regulated Activities Order, including entry into credit and hire agreements, credit brokerage and debt counselling and regulated mortgage contracts.

79. The starting point is that an agreement entered into in breach of the general prohibition is unenforceable by the person who has concluded the agreement acting in breach of the general prohibition against the other party.[147] For these purposes, an agreement is one the making of or performance of which constitutes or is part of a regulated activity.[148]

80. Since entering into a credit agreement (other than an exempt agreement) in the course of business is a regulated activity, then if the lender fails to obtain the necessary authorisation from the FCA, the agreement is prima facie unenforceable against the borrower. This mirrors the position under section 40 of the Consumer Credit Act 1974 in respect of a lender that failed to obtain a consumer credit licence.[149]

Entry into agreements with persons with insufficient authorisation

81. The general prohibition applies in circumstances when a firm without *any authorisation at all* enters into an agreement in the course of an activity for which authorisation was required. Note that it is not in breach of the general prohibition for an authorised person to enter into an agreement that is outside the scope of his or her authorisation.

82. However, by way of specific provision, an agreement that is in respect of 'credit-related regulated activities' will be unenforceable if entered into by someone without the appropriate authorisation that covers the appropriate credit-related regulated activity.[150]

83. A credit-related regulated activity, in accordance with section 23(1B), is defined by the Financial Services and Markets Act 2000 (Consumer

146 Section 19(1) Financial Services and Markets Act 2000.
147 Section 26(1) Financial Services and Markets Act 2000.
148 Section 26(3) Financial services and Markets Act 2000.
149 Section 40 Consumer Credit Act 1974.
150 Section 26A Financial Services and Markets Act 2000.

Credit) (Designated Activities) Order 2014.[151] It is confined to entering into credit agreements within article 60B of the Regulated Activities Order and debt collecting in accordance with article 39F(1) of the Regulated Activities Order.

84. Accordingly, a loan agreement will not be enforceable if the authorisation of the lender does not cover lending activities. This also mirrors the position under the Consumer Credit Act 1974 whereby a loan was unenforceable if the consumer credit licence did not cover the specific activity engaged in.[152]

85. Other types of activity, such as entry into regulated mortgage contracts, hire agreements and credit brokerage, although connected with credit, are not 'credit-related regulated activities'.

86. Section 26A(5) provides that: 'If the taking of steps to procure payment of debts due under an agreement involves the carrying out of a credit-related regulated activity, the agreement may not be enforced by a person for the time being exercising the rights of the lender under the agreement unless the agreements is enforced in accordance with permission – (a) given under Part 4A to the person enforcing the agreement, or (b) resulting from any other provision of this Act.' Now debt collecting is a credit-related regulated activity. It follows that if the lender has engaged a debt collector that does not have the required authorisation, then the lender will not be able to enforce the agreement.

87. Section 26A(4) refers to a situation where the *administration of an agreement* involves the carrying of a credit-related regulated activity, but in the light of the definition in the Financial Services and Markets Act 2000 (Consumer Credit) (Designated Activities) Order 2014,[153] which does not extend to the activity of administering an agreement, this does not arise.

Agreements made through unauthorised persons

88. Similar consequences apply where an agreement is entered into by an authorised person in the course of carrying on a regulated activity but is made 'in consequence of something said or done by another person ("the third party")' when acting in the course of a regulated activity in contravention of the general prohibition or when acting in the course of a credit-related regulated activity without authorisation for that activity.[154]

89. Thus, if a lender enters into a loan agreement with a borrower as a result of an introduction by a credit broker that is not an authorised person, then the agreement will be unenforceable by virtue of section 27. However,

151 SI 2014/334.
152 Section 40(1A)(b) Consumer Credit Act 1974.
153 SI 2014/334.
154 Section 27(1)(d) Financial Services and Markets Act 2000.

since credit brokerage is not a credit-related regulated activity, if the introduction is made by a credit broker with authorisation but not extending to credit brokerage, the agreement will be enforceable.

90. This also mirrors the provisions in the Consumer Credit Act 1974 relating to the unenforceability of a credit agreement entered into as a result of an introduction by an unlicensed credit broker.[155]

Consequences of unenforceability

91. Plainly, the lender will not be able to sue on an enforceable agreement. The consequences of unenforceability were discussed in the context of the Consumer Credit Act 1974 in *McGuffick v The Royal Bank of Scotland plc*,[156] the court holding that the rights and liabilities of the creditor and lender continued to exist during the period of unenforceability, notwithstanding that they were unenforceable.

92. Furthermore, by virtue of sections 26(2) and 26A(2), the party contracting with the unauthorised or incorrectly authorised person is entitled to recover any money or other property paid under the agreement together with compensation for having parted with the money or property.[157] However, this will not normally apply in connection with a loan agreement in which monies are normally paid *to* and not *by* the borrower. It would apply to security provided by the borrower to the lender. Insofar as property has been transferred by the unauthorised person to a third party following entry into the agreement so that it cannot be returned to the borrower, the reference to the property is to be read as a reference to the value of the property at the date of the agreement. The amount of compensation to be paid is that agreed between the parties or fixed by the court to be paid.[158] If the person elects to treat the agreement as unenforceable and requires return of money or property made under the agreement, that person must give credit for and return any money or property previously received under the agreement.

93. The remedy conferred by sections 26(2) and 26A(2) is restitutionary; it is not a remedy in damages. If the terms of the relevant loan agreement required the borrower to hand over monies or property not to the lender, but to a third party, section 26(2) does not give a right against the third party for return of the property or monies.[159] The remedy lies against the lender alone.

155 Section 149 Consumer Credit Act 1974.
156 2009 EWHC 2386 (Comm).
157 Section 26(2) Financial Services and Markets Act 2000.
158 Section 28(2) Financial Services and Markets Act 2000.
159 *Brown and others v Innovatorone Ltd* 2012 EWHC (Comm) 1321 paragraphs 1235–1239.

Discretionary enforcement by the court

94. The court has discretion to permit an agreement entered into by an unauthorised person to be enforced if it considers it just and equitable to do so.[160] However, this does not apply to agreements relating to credit-related activities. The court's discretionary powers are therefore relevant to regulated mortgage contracts, credit brokerage contracts and hire agreements. In the case of *Helden v Strathmore Ltd*,[161] the Court exercised its discretion to permit enforcement of certain regulated mortgage contracts, notwithstanding that the lender was not authorised.

95. In this regard, the court must 'have regard' to whether the person entering into the agreement reasonably believed that it was not contravening the general prohibition in entering into the agreement.[162] In *Helden v Strathmore Ltd*,[163] the question was raised whether someone could reasonably believe that he or she was not contravening the general prohibition if he or she did not know about the general prohibition.[164] The Court of Appeal did not find it necessary to decide the point, but considered that there were powerful arguments in favour of saying that knowledge of the general prohibition was necessary before someone could say that he or she had acted reasonably in thinking it did not apply. But the Court of Appeal made it clear that this was only one consideration and upheld the judge's decision to allow enforcement of some of the agreements in contention.

96. The court also made it clear that if a party is driven to seek the relief of the court under section 28, then this is likely to have adverse consequences in relation to the costs order made at the conclusion of proceedings.[165]

97. The court also has a discretion to allow property to be retained if it is just and equitable;[166] the court will particularly have regard to whether the person reasonably believed he was not contravening the general prohibition in not entering into the agreement.

98. A similar discretion is given to the court in a case under section 27 when an agreement is unenforceable as a result of having been made *through* an unauthorised person; the court can, in the same way, allow the agreement to be enforced or property to be retained where it is just and equitable to do so. But in this case, the court will have regard to the issue of whether the party entering into the agreement knew that the third party responsible for bringing about entry into the agreement was acting in breach

160 Section 28(3)(a) Financial Services and Markets Act 2000.
161 2011 EWCA Civ 542.
162 Section 28(5) Financial Services and Markets Act 2000.
163 2011 EWCA Civ 542 para 46 to 52.
164 [46].
165 *Helden v Strathmore Limited* 2011 EWCA Civ 542 at para 61.
166 Section 28(3)(b) Financial Services and Markets Act 2000.

of the general prohibition when that third party brought about the agreement in the course of carrying on a regulated activity.[167] It is striking that there is reference to the reasonableness of that belief in relation to section 28(6), by contrast with section 28(5). However, a court is likely to find that it is incumbent on a person accepting introductions from a credit broker to ensure that the broker is properly authorised.

Discretionary enforcement by the FCA

99. However, the court has no discretionary power to allow enforcement of prima facie unenforceable credit-related regulated activities. In these circumstances, the FCA, not the court, may decide that it is just and equitable for the agreement to be enforced or money or other property transferred under the agreement to be retained. This is akin to the discretionary power given to the Office of Fair Trading under the Consumer Credit Act to authorise agreements entered into by persons without the required consumer credit licence.[168]

100. A finding made by the FCA must follow an application by the firm, or by someone exercising rights under the agreement. It is clear that the firm may apply in relation not just in respect of one agreement, but in relation to a range of agreements. Certain parts of section 55U apply to the procedure in accordance with the Financial Services and Markets Act 2000 (Consumer Credit) (Miscellaneous Provisions) Order 2014.[169] The FCA will give its decision in a written notice.[170] In the case of an unauthorised person entering an agreement, the FCA will have regard to whether it was reasonable for the party entering an agreement without authorisation to believe that no authorisation was required.[171] In the case of an agreement concluded as a result of third party involvement, the FCA will consider whether the party seeking to enforce the agreement or agreements knew that the third party did not have necessary authorisation.[172]

101. The FCA has the ability to make a finding limited to certain agreements or types of agreements or to attach conditions on the doing of acts by the applicant.[173] The FCA is also given the power to fix the amount of compensation by notice on application by either party.[174] The parties are also able to agree the amount of compensation.

167 Section 28(6) Financial Services and Markets Act 2000.
168 Section 40(2) Consumer Credit Act 1974.
169 SI 2014/208.
170 Section 28A(3) Financial Services and Markets Act 2000.
171 Section 28A(4)(a) Financial Services and Markets Act 2000.
172 Section 28A(4)(b) Financial Services and Markets Act 2000.
173 Section 28A(9) Financial Services and Markets Act 2000.
174 Section 28A(2)(b) Financial Services and Markets Act 2000.

102. Insofar as the FCA makes a determination as to the enforcement of a credit-related regulated agreement, it must give reasons and also point out the right to refer the matter to the tribunal.[175] Thereafter, if aggrieved by the decision, the firm can refer the matter to the tribunal.[176]

175 Section 28B Financial Services and Markets Act 2000.
176 Section 28B(3).

5 Continuing regulatory powers and obligations after authorisation

Cancellation or variation of authorisation by the FCA

1. There are circumstances in which the FCA can unilaterally cancel or vary an authorisation, namely:

(a) where the authorised person is either contravening the threshold conditions or is likely to do so;
(b) where the authorised person has not carried on a regulated activity for the last 12 months at least; and
(c) where a variation is desirable in order for the FCA to be able to advance its operational objectives.[1]

2. The type of circumstance in which these powers may be exercised are[2] if:

(a) the FCA considers that the firm's management, business or internal controls are giving rise to risks that are not adequately controlled;
(b) the FCA considers the firm is becoming involved in new products or practices that are not adequately addressed by existing requirements;
(c) the FCA consider changes in a firm's structure imposes unacceptable risks; or
(d) to assist an overseas regulator.

3. The powers conferred on the FCA by these provisions are known, rather inelegantly, as the 'own initiative variation power'.[3]

4. In addition the FCA can impose a requirement on an authorised person known as the 'own initiative requirement power'.[4] The circumstances in which the FCA can impose a requirement mirror those in which the

1 Section 55J(1) Financial Services and Markets Act 2000.
2 SUP 7.3.2.
3 Section 55J(12) Financial Services and Markets Act 2000.
4 Section 55L Financial Services and Markets Act 2000.

FCA can impose a variation. The requirements that can be imposed include a direction to the person concerned either to take or to refrain from taking relevant action,[5] including requiring the taking of remedial action in respect of past conduct. The requirement may take effect over a limited period of time but if it so, this does not inhibit the imposition of a new requirement.[6]

5. The authorised person must be given a written notice of the proposed or actual variation, or of the imposition of a requirement.[7] Such a notice is referred to as a 'supervisory notice'.[8] This notice must give the FCA's reasons and inform the authorised of the right to make representations to the FCA, of the timescale when the variation or requirement takes effect. The supervisory notice must also inform the authorised person of his or her right to take the matter to the tribunal.[9]

6. Normally, the FCA seeks to give reasonable notice of exercising its own initiative powers.[10] But a variation or cancellation or the addition of a requirement can take effect immediately, or after a stated interval, as the FCA may decide.[11] But a variation should only take effect immediately if the regulator considers this to be necessary.[12]

7. If the FCA intends to cancel an authorisation, it must first serve a warning notice to this effect.[13] The decision to serve a warning notice must be taken by the Regulatory Decisions Committee.[14] If the Regulatory Decisions Committee decide to confirm the decision having heard any representations, it must serve a decision notice.[15] Having served such a warning notice, the FCA has an obligation in normal circumstances to make available to the authorised person the material on which it relied in order to take the decision[16] and to any secondary material that might undermine that decision.[17] This right should have been referred to in the warning notice. There is an exception to this if the FCA considers that release of the material would not be in the public interest, or would not be fair having regard to the significance of the material and to the potential prejudice that may be caused to the commercial interests of others.[18] In this event, the FCA must

5 Section 55N Financial Services and Markets Act 2000.
6 Section 55N(4) Financial Services and Markets Act 2000.
7 Section 55Y(4).
8 SUP 7.2.5.
9 Section 55Y(5).
10 SUP 7.3.4.
11 Section 55Y(2).
12 Section 55Y(3).
13 Section 55Z(1) Financial Services and Markets Act 2000.
14 DEPP 2.
15 Section 55Z(2) Financial Services and Markets Act 2000.
16 Section 394(1)(a) Financial Services and Markets Act 2000.
17 Section 394(1)(b) Financial Services and Markets Act 2000.
18 Section 394(4) Financial Services and Markets Act 2000.

give written notice of a refusal to give access to this material and the reason for that refusal.

8. If FCA makes a fundamental variation to an authorisation or imposes a fundamental requirement, then the decision must be taken by the Regulatory Decisions Committee of the FCA; otherwise, the decision can be made by the FCA staff acting under executive procedures.[19] It is a fundamental requirement to remove an activity from the scope of an authorisation.[20]

9. A person can appeal to the tribunal if dissatisfied with the outcome of the exercise of these powers.[21]

10. Once a supervisory notice has taken effect, it should be publicized to the extent that the FCA considers appropriate.[22]

Prohibition order

11. The FCA may make a prohibition order addressed to an individual where it appears to the FCA that that individual is not a fit and proper person to perform functions in relation to a regulated activity carried on by an authorised person, an exempt person or a professional firm.[23] The prohibition order will prohibit the individual from performing a function specified in the order.[24]

12. It is a criminal offence to disobey a prohibition order,[25] although it is a defence for an accused person to show that he or she took all reasonable precautions and exercised all due diligence to avoid committing the offence.[26]

13. Prior to making a prohibition order, the FCA must serve a warning notice on the individual concerned setting out the terms of the proposed prohibition order.[27] The decision will be made by the Regulatory Decisions Committee of the FCA.[28] The individual concerned will, subject to the limitations of public interest and proportionality, have the right to inspect the material available to the FCA.[29]

14. This can then be followed by a decision notice identifying the individual and setting out the terms of the prohibition.[30] The individual subject to the prohibition order may take the matter to the tribunal.[31]

19 DEPP 2.5.7.
20 DEPP 2.5.8.
21 Section 55Z3(2) Financial Services and Markets Act 2000.
22 Section 391(5) Financial Services and Markets Act 2000.
23 Section 56(1) Financial Services and Markets Act 2000.
24 Section 56(2) Financial Services and Markets Act 2000.
25 Section 56(4) Financial Services and Markets Act 2000.
26 Section 56(5) Financial Services and Markets Act 2000.
27 Section 57(1) Financial Services and Markets Act 2000.
28 DEPP 2.
29 Sections 392 and 394 Financial Services and Markets Act 2000.
30 Section 57(4) Financial Services and Markets Act 2000.
31 Section 57(5) Financial Services and Markets Act 2000.

15. An individual subject to a prohibition order may apply to the FCA to have the order revoked or varied.[32] If the application is granted, then the FCA will give a written notice to that effect. If the FCA proposes to refuse, it must give a warning notice.[33] Thereafter, having heard any relevant representations that may have been made, the FCA may confirm the decision in a decision notice.[34] The matter may then be referred to the tribunal.[35]

16. The individual the subject of a prohibition order and its terms must be entered on the register kept by the FCA.[36]

Disciplinary action against an authorised person

17. The FCA has a number of possible remedies available in the event that an *authorised* person breaches a 'relevant requirement'. The FCA has fewer options available if a person is entirely unauthorised.

18. A relevant requirement is one imposed by the Act or by a relevant EU provision stipulated by the Treasury.[37] Requirements imposed by the Consumer Credit Act 1974 also come within the definition of relevant requirement for this purpose.[38]

19. In relation to the disciplinary action to be taken for breach of relevant requirements, the FCA must prepare a statement of policy.[39] Likewise now in relation to breaches of the Consumer Credit Act 1974.[40] These policy statements are contained in DEPP. The types of disciplinary action that the FCA may take are as follows.

20. The FCA may consider it sufficient deterrent to publish a statement setting out the contravention that has occurred.[41] This is referred to as public censure.[42] If the FCA follows this course, it must provide a copy of the statement to the authorised person.[43]

21. If the FCA considers that an authorised person has breached a relevant requirement, then it may impose a financial penalty in such amount as it considers appropriate.[44]

22. The factors that the FCA will take into account in deciding whether or not to proceed by way of financial penalty or public censure are set out

32 Section 58(1) Financial Services and Markets Act 2000.
33 Section 58(3) Financial Services and Markets Act 2000.
34 Section 58(4) Financial Services and Markets Act 2000.
35 Section 58(5) Financial Services and Markets Act 2000.
36 Section 347 Financial Services and Markets Act 2000.
37 Section 204A Financial Services and Markets Act 2000.
38 Article 3 Financial Services (Consumer Credit) Order 2013 SI 2013/1882.
39 Section 210 Financial Services and Markets Act 2000.
40 Article 4 Financial Services (Consumer Credit) Order 2013 SI 2013/1882.
41 Section 205 Financial Services and Markets Act 2000.
42 Section 205 Financial Services and Markets Act 2000.
43 Section 209 Financial Services and Markets Act 2000.
44 Section 206 Financial Services and Markets Act 2000.

at DEPP 6.2.1. As between the choice between financial penalty and public censure, the FCA will consider those factors listed at DEPP 6.4. The level of financial penalty is fixed by considering the factors referred to at DEPP 6.6; the penalty will be a combination of financial disgorgement and penalty. The FCA can also offer a discount for settlement of the matter by agreement, on principles set out at DEPP 6.7. The level of discount will be dependent on the stage at which the investigation has reached when settlement is concluded.[45]

23. The FCA also has the option of suspending a permission to carry on a regulated activity or to impose additional restrictions.[46] This option also exists in the event of non-compliance with the Payment Services Regulations 2009 or the Electronic Money Regulations 2011.[47] The factors that the FCA will take into account in respect of suspension or imposing restrictions are set out at DEPP 6A.

24. If the FCA contemplates any of these steps, it must first serve a warning notice on the authorised person.[48] This must be in writing and state the action that the FCA intends to take and the reasons for it.[49]

25. The decision to serve a warning notice must be taken by the Regulatory Decisions Committee of the FCA[50] after receipt of a recommendation to this effect from FCA staff.[51] The Regulatory Decisions Committee will sit in a panel of at least three, of which one will be the Chairman or Deputy Chairman of the Committee.

26. The warning notice will point out the right of the recipient to make representations including oral representations. The notice will stipulate the time in which written representations must be made, which must not be less than 14 days.[52] The recipient may apply for an extension of time and any request for an extension will be considered by the Chairman or Deputy Chairman of the Regulatory Decisions Committee.[53] Neither the FCA or the person receiving the warning notice may publish it or any details concerning it.[54]

27. The FCA has an obligation in normal circumstances to make available to the authorised person the material on which it relied in order to take the decision[55] and to any secondary material that might undermine that

45 DEPP 6.7.3(3) G.
46 Section 206A Financial Services and Markets Act 2000.
47 Section 206A(1A) Financial Services and Markets Act 2000.
48 Section 207 Financial Services and Markets Act 2000.
49 Section 387(1) Financial Services and Markets Act 2000.
50 DEPP2 in accordance with a procedure laid down to comply with section 395 Financial Services and Markets Act 2000.
51 DEPP 2.2.1.
52 Section 387(2) Financial Services and Markets Act 2000.
53 DEPP 3.2.16.
54 Section 391(1ZA) Financial Services and Markets Act 2000.
55 Section 394(1)(a) Financial Services and Markets Act 2000.

decision.[56] This right should have been referred to in the warning notice. There is an exception to this if the FCA considers that release of the material would not be in the public interest, or would not be fair having regard to the significance of the material and to the potential prejudice that may be caused to the commercial interests of others.[57] In this event, the FCA must give written notice of a refusal to give access to this material and the reason for that refusal.

28. It may be that having served a warning notice, the FCA, perhaps after reflecting on representations made, decides not to go any further with an investigation. In these circumstances, the FCA may serve a notice of discontinuance.[58]

29. Once the FCA has reached a decision to publish a statement, or impose a penalty or suspend an authorisation or impose a restriction, then it must, without delay, give the authorised person a decision notice.[59] The decision to give a decision notice will be taken by the Regulatory Decisions Committee.[60] The decision notice must be in writing and state reasons.[61] It must also draw attention to the right of the authorised person to refer the matter to the tribunal. A person to whom a decision notice is given may not publish the notice or any details concerning it unless and until the FCA has published details of the notice.[62]

Duties and disciplining of approved persons

30. In accordance with section 64 of the Financial Services and Markets Act 2000, the FCA has promulgated Statements of Principle and Codes of Practice to which approved persons should adhere. Section 64 will be repealed by the Financial Services (Banking Reform) Act 2013[63] on a date to be appointed but the principles behind the Statements of Principle should remain in force.

31. These are to be found in the module of the Handbook entitled APER. The Statements of Principle are at APER 2.1A.3 P. Thus, Principle 6 provides, by way of example, that: 'An approved person performing an accountable significant-influence function must exercise due skill, care and diligence in managing the business of the firm for which he is responsible in his accountable function.' The supplemental Codes of Practice are to be found at Chapter 4 of APER.

56 Section 394(1)(b) Financial Services and Markets Act 2000.
57 Section 394(4) Financial Services and Markets Act 2000.
58 Section 389 Financial Services and Markets Act 2000.
59 Section 208 Financial Services and Markets Act 2000.
60 DEPP 2.
61 Section 388 Financial Services and Markets Act 2000.
62 Section 391(1A) Financial Services and Markets Act 2000.
63 Section 30.

32. A regulator may take disciplinary action against those approved persons it suspects of misconduct and the regulator is satisfied that this is an appropriate course to take.[64]

33. A person is guilty of misconduct where the FCA is the regulator if a person has failed to comply with a Statement of Principle issued by the FCA under section 64 of the 2000 Act or has breached some other requirement imposed by the Act or a relevant requirement under the Consumer Credit Act 1974.[65]

34. However, no action must be taken after a period of three years from the time that the FCA had knowledge of the contravention.[66] In this context, the FCA is treated as knowing of misconduct if it has knowledge of matters from which the misconduct could reasonably be inferred. Action is treated as commencing for the purposes of proceedings for misconduct when a warning notice is given to the person under section 67(1).

35. If the FCA is entitled to take action, the FCA may consider a public censure or impose a financial penalty or may suspend any authorisation of any function or impose such limitations or restrictions as it considers appropriate. As required by section 68 of the Financial Services and Markets Act 2000, the FCA has published guidance on its approach to taking disciplinary action under section 66, contained in the Handbook at DEPP 6.2.4 to 6.2.9 G. DEPP 6.2.9 G states expressly that the burden will be on the FCA to show that the approved person has been guilty of misconduct.

36. If the FCA decides to suspend authorisation, the period of suspension may not exceed two years.[67] Once a suspension or restriction has been imposed, it can be later withdrawn or curtailed by the FCA.[68] Guidance on the stance taken by the FCA when considering imposition of a suspension or restriction is contained at Chapter 6A of DEPP.

Reporting

37. The Financial Services and Markets Act 2000 imposes more extensive reporting requirements than applied under the Consumer Credit Act regime, where the requirements were limited to changes to the particulars appearing on the consumer credit register or to those controlling a person holding a licence.[69] FCA regulated firms have to report information to the FCA on a regular basis in order to enable the FCA to monitor the activities

64 Section 66(1) Financial Services and Markets Act 2000.
65 Financial Services Act 2012 (Consumer Credit) Order 2013 SI 2013/1882 art 3(3).
66 Section 66(4) Financial Services and Markets Act 2000.
67 Section 66(3A) Financial Services and Markets Act 2000.
68 Section 66(3D) Financial Services and Markets Act 2000.
69 Section 36, 36A Consumer Credit Act 1974.

of the firm. The reporting requirements are contained at SUP16 of the FCA Handbook. These have been modified to accommodate the newly regulated (by the FCA) consumer credit sector.

38. Reporting requirements take effect from 1 October 2014. They do not apply to firms operating on the basis of interim permission. Reporting is to take place either annually or six-monthly, adjusted to the financial year end, depending on the turnover of the firm. Reporting will take place using the GABRIEL[70] electronic reporting system. The extent of the reporting required will depend on the nature of the activity carried on by the firm; firms with only limited permission will have lesser continuing reporting requirements.

39. Reporting has two aspects, namely regulatory reporting and product sales data reporting. Product sales data will help the FCA understand the market. The FCA also wishes to use the data to build up an understanding of the relationship between brokers and lenders in the distribution of loan products.[71] The regulatory data are to be used to enable the FCA to understand the risks posed by consumer credit firms.[72]

40. Product sales data have previously been collected in respect of regulated mortgage contracts, home purchase plans and home reversion plans entered into by home finance providers.[73] Such providers have had and will continue to have to submit a Mortgage Lending Administration Return. As from 1 October 2014, it is to be collected in addition in respect of high-cost short-term credit and home collect credit.[74] The relevant information that has to be reported is contained at SUP 16 Annex 21R.

41. Regulatory data has to be provided for firms carrying out credit-related activities in accordance with SUP 16.12.29C. However, there is no regulatory reporting requirements relevant to:[75]

(a) credit reference agencies;
(b) not-for-profit firms other than debt advice agencies; and
(c) activities secured by a land mortgage.

42. To comply with its regulatory reporting requirement, the firm has to complete forms CCR001 to CCR007 as appropriate. The applicability of these forms is set out in notes to the table at SUP 16.12.29C. CCR 001, for instance, relates to financial reporting, applicable to all firms except for those whose activity is confined to electronic systems in relation to

70 Gathering Better Regulatory Information Electronically.
71 FSA Consultation Paper 13/7 para 9.36.
72 FSA Consultation Paper 13/7 para 9.37.
73 SUP 16.11.5; the data must comply with SUP 16 Annex 21 R.
74 SUP 16.11.1 R.
75 SUP 16.12.29B R.

lending or to firms with limited permission unless it is a not for profit debt advice body that has held client monies exceeding £1 million in the last 12 months or is projected to hold this sum during the course of the next 12 months. CCR005 applies to all lenders and CCR006 applies to all debt collectors and those operating an electronic system in relation to lending.

Notification of change in control

43. The Financial Services and Markets Act 2000 imposes a general requirement to report to the FCA a proposed acquisition or increase in control of an authorised firm before it occurs.[76] Acquiring control in this context means acquiring more than 10 per cent of the shareholding in the firm[77] and increasing control means going from holding less than 20 per cent of the voting power to more than 20 per cent, or going from less than to more than 30 per cent, or going from less than to more than 50 per cent.[78]

44. Notification must be in the form and contain the information specified by the FCA.[79] These requirements are set out in SUP 11.

45. Once the regulator has been notified, it is then the duty of the regulator to consider whether or not to approve the proposed change in control[80] in accordance with the statutory criteria set out in section 186. There is an assessment period of 60 days during which time the FCA must decide whether or not to give approval and, if so, on what terms.[81]

46. A proposed reduction in control must also be notified[82] in circumstances where the person previously with more than 20 per cent intends to have less than 20 per cent.

47. These requirements all apply to firms carrying on consumer credit regulated activities.

48. However, the requirements are lessened in the case of a firm with limited permission. The notification requirement only applies in these circumstances if the shareholding of the person intending to acquire or increase control will go above 33 per cent, or fall below 33 per cent.[83]

76 Section 178 Financial Services and Markets Act 2000.
77 Section 181 Financial Services and Markets Act 2000.
78 Section 182 Financial Services and Markets Act 2000.
79 Section 179 Financial Services and Markets Act 2000.
80 Section 185 Financial Services and Markets Act 2000.
81 Section 189 Financial Services and Markets Act 2000.
82 Section 191D Financial Services and Markets Act 2000.
83 Financial Services and Markets Act 2000 (Controllers) (Exemption) Order 2009 Article 6A as added by the Financial Services and Markets Act 2000 (Regulated Activities) (Amendment No 2) Order 2013 SI 2013/1881.

49. It is a criminal offence for a person to acquire or increase or reduce control contrary to these requirements.[84]

50. As a separate matter, *the firm* must notify the FCA when a person becomes controller or a person ceases to be controller of a firm (see SUP 11.4.2A R). This applies to a firm with limited permission as well as other firms.

84 Section 191F Financial Services and Markets Act 2000.

6 Advertisement and financial promotion

Advertisements and other forms of financial promotion

1. The Consumer Credit Act 1974 regulated the form and content of *advertisements* by reference to the Consumer Credit (Advertisement) Regulations 2004[1] and 2010.[2] The relevant statutory provisions have now been repealed and with them have gone the Regulations. Only certain criminal provisions remain unrepealed from Part IV of the Consumer Credit Act 1974 that deals with 'Seeking Business'.

2. On the face of it, the Financial Services and Markets Act has a different approach. It controls credit advertising by rules made under the FCA Handbook CONC.

3. The approach under the 1974 Act was to control advertisements, which have a very wide definition under the Act, advertising including:[3] 'every form of advertising, whether in a publication, by television or radio, by display of notices, signs, labels, show cards or goods, by distribution of samples, circulars, catalogues, price lists or other material, by exhibition of pictures, models or films, or in any other way'. Although the definition is wide, it does not include direct speech whether by way of telephone calls or visits undertaken for promotional purposes.

4. By way of contrast, the terminology employed in CONC and the Financial Services and Markets Act 2000 is to regulate *communications* with a potential borrower or hirer, a wide term embracing all forms of contact. The FCA Glossary makes it clear that communication can take any form, including causing a communication to be made or directed. Further guidance on the meaning of the term *communicate* is at PERG 8.6.[4] CONC also refers to the regulation of *financial promotions*, defined in the Glossary,

1 SI 2004/1484.
2 SI 2010/1970.
3 Section 189(1).
4 The Perimeter Guidance forming part of the FCA Handbook.

as an invitation or inducement to engage in investment activity communicated in the course of business. PERG 8.4 also gives guidance on the meaning of the various terms comprised in the definition of financial promotion.

5. In fact, the change made by the repeal of the Advertisement Regulations is more apparent than real because, as will be seen, CONC largely repeats the effect of the Advertisement Regulations, incorporating them as Rules in CONC 3.

6. However, there is a difference in sanction between the Advertisement Regulations and the Rules contained in CONC. The 1974 Act made it a criminal offence for credit and hire advertising not to comply with the Advertisement Regulations.[5] In practice, the Regulations were so complicated that the number of prosecutions was very small and there was no other sanction. By contrast, breach of the Rules does not give rise to criminal sanctions, but may give rise to civil remedies under section 138D (save where that remedy is specifically excluded in the Rules). The FCA can also enforce the Rules directly as appropriate.

General provisions

7. The Rules in CONC 3 apply to advertisements of regulated credit and hire agreements. It does not apply to exempt agreements (which category includes regulated mortgage contracts and home purchase contracts,[6] which have their own regulatory regime in MCOB).

8. It is a fundamental rule that a firm must ensure that a communication or financial promotion is clear, fair and not misleading; however, provided reasonable care is taken, breach of this does not give rise to a right of damages under section 138D of the Act.[7] But of course it may be difficult to show reasonable care and then a civil remedy will be available under section 138D.

9. As part and parcel of this, the communication must use plain and intelligible language, must be easily legible and the name of the person making the communication must be specified.[8] If the advertisement is published by a credit broker, the advertisement must also specify the name of the lender if this is known. Important information must not be hidden by putting it in small type or tucked away in parts of the document not likely to be read.[9]

5 Section 167(2).
6 Art 60C RAO.
7 CONC 3.3.1 R.
8 CONC 3.3.2 R.
9 CONC 3.3.5 G.

10. If mention is made of a premium rate telephone number, the cost per minute and likely duration of any telephone call must be given so that the caller can work out the likely cost of the call.[10]

11. An example of misleading conduct is for a broker to publish an advertisement suggesting that the broker will introduce the borrower to a personal loan on instalment payments or to a bank overdraft facility when instead the intention is to introduce the borrower to a provider of high-cost short-term finance.[11]

12. It is a mandatory requirement that an advertisement must *not* state, either expressly or by implication, that credit is available regardless of financial status.[12] Moreover, such an implication could arise by virtue merely of the firm's name.[13]

Advertisement of regulated credit agreements not secured on land

13. An advertisement may not offer goods or services as being available on credit if the supplier is not also prepared to supply these for cash.[14] This provision was previously found in section 45 of the Consumer Credit Act 1974.

14. If an advertisement mentions a rate of interest[15] or an amount relating to the cost of credit, this triggers the need to give a representative example in the advertisement as well as the postal address of the advertiser.[16] But the requirement to give a postal address does not apply to a radio or television advertisement or to an advertisement that gives the name of a credit broker.[17]

15. There are detailed requirements specifying the information that the representative example must contain.[18] Further guidance is given.[19] The representative example must be labelled as such and given greater prominence than other financial information.[20] The information must include the rate of interest and whether it is variable or not and a representative APR.

16. There are other circumstances when an APR must be referred to.[21] An APR must be referred to if the communication states or infers that:

10 CONC 3.3.9 G.
11 CONC 3.3.11 G.
12 CONC 3.3.3 R.
13 CONC 3.3.4 G.
14 CONC 3.5.2 R.
15 This need not be an annual rate: CONC 3.5.4 G.
16 CONC 3.5.3(1) R.
17 CONC 3.5.3(3) R.
18 CONC 3.5.5 R.
19 CONC 3.5.6 G.
20 CONC 3.5.5 R.
21 CONC 3.5.7 R.

(a) credit is available to those who might otherwise consider their access to credit restricted;
(b) the terms on which credit is offered, or the way in which credit is offered, is more favourable than the terms or way in which credit is generally on offer from other lenders; and
(c) there are incentives to applying for credit, including as to the speed or manner in which an application is processed.

17. APR must be referred to as %APR and if variable or representative must be labelled as such, respectively.[22] There are rules about the assumptions that must be applied in the calculation of APR.[23]

18. The use of a number of expressions is subject to limitations so that the term can only be used in specified circumstances, namely:[24] 'overdraft', 'interest free',[25] 'no deposit',[26] 'loan guaranteed', 'pre-approved', 'no credit checks', and 'gift' or 'present'.

Promotion of credit agreements secured on land

19. CONC 3.6 sets out the rules applicable to loans intended to be secured on land. These rules do not apply to regulated mortgage contracts (i.e. domestic mortgages) to which MCOB applies. Many of the same rules apply to credit agreements secured on land as apply to regulated credit agreements not secured on land; for instance, as to the requirement to provide a typical APR.[27] Likewise, there are identical rules on the use of certain expressions, such as 'interest free'.[28] There are similar rules as to the information that must be provided in a credit advertisement of this type.[29]

20. Differences that there are largely reflect differences that existed between the Consumer Credit (Advertisement) Regulations 2004 and 2010.

21. However, there are some specific risk warnings that must be included, prominently.[30]

22. Where the loan is secured by a mortgage on someone's home, there must be a warning: 'YOUR HOME MAY BE REPOSSESSED IF YOU DO NOT KEEP UP YOUR REPAYMENTS ON A MORTGAGE OR ANY OTHER DEBT SECURED ON IT.'

22 CONC 3.5.9 R.
23 CONC 3.5.13 R.
24 CONC 3.5.12 R.
25 This can only be used if the amount the customer has to pay is no more than the cash price.
26 This can only be used where no advance payment is to be made.
27 CONC 3.6.6 R.
28 CONC 3.6.8 R.
29 CONC 3.6.10 R.
30 CONC 3.6.5(5) R.

23. In the case of a financial promotion aimed at refinancing debts, there must be a further warning before the earlier one:[31] 'THINK CAREFULLY BEFORE SECURING OTHER DEBTS AGAINST YOUR HOME.'

24. Where the credit is of the type that only has to be repaid on moving house or death, the warning is:[32] 'CHECK THAT THIS MORTGAGE WILL MEET YOUR NEEDS IF YOU WANT TO MOVE OR SELL YOUR HOME OR YOU WANT YOUR FAMILY TO INHERIT IT. IF YOU ARE IN ANY DOUBT, SEEK INDEPENDENT ADVICE.'

25. In the case of a foreign currency loan, the warning is:[33] 'CHANGES IN THE EXCHANGE RATE MAY INCREASE THE STERLING EQUIVALENT OF YOUR DEBT.'

Promotions by credit brokers

26. It is an important principle that a promotion by a credit broker must make it clear the extent of the services provided and whether the broker is tied to a particular lender or is working independently.[34] An independent credit broker must genuinely have access to a range of products that it is able to offer impartially.[35]

Unfair practices by lenders

27. A number of unfair promotional practices by lenders are specifically prohibited.[36]

28. It is unfair to provide a pre-completed credit application form with an amount of credit specified unless that amount has been arrived at following a creditworthiness assessment of the borrower.[37]

29. It is also unacceptable to state that the amount of credit is solely dependent on the amount of equity in a property.[38]

30. It is likewise unacceptable to promote credit in circumstances where the firm has reason to believe it would be unsuitable;[39] for example, to promote high-cost short-term borrowing for longer term lending.[40]

31 CONC 3.6.5 R.
32 CONC 3.6.5(2)(c) R.
33 CONC 3.6.5(4) R.
34 CONC 3.7.3 R.
35 CONC 3.7.4 G.
36 CONC 3.8.
37 CONC 3.8.2(1) R.
38 CONC 3.8.2(2) R.
39 CONC 3.8.2(3) R.
40 CONC 3.8.3(2) G.

Financial promotion of debt adjusting and debt counselling

31. There are rules applying to the contents of communications and promotions of those engaged in debt adjusting and debt counselling.[41] There must be a statement of the level of fees charged and the services they cover and a reasonable estimate of the overall anticipated cost.[42]

32. If the firm is profit seeking, this must be stated.[43] Equally, it must not be stated that the service is free, impartial or independent, if this is not the case.[44] Nor may a favourable outcome of negotiations with lenders be guaranteed.[45] A profit-seeking body must give details of impartial free advice services available including publications produced by the Insolvency Service and the Department of Enterprise.[46]

33. Where the financial promotion sets out options, the advantages and disadvantages of each approach must be given.[47] If a financial promotion promotes the possibility of an individual voluntary arrangement or protective trust, the specific drawback with these must be pointed out.[48]

Promotions not in writing

34. An authorised person must not permit an unauthorised person to make a promotion during a telephone call, visit or other form of interactive communication.[49] If an authorised person makes a visit outside the firm's premises, it must make the visit at an appropriate time of day and must identify him or herself and his or her firm at the outset of the visit.[50]

Quotations

35. The Consumer Credit Act 1974, by sections 52 and 152, imposed an obligation on a lender, hirer or credit broker of a regulated agreement to provide a written quotation on request. The required content of a quotation was laid out in the Consumer Credit (Quotations) Regulations 1989. These, however, were later revoked by the Consumer Credit (Quotations) (Revocation) Regulations 1997. Subsequently, the content of quotations for prospective credit and hire agreements secured on land were prescribed

41 CONC 3.9.3 R.
42 CONC 3.9.3(3) R.
43 CONC 3.9.3(6) R.
44 CONC 3.9.5(1) R.
45 CONC 3.9.5(4) R.
46 CONC 3.9.4 G.
47 CONC 3.9.3(9) R.
48 CONC 3.9.3(14) R.
49 CONC 3.9.11 R.
50 CONC 3.9.10 R.

by the Consumer Credit (Content of Quotations) and Consumer Credit (Advertisement) Regulations 1999.[51]

36. The requirement to provide a quotation in respect of regulated credit and hire agreements secured on land is now contained in the Handbook at CONC 4.1 embodying the requirements of the 1999 Regulations notwithstanding that sections 52 and 152 have been repealed by virtue of the Financial Services and Markets Act 2000 (Regulated Activities) (Amendment) Order 2013.[52]

37. A quotation is a document containing the proposed terms on which a lender or owner is prepared to do business. It must not be capable of being signed to form a contract nor must it comprise a financial promotion.[53]

38. A quotation for a contract secured on land must contain the same warning statements as are required for a financial promotion as explained earlier.[54] The same warnings apply to a prospective hire agreement that will be secured on land.

39. Where a credit broker gives a quotation and the loan may required to be secured on land, the quotation must state this.[55] Where an agreement will be secured on land, the quotation provided by the credit broker must contain the same warning statements as is required in the case of a lender.[56]

Canvassing borrower-lender and ancillary credit agreements off trade premises

40. It is a criminal offence to canvass regulated borrower-lender agreements off trade premises.[57]

41. Canvassing off trade premises comprises making oral representations during a visit that takes place away from trade premises; the purpose of the visit must be to solicit an individual to enter into a regulated agreement and the visit must not have been carried out in response to a prior request.[58] The representations need not necessarily be made to the same individual that is intended should enter into the regulated agreement.

42. Trade premises for these purposes comprise premises where the lender or owner, or a supplier, or the canvasser, or the canvasser's employer or principal, or the consumer, carry on business.[59] It is sufficient if the place

51 SI 1999/2725.
52 SI 2013/1881.
53 CONC 4.1.5(2)(d) R.
54 CONC 4.1.3 R.
55 CONC 4.1.4(1) R.
56 CONC 4.1.4(2) R.
57 Section 49 Consumer Credit Act 1974.
58 Section 48(1).
59 Section 48(2).

of business is only temporary. The supplier in this context refers to the person, both in respect of restricted use and unrestricted use credit, known to be supplying the goods and services to be financed by credit.[60]

43. 'Representation' encompasses most types of statement and specifically includes any condition or warranty, or any other statement or undertaking.[61]

44. It is an offence to canvass borrower-lender agreements off trade premises, as so defined.[62] It is not an offence to canvass a borrower-lender-supplier agreement (i.e. one where the credit is tied up with the supply of goods and services). On indictment, the offence carries a maximum prison sentence of one year.[63]

45. It is a separate offence to make a visit in response to a request that is not *in writing and signed*, in circumstances such that if no request at all had been made, the visit would have amounted to canvassing off trade premises.[64] The request must be signed by or *on behalf* of the person being canvassed. This also carries a maximum penalty of imprisonment of one year when tried on indictment.

46. The Act permits an exception to be made in some circumstances in respect of canvassing a borrower to overdraw on a current account, provided that the borrower already has an account with that lender (not necessarily a current account). The FCA must have determined that current accounts of a particular description are to be excluded from the prohibition, provided the FCA considers this is not contrary to the interests of borrowers. The FCA can lay down conditions.[65] Failure to comply with the conditions means that the exemption from the prohibition is lost[66] and a criminal offence will be committed. The FCA may vary or withdraw a determination once made.[67]

47. There is a like offence for canvassing *ancillary credit business* off trade premises.[68] Canvassing, as before, entails the making of oral representations during a visit, the purpose of which is to solicit the entry by an individual into an agreement for ancillary credit business. Ancillary credit business comprises credit brokerage, debt adjusting, debt counselling, debt collecting, debt administration, the provision of credit information services and the operation of a credit reference agency.[69] Trade premises for these

60 Section 189(1), Consumer Credit Act 1974.
61 Section 189(1).
62 Section 49(1).
63 Schedule 1.
64 Section 49(2).
65 Section 49(3).
66 Section 49(5).
67 Section 183.
68 Section 154.
69 Section 145(1).

purposes are premises where an ancillary business is carried on, or where the canvasser or the canvasser's employer or principal carries on business, or where the consumer carries on business.[70] The offence carries the same maximum penalty as for the offence of canvassing borrower-lender agreements off trade premises, namely a prison sentence of one year.[71]

48. One difference between the offence of canvassing borrower-lender agreements and the offence of canvassing ancillary credit business off trade premises is that it is not a separate offence to canvass ancillary credit business without being in receipt of a *written request* (i.e. it will be a defence to the offence if canvassing ancillary credit business off trade premises that the consumer made a purely oral request).

49. In respect of all of these offences, it is a defence for the person proved to charge that his or her act was due to a mistake, or on reliance on incorrect information supplied or to an act or omission by another person or to an accident or some other cause beyond his or her control, and that he or she took all reasonable precautions to avoid such an act or omission, including by persons under his or her control.[72]

50. So in relation to a canvassing offence, it would be a defence for the person charged to prove on the balance of probabilities that he or she had been incorrectly told that the person canvassed had requested the visit (or, in the case of a borrower-lender canvassing offence, had signed a request for a visit), provided that the person charged had reasonably believed what he or she had been incorrectly told.

51. However, where the defence is based on wrong information supplied by a third party, the person charged shall not be entitled to rely on this as a defence unless, seven days prior to the hearing, the person charged has served a written notice on the prosecutor identifying the source of the incorrect information or giving such information as is in his or her possession to assist in the identification of that other person as was then in his or her possession. The Act does not define what is meant by the hearing in this context; it must refer to the first day of the trial.

Circulars to minors

52. It is an offence to send a prohibited circular to a minor with a view to financial gain.[73] The offence replaces a similar offence contained in the now repealed Betting and Loans (Infants) Act 1892. The offence is triable either summarily or on indictment, and when tried summarily there is a maximum prison sentence of one year.

70 Section 153(2).
71 Schedule 1.
72 Section 168(1).
73 Section 50, Consumer Credit Act 1974.

53. The ingredients of the offence are as follows:

(a) One or more documents must be sent. Sending is not confined to sending by post; where the Act wishes to specify sending by post or by other appropriate method, it states this expressly. The word 'send' is not defined by the Act but it would seem to preclude personal delivery to an address.
(b) The document must be of the prohibited type (i.e. the document must invite the minor to borrow money, or to obtain goods on credit or hire, or to obtain services on credit, or to apply for information or advice on borrowing money or otherwise obtaining credit or hiring goods).[74]
(c) The motive for sending the document must be financial gain for the sender, but the sender need not necessarily be a profit-making organisation.
(d) The document must be sent to a minor (i.e. someone under the age of 18). It is a defence for the sender to prove that the sender did not know and had no reasonable cause to suspect that the person to whom the circular was sent was a minor. The burden of proof is on the defendant to show this on the balance of probabilities.[75]

54. Special rules apply when a document is sent to a minor at a school or other educational establishment for minors. If the person sending the document either knows or has reasonable cause to suspect that the address of the person to whom the document is sent is a school, then that person is deemed to have reasonable cause to suspect that the person to whom the document is sent is a minor. If the other criteria are satisfied, then the offence is committed. The person charged may assert that he or she did not know and did not have reasonable cause to suspect that the document was addressed to a school or other educational institution for minors; the person charged bears the burden of proof in this respect on the balance of probabilities.[76]

55. The title to the section implies that the offence is only committed when the person charged initiates the sending out of a circular to a minor, and this undoubtedly is the most serious circumstance when the offence is committed. Nevertheless, it is clear that the offence may be committed by *responding* in writing to a request for a loan or hire initiated by a minor.

56. It is a defence to prove on the balance of probabilities that the document was sent to a minor by mistake or by accident provided that reasonable precautions have been put in place and all due diligence

74 Section 50(1).
75 *R v Carr-Briant* 1943 2 All ER 156.
76 Section 171(5).

exercised to ensure that the document was not sent to a minor.[77] It will be for the person charged to prove on the balance of probabilities that all reasonable precautions were taken and all due diligence exercised. The prospective lender or owner will have to show, for instance, that suitable training has been given to staff when sending out or responding to requests for credit.

57. If someone seeks to rely on this defence on the basis of misinformation provided by a third party, the person charged will have to notify the prosecution at least seven days in advance of the hearing of the source of the information or of all information available to the person charged identifying the source of the information. Failure in this respect will mean that the defence cannot be relied upon without leave of the court.

58. This offence may of course be committed by a body corporate in circumstances where the body corporate sends out the offending circular. Obviously, a body corporate only acts through human agency and someone acting as a director, manager, secretary or similar officer will also be criminally liable if the offence has occurred through either the active consent of that person or through the neglect of that person.[78]

Unlawful financial promotions

59. The basis proposition is this. If someone acting in the course of business promotes entry into a loan or hire agreement and the person making the communication is not an authorised person, and the communication has not been approved by an authorised person, then the communication is unlawful, and if the borrower or hirer enters into a loan or hire agreement on the basis of that unlawful communication, then the loan or hire agreement will be unenforceable against the borrower or hirer. This proposition derives from sections 21 and 30 Financial Services and Markets Act 2000; section 21 establishes the unlawfulness of the communication and section 30 sets out the consequences that flow from reliance on that unlawful communication.

60. Section 21 provides that a person making the communication referred to as 'A' 'must not when acting in the course of business communicate an invitation or inducement to engage in investment activity'.[79] However, this prohibition does not extend to a case where 'A' is an authorised person, or when the content of the communication had been approved for the purposes of section 21 by an authorised person.

77 Section 168(1).
78 Section 169(1).
79 Section 21(1), Financial Services and Markets Act 2000.

61. The Act has given the Treasury the right to exempt certain types of communication from this general rule and the exemptions have been made that are set out in the FPO.[80] These will be considered briefly later.

62. In order to label a communication by 'A' as unlawful, the following requirements must be satisfied:

(a) 'A' must be acting in the course of business;
(b) there must be a *communication*;
(c) the communication must be *an invitation or inducement*;
(d) the invitation must relate to an *investment activity*;
(e) 'A' must not be authorised;
(f) the communication must not have been approved by an authorised person; and
(g) none of the exemptions in the FPO must apply.

63. These requirements deserve further comment.

64. As to the requirement that 'A' must be acting in the course of business, the Treasury is given power to specify the circumstances when someone is or is not acting in the course of business.[81] No order has been made.

65. As to the requirement that 'A' must *communicate* the invitation or inducement, a communication can take any form; it can be oral or in writing. Further, it is sufficient if 'A' 'causes a communication to be made'.[82] Thus, the communication can be indirect. Further, a communication made abroad counts if capable of having effect within the United Kingdom.[83] PERG 8 in the FCA Handbook gives illustrations of the type of communication that may be made.

66. The terms 'invitation or inducement' are not defined in the Act and PERG 8 gives guidance as to what is included.

67. An important qualification is that the 'invitation or inducement' must relate to 'investment activity'. This is given a specific meaning in section 21 and its definition entails two further defined expressions, namely 'controlled activity' and 'controlled investment'. Section 21 provides that 'engaging in investment activity' means as follows: '(a) entering or offering to enter into an agreement the making or performance of which by either party constitutes a controlled activity, or (b) exercising any rights conferred by the controlled investment to acquire, dispose of, underwrite or convert a controlled investment.'[84]

80 Financial Services and Markets Act 2000 (Financial Promotions) Order 2001, SI 2001/1335 as amended.
81 Section 21(4).
82 Section 21(13).
83 Section 21(3).
84 Section 21(8).

68. A controlled activity is an activity of a specified kind relating to an investment of a specified kind (i.e. a controlled investment). The FPO specifies what controlled activities and controlled investments are.

69. It can be seen, therefore, that the FPO has a dual overall purpose. It sets out those investments and activities that constitute investment activity for the purpose of the prohibition in section 21(1). This therefore defines the ambit of the prohibition. Second, the FPO, having defined the ambit of the provision, also provides a number of exemptions from the prohibition.

Controlled activities and controlled investments

70. The Financial Promotions Order[85] specifies, at Schedule 1, those activities and investments that are 'controlled' for the purposes of section 21; this is relevant to ascertain what constitutes 'investment activity' for the purposes of section 21. This in turn is relevant because it is only communications that invite or induce participants to engage in investment activity that are unlawful under section 21.

71. The Financial Services and Markets Act 2000 (Regulated Activities) (Amendment) (No 2) Order 2013[86] amended Schedule 1 of the FPO to include a number of credit- and hire-related activities and investments to the list of controlled investments and activities. Indeed, the list closely follows the list of credit and hire activities that are regulated activities for the purposes of the RAO. The principal difference between the list of controlled activities and investments in Schedule 1 of the FPO and the list of regulated activities in the RAO is that many of the controlled activities specified by the FPO are not subject to the same exemptions as apply to the equivalent regulated activities within the RAO. The reason for this is that many of the exclusions from the scope of regulated activities are not appropriate when it comes to specifying what advertisements should be subject to control by virtue of the FPO.

72. It will be remembered that engaging in investment activity is defined as offering to enter into an agreement the entry into which is a controlled activity, *or* exercising rights under a controlled investment to dispose of it or acquire it.[87]

Types of controlled activities and controlled investments

73. Providing credit is a controlled activity. Paragraph 10BA of Schedule 1 of the FPO provides that the activity of 'entering into a relevant credit

85 Financial Services and Markets Act 2000 (Financial Promotions) Order 2005 SI 2005/1529.

86 SI 2013/1881.

87 Section 21(8).

agreement, other than an agreement under which qualifying credit within the meaning of paragraph 10 is provided as lender or exercising or having the right to exercise the rights of the lender under such an agreement' is a controlled activity. A relevant credit agreement is defined in paragraph 28 of Schedule 1 to mean a credit agreement within Article 60B of the RAO other than a regulated mortgage contract. This definition embraces all credit agreements entered into with an individual, including all exempt agreements, other than regulated mortgage contracts.

74. But in fact the exclusion of the entry into 'qualifying credit agreements' from the category of entry into relevant credit agreements is of little direct consequence as entry into such agreements forms a separate category of controlled activity under paragraph 10 of Schedule 1.

75. The FPO defines 'qualifying credit' as occurring when a lender carries on the business of entry into regulated mortgage contracts[88] and when, in respect of loans, the obligation of the borrower is secured at least in part on land.[89] Entry into regulated mortgage contracts comes within this activity but the activity is not confined to entry into regulated mortgage contracts since it extends to agreements whereby loans are secured on land as a second charge provided that the lender is also in the business of entering into regulated mortgage contracts (which relate only to first charges).[90] Entry into, arranging or advising on qualified credit are all controlled activities.[91]

76. Entry into hire agreements is a controlled activity. Paragraph 10BB of Schedule 1 of the FPO provides that entry into 'regulated consumer hire agreement or an agreement that would be such an agreement but for article 60O . . . or 60Q of the Regulated Activities Order as owner, or exercising the rights or having the right to exercise the rights of the owner under such an agreement' is a controlled activity. The exemption in article 60O exempts agreements for business purpose when the hire payments will exceed £25,000. Article 60Q exempts agreements with a high net worth individual when the hirer makes a declaration agreeing to forego the protection of the Consumer Credit Act. These exemptions have no relevance for the purpose of rendering a hire advertisement or other form of financial promotion unlawful.

77. However, advertisements that state they are directed solely at bodies corporate are not caught by section 21.[92]

78. Likewise, entering into, arranging or advising on home reversion plans, home purchase plans, sale and rent back agreements[93] are all controlled activities.

88 As defined in article 61 RAO.
89 Paragraph 10 Schedule 1, FPO.
90 PERG 8.17.3.
91 Paragraph 10, 10A, 10B Schedule 1 FPO.
92 Article 46 FPO.
93 Paragraph 10C to 10K Schedule 1 FPO.

79. Credit broking in respect of relevant credit agreements, as defined and explained above, is a controlled activity.[94] The definition mirrors the definition of credit broking in the RAO in that there are the same six categories of activity classified as credit broking.[95] Likewise, debt adjusting and debt counselling in respect of relevant credit agreements are controlled activities to the same extent as with the RAO.[96]

80. Operating a peer-to-peer electronic lending system to match borrowers and lenders to enable them to into a loan agreement is also a controlled activity by virtue of Article 4C of Schedule 1. This matches the regulated activity prescribed by Article 36H of the RAO. It is not a controlled activity if the loans are concluded only with bodies corporate, or where the amount of credit is not less than £25,000 and are for predominantly business purposes. This mirrors the position in relation to the RAO.[97] Indeed, communications for business purposes in connection with peer-to-peer lending are subject to an important specific exclusion exempting communications from the effect of section 21 that state that they are purely for business purposes.[98]

Exempted communications

81. The FPO renders certain types of communication lawful even if the communication relates to an invitation to engage in an investment activity (as defined) and even if the person making the communication is not authorised or had the communication approved by an authorised person.

82. However, these exemptions are unlikely to apply in many situations involving credit or hire agreements, although this cannot be ruled out. There are exemptions relating to generic promotions,[99] one-off non-real time communications or solicited communications,[100] real-time communications involving introductions,[101] communications when the person is acting as a mere conduit,[102] certain communications to certified high net worth individuals[103] and to sophisticated investors.[104]

94 Paragraph 4B Schedule 1 FPO.
95 Article 36A RAO.
96 Paragraph 5A and 5B Schedule 1 FPO.
97 Paragraph 4C(5), (6) Schedule 1 FPO.
98 Article 46A FPO.
99 Article 17 FPO.
100 Article 27 FPO.
101 Article 28B FPO.
102 Article 18 FPO.
103 Article 48.
104 Article 50 FPO.

Consequences of unlawful financial promotion

83. Section 21 of the Act provides that any relevant financial promotion of an investment activity must either be communicated by an authorised (or exempt) person, or must have been approved by an authorised or exempt person. Investment activity must in this context be either a controlled activity or controlled investment specified by the Financial Promotions Order[105] as amended.

84. A financial promotion entered into contrary to these requirements is referred to in the Act as an 'unlawful communication'.[106]

85. Section 30 provides for the situation where someone enters into a *controlled*[107]agreement 'in consequence of an unlawful communication'[108] This raises the familiar test of causation; it should be sufficient in order to attract the consequences of the provision that someone has entered into a relevant agreement *in reliance* upon such a communication.

86. Section 30 provides the basic rule that the controlled agreement is rendered unenforceable and that any monies paid or property transferred under it are returnable and compensation is payable.[109] Accordingly, a lender will be unable to recover loan repayments if the borrower was induced to take out a loan by an unlawful financial promotion. It is to be noted that not only regulated agreements may be rendered unenforceable, but exempt agreements also.

87. Any security handed over by the borrower must also be returned.[110]

88. Section 30 also covers the situation where someone exercises a contractual right as a result of an unlawful communication. Such obligations are not enforceable and money or property transferred consequential upon exercise of the right is returnable.[111] Accordingly, a lender would not be entitled to terminate an unenforceable hire-purchase agreement.

89. If the borrower elects to treat a loan agreement or hire agreement as unenforceable, the borrower or hire must return any monies or property already received.[112] Section 30(11) says nothing about the recipient of monies having to pay any interest on the monies returned.

90. The court has discretion to allow enforcement of the agreement insofar as enforcement is just and equitable in the circumstances of the case.[113] The court is required in particular to consider the two matters referred to

105 Financial Services and Markets Act 2000 (Financial Promotions) Order SI 2001/1335.
106 Section 30(1) Financial Services and Markets Act 2000.
107 As specified by the FPO.
108 Section 30(2) Financial Services and Markets Act 2000.
109 Section 30(2) Financial Services and Markets Act 2000.
110 Section 30(3).
111 Section 30(3) Financial Services and Markets Act 2000.
112 Section 30(11).
113 Section 30(4).

in section 30(6) and 30(7). If the lender or owner was responsible for the unlawful communication that led to entry into the credit or hire agreement, then by section 30(6), the issue is whether it reasonably believed that it was not making such a communication. It might be that the lender or owner reasonably but incorrectly believed that it fell within an exemption specified in the FPO. If the lender or owner was not responsible for the unlawful communication, then, by section 30(7), the issue is whether the lender or owner knew that the loan or hire agreement was entered into as a result of the communication. It also ought to be an issue, although not specifically referred to in section 30(7), whether the lender or owner reasonably believed that the communication was by, or approved by, an authorised person.

Criminal sanctions

91. It is a criminal offence to communicate an invitation or inducement in breach of section 21 punishable with imprisonment.[114] It is a defence for the defendant to show on a balance of probabilities that he or she believed on reasonable grounds that the content of the communication had been prepared or approved by an authorised person, or that he or she had taken all reasonable precautions and exercised all due diligence to avoid committing the offence.

Misleading statements

92. Section 89 of the Financial Services Act 2012 makes it an offence knowingly or recklessly to make a statement that is false and misleading with a view to inducing another to offer to enter into a relevant agreement.[115] The activities that are specified for the purposes of the offence are controlled activities within Part 1 and controlled investments within Part 2 of Schedule 1 to the Financial Promotions Order.[116] These activities include entering into regulated credit and hire agreements, credit brokerage and other ancillary credit activities. The offence is punishable by up to 12 months in prison in respect of trial on indictment.[117]

114 Section 25.
115 Replacing the previous offence at section 397 Financial Services and Markets Act 2000.
116 Financial Services Act 2012 (Misleading Statements and Impressions) Order 2013, SI 2013/637.
117 Section 92 Financial Services Act 2012.

7 Pre-contract requirements

Disclosure of pre-contract information

1. Section 55 of the Consumer Credit Act 1974, which entitles the Secretary of State to make Regulations prescribing information to be disclosed to a consumer prior to entry into a regulated agreement, lay dormant for 30 years.

2. However, the utility of requiring the disclosure of pre-contractual information prior to entry into a credit or hire agreements was eventually recognised and pre-contract disclosure requirements binding on lenders and owners were introduced by reference to the Consumer Credit (Disclosure of Information) Regulations 2004.[1] However, the end result is complicated.

Applicability of the Disclosure of Information Regulations 2004

3. When these Regulations were initially promulgated, they applied to all regulated agreements (other than non-commercial agreements) entered into after 31 May 2005. These Regulations are still in force but their initial wide ambit is reduced in scope following amendments made by the Consumer Credit (EU Directive) Regulations[2] and the introduction of the Disclosure of Information Regulations 2010.

4. Now the Regulations apply only to consumer hire agreements[3] and to consumer credit agreements entered into wholly or predominantly for business purposes.[4] As is not uncommon for the purposes of the Financial Services and Markets Act 2000, there is a presumption that an agreement is entered into wholly or predominantly for business purposes if the borrower signs a declaration to this effect. But if the lender or a person

1 SI 2004/1481.
2 SI 2010/1010.
3 Reg 2(1)(b).
4 Reg 2(1)(c).

acting for the lender has reason to believe that the declaration is untrue, then the lender cannot rely upon it.[5]

5. The Regulations also apply to agreements where the amount of credit is over £60,260 and where it is a restricted use small agreement (i.e. where the credit advanced is less than £50). They also apply to consumer credit agreements secured on land[6] except for agreements governed by section 58 of the Consumer Credit Act 1974. However, the category of agreements that are secured on land and are regulated and are not within section 58 is small.

6. There are other types of contract to which the 2004 Regulations do not apply: distance contracts[7] and authorised non-business overdraft agreements (extended to the case where credit is not repayable on demand or within three months).[8] These exceptions exist because special rules imposing different, more onerous obligations apply to these situations.

7. Where the Regulations apply, the prescribed information must be given before the regulated agreement is 'made'.[9] This must mean before the consumer commits him or herself to an agreement by signing it even if the lender or owner has not countersigned it by that stage; once the customer's signature is obtained, then the lender or owner has it within its power to conclude the agreement.

Information that must be provided under the Disclosure of Information Regulations 2004

8. The information that must be provided is the same as the information that is prescribed for the purpose of the document comprising the agreement as set out in relevant parts of the Agreements Regulations and to which reference is made hereafter.[10] This information includes information as to the terms of the proposed agreement and the remedies available in accordance with the Agreements Regulations.

9. In the case of a consumer credit agreement other than that secured on land, the borrower must be informed that if entry into a consumer credit agreement is refused because of an adverse report from a credit reference agency, then the borrower must be informed of this by the lender, together with details of the agency.[11] The lender is bound to give this information in any event by virtue of section 157(1) of the 1974 Act.

5 Reg 2(2).
6 Reg 2(1)(a).
7 Reg 2(3)(a).
8 Reg 2(3)(b), (c).
9 Reg 3(1).
10 Reg 3(1).
11 Reg 3(1A).

10. The information must be presented in a separate[12] document headed 'Pre-contract disclosure'[13] and must not contain any other information apart from that specified.[14]

Sanctions for non-compliance

11. If the Regulations are not complied with in relation to any agreement, the agreement may only be enforced following an order of the court.[15] It will be necessary for the lender to apply to the court for an enforcement order to be able to enforce the agreement.[16]

Distance contracts and distance marketing

12. Special care is needed with credit and hire distance contracts. 'Distance contracts' have been regulated since the Consumer Protection (Distance Selling) Regulations 2000[17] implementing EU Directive 97/7/EC. These Regulations came into force on 31 October 2000. The essence of the regulation was to require certain information to be disclosed pre-contract and to confer a right of cancellation in the case of distance contracts. A consumer who contracted at a distance was felt in need of particular protection.

13. A 'distance contract' in all these regulations is a contract 'concluded between a supplier and a consumer under an organised distance sales or service provision scheme run by the supplier who, for the purpose of the contract, makes exclusive use of one or more means of distance communication up to and including the moment at which the contract is concluded'.

14. Thus, a distance contract is one between a 'supplier'[18] and a 'consumer'. 'Consumer' has a specialised meaning throughout all these Regulations. It refers to any natural person who, in contracts to which the various Regulations apply, is acting for purposes that are outside his or her business. Accordingly, contracts concluded for business purposes or with a limited company are outside the scope of the Regulations.

15. A distance contract arises only when a supplier makes exclusive use of one or more 'means of distance communication' in order to conclude the contract. This phrase is defined in the 2000 Regulations to refer to any means 'which, without the simultaneous physical presence of the supplier and the consumer, may be used for the conclusion of a contract between

12 Reg 4(d)(i).
13 Reg 4(d)(ii).
14 Reg 4(d)(iii).
15 Section 55(2) Consumer Credit Act 1974.
16 Section 127(1)(za).
17 SI 2000/2334.
18 Or trader in the context of the 2013 Regulations.

those parties'. An indicative list of such means of distance communication is given at Schedule 1 of those Regulations and both email and telephone are included within the categories of distance communication listed. The phrase is not defined in later Regulations, but its meaning must be constant throughout.

16. It can be seen that potentially both credit and hire agreements could be distance contracts for the purpose of the definition and initially the 2000 Regulations applied to credit and hire distance contracts.

17. However, credit agreements were taken out of the ambit of the 2000 Regulations by the Financial Services (Distance Marketing) Regulations 2004. Financial services had always been excluded from the ambit of the 2000 Regulations[19] but the definition was changed to bring credit agreements within the scope of the exclusion.[20]

18. Hire agreements, however, remained regulated by the 2000 Regulations. So it seems did a credit brokerage agreement since such a contract facilitates the obtaining of credit without providing credit itself.

19. Further, the pre-contract disclosure of information requirements contained in the 2004 Regulations do not apply to circumstances where the 2010 Disclosure of Information Regulations apply,[21] save in the context of authorised non-business overdraft agreements. The 2010 Regulations, which came into force on 30 April 2010, apply to most credit agreements but not to those secured on land or where the credit is more than £60,260.[22] It is in this residual category of cases that the 2004 Financial Services (Distance Marketing) Regulations continue to have effect.

20. The 2010 Disclosure of Information Regulations contain particular disclosure of information requirements for contracts entered into following distance marketing.[23]

21. The 2000 Regulations have been replaced by the Consumer Contracts (Information, Cancellation and Additional Charges) Regulations 2013[24] with effect from 13 June 2014.[25] The 2013 Regulations do not apply to agreements of a 'credit nature'[26] so that credit and credit brokerage agreements are both outside the ambit of these Regulations. The distance marketing of hire agreements will, however, fall within the ambit of the 2013 Regulations.

19 Reg 5 2000 Regulations SI.
20 Reg 3(1) 2000 Regulations.
21 Reg 7(6) 2004 Regulations SI 2004/.
22 Although even in relation to these categories, there is a right to comply voluntarily, in which case the 2010 Regulations do apply to these categories as well.
23 Regs 4, 5 and 6 2010 Regs SI 2010/1013.
24 SI 2013/134.
25 Reg 2 2013 Regs 2013/3134.
26 Reg 6(b) 2013 Regs 2013/3134.

Disclosure of Information Regulations 2010

22. The Consumer Credit (Disclosure of Information) Regulations 2010[27] were made under powers conferred on the Secretary of State by section 55 of the Consumer Credit Act 1974 and in order to give effect to part of EU directive 2008/48. The effect of the directive was not to repeal the Consumer Credit (Disclosure of Information) Regulations 2004,[28] but to narrow their scope considerably. Moreover, these Regulations supplement and go further than the 2004 Regulations in a number of respects in that the 2010 Regulations demand more extensive initial disclosure than the 2004 Regulations. Furthermore, it is expressly provided that where the 2010 Regulations apply, the 2004 Regulations do not.[29]

23. If these Regulations are not complied with, the agreement entered into in breach of the Regulation may be enforced on order of the court only.[30] It will be necessary for the lender to apply to the court for an enforcement order under section 127.[31]

24. These Regulations apply to all consumer credit agreements entered into after 1 February 2011 except a number of restricted categories[32] for the most part covered by the 2004 Regulations.

25. Thus, the 2010 Regulations do not apply to consumer credit agreements made predominantly for business purposes, or where the credit exceeds £60,260, or where it is secured on land.[33] (When a borrower makes a declaration that an agreement has been entered into predominantly for business purposes, there is a presumption to this effect unless the lender has reasonable cause to believe that this is not the case.)[34]

26. But even in the case of these categories of agreements, the lender may decide to voluntarily supply the stipulated pre-contract information, in which case the Regulations then apply.[35]

27. The Regulations do not apply to credit agreements secured on land to which section 58 applies because section 58 provides for its own disclosure requirements.[36] Nor do they apply to authorised non-business overdraft agreements where the credit exceeds £60,260 or that is secured on land.

27 SI 2010/1010.
28 SI 2004/1481.
29 Reg 2(1) Consumer Credit (Disclosure of Information) Regulations 2004.
30 Section 55(2) Consumer Credit Act 1974.
31 Section 127(1)(za).
32 Reg 2(1).
33 Reg 2(3).
34 Reg 2(6).
35 Reg 2(5).
36 Reg 2(2).

The pre-contract information

28. The 2010 Regulations impose particular requirements in a number of specific situations involving various specific times of agreement. But where these do not apply, the general rule laid down by the 2010 Regulations is as follows:[37] 'In good time before the agreement is made, the creditor must disclose to the debtor in the manner set out in regulation 8, the pre-contract information.'

29. There is a long list of information in regulation 3, referred to throughout the Regulations as the 'pre-contract credit information'. Regulation 8 requires that the information is presented in writing on a form set out in Schedule 1 headed 'Standard European Credit Information'. If the lender wishes to provide additional information, it must be on an additional sheet.[38] Where the contract is a distance contract, this information must include the contractual terms and conditions.[39]

30. The general rule is that the information has to be provided in good time before the agreement is made. There is no definition as to what is meant by 'in good time' in this context but it clearly means in good time for the prospective borrower to be able to consider the contents of the information communicated.

31. There is one exception to the requirement that the form must be provided in advance and that is when a distance contract is entered into predominantly for business purposes; in this instance, it is sufficient for the pre-contract information to be provided immediately after the contract is entered into.[40]

Telephone contracts

32. Some modification is made to the requirement to disclose the entirety of the pre-contract information where there is a telephone contract (i.e. one made 'by way of a voice telephone communication'). The Regulations distinguish between distance contracts (i.e. one made over the telephone during a distance marketing scheme) and other situations. They also distinguish between distance contracts made predominantly for business purposes and other contracts.

33. Where there is a telephone contract that is not concluded as part of a distance marketing scheme, the information that must be disclosed before the agreement is made is not as extensive as that required by regulation 3,

37 Reg 3(2).
38 Reg 8(4).
39 Reg 7(2).
40 Reg 6(2).

being limited to the total amount of credit, the duration of the agreement, any goods to be acquired by the credit, the rate or rates of interest, the APR, the frequency of repayments and the amount of each repayment in the case of running account credit.[41]

34. In the case of a distance telephone contract, limited information can be provided in circumstances where *the customer explicitly consents*.[42] This includes all the information that would have been required had the contract not been a distance contract,[43] but there must also be included the identity of the person making the telephone call and that person's link with the creditor,[44] and the total amount to be paid by the borrower,[45] and a statement of any right of the borrower to withdraw[46] or cancel[47] the agreement.[48] The borrower must also be told that he or she can obtain further information on request.[49] The explicit consent of the borrower may be obtained orally, and once obtained the required information may then be communicated orally.

35. In the case of a distance contract, if the customer does not give explicit consent, then full information has to be provided as set out in regulation 3 (i.e. the specified form in writing has to be provided in advance of the agreement being entered into) (unless it is predominantly for business purposes).[50] In the case of a distance contract entered into predominantly for business purposes, no pre-contract information has to be provided.[51]

36. Following the conclusion of the contract, the pre-contract credit information stipulated in regulation 3 has to be presented to the borrower on the form required by regulation 8[52] *immediately* (so as to enable the borrower to exercise any right of withdrawal conferred by section 66A). The contractual terms and conditions must also be furnished.[53] Consequently, in the case of a telephone contract, information must be given both before and after the contract is concluded.

41 Reg 4(3).
42 Reg 4(2).
43 Reg 4(2)(b).
44 Reg 4(2)(a).
45 Reg 4(2)(c).
46 Under section 66A Consumer Credit Act 1974.
47 Under Financial Services (Distance Marketing) Regulations 2004.
48 Reg 4(2)(e).
49 Reg 4(2)(f).
50 Reg 3(1).
51 Reg 6.
52 Reg 4(4).
53 Reg 7(2).

Other types of distance contract

37. There are some types of distance contract, entered into at the borrower's request other than by telephone, that do not permit of an opportunity to supply the pre-contract credit information in advance of the conclusion of the agreement. In these circumstances, the information can be supplied in accordance with regulation 8 immediately after the agreement is made.[54]

38. Moreover, if a distance contract has been entered into for business, or predominantly business purposes, it suffices that the information is supplied immediately after the agreement is entered into.[55] This applies to telephone distance contracts as well as other distance contracts. There is a presumption that a contract is made predominantly for business purposes when the borrower makes a declaration to this effect unless the lender has reason to believe the contrary.[56]

Pawn agreements

39. Special rules apply to pawn agreements, which allow a more relaxed approach to be taken with a customer that is not a new client (i.e. a new customer being defined as one that has not entered into an agreement with the lender within the preceding three years).[57] If the customer is a new customer, then the general requirements in regulation 3 apply. If the customer is not a new customer, then the customer must be told of his or her right to receive the pre-contract credit information free of charge on request.[58] If such a request is received, then pre-contract information must be supplied; otherwise, it need not.[59]

Authorised non-business overdraft agreement

40. These agreements are subject to special, somewhat complicated rules. An authorised non-business overdraft agreement is one entered into with a consumer for a non-business purpose on the basis that the credit is either repayable on demand or within a period of less than three months.[60]

41. The general rule is that before an agreement of this type is entered into, the prospective borrower must be provided with the information set out at regulation 10(3) in the written form provided for by regulation 11 and Schedule 3.[61] The prescribed information includes many detailed

54 Reg 5.
55 Reg 6(2).
56 Reg 6(3).
57 Reg 1(6).
58 Reg 9(2).
59 Reg 3(1)(c).
60 Section 189(1) Consumer Credit Act 1974.
61 Reg 10(2).

aspects of the overdraft arrangement. Schedule 3 requires the form to be headed 'European Consumer Credit Information'.

42. The information specified in regulation 10(3) includes, in the case of a distance contract, information about the right of cancellation provided for by the Financial Services (Distance Marketing) Regulations 2004.[62]

43. In the case of a telephone agreement for an authorised non-business overdraft that is not a distance contract, the requirements are somewhat reduced; the creditor must provide, orally or in writing, certain specified information about the terms of the arrangement before the agreement is made; there is no need to provide the full document in the form set out in Schedule 3.[63]

44. In the case of a telephone agreement that is a distance contract, it is permissible to disclose more limited information orally prior to the agreement without using the Schedule 3 form, if the prospective borrower explicitly agrees.[64] If there is no explicit agreement, then the Schedule 3 form must be provided prior to the agreement.[65]

45. If the customer says that he or she wants an overdraft immediately, a Schedule 3 form must be used prior to the agreement but it needs only set out the key terms of the overdraft agreement.[66]

46. In the case of a joint overdraft agreement, the necessary information can be given to only one of them if both agree to this.[67]

Financial Services (Distance Marketing) Regulations 2004: disclosure of information

47. The 2004 Regulations contain requirements for the disclosure of pre-contract information in respect of the limited number of distance marketing contracts to which they apply: breach of the Regulations is a criminal offence. The effect of these Regulations is replicated at CONC 2.7, although the Regulations remain in force. The Regulations do not apply to those agreements to which the Disclosure of Information Regulations 2010 apply.[68] This leaves, in effect, consumer credit agreements where the amount of credit exceeds £60,260 or that are secured on land, although even in these instances a lender can opt to apply the 2010 Regulations by voluntary compliance with those Regulations.[69]

62 Reg 10(5)(e).
63 Reg 10(6).
64 Reg 10(5).
65 Reg 10(5A).
66 Reg 10(8).
67 Reg 10(9).
68 Reg 7(6); CONC 2.7.2(3) R.
69 Reg 2(5) Disclosure of Information Regs 2010 SI 2010/1013.

48. The Regulations provide, in the case of a distance contract for financial services, for the disclosure of the contractual terms and information in the written format stipulated in Schedule 1, also appearing at CONC 2 Annex 1 R. The information is to be given in 'clear and comprehensive manner appropriate to the means of distance communication used, with due regard in particular to the principles of good faith in commercial transactions and the principles governing the protection of those who are unable to give their consent such as minors'.[70] Further, at the time of supplying this information, the supplier must make his or her commercial purpose clear.[71] Disclosure must be in a durable medium.

49. In the case of telephone distance selling, the supplier must at the outset of any call initiated by the supplier make clear the identity of the caller and the purpose in telephoning[72] but, if the consumer explicitly consents, the information supplied may be limited to that more limited information in Schedule 2 to the 2004 Regulations (also found at CONC 2 Annex 2 R).[73]

50. In the case of an agreement involving an initial agreement and successive operations thereafter,[74] it is sufficient for the lender to comply at the time of the initial agreement and there is no need to comply at the time of each successive operation.[75]

51. In the case of an authorised business overdraft agreement, it is sufficient if the information required by regulation 10 of the 2010 Disclosure Regulations has been provided, including in the case of such an agreement concluded over the telephone, a copy of the agreement.[76]

Disclosure of information with hire contracts

52. Hire contracts are covered by the Consumer Credit (Disclosure of Information) Regulations 2004.[77] The Consumer Contracts (Information, Cancellation and Additional Charges) Regulations 2013,[78] implementing EU Directive 2011/83/EU, govern pre-contract disclosure of information in the context of on-premises, off-premises and distance contracts as from 13 June 2014. But they do not apply to agreements of a 'credit nature'.[79] However, they do potentially apply to hire contracts. There seems to be a

70 Reg 7(2); a requirement repeated at CONC 2.7.3 R.
71 Reg 7(3); CONC 2.7.3 R.
72 CONC 2.7.4 R.
73 Reg 7(4); CONC 2.7.11 R.
74 For instance, as with a bank account.
75 CONC 2.7.9 R.
76 Reg 7(7).
77 SI 2004/1481.
78 SI 2013/3134.
79 Reg 6(b).

probably unintentional overlap between the 2004 and 2013 Regulations so that technically both need to be complied with.

53. The 2013 Regulations cover distance contracts, 'off-premises contracts' and 'on-premises contracts' concluded between traders and consumers, defined as previously discussed.[80]

54. An off-premises contract is one:

(a) that is concluded in the physical presence of the trader and customer in a place other than the business premises of the trader;
(b) where an offer is made by the consumer in the physical presence of the trader and consumer in premises not the business premises of the trader;
(c) that is concluded on the business premises of the trader or using a distance communication in circumstances where the consumer had immediately before the conclusion of the agreement been addressed (i.e. spoken to) in a place not the trader's business premises in the physical presence of the trader; or
(d) where a contract is entered during an excursion organised by the trader for the purpose of promoting the trader's services.

55. An on-premises contract is one that is neither a distance contract nor an off-premises contract. So distance contracts, off-premises contracts and on-premises contracts together comprise the entirety of consumer contracts of the relevant types.

Information requirements

56. Part 2 of the Regulations requires information to be presented or made available to the consumer before the various types of contract are entered into. Any information given is to be treated as a term of the contract.[81] The information required in respect of on-premises contracts and off-premises contracts is set out in Schedules 1 and 2 of the Regulations, respectively.

57. The information set out in Schedule 2 also has to be supplied in the case of a distance contract.[82] Further, a cancellation form must be provided if a right to cancel exists.[83]

Pre-contract explanations

58. As has been explained, the Consumer Credit (Disclosure of Information) Regulations 2004 and 2010, made under section 55 of the Consumer

80 Reg 4, 5.
81 Reg 9(3), 10(5), 13(6).
82 Reg 13.
83 Reg 13(1)(b).

Credit Act 1974, are not substantively amended by the recent reforms and continue to have effect. In addition to these Regulations, there are other provisions that, in limited circumstances, require disclosure of yet further information, notably the Financial Services (Distance Marketing) Regulations 2004[84] (distance marketing of certain types of credit) and the Consumer Contracts (Information, Cancellation and Additional Charges) Regulations 2013[85] (in relation to hire agreements).

59. However, section 55A of the Consumer Credit Act 1974 Act went further and placed an obligation on the lender pre-contract not only to *inform*, but also to *explain*. Section 55A has been repealed but the substantive requirements of that section are now replicated and supplemented at CONC 4.2.

60. These requirements do not apply where the amount of credit is either in excess of £60,260 or is secured on land[86] but it is of course good practice to comply with these requirements even in these circumstances.[87] The requirements can be satisfied either by the prospective lender or by a credit broker acting in relation to the transaction.[88] Before the lender considers itself relieved of the obligation to provide a pre-contract explanation, it must take reasonable steps to satisfy itself that the lender has provided the necessary explanation.[89]

61. In addition to the explanations that have to be provided, the prospective lender must advise the prospective borrower to give consideration to the information that will be provided and must point out to the borrower that the document containing the information may be taken away; further, the lender must provide the borrower with an opportunity to ask questions and advise the customer how to obtain further information[90] (which, if requested, must be provided without undue expense or delay).[91] It is an unfair practice and prohibited to encourage or incentivise the borrower to enter into an agreement quickly with a view to discouraging the borrower from giving proper consideration to the information.[92]

62. The matters that should be explained are:[93]

(a) features of the agreement that may make it unsuitable for the customer;
(b) how much the customer will have to pay periodically and, so far as it can be determined, the total amount payable;

84 SI 2004/2095.
85 SI 2013/3134.
86 CONC 4.2.1 R.
87 CONC 4.2.2 G.
88 CONC 4.2.5.(2)(5) R.
89 CONC 4.2.11 R.
90 CONC 4.2.5(1) R.
91 CONC 4.2.12 R.
92 CONC 4.8.2 R.
93 CONC 4.2.5(2) R.

(c) those features of the agreement that may operate adversely to the customer in a way that the customer may not be able to foresee;
(d) the principal consequences to the customer of failing to make the due payments, including the possibility of legal proceedings or repossession of the customer's home; and
(e) how the right to withdraw may be exercised and its consequences.

63. The lender or credit broker should continue to explain even if the prospective borrower should say that he or she does not *need* an explanation.[94] It is different, however, if the prospective customer should say he or she does not *want* an explanation, although the creditor or credit broker must not encourage a customer to waive his or her rights.[95]

64. These explanations can be given orally or in writing[96] save that if the features of the agreements or of the right to withdraw are communicated orally or in person, then the rest of the information must also be given orally.[97]

Copy of prospective agreement

65. As from 1 February 2011, a prospective borrower in respect of a regulated consumer credit agreement (not a hire agreement) has a right to have a copy of a prospective agreement or so much of the agreement as has been reduced into writing.[98] However, the lender does not have to supply a copy of the agreement if the lender does not intend to proceed with the agreement.[99] Nor does this apply if the agreement is secured on land, or under which an article is taken in pawn or where the amount of credit exceeds £60,260 or where the agreement is wholly or predominantly for business purposes.[100]

66. As to the purpose of the loan, the lender is entitled to rely on a declaration from the borrower unless the lender has reason to believe that the declaration is false.[101]

67. If the lender fails to comply with this requirement, then the lender is liable for breach of statutory duty.[102] But it is hard to imagine that any damage could ensue.

94 CONC 4.2.9 R.
95 CONC 4.2.10 R.
96 CONC 4.2.5(3) R.
97 CONC 4.2.5(4) R.
98 Section 55C; this remains in force.
99 Section 55C(2).
100 Section 55C(4).
101 Section 55C(5).
102 Section 55C(3).

Creditworthiness assessment

68. Prior to concluding a contract, the firm must assess the creditworthiness of a prospective borrower in accordance with CONC 5.[103] The assessment must take into account:[104]

(a) the prospect that payments due under a credit agreement may adversely affect the borrower's financial situation; and
(b) the ability of the prospective borrower to make payments throughout the duration of the agreement.

69. This requirement has no application to hire agreements[105] or to small agreements for restricted use credit, or to non-commercial agreements, or to agreements secured on land, or to pawn agreements, or to agreements allowing the borrower to overdraw on a current account.[106] A creditworthiness assessment is, however, needed in the case of an authorised business or non-business overdraft agreement or an agreement that would be an authorised non-business overdraft agreement if the credit was not repayable on demand or within three months.[107] But even in these excluded cases, it is still necessary for the lender to assess the potential of an agreement to impact on the customer's financial situation so that the exclusions are not of great significance.[108]

70. According to CONC 5.2.1(3) R, the assessment of creditworthiness must be based on sufficient information and two sources are identified, from the customer where appropriate, and from a credit reference agency where *necessary*. This implies that a lender sometimes must actively seek to obtain information from one or more credit reference agencies in order to perform this task. However, it is clear that insofar as the lender has access to other information, it may be taken into account, including from other lenders.

71. CONC says at 5.3.1 G: 'Subject to the relevant legal constraints, FCA encourages the sharing between lenders of accurate data about the performance of a customer's account and the settlement of outstanding debts, as the process of making the assessments in this chapter is assisted by lenders registering such data with credit reference agencies, in a timely manner.' In the past, lenders have been reluctant to share information, particularly in the high-cost short-term sector.

103 A requirement initially introduced in 2011 pursuant to section 55B Consumer Credit Act 1974.
104 CONC 5.2.1(2) R.
105 CONC 5.1.1 R.
106 CONC 5.2.1.
107 CONC 5.2.1(6).
108 CONC 5.2.2 R.

72. Guidance at CONC 5.2.3 demonstrates what factors will need to be taken into; these will of course include an analysis of existing financial commitments, the income position and credit history. The assessment may also look to the future in both a positive and negative way, both in relation to future income and future commitments.

73. A high level of scrutiny should be undertaken where a lender takes a second or subsequent charge secured on the borrower's home.[109]

74. The creditworthiness must involve more than the borrower's ability to make the repayments. The lender has to ensure that the repayments are *sustainable*[110] (i.e. can be made without undue difficulty).[111]

75. The creditworthiness assessments are important and a firm must lay down clear policies for undertaking them based on accurate and complete information.[112]

76. It is *not* enough to make lending policies dependent merely on the value of security.[113]

77. A creditworthiness assessment will need to be undertaken if, during the course of an agreement, the borrower wishes to increase the amount of credit made available to him or her, or his or her credit limit.[114]

109 CONC 5.2.4(4) G; note CONC 5.2 does not apply to an agreement secured on land.
110 CONC 5.3.1(2) G.
111 CONC 5.3.1(6) G.
112 CONC 5.3.2 R.
113 CONC 5.3.4 R.
114 CONC 6.2.1 R.

8 Requirements governing entry into agreements

1. The Act imposes requirements on the form and content of regulated agreements. It also requires that certain information be given to the borrower or hirer in advance of the agreement and that the borrower or hirer be supplied with copies of the agreement. This chapter is concerned with these requirements.

2. These formalities requirements are to be found in Part V[1] of the Act. These provisions will continue in force almost unamended after 1 April 2014. Before these requirements are considered, it is important to realise that there are certain types of agreements that are, for the most part, not subject to these provisions as set out in section 74, Consumer Credit Act 1974.

Agreements outside the formalities requirements

3. The formalities requirements do not apply to non-commercial agreements[2] (i.e. where the lender does not enter the agreement in the course of a business carried on by it).[3] From the lender's point of view, the credit or hire agreement is likely to be an isolated transaction and the lender is unlikely to be aware of any formalities required, nor be in a position readily to comply with them in any event. For these reasons, the legislation has completely exempted such transactions from the requirements relating to formalities, the supply of copies or the rights of cancellation.

4. There is also exemption for a debtor-creditor agreement to overdraw on a current account where no particular purpose for the overdraft is proscribed.[4] Such agreements are by their very nature often made ad hoc. However, both authorised business and non-business overdraft agreements are subject to significant regulation in relation to the form of the agreement, the supply of information and copies.[5] This regulation is even more

1 Section 55 to 74, Consumer Credit Act 1974.
2 Section 74(1)(a).
3 Defined at section 189(1).
4 Section 74(1)(b).
5 Section 74(1B) , (1C).

extensive where the overdraft agreement is a non-business agreement and the credit is not repayable for three months or more or on demand.[6]

5. There is also important exemption for 'small' debtor-creditor-supplier agreements for restricted use credit.[7] This exemption applies to shopkeepers that give credit to customers for the supply of items (e.g. the newspaper delivery where the amount of credit involved is less than £50).[8] Hire purchase and conditional sale agreements are not included within 'small' agreements and will always have to comply whatever the amount of the credit advanced (although the number of transactions of this type involving credit of this small amount must be tiny).[9]

6. Moreover, by virtue of section 74(4), if any term of such a 'small' agreement is expressed in writing, the Agreements Regulations 'apply' to that term. The gist of section 74(4) would seem to be that in a case where written information is provided in relation to a term of the agreement, the presentation and detail of the information must be in compliance with the Regulations. For example, if a lender sets out written repayment terms, he or she must do so in accordance with paragraphs 12 to 14 of Schedule 1 to the Agreements Regulations (i.e. the lender must give full details of the amounts and timing of repayments). If this requirement is too burdensome, a lender or owner can apply for exemption from the requirement to comply under section 60(3).

7. One other type of agreement is given *discretionary* exemption; in each case, the final decision now rests with the FCA. The exemption is for loans provided in connection with the death of a person.[10] The types of loans connected with the death of a person capable of exemption are those specified in the Consumer Credit (Payments Arising on Death) Regulations 1983.[11] The loans must relate to specific purposes, namely to finance amounts owing in respect of inheritance tax or probate fees payable to the court. It is considered that these loans have to be provided speedily and without complication. It is thought that the imposition of formalities might cause delay, which would prejudice borrowers.

8. It is not enough for a loan to fall into this category for it to gain exemption. The FCA must still give its sanction and will only do so if it determines that this will not be contrary to the interests of borrowers.[12]

6 Section 74(1D).
7 Section 74(1)(d).
8 If the type of transaction is one to which the Cancellation of Contracts in a Consumer's Home Regulations 2008 apply (i.e. a off-premises contract), the limit is £35; section 74(2A). These Regulations have now been replaced by the Information, Cancellation and Additional Charges Regulations 2013.
9 Section 17(1).
10 Section 74(1)(c).
11 SI 1983/1554.
12 Section 74(3).

Waiver

9. On top of these specific exemptions, there exists a general power in the FCA to waive any particular requirements in the Agreements Regulations (and to impose conditions) where compliance is 'impracticable'.[13] However, as from 1 February 2011, this right to be granted a waiver is restricted to a limited range of agreements, namely credit agreements secured on land, agreements where articles are taken in pawn, agreements where the credit exceeds £60,260 and agreements predominantly for business purposes.[14] This is because a waiver in other circumstances is not consistent with the requirements of the EU Directive.

Operation of the Agreements Regulations

10. There are two sets of Agreements Regulations that govern the form and content of regulated agreements, namely the Agreements Regulations 1983[15] and the Agreements Regulations 2010.[16] The Agreements Regulations 2010 were brought in to implement EU Directive 2008/48 and apply to all regulated credit agreements other than excluded agreements after 1 February 2011. The 2010 Agreement Regulations overall are less prescriptive than the 1983 Regulations and so less complicated for the lender to comply with. The 1983 Regulations apply only when the 2010 Regulations do not.[17] The 1983 Regulations also continue to apply to all regulated consumer hire agreements.

11. The 2010 Regulations do not apply to credit agreements in which the credit is secured on land or exceeds £60,260 or entered into for predominantly business purposes.[18] Nevertheless, in relation to these situations, the 2010 Regulations will apply if the lender has, prior to the agreement, voluntarily disclosed the information required by the Disclosure of Information Regulations 2010.[19] (The Disclosure of Information Regulations 2010 do not apply in the case of agreements secured on land or when the credit exceeds £60,260, or is intended predominantly for business purposes.)

12. The 2010 Agreements Regulations also apply to a limited range of agreements in respect of which section 58[20] applies where the borrower has

13 Section 60(3).
14 Section 60(5).
15 SI 1983/1553 as amended.
16 SI 2010/1014.
17 Reg 8(1A) Agreements Regulations 1983.
18 Art 60(c)(5), (6) of the RAO applies to a declaration made that the loan is for a business purpose.
19 Reg 2(2), 2(3) of the 2010 Regulations.
20 The provision in the Consumer Credit Act specifying the formalities required for entry into a regulated credit agreement secured on land.

been given for signature a copy of the unexecuted agreement compliant with the 2010 Regulations.[21]

13. Assuming that the Regulations apply, how do they operate?

14. In respect of both sets of Regulations, there is a statutory requirement that the document and its terms must be readily legible at the time that it is presented to the borrower for signature.[22] In the case of a borrower that is a partnership or unincorporated association, the borrower may sign by an agent.[23] The inference must be that when the borrower is an individual, the borrower should sign personally and not by agent.

15. Furthermore, in respect of both sets of Agreements Regulations, it is a requirement that the document must embody 'all terms in the agreement other than implied terms'.[24] If there is a failure to incorporate all express terms into the agreement, the agreement will be improperly executed and will be unenforceable except by application to the court for an enforcement order. Previous decisions under section 6 of the Moneylenders Act 1927 give some guidance on the scope of the requirement that the document must embody all the terms of the agreement. Thus, it was a breach of a similar requirement in the 1927 Act for a lender to fail to stipulate the purpose for which monies lent must be used in the case of a restricted use agreement.[25] But it was not a breach to omit purely administrative arrangements relating to the mechanics of payment of the monies loaned.[26]

16. The provisions of section 61(1)(b) may cause difficulty in hire purchase, conditional sale and credit sale agreements. By section 56, the dealer in these situations acts as deemed agent of the lender, at least in relation to representations made in relation to the goods to be supplied. Such representations may, in some circumstances, have the status of contractual warranties[27] and it would seem therefore that any contractual warranties given by the dealer should be expressly incorporated into the written agreement in order to comply with the requirement that the written agreement should contain all the express terms.

17. It might be that the court could interpret section 61(1)(b) to restrict the requirement to state only terms relating to the provision of credit and not to the provision of goods; this distinction is drawn in the deemed agency provisions of section 56. It is unlikely, however, that this is a permissible construction of the subsection since the supply of goods in a hire purchase or conditional sale transaction is an integral part of the credit agreement.

21 Reg 2(1A) Agreements Regulations 2010.
22 Section 61(1)(c).
23 Section 61(4).
24 Section 61(1)(b).
25 *Egan v Langham Investments Ltd.* [1938] I K.B. 667.
26 *Hanyet Securities Ltd v Mallett* [1968] 1 W.L.R. 1265.
27 See *Oscar Chess Ltd v Williams* [1957] I W.L.R. 370.

However, a more convincing way around the problem would be to treat a representation as constituting a *collateral warranty* and therefore outside the ambit of section 61(1)(b).

18. There is also a statutory requirement that certain terms, considered to be of particular importance to be specified in regulations, must be present in the agreement at the time of signature.[28] This was of more importance formerly than now because it was previously the case that non-compliance with this requirement was fatal to the enforcement of the agreement.[29] The agreement became irredeemably unenforceable. This absolute bar to enforcement is fortunately no longer the law in respect of agreements entered into after 6 April 2007.[30]

The Agreements Regulations 2010

19. The documents embodying the regulated consumer credit agreement must contain the required information,[31] which will vary depending on the type of agreement, and that information must be presented in a clear and precise manner.[32] In this context, 'clear' includes a requirement that the wording is easily legible.[33]

20. By way of example, the agreement must contain details of the length of the agreement or if there is no fixed term, it must be said to be open-ended and any minimum term must be stated.[34] Likewise, the APR must be stated and any assumptions used in its calculation.[35] Schedule 4 to the Regulations contains provisions relating to the calculation and disclosure of the APR.

21. The document must also contain prescribed statements of the protection and remedies available to the borrower, again as appropriate to the particular agreement type.[36] So, for example, in the case of a pawn agreement, the agreement must contain a form making reference to the 'notice to debtor'.[37] A cancellable agreement will contain a form referring to cancellation rights. These forms must be reproduced without alteration[38] and must be completed in accordance with any note that may require

28 Section 61(1)(a).
29 Section 127(3); repealed by the Consumer Credit Act 2006.
30 The commencement date of the Consumer Credit Act 2006.
31 Reg 3(1).
32 Reg 3(2).
33 Reg 3(3).
34 Schedule 1, paragraphs 3, 4.
35 Schedule 1, paragraph 13.
36 Reg 2(4).
37 Schedule 2, para 6.
38 Reg 7(1).

wording to be added or deleted.[39] Words in capital letters in the forms contained in the Schedules to the Regulations must be given particular prominence in the agreement.[40]

22. Moreover, in a case where a borrower has provided security, then details of that security must be given.[41]

23. There is also special provision made for loan agreements that provide or contain the option for insurance to cover repayments in the event of accident, sickness and unemployment where the insurance premium will be financed out of the loan (as will be almost invariably the case).[42] The agreement need only have the heading and statements of protection applicable to the principal loan agreement.[43]

24. The agreement must of course be signed by both lender and borrower. A space must be left for the signature of the borrower and the date the borrower signs.[44] The Regulations spell out what terms have to be inserted into the agreement prior to signature by the borrower, the 'prescribed terms' for the purpose of section 61(1)(a). The APR is not one of these terms, but the amount of credit to be provided is.

25. The Regulations also provide for the formalities to be complied with in respect of a modifying agreement.[45]

The 1983 Agreements Regulations

26. These Regulations, not surprisingly, follow the same structure as the 2010 Regulations but with more detail. Thus, the order in which information must be provided within the agreement is laid down.[46]

27. Financial information must be shown together as a whole in the agreement.[47] This is not something specified in the 2010 Agreements Regulations. The APR can be referred to as the APR or the 'annual percentage rate' or the 'annual percentage rate of the total charge for credit'.[48] The APR is sufficiently stated if calculated in accordance within the assumptions required and tolerances permitted by Schedule 7.

28. Just as with the 2010 Agreements Regulations, every agreement has to reproduce the statutory notices of protection and remedies that are set out in the Schedules to the Agreements Regulations. These statutory notices explain the rights and duties of the borrower or hirer in various types

39 Reg 7(2).
40 Reg 7(4).
41 Reg 3(5).
42 Reg 3(6).
43 Reg 3(7).
44 Reg 4(3).
45 Reg 8.
46 Reg 2(4).
47 Reg 2(4).
48 Reg 2(6).

of situation. Regulation 5 sets out how the forms are to be reproduced, applying the same principles as with the 2010 Regulations.

29. Every agreement concluded under the 1983 Agreements Regulations must contain a signature box.[49] This is not a requirement in the 2010 Agreements Regulations. This must be in the statutory form prescribed by Schedule 5 and contain the required wording. The borrower must sign inside and the lender outside the signature box.[50] There are also requirements about the insertion of dates on the document.[51]

30. In three sets of circumstances (where an article is taken in pawn, where an agreement is cancellable and where an agreement is to be secured on land), certain statutory forms must be reproduced next to the signature box. For example, a form setting out a general statement of the borrower's rights of cancellation must be placed next to the signature box in the case of a cancellable agreement.[52] Where more than one description of goods, services or land are comprised in a restricted use debtor-creditor-supplier agreement (such as hire purchase or connected landing transactions), the descriptions of each may be contained in a Schedule to the agreement referred to alongside the financial information.[53]

31. Schedule 6 contains details of what terms must be completed prior to signature by the borrower or hirer, 'the prescribed terms' required by section 61(1)(a). This information includes information as to any initial payment required from the borrower and a statement of the amount of credit. Moreover, just as with the 2010 Agreements Regulations, a statement of the APR is not a prescribed term, but the rate of interest is.

Failure to comply with the Agreements Regulations

32. Failure to comply with either of the Agreements Regulations or the signature requirements renders the agreement improperly executed.[54] It can then only be enforced by application to the court for an enforcement order.[55]

Duty to supply a copy of the executed agreement

33. With the introduction of section 61A to the Act, there is a new requirement to provide a copy of a concluded credit agreement that largely supersedes the previous regime in the case of regulated consumer *credit* agreements (the provision has no application to hire agreements) with effect from 10 February 2011. The core obligation is that the lender must give

49 Reg 2(7).
50 Reg 6(3).
51 Reg 6(3).
52 Reg 2(7).
53 Reg 2(5).
54 Section 61(1).
55 Section 65(1).

to the debtor 'a copy of the executed agreement and any other document referred to in it'.[56]

34. The nature of the copy must comply with the Consumer Credit (Cancellation Notices and Copies of Documents) Regulations 1983[57] by virtue of regulation 3(1) thereof. The requirements of these Regulations are discussed in more detail later. Every copy provided must be a 'true copy'. The obligation to supply copies of all documents referred to in the agreement is modified by regulation 11 of the 1983 Regulations.

35. The new provision does not apply to 'excluded' agreements entered into after this date in respect of which the original regime (at sections 62 and 63) continues to apply.

36. A cancellable agreement is one category of excluded agreement.[58] Other excluded agreements are those where the borrowing is secured on land, where the amount of credit exceeds £60,260 or where the loan is made predominantly for business purposes.[59] However, section 61A applies even in respect of these last types of excluded agreements where the lender has complied or purported to comply with the 2010 Disclosure of Information Regulations by providing the information required by those Regulations.

37. Section 61A does not apply if, prior to the conclusion of the regulated consumer credit agreement, the lender had already supplied a copy of the unexecuted agreement (perhaps pursuant to a request made under section 55C) and if, thereafter, the lender informs the borrower in writing that the agreement has been concluded in the same terms as the unexecuted agreement, giving the borrower the right to seek a copy of the executed agreement within the 14-day withdrawal period specified by section 66A.[60] If such a request is made, then the lender must supply the borrower with a copy of the executed agreement without delay.[61]

38. If these requirements are not met, then the agreement is not properly executed and can only be enforced with an order of the court.[62]

Authorised business and non-business overdrafts

39. There are particular rules applicable to these types of agreements set out at section 61B; these are further discussed hereafter under the heading of overdraft agreements.

56 Section 61A(1).
57 SI 1983/1557.
58 Section 61A(6)(a).
59 Section 61A(6)(b).
60 Section 61A(3).
61 Section 61A(4).
62 Section 61A(5).

40. An authorised business overdraft is one where the overdraft is agreed in advance to be drawn on a current account and is not entered into wholly or predominantly for the purposes of the borrower's business, and in addition the overdraft must be repayable on demand or within three months.[63] An authorised non-business overdraft has the same attributes except that it must be entered into other than for the purposes of business.[64] The lender may place reliance on a declaration from the borrower in order to ascertain the purpose of the overdraft save where the lender has reason to believe that the declaration is untrue.[65]

41. Section 61A does not apply to these types of agreements.[66]

42. With these agreements, section 61B provides that a document containing the terms of the agreement (i.e. not the executed agreement) must be given before or at the same time as the agreement. However, there are exceptions allowing the copy of the relevant terms to be provided subsequent to the conclusion of the agreement.

43. Thus, if the comprehensive information set out at regulation 10(3) of the Consumer Credit (Disclosure of Information) Regulations 2010 has been provided prior to entry into the agreement, then the copy agreement may be provided afterwards.[67]

44. However, if the more limited information provided in advance of agreement is confined to that required in respect of a telephone agreement or an overdraft agreed in an emergency,[68] being the core financial information other than the rate of interest, then the document containing the terms of the agreement must be provided *immediately* following the conclusion of the agreement.[69]

45. If an agreement is made using a means of distance communication other than by telephone other than at the borrower's request, then the copy agreement must be given immediately after the agreement is made.[70]

46. If there is a contravention of this provision, the agreement can be enforced on an order of the court only, and a retaking of goods or land to which the agreement relates is enforcement for these purposes.[71] The section does not specifically provide that the agreement is not properly executed if section 61B is not complied with, but it has the same effect.

63 Section 189(1).
64 Section 189(1).
65 Section 189(2A).
66 Section 74(1B), (1C).
67 Section 61B(2)(a).
68 Disclosure of Information Regulations 2010, reg 10(5), 10(8).
69 Section 61B(2)(b).
70 Section 61B(2)(c).
71 Section 61B(2).

The supply of copies: the original requirements

47. The 1974 Act as originally enacted provided that every borrower or hirer must be furnished with at least one copy of the agreement and usually two. This still has application in cases where the requirement to provide a copy credit agreement under section 61A does not apply. In other words, it applies to the category of credit agreements known as 'excluded agreements' for the purposes of section 61A,[72] namely cancellable agreements, agreements secured on land, where the credit exceeds £60,260 and agreements predominantly for business purposes.[73] The original provisions at sections 62 and 63 also apply to all regulated hire agreements.

48. The number and timing of the copies depends on whether:

(a) the agreement is presented personally to the borrower or hirer for his signature; or
(b) the signature of the borrower or hirer executes the agreement.

49. There are four possible situations that the Act regulates:

(a) Where the form of agreement is presented personally to the borrower or hirer and the borrower or hirer's signature executes the agreement. It is submitted that the unexecuted agreement is 'presented personally for his signature' within section 62(1) even if the borrower or hirer, having been presented personally with the agreement, takes it away to sign.
(b) Where the form of agreement is presented personally to the borrower or hirer but the borrower or hirer's signature does not execute the agreement. In this case, the agreement will be executed when the lender or owner later signs the agreement.
(c) Where the form of agreement is sent to the borrower or hirer and his signature executes the agreement.
(d) Where the form of agreement is sent to the borrower or hirer for him to sign but his signature does not execute the agreement, the form being returned to the lender or owner for his signature.

50. The copies that have to be supplied in respect of each of these situations are as follows:

(a) The borrower or hirer must there and then be handed a copy of the fully executed agreement.[74]

72 Section 62(1), 63(1).
73 Section 61A(6).
74 Section 63(1).

(b) A copy of the unexecuted agreement must be given to the borrower or hirer, there and then when he or she signs it. A further copy of the executed agreement must be given to the borrower or hirer within seven days after the conclusion of the agreement.[75] If the agreement is cancellable, the lender or owner has no choice but to send the copy of the executed agreement by post or other agreed form of electronic communication.[76]

(c) A copy of the unexecuted agreement must be sent with the form of agreement that the borrower or hirer has to sign. This is the only copy that needs to be supplied.[77]

(d) A copy of the unexecuted agreement must be sent with the form of agreement that the borrower or hirer has to sign. If the lender or owner subsequently signs the agreement, a further copy of the executed agreement must be given to the borrower or hirer within seven days of execution.[78] If the agreement is cancellable, the lender or owner has to send the second copy of the executed agreement by post or agreed form of electronic communication.[79]

51. However, in the case of a credit token agreement, the seven-day time limit does not apply if the copy is supplied with or before the credit token.[80]

52. In assessing the seven-day time limit applicable, the date that the lender or owner signs the agreement is ignored.[81] Furthermore, as was explained in relation to service under the Act, it is the time that the borrower or hirer *receives* the copy of the executed agreement, not the time that it is put in the post, that marks the end of the seven-day period.

The form of copies to be supplied

53. Lenders and owners have to provide copies of agreements, sometimes one, sometime two. The Consumer Credit (Cancellation Notices and Copies of Documents) Regulations 1983[82] set out the required nature of these copies. Every copy must be readily legible and its lettering must be in a colour readily distinguishable from the rest of the paper.[83]

54. The wording of every form prescribed by the Regulations has to be reproduced in all the copies thereof without any alteration or addition.[84]

75 Section 62(1), 63(2).
76 Section 63(3).
77 Section 62(2), 63(2)(b).
78 Section 62(2), 63(2).
79 Section 63(3).
80 Section 63(4).
81 *Goldsmiths Co. v West Metropolitan Railway Co.* [1904] 1 K.B. 1.
82 SI 1983/1557; made under section 180 of the Act.
83 Reg 2.
84 Reg 2(2).

Furthermore, the form must be completed in accordance with any footnote.[85] Whether this latter requirement had been satisfied was in contention in the case of *Goshawk Dedicated (No 2) Ltd v Bank of Scotland*.[86]

55. Virtually every cancellable agreement will involve three different types of cancellation notice to be inserted in the agreement and in the copies given:

(a) the form included in the original agreement signed by the borrower or hirer;
(b) the form included in the first copy given to the borrower or hirer;
(c) the form included in the second copy, including with it the cancellation form.

56. Each form is progressively more explicit in describing the cancellation rights of the borrower or hirer. Only the second copy of the agreement contains a cancellation form. The form (a) is set out in the Schedules to the Agreements Regulations, the remainder, (b) and (c), are to be found in the Schedule to the Cancellation Notices and Copies of Documents Regulations.

57. A difficulty arises when cancellation notices are inserted into agreements that are not cancellable in the sense that the circumstances in which the agreement came to be concluded are not within section 67. If the circumstances in which an agreement comes to be entered into may vary, the lender or owner may incorporate a cancellation notice into an agreement for safety's sake. The presence of 'unnecessary' cancellation forms in the agreement and in the copies of it provided to the borrower or hirer does not mean that the agreement is improperly executed: this is the effect of the Consumer Credit (Cancellation Notices and Copies of Documents) (Amendment) Regulations 1984,[87] which added regulation 5(4) to the Cancellation Notices and Copies of Documents Regulations 1983. In fact, if copies of the agreement given to the borrower or hirer contain cancellation notices, it is likely that a court will construe the agreement as conferring upon the borrower or hirer a *contractual* right to cancel equivalent to the statutory right of cancellation. Such cancellation notices should be in the form of and follow the wording laid down in the Cancellation Notices and Copies of Documents Regulations.[88] Where two copies of the agreement have to be provided to the borrower or hirer, the cancellation notices in each should differ in the usual way and the second copy should also contain a cancellation form. Where the borrower or hirer's signature executes the

85 Reg 2(2)(b).

86 2006 2 All 2010. A note on the form in question said that an insurance policy would not be affected by cancellation. This was held to be an accurate statement for the purposes of the form.

87 SI 1984/1108.

88 Amendment Regulation reg 2(b).

agreement, only *one* copy of the agreement need be given. With a truly cancellable agreement, the lender or owner would then have to send a separate cancellation notice and cancellation form by post in accordance with section 64(1)(b) and following the wording prescribed by the Regulations. Although the Amendment Regulations do not expressly impose a further requirement that a separate cancellation notice and cancellation form has to be sent thereafter (i.e. there is nothing applying the requirements of section 64(1)(b) to agreements that contain cancellation notices but are not in fact cancellable within section 67), this is likely to be a *contractual* obligation on the lender or owner.

58. Every copy of the agreement must be a 'true copy' of the agreement.[89] There are limited exceptions to this rule contained in regulation 3(2). These are:

(a) As has been noted, the cancellation notices will vary.
(b) Information inserted into the form of agreement solely for the benefit of the lender or owner and not prescribed by the Agreements Regulations may be omitted.
(c) A copy of an unexecuted agreement need not contain the name and address of the borrower or hirer.
(d) The signature box, signatures of borrower and lender and dates of signatures may be omitted. There is just one situation where the date of the borrower's signature has to be reproduced. This arises in the rather rare case where the agreement is cancellable and the period of cancellation commences with the date of the borrower's *signature*. With such cases, the period of cancellation is differently calculated and is 14 days, not the usual five days. With such cases, it is obviously crucial that the borrower or hirer be reminded of the date that he or she signed. Accordingly, this date has to be reproduced.

59. The Act (in sections 61A, 62 and 63) refers not only to the lender's obligation to supply copies of the *agreement*, but also to supply copies of *documents referred to* in the agreement. If this obligation went unmodified, it might necessitate the supply of a large volume of documentation every time an agreement was entered into. At the very least, a copy of the Consumer Credit Act would have to be supplied with every agreement. Fortunately, regulation 11, in accordance with section 180(3), restricts the classes of documents the lender has to supply.

60. Regulation 11 curtails the possibility of a vast volume of paper being supplied with every agreement. Statutes are excluded, as are documents of

89 Reg 3(1).

title. Land Registry certificates do not therefore have to be supplied with copies of a registered land mortgage. Copies of documents furnished by the borrower or hirer him or herself and documents evidencing rights over goods and land are excluded. Thus, there will be no need to append insurance policies and maintenance contracts.

Consequences

61. If there is a breach of the above requirements, whether in relation to the supply of copies or the form of the copies, then the agreement is not properly executed and can only be enforced with permission of the court.[90]

Formalities involving agreements secured on land

62. Certain very special procedures apply to certain types of agreement that are secured on land laid down in sections 58 and 61. These apply to both regulated hire and credit agreements secured on land. 'Secured on land' almost inevitably means secured by way of mortgage. It is irrelevant whether the security is provided by the borrower or hirer personally, provided that it is provided at his or her request.

63. The point to note at the outset is that section 58 agreements are not cancellable.[91] This was for the convenience of the Land Registry, which feared the additional amount of work if mortgages were registered in respect of transactions that were subsequently cancelled. However, sections 58 and 61(2) substitute a consideration period for a cancellation period,[92] designed to give the borrower or hirer a similar period of reflection to that that he or she would otherwise have during the cancellation period. It is not the case, however, that the special procedures apply only where the agreement would in other circumstances be cancellable; they apply whenever an agreement is concluded coming within the ambit of section 58.

64. Perhaps the most important category of agreements to which section 58 applies is agreements secured on land where the borrowing constitutes a second charge over the property. It will also apply to the creation of charges over property previously held unencumbered.

To what agreements the procedures apply

65. It applies only to regulated credit agreements secured on land but subject to some important exclusions.

90 Section 63(5).

91 Such agreements are not cancellable by virtue of section 67(1)(a) and there is no right of withdrawal under section 66A by virtue of section 66A(14).

92 Section 61(3).

66. Thus, it does not apply to agreements that are exempt agreements for the purposes of the RAO.[93] These categories include:

(a) the important categories of regulated mortgage contracts and home purchase plans that are classified as exempt agreements;[94]
(b) agreements secured on land for business purposes when the amount of credit exceeds £25,000;[95]
(c) agreements in which the loan is to be used for the purchase of land for non-residential purposes (in that less than 40 per cent will be used as a dwelling by the borrower or relative);[96]
(d) agreements secured on land with certain specified lenders such as housing associations and local authorities;[97] and
(e) agreements for the purchase of land limited to four repayments.

67. Nor does the regime imposed by section 58 apply to agreements of the type exempted by section 58(2). This excludes restricted use credit agreements for the purchase of land and an agreement of a bridging loan in connection with the purchase of this or other mortgaged land. (Some of the categories of exempt agreement are also excluded by section 58(2).)

68. Finally, section 58 does not apply to agreements of a type rendered exempt from the formalities requirements contained in Part V of the Consumer Credit Act 1974 by virtue of section 74. This relates to non-commercial agreements[98] and overdraft agreements.[99] The exemption of both is significant; it is not uncommon for loans between friends or family members, likely to be non-commercial agreements, to be secured on land in which case the requirements imposed by section 58 of the Act will not apply.

Pre-contract requirements

69. These are governed by the FCA Handbook. CONC 15 contains requirements specifically directed at loans secured by second charges that will be subject to section 58.

70. Any promotion of the lending must comply with CONC 3, as to which see earlier.[100]

93 See the definition of regulated credit agreement in article 60B(3) RAO.
94 Article 60C(2) RAO.
95 Article 60C(3) RAO.
96 Article 60D RAO.
97 Article 60E RAO.
98 Section 74(1)(a).
99 Section 74(1)(b); this is confined to borrow-lender agreements on a current account. Most overdrafts are of this nature.
100 CONC 15.1.3 R.

71. Neither the Consumer Credit (Disclosure of Information) Regulations 2004 nor the 2010 Regulations apply to agreements within section 58.[101] Nevertheless, it is incumbent upon the lender, prior to the contract, to disclose the key contract terms and conditions of the prospective agreement, as well as any features that pose a particular risk for the customer.[102] The lender must also inform the customer of certain specific matters such as the consequences of missing payments and the risk of default,[103] the circumstances in which interest rates may change, the latter information being given orally.[104] The nature of the fees to be charged by the firm must be set out, including default fees.[105]

72. The firm should encourage the customer to read the contract and other information; the firm should also take reasonable steps to ensure that the customer has fully appreciated the risks involved in the transaction.[106] Indeed, the firm should encourage the customer to take independent advice before entering into the agreement.[107]

73. The firm will have a duty in this context to give the customer the pre-contractual explanation of the agreement required by CONC 4.2 and to carry out a creditworthiness assessment in accordance with CONC 5.2.2 R.[108] If it appears that it is not in the best interests of the customer to enter into an agreement secured on land, this should be explained.[109] The firm should encourage the customer to consider whether the agreement can be afforded including in the event of a change of circumstances.[110]

The formalities of entering into an agreement

74. The essence of the requirements is that in addition to the normal requirements applicable to regulated agreements, the borrower must be provided with an additional advance copy of the unexecuted agreement, which must be sent to the borrower or hirer prior to the unexecuted agreement being sent, and the borrower or hirer is protected from communication with the lender or owner during a period following receipt of this copy, known as the 'consideration period'. The consideration period is intended to be a period of reflection and, if the prospective borrower so decides, withdrawal.

101 Reg 2.1 of the 2004 Regulation; Reg 2(2) of the 2010 Regulations.
102 CONC 15.1.5(1), (2) R.
103 CONC 15.1.5(3) R.
104 CONC 15.1.5(6) R.
105 CONC 15.1.11 R.
106 CONC 15.1.8(2) R.
107 CONC 15.1.8(3) R.
108 CONC 15.1.9 G.
109 CONC 15.1.10(2) G.
110 CONC 15.1.10(3) G.

75. The statutory procedure must be carefully followed by the lender or owner; if the lender or owner fails to follow the procedure, the agreement is not properly executed and can only be enforced upon an application to the court for an enforcement order.[111]

76. Once the lender has been through the required pre-contractual steps, the lender must give a potential borrower or hirer an advance copy of the agreement he or she is to be asked to sign.[112] The normal rules of service apply as specified in section 176, discussed later.

77. The copy must be in the form required by the Agreements Regulations 1983,[113] not the Agreements Regulations 2010. The total charge for credit shall be calculated in accordance with the rules applicable to agreements secured on land set out at FCA Handbook CONC Appendix 1.1.1 R made under Article 60M of the RAO.[114]

78. The copy given to the prospective borrower must follow the requirements of regulation 4 of the Consumer Credit (Cancellation Notices and Copies of Documents) Regulations 1983.[115] The heading must refer to section 58 of the Act. The advance copy must contain a detailed statutory notice setting out the rights of withdrawal.[116] Rather surprisingly, a withdrawal form is not included for the borrower or hirer to fill in and send off.

79. With the agreement for execution must be sent a copy of the mortgage document. Fortunately, documents of title, copies of Land Registry Certificates and copies of local searches will not have to be supplied with every copy of every credit or hire agreement as the need to supply these is excluded by regulation 11 of the Cancellation Notices and Copies Regulations 1983. It will, however, be necessary to supply a copy of the mortgage deed as security instruments do not fall within the exempting provisions of regulation 11.

80. There then follows the period of reflection known as the 'consideration period'.

81. The lender or owner must not communicate in any way with the borrower or hirer during this period.[117] The 'consideration period' runs from the time that the advance copy was given to the borrower or hirer until a time seven days after the agreement sent to the borrower or hirer to sign was received by him. If the borrower or hirer, however, specifically requests information from the lender or owner, this can of course be provided without infringing the requirements of sections 58 and 61.

111 Section 61(2).

112 Section 58(1).

113 Reg 8(1A) 1983 Regulations.

114 These follow the Total Charge for Credit Regulations 1980.

115 SI 1983/1557.

116 Form No 2, Part I, Schedule. Cancellation and Copies of Documents Regulations 1983.

117 Section 61(2)(c).

82. At least seven days must then elapse before he or she is sent the unexecuted agreement for his signature, which must be sent by 'an appropriate method'.[118] defined in section 189(1) as sending by post, or transmitting by electronic communication provided that the preconditions in section 176A are satisfied. The seven days is measured from the time that the potential borrower receives the advance copy of the unexecuted agreement that he or she is to sign (see my remarks on service in this chapter).

83. The lender may or may not have already signed the unexecuted agreement. If the lender has already signed, then the agreement will be concluded once the prospective borrower has signed the document and returned it.[119] If the lender has not already signed the document at the time it is sent to the prospective borrower, then the agreement will only be concluded once the document has been returned by the prospective borrower and later signed by the lender.

84. The form of the unexecuted agreement must normally comply with the Agreements Regulations 1983. The only instance when the Agreements Regulations 2010 apply to an agreement subject to section 58 is if the lender has given the prospective borrower an advance copy of an unexecuted agreement purporting to comply with the 2010 Regulations.[120] The withdrawal notice set out in the advance copy agreement is not repeated in the form of agreement sent to the borrower or hirer to sign since the borrower or hirer will no longer be able to withdraw once he or she signs in any event. The agreement must, however, contain a statement in the prescribed form informing the prospective borrower that he or she ought to have received a copy of the agreement at least seven days earlier and that the agreement will not be enforceable except by order of the court if he or she was not supplied with one.[121]

85. A copy of the agreement for the borrower must be included along with the document for execution,[122] complying with the Cancellation Notices and Copies of Documents Regulations. The notice advising the prospective borrower of the right to withdraw will now be excluded. However, there is no need to include a further copy of the mortgage document.[123]

86. The lender or owner can make contact with the prospective borrower only once the form of agreement has been signed by the borrower or hirer and it has been returned back to the lender owner. The purpose of this

118 Section 61(2)(b).

119 The agreement will be subject to the formalities requirements contained in section 2(1) Law of Property (Miscellaneous Provisions) Act 1989.

120 Reg 2(1A) Agreements Regulations 2010.

121 Form 1, Part I, Schedule 2, Agreements Regulations 1983.

122 In accordance with section 62(2), the requirements to serve a copy under section 61A do not apply.

123 Reg 11(h) Cancellation and Copies of Documents Regulations 1983.

procedure is to enable the borrower or hirer to think carefully about the wisdom of the agreement undisturbed by pressures from the lender or owner and to allow the borrower or hirer every opportunity to withdraw if he or she so wishes.

87. If the lender or owner signs after the borrower or hirer, which is perhaps more usual, not only will a copy have to have been sent at the time that the unexecuted agreement is sent for the borrower or hirer to sign, but a further copy must be given within seven days after execution by the lender or owner.[124] In this latter circumstance, the borrower or hirer will have to be supplied with no less than three copies (one under section 58, one under section 62(2) and one under section 63(2)). This third copy is not required if the copy sent by the lender to the borrower's signature has already been signed by the lender.[125]

Following the agreement

88. Interest rates can only be increased to recover genuine increases in costs that have an effect on the credit provided.[126] The firm must allow early repayment, including repayment of capital.[127] Charges for early repayment must be reasonable to reflect the firm's costs.[128] If the security has to be sold, and there is still a shortfall, the borrower should be notified of the shortfall as soon as possible.[129]

Modifying agreements and variation

89. Section 82 of the Consumer Credit Act 1974 is headed 'Variation of agreements' but this does not fully describe the ambit of the section. The section deals with two different concepts, variations and modifying agreements. A variation, as that term is used in this context and contrary to the normal meaning, involves a unilateral change to the manner of operation of the contract; a modifying agreement involves the consensual variation to the terms of a contract on the other.

Variation

90. Generally in the law of contract, a variation to a contract is a consensual alteration to the terms of that contract. Moreover, both sides must give

124 Section 63(2).
125 Section 63(2)(b).
126 CONC 15.1.12(2) R.
127 CONC 15.1.13(3) R.
128 CONC 15.1.13(1) R.
129 CONC 15.1.15 R.

consideration in order for a contractual variation to be binding, albeit that the variation is often capable of generating its own consideration. An example of such a contractual variation might be an agreement to extend the term of a loan in consideration for an alteration to other credit terms. Sometimes, under the general law of contract, a variation to a contract can have the effect of rescinding the earlier contract and its replacement by a new one; this will occur *if* the variation goes to the root of the contract,[130] although it is often a difficult question whether any particular variation has this effect.

91. But the Consumer Credit Act does not use the standard contractual terminology. An agreement varying or supplementing the terms of a regulated consumer credit or consumer hire agreement is known as a 'modifying agreement'.[131] Moreover, under the Act, the effect of such a contractual variation is normally to revoke the original agreement and replace it with a new agreement combining the terms of both agreements.[132]

92. The term 'variation', when used in section 82(1) of the Consumer Credit Act, does not refer to a contractual variation as described above. It applies 'where under a power contained in a regulated agreement, the creditor or owner varies the agreement'. This language is inexact because it implies that the creditor or owner may have the power to vary the *terms* of an agreement, whereas a creditor or owner could have no such power without the consent of the borrower or hirer. However, it is clear that what is being referred to is the exercise by the lender or owner to a power conferred by the contract to modify the manner of operation of the contract.[133] There is no variation of the *contractual terms* involved in a variation in this sense.

93. The classic instance of this type of variation is where the loan agreement gives the right to the lender to vary the interest rate.

94. Such a situation arose in *Lombard Tricity Finance v Paton*,[134] where the finance agreement provided that the interest rate was subject to variation 'as may from time to time be notified'. At the time of the agreement, the interest rate was 2.433 per cent a month and later rose to 2.4345 per cent a month following notification of the increase by the lender. The Court of Appeal accepted that this adjustment of the interest rate was a variation within section 82(1).

95. A similar provision was considered by the Court of Appeal in *Nash v Paragon Finance plc*,[135] where a mortgage agreement provided for the interest rate payable to be 'such rate as the [lender] shall apply to the category of business to which the [lender] considers the Mortgage belongs'.

130 *Morris v Baron & Co* 1918 AC 1 and following cases.
131 Section 82(2).
132 Section 82(3).
133 Section 82(1).
134 1989 1 All ER 918.
135 2002 1 WLR 685.

96. Such a provision does not, however, give a lender a completely free hand; the agreement will be subject to an implied term that the interest rate will not be fixed for an improper purpose, capriciously or arbitrarily.[136] There is also an implied term that any increase shall be reasonable in the limited sense that it must not be an increase that no reasonable lender would impose.[137] Reasonableness in this sense would doubtless need expert evidence to assess.

97. In fact, in respect of a regulated credit agreement, CONC provides that the lender can only increase interest rates when it has a *valid* reason to do so.[138] This seems a narrower test than that implied by *Nash*. Examples of such valid reason will be where the lender has increased costs (typically increased borrowing costs) or where the borrower genuinely represents an increased risk.[139] However, where the reason for the increase is that the borrower presents an increased risk, the borrower must be informed of this and given an explanation.[140]

Varying the interest rate

98. The Consumer Credit (EU Directive) Regulation[141] introduced a new regime for the notification of interest rate variations, adding section 78A to the Act with effect from 1 February 2011. Section 82 now only applies to interest rate variations where the agreement is secured on land.[142] Section 82 also applies to other types of provision enabling the lender or owner to adjust the operation of the agreement, whereas section 78A is concerned only with interest rate variations.

99. Section 78A does not, however, apply to agreements secured on land or where an overdraft arises on a current account without a prearranged overdraft limit having been arranged.[143]

100. In respect of other agreements to which section 78A applies, the key principle is that the lender must 'inform the debtor in writing' of the interest rate change before the change can 'take effect'.[144] It is therefore a requirement that the borrower actually *receives* the information before the variation can take effect. The matters of which the borrower must be informed are the new interest rate, the new payment amounts and the new frequency of payments (insofar as these vary).[145]

136 *Nash* at [36].
137 *Nash* at [42].
138 CONC 6.7.14 R.
139 CONC 6.7.15 G.
140 CONC 6.7.16 R.
141 SI 2010/1969.
142 Section 82(1A).
143 Section 78A(6).
144 Section 78A(1).
145 Section 78A(3).

101. There is a relaxation of these requirements where the interest rate is to vary in accordance with a 'reference rate'. This is not defined, but presumably it extends to a situation where a bank sets a base rate as a benchmark for its interest charges. There are also requirements that the reference rate is publicly available and that information about the rate is available 'on the premises of the creditor'. There is no requirement that it is displayed in any particular way or that it be available at *all* the branches of the bank. Provided that the contract provides for the borrower to be periodically notified of these matters, then the requirement of notification in section 78A(1) does not apply.[146] This means that a bank can changes its interest rate by reference to a base rate and it can take effect immediately without waiting until the borrower is informed of the change in the periodic statement.

102. There is a lessening of the requirement in the case of authorised business and non-business overdrafts[147] and also in respect an overdraft that would be a non-business overdraft but for the fact that the credit is not repayable on demand or within three months.[148] In these instances, all that has to be notified is an *increase* in interest rates; the other matters do not have to be notified.[149] The requirements do not apply at all to an overdraft that has arisen without prior agreement.[150]

Section 82(1) variations

103. Section 82(1) sets out the procedure to be followed in the case of other types of variation, including the variation of an interest rate in respect of an agreement secured on land. Neither section 78A nor section 82(1) applies to unauthorised overdrafts on a current account.[151] Nor does section 82 apply to a non-commercial agreement.[152]

104. Nor does it apply to an authorised business or non-business overdraft agreement[153] or an agreement that would be an authorised non-business overdraft agreement but for the fact that the credit is not repayable on demand or within three months, *provided* that the interest rate or other charges are going to be *reduced*.[154]

105. The principle is that 'the variation shall not take effect before notice of it is given to the debtor in the prescribed manner'.[155] The prescribed

146 Section 78A(2).
147 As defined in section 189(1).
148 Section 78A(5).
149 Section 78A(4).
150 Section 78A(6).
151 Section 82(1E).
152 Section 82(7).
153 Defined in section 189(1).
154 Section 82(1B), (1C), (1D).
155 Section 82(1).

manner is that laid down in the Consumer Credit (Notice of Variation of Agreements) Regulations 1977.[156]

106. Regulation 2 requires that notice must set out the particulars of the variation and must be served on the borrower or hirer before the variation is to take effect.

107. There is a special rule applicable in the case of an agreement secured on land where interest is charged daily on the account balance established daily. If the lender wishes to vary the rate of interest, the lender may give notice of the variation in at least three daily national newspapers.[157] The minimum dimensions of the notice are given. If this is not practicable, notice may be given in the *London Gazette*. Moreover, if practicable, the notice of variation must be put on display on the relevant premises of the lender.[158]

108. There is also a provision catering for changes to hire payments reflecting an increase or decrease in the rate of VAT.[159] This provides that the VAT increase or decrease can be reflected provided either that the notice is served on the hirer *or* 'the notice of variation is prominently displayed so that it may easily be read in the part of the premises of the owner where the hirer or a person on his behalf ordinarily makes payments under the agreement in person'. This latter alternative presupposes or ordinarily attends in person in order to make hire payments, perhaps no longer a frequent occurrence.

Modifying agreements

109. Section 82(3) says that whenever the parties enter into a subsequent agreement varying the terms of a regulated credit or hire agreement, the effect of this is to treat the earlier agreement as revoked and replaced by a later agreement. Obligations outstanding under the earlier agreement shall be treated as outstanding under the later agreement. This rule does not, however, apply if either the earlier agreement or later agreement is a regulated mortgage contract, a home purchase plan or an investment property purchase where less than 40 per cent of the property is to be used as a dwelling.[160]

110. Furthermore, except in the case of these categories of agreement or in the case of a running account credit agreement, if the earlier agreement is regulated, so will be the modifying agreement.[161] This principle has, however, lost some significance with the general abolition of financial ceilings for the purpose of the definition of regulated consumer hire and consumer credit agreements.

156 SI 1977/328.
157 Reg 3(2)(a).
158 Reg 3(2)(b).
159 Reg 4.
160 Section 82(2A), (8).
161 Section 82(3).

111. This situation arose in *Swift Advances v McKay*.[162] On the facts of that case, Mr McKay entered into three loan agreements. The first loan agreement was for £25,000 and was regulated, and the second and third loan agreements were entered into in 2007 before the coming into force of the Consumer Credit Act 2006 and the abolition of financial ceilings on 6 April 2008. The second and third agreements were entered into for sums of over £100,000 and were treated as unregulated agreements. The agreements were entered into on the basis that they were separate agreements but each paid off the credit outstanding in relation to the previous agreement. The argument for Mr McKay was that each of the agreements should have been treated as if they were regulated by virtue of section 82(3) as the two subsequent agreements, Mr McKay argued, amounted to modifying agreements of the first agreement. The argument of Mr McKay was rejected by the Court of Appeal of Northern Ireland, which held that all the agreements were intended to be separate agreements and had been executed as such. They were not, therefore, modifying agreements. It made no difference that each of the agreements had discharged the credit due under the earlier agreements.

112. Special rules apply to the cancellation and withdrawal from modifying agreements. Modifying agreements are not cancellable or capable of withdrawal under section 66A unless they were entered into during the cancellation or withdrawal period applicable to the original agreements. Furthermore, notice of cancellation or withdrawal may be given only during the original cancellation or withdrawal period.[163] However, these special rules likewise do not apply to regulated mortgage contracts, a home purchase plan or investment property purchase.[164] The Agreements Regulations make separate provision for modifying agreements.

Service under the Consumer Credit Act 1974

113. The Consumer Credit Act 1974 refers in many places to documents and information to be provided either from the lender/owner to the borrower/hirer or vice versa. Questions arise as to the proper *manner* of service of the documents. Questions may also arise as to the *timing* of service in conjunction with time limits. References, using a variety of different terminology, include the following:

(a) Section 61A refers to the lender 'giving' a copy of the unexecuted agreement to the borrower; likewise, section 61B refers to giving a document with the terms of the agreement to the borrower.

162 2013 NICA 72.
163 Section 82(5), (6A).
164 Section 82(5A).

(b) Sections 62(2) refers to 'sending' a copy of the unexecuted agreement for signature and section 63(3) says that a copy of the executed agreement must be 'given' within seven days following the making of the agreement.

(c) Section 63(3) refers, in the case of a cancellable agreement, to a copy being 'sent by an appropriate method' to the borrower within seven days; likewise, where there is a separate cancellation notice, this must be 'sent by an appropriate method' in accordance with section 64(1).

(d) Section 69(1) refers to the borrower 'serving' a notice of cancellation on the lender, which has to be done 'within' the cooling off period prescribed by section 68.

(e) Section 78 refers to the lender 'giving' a statement of information to the borrower under a running account agreement.

(f) Section 87 refers to a 'service' of a default notice on a borrower or hirer before enforcement action can be taken.

(g) Section 99 entitles the borrower to 'give' written notice terminating a hire purchase or conditional sale agreement.

(h) The Financial Services (Distance Marketing) Regulations 2004 refer to the supplier 'providing' information to the consumer and provides for the consumer to 'give' written or oral notice of cancellation during the relevant period.

(i) The Consumer Contracts (Information, Cancellation and Additional Charges) Regulations 2013 refer to the 'giving' of required information and notice of cancellation rights to the borrower; the Regulations refer to the consumer 'cancelling' within the cancellation period.

Manner of service

114. 'Serve on' is defined in section 189(1) as 'deliver or send by an appropriate method to'. The word 'give' has precisely the same definition in section 189(1) and it is clear the terms 'serve' and 'give' are synonymous, a point also made clear by section 176(8).

115. By contrast, the term 'deliver' is undefined in the Act. However, section 176(1) allows service under the Act to take place in any of the modes stated in section 176(2), namely by delivery, sending by an 'appropriate method' or additionally by leaving the document addressed to the person at his or her proper address.

116. 'Appropriate method' is defined in section 189(1) as sending by post or transmitting as an electronic communication in compliance with section l76A. Section 176A was introduced into the Act in 2004 to enable documents to be served electronically. However, there are a number of preconditions that must be met before this can be done, the first being that the intended recipient of the document must agree to it being transmitted to a particular electronic address (e.g. an email address) in that form (e.g.

as an attachment to an email).[165] The second is that it must have been transmitted in accordance with that agreement. The third is that the information must be sent in such a way that it is capable of being stored for reference purposes for an appropriate period without charge.[166]

117. Sending by post or by delivery to the address of a person is good if made to the address of the party to be served last known to the server.[167] If it is sought to serve someone with an interest on land, and the address of that person cannot reasonably be discovered, service can take place by addressing the document to the person and either by affixing it in a prominent position on the land or by leaving it with a responsible person thereon.[168] A responsible person in this context is presumably someone who can reasonably be relied upon to ensure that the document reaches the attention of the person for whom it is intended. Both the identity of the person and the context in which the document is handed to him or her are clearly relevant to this.

118. Service can take place on someone who has died by sending it to or leaving at that person's address as if that person had not died, even if that person's death is known about.[169] Service can also be affected on the executors or administrators of the deceased, since once they are appointed, they stand in the same position as the deceased for the purposes of the Act (see the definitions of creditor, owner, debtor, hirer and surety in section 189). But it is not possible to serve documents on the Public Trustee.[170] If a party becomes bankrupt, the creditor or owner may serve on that party if unaware of his or her bankruptcy.[171] Otherwise, the lender or owner must serve on the trustee in bankruptcy.

Timing of service

119. In many instances in the Act it is important to know *when* service takes place. It may be necessary for service to take place *within* a given period or sometimes steps have to be taken within a given time *after* service. In the case of physical delivery, it is clear that the time of service is when physical delivery takes place. In the case of sending by post, the position is governed by section 7 of the Interpretation Act 1978. There is a presumption (no more than that) that it arrives at the time of a letter sent in the ordinary course of post. However, this is not conclusive; it is open to a party to

165 Section 176A(1)(a).
166 Section 176A(1).
167 Section 176(3).
168 Section 176(4).
169 Section 176(6).
170 Section 176(7).
171 Section 176(5).

establish that the letter arrived later than this or not all.[172] The burden of proof is the balance of probabilities.[173]

120. However, by way of contrast, if the statutory provision does not fix a time limit in which service has to take place but only requires that service be affected, then deemed service takes place on posting and it will avail the other party nothing to say that the document was not in fact received.[174]

121. In the case of sending by electronic communication, it is deemed, unless the contrary is proved, to have arrived on the following *working* day after the day on which the communication is transmitted.[175] Sometimes a statutory provision expressly provides that the document is deemed to have been received on the date when it is posted or transmitted by electronic communication. So a notice of withdrawal under section 66A is deemed to have been received at the time that it was sent whether by post or electronic transmission.[176] A similar assumption is made in connection with a document transmitted under the Financial Services (Distance Marketing) Regulations 2004.[177]

172 *R v County of London Quarter Sessions Appeal Committee* 1956 1 QB 682.
173 *Calladine-Smith v Saveorder Ltd* 2011 EWHC 2501 in which Mr Justice Morgan examines the authorities.
174 *Moody v Godstone* 1966 1 WLR 1085 explained in the *Calladine-Smith* case.
175 Section 176A(2).
176 Section 66A(5), (6).
177 Reg 9(4), SI No 2004/2095.

9 Withdrawal and cancellation

Common law right of withdrawal

1. At common law, a party making a contractual offer is at liberty to withdraw it at any time before it is accepted. Until the contract is concluded, the offeror is not bound (unless he entered into a separate contract to keep the offer open).

2. Problems of withdrawal arise particularly frequently with credit and hire transactions because of the lengthy time often passing between the signatures of the borrower and lender (or hirer and owner). In many hire purchase (and leasing) transactions, for example, it is common for the borrower to sign the form of agreement at the trade premises of the dealer. The borrower in so signing is making an offer to the lender to enter into the agreement. The lender can accept the offer by signing in turn. But such signature may only take place, if it takes place at all, several days later. In the meantime, the dealer has to transmit the signed forms to the lender, who will then scrutinise them, and probably investigate the creditworthiness of the prospective borrower. Only if satisfied in all necessary respects will the lender eventually sign, thereby concluding the agreement. And up until this time, the borrower is free to withdraw from the agreement.

3. At common law, a party seeking to withdraw from a contract must normally communicate its withdrawal in order for it to be effective.[1] Communication must be to the other intended contracting party or alternatively to its duly authorised agent. Exactly who is an authorised agent for the purpose of receiving notice of withdrawal is a question of fact in every case. In the case of *Financings Ltd v Stimson*,[2] it was held that in the case of a hire purchase or conditional sale agreement, notice of withdrawal could be given not only to the finance company who were the intended contracting party, but also to the dealer who was to deliver the goods to

1 *Byrne & Co v Leon van Tienhoven* 1880 5 CPD 344.
2 1962 1 WLR 1184.

the borrower. This decision was followed in the Court of Appeal decision of *CF Asset Finance Ltd v Okonji*.[3]

4. The consequences of withdrawal at common law are that the transaction is to be unravelled, any property handed over in anticipation of the contract must be returned to the party and any monies already received must be repaid. This applies to the borrower and lender equally. The right to restitution arises as a result of total failure of consideration.

Withdrawal under the Consumer Credit Act

5. Section 57 of the Consumer Credit Act supplements these common law rights in the case of withdrawal by a borrower or hirer. Withdrawal by a lender or owner, in the case where this arises, will be governed solely by the rules of the common law, as will be the case with agreements falling outside the ambit of section 57.

6. The basic principle is that section 57 equates a withdrawal with a cancellation.[4] Section 57 makes three principle changes to the common law position:

(a) it expands the range of persons to whom the borrower or hirer may give notice of withdrawal;
(b) it operates to withdraw the borrower or hirer from linked transactions already concluded; and
(c) it alters the financial consequences of withdrawal in certain instances in favour of the borrower or hirer.

7. Section 57 applies to all regulated agreements except those taken out of its ambit by section 74. This section was discussed previously when considering those agreements caught by the formalities requirements; the principal effect is to exclude non-commercial agreements and small debtor-creditor-supplier agreements from the operation of section 57.

Upon whom may notice of withdrawal be served?

8. Notice to withdraw can either be oral or in writing. It need not be formally expressed, but need only express the borrower or hirer's intention not to proceed with the agreement.[5] The 'giving' of a notice operates as a withdrawal.[6] A notice sent to a person's proper address is treated as properly served.[7]

3 2014 EWCA Civ 870.
4 Section 57(1).
5 Section 57(2).
6 Section 57(2).
7 Section 176(2).

9. Notice can be served upon the lender or owner him or herself; this is in accord with the common law position. It can also be served upon a credit broker or supplier who acts as a 'negotiator' within the meaning that that term is given in section 56.[8] The term will be discussed more fully in that context where it will be seen that it relates only to debtor-creditor-supplier transactions in which there is a third party involved in the transaction.

10. The final category of persons upon whom notice of withdrawal may be served is any person who acted for the borrower or hirer in negotiating the agreement and in the course of a business carried on by him or her.[9] The classic example of such a negotiator is the solicitor engaged by the borrower or hirer. But it is not enough in order for him or her to be properly served with a notice of withdrawal that he or she merely advised the borrower or hirer on the effects of an agreement. The solicitor must actually have entered into the negotiations, the essence of which is some form of communication with the lender or owner.[10]

11. It is a difficult question whether a citizens advice bureau could be said to be acting in the course of a 'business' in this context if a member of its staff entered into negotiations with a lender or owner. But it seems that a citizens advice bureau is carrying on a business within the meaning of the Act. The definition of 'business' in the Act[11] includes that of profession or trade but makes it unclear whether the definition encompasses non-profit-making activities.

12. All of these are deemed to be agents of the lender or owner for the purpose of receiving notice of withdrawal. All are under a deemed contractual duty to transmit the notice of withdrawal to the lender or owner as soon as they receive it – 'forthwith'.[12] They can be liable for breach of contract for any losses arising if they fail to pass on the notice of withdrawal.

The effect on linked transactions

13. Withdrawal in accordance with the Act has wider consequences than withdrawal at common law. The borrower or hirer becomes released on withdrawal from linked transactions previously entered into.[13] This rule does not apply to agreements otherwise exempted from section 57 by section 74, such as non-commercial agreements. An example will illustrate this.

14. A borrower enters into a concluded contract for double glazing. The double glazing is to be financed by a loan from a finance company. The

8 Section 57(3)(a).
9 Section 57(3)(b).
10 Section 56(4).
11 Section 189(1).
12 Section 175.
13 Section 57(1); this is also the effect of section 19(3).

finance company is introduced by the double glazing salesman who presents the borrower with a form of agreement to sign. Under the agreement, the loan moneys are to be paid directly to the double glazing company. Once the borrower has signed, the salesman sends the signed form of agreement on to the finance company. But having signed, the borrower then reconsiders. He informs the salesman, before the finance company has signed the agreement, that he wishes to pull out of the transaction.

15. *Analysis*. The borrower's remarks to the salesman will constitute a valid withdrawal from the agreement by virtue of section 57(3)(a). The double glazing company will be under a contractual duty to transmit notice of the withdrawal to the finance company forthwith (section 175). The withdrawal will have the effect of withdrawing the borrower not only from the loan agreement, but *also* from the contract of double glazing (section 19(3)). The borrower will not, therefore, have any liability under that contract. The double glazing company will not be able to claim (e.g. for loss of profit) when the borrower resiles from it.

16. There are only three types of linked transaction, the validity of which is preserved despite withdrawal from the principal agreement. These exceptions are contained in the Consumer Credit (Linked Transactions) (Exemptions) Regulations 1983.[14] The three exceptions created thereby are:

(a) *Contracts of insurance*. Insurance contracts are divided into long-term and general insurance contracts as explained at regulation 3 of the Regulated Activities Order to which reference should be made for the purposes of this Regulation.[15] This exception was created to remove a potential difficulty to the borrower that would otherwise exist if insurance cover was held to be invalid. This could have particularly unfortunate implications in the case of motor insurance.
(b) *Contracts of guarantee*. 'Guarantee' here is used in the commercial sense to refer to any promise or assurance to rectify or repair or compensate for defects in goods.[16] It does not refer to security instruments. This exemption is also included for the protection of the borrower or hirer.
(c) *Deposit and current accounts opened pursuant to the agreement*. These accounts continue in effect despite withdrawal from the principal agreement. If this provision were not made, commercial institutions, principally banks, could be put to a great deal of inconvenience and commercial embarrassment. A situation can be envisaged where it is a precondition of a credit agreement that the borrower open a bank account.

14 SI 1983/1560.
15 Reg 1(2A).
16 Reg 1(2).

Financial consequences of withdrawal

17. The financial consequences of withdrawal are the same as those of cancellation.[17] The financial consequences apply even where the agreement is not cancellable; it is assumed that it is.[18]

18. The financial adjustment to be made at common law is straightforward; both sides have to restore any moneys or goods obtained prior to and in expectation of the future contract being concluded. The financial consequences under section 57 do not differ greatly from the common law approach, although some modifications are made.

19. The borrower's obligation to repay credit advanced by instalments only arises once the first instalment date has elapsed and once the borrower has been served with a notice in the prescribed form setting out the schedule of repayments required.[19] The prescribed form of notice must contain the information set out in Schedule 2 to the Consumer Credit (Repayment of Credit on Cancellation) Regulations 1983.[20] Schedule 2 specifically relates to withdrawal from the agreement.

Withdrawal from a concluded agreement

20. A statutory right of withdrawal contained in section 66A was inserted into the 1974 Act as from 1 February 2011 to give effect to the requirements of the Consumer Credit Directive 2008/48/EC. This right is very extensive and differs significantly from the right of withdrawal at common law.

21. It applies to regulated consumer credit agreements. It has no relevance, therefore, to consumer hire agreements. It gives an unfettered right of withdrawal without the need for the borrower to give any reason in the case of any agreement within the scope of this provision.

22. However, the right to withdraw does not apply to the following categories of agreements:[21]

(a) where the credit exceeds £60,260;
(b) where the credit advanced under the agreement is secured on land;
(c) in the case of a restricted use credit agreement to finance the purchase of land; and
(d) in the case of an agreement for a bridging loan in connection with the purchase of land.

17 Section 57(1).
18 Section 57(4).
19 Section 71(3).
20 SI 1983/1559.
21 Section 66A(14).

23. Notice of withdrawal can be given orally or by notice in writing. Oral notice must be given in the manner stipulated by the agreement. Written notice can be given at the electronic address or to the fax number stipulated in the agreement.[22] The relevant notice can also be posted to the postal address specified for the purpose in the agreement. It is taken to be received by the lender at the time of sending even if post is used.[23] Notice must be given to the lender or to a person stipulated by the lender in the agreement.[24]

24. It must be given within 14 days beginning with the day after the relevant date.[25] The relevant date is the latest of:[26]

(a) the agreement date;
(b) where this is required, the date of communication of the credit limit; or
(c) in circumstances where a copy of the executed agreement has to be supplied, when this is done.

25. The effect of withdrawal is that the agreement is treated as if it had never been entered into and any agreement for any ancillary service is also treated as if it had never been entered into.[27] The lender must notify the supplier of the ancillary service of the withdrawal.[28] An ancillary service is one that relates to the provision of credit and expressly includes an insurance or payment protection policy.[29]

26. The borrower is obliged to repay any credit provided together with interest accrued at the contractual rate.[30] However, no other compensation or charges are payable except non-returnable charges payable to a public administrative body.[31] The credit has to be repaid 'without undue delay' and in any event within 30 days.[32]

27. Once the borrower has repaid the credit and interest in the case of a conditional sale, credit sale or hire purchase agreement, then the borrower acquires title to the goods on the same terms as would have applied if the borrower had not withdrawn from the agreement.[33]

22 Section 66A(5)(a).
23 Section 66A(6)(b), so that the Interpretation Act 1976 does not apply.
24 Section 66A(12).
25 Section 66A(2).
26 Section 66A(3).
27 Section 66A(7).
28 Section 66A(8).
29 Section 66A(13).
30 Section 66A(9)(a).
31 Section 66A(9)(b).
32 Section 66A(10).
33 Section 66A(11).

Withdrawal from a modifying agreement

28. Where a consumer credit agreement is modified, the effect of the Act is to revoke the earlier agreement and to treat the modifying agreement as a fresh agreement incorporating the original terms as modified[34] (see the discussion under the definition of 'modifying agreements'). It is not possible to withdraw from a modifying agreement unless the original agreement was one in respect of which there is a right of withdrawal and the modifying agreement is concluded during the period for withdrawal in respect of the original agreement.[35] Where this applies, it is possible for the borrower to withdraw from the modifying agreement during the withdrawal period appertaining to the original agreement.[36] There is no extension of the period. Otherwise, there is no right of withdrawal.[37]

The right of cancellation under the Consumer Credit Act 1974

29. In certain circumstances, the borrower is allowed a period of reconsideration, subsequent to having signed the agreement and after copies have been supplied. The borrower may still be given, by law, a limited period to resile. This period is known as the 'cancellation' period or 'cooling-off' period, during which time, in theory at least, the borrower is presumed to be calmly reflecting upon the wisdom of entering into the agreement. At any time during this period, the borrower may notify the lender of his or her desire to cancel.

30. The borrower's right to cancel, however, is confined only to *regulated* agreements (which includes consumer hire agreements) that are entered into in closely defined circumstances.

31. The law has now, as from 2010, given a more general right of withdrawal under section 66A of the Act and where this applies, which it often will in the case of regulated credit agreements, then the cancellation provisions do not take effect.[38]

What is a cancellable agreement?

32. An agreement capable of cancellation by the borrower is known as a 'cancellable agreement'.[39] The following conditions (specified in section 67) must be satisfied before an agreement is cancellable.

34 Section 82(2).
35 Section 82(6A).
36 Section 82(6A).
37 Section 82(6B).
38 Section 67(2).
39 Section 189(1).

33. First, the agreement must be a regulated agreement. Both consumer credit and consumer hire agreements can be cancellable.

34. Second, it must not be an agreement of the type specifically excluded from the cancellation provisions. Such agreements are those excluded either by section 74 (which has been discussed earlier) or by section 67(1)(a).

35. It will be remembered that the agreements excluded by section 74 are:

(a) non-commercial agreements;
(b) small debtor-creditor-supplier agreements;
(c) most agreements for the provision of an overdraft on a current account; and
(d) most agreements providing for payments to be made on death.

36. Agreements specifically excluded from the cancellation provisions by section 67(1)(a) are those secured on land, or to provide finance or a bridging loan for the purchase of land. It was largely for the convenience of the Land Registry that these agreements were taken out of the cancellation provisions. In many agreements of this type, the borrower is in any event protected by the special provisions of section 58, which provide for a period of isolation while the borrower considers whether or not to sign the agreement. The situations in which the borrower is neither protected by the cancellation provisions nor by section 58 are situations where credit is advanced for the purchase of land. In these circumstances, the borrower is likely to have independent legal advice in any event.

37. The third requirement for a cancellable agreement is that there must have been: (a) oral representations made during the course of antecedent negotiations in the presence of the borrower by the negotiator or someone acting on his behalf; and (b) the agreement must not have been signed at appropriate trade premises.

38. As to (a), oral representations must be made by a negotiator. Who the 'negotiator' is in any particular transaction is defined in section 56(1). The negotiator is defined to be:

(a) The lender (or the owner in a hire transaction).
(b) A credit broker who proposes to sell goods to the lender that will then be supplied by the lender as part of the eventual credit agreement entered into with the borrower. This provision is designed to make the dealer in a hire purchase, conditional sale, credit sale situation a 'negotiator'. In such a situation, the dealer intends to sell the goods to the finance company who will then supply them to the borrower. Pre-contractual statements made by the dealer will therefore be made by him or her as 'negotiator'.
(c) A supplier under a debtor-creditor-supplier agreement.

39. It will be remembered that a debtor-creditor-supplier agreement only arises where, with an unrestricted use agreement, there are pre-existing arrangements between lender and supplier, or where, with a restricted use agreement, there is alternatively the contemplation of future arrangements between them. In practice, the 'connected lending' transaction (e.g. the double glazing company who also introduces a source of loan finance) provides the most frequent example of a supplier in this context. The supplier will then be a 'negotiator'.

40. The negotiator must make *oral representations* in the presence of the borrower. At common law, a 'representation' is confined to a statement of fact.[40] The Act, however, defines the term in section 189 to include also 'conditions or warranties', so that promises for the future are covered by the term (e.g. an anti-rust guarantee), and 'any other statements or undertakings whether oral or in writing'. Thus, virtually anything said about the goods or the credit provided its content is concrete enough for it to be called a statement will amount to 'oral representations'.

41. Perhaps the crucial factor is that these oral representations must be made in the *presence* of the borrower. It is where there is personal contact between borrower and negotiator that the borrower needs protection. Where contact is only postal, or over the telephone, the agreement will not be trade premises of a negotiator.

42. However, a further requirement is that the borrower must *not* sign the unexecuted agreement at appropriate premises at which business is being carried on.[41] Appropriate premises are the business premises of one of the following:

(a) The lender or owner.
(b) The negotiator (if different from the lender or owner). Thus, the showroom of a car dealer in a hire purchase transaction or the offices of a double glazing company in a connecting lending transaction will be appropriate trade premises for the purposes of rendering an agreement not cancellable.
(c) The party to a linked transaction. This will be rather unusual. It will cover the situation, for example, where an agreement is signed at the offices of an insurance company who may be insuring the goods pursuant to the agreement.

43. Any place where one of the above carry on any business is included. The place of business can be either permanent or temporary.[42] The essence of this qualification excluding the cancellation provisions is that the place

40 See for instance *Edginton v Fitzmaurice* 1885 29 ChD 459.
41 Section 67(1)(b).
42 Section 67(1)(b).

must be a place where the borrower has made the effort to attend rather than one where the lender has sought out the borrower.

The modifying agreement

44. Where a credit agreement is modified, the effect of the Act is to revoke the earlier agreement and to treat the modifying agreement as a fresh agreement incorporating the original terms as modified[43] (see the discussion under the definition of 'modifying agreements'). Modifying agreements are not cancellable even though the conditions discussed above apply, unless it was concluded during the cancellation period applicable to the original agreement.[44] Where this exception applies, the modifying agreement is cancellable up until the end of the cancellation period appertaining to the original agreement.[45] Furthermore, if the modifying agreement is an exempt agreement, it is not cancellable at all.[46]

The formalities required with a cancellable agreement

45. It has already been seen that at least one copy of the regulated agreement must be given to the borrower, sometimes two. In every copy given, a cancellation notice must be inserted in the copy agreement.[47] The form of notice is as set out in the Consumer Credit (Cancellation Notices and Copies of Documents) Regulations 1983.[48] The notices must be reproduced without any 'alteration or addition'[49] and in accordance with the footnotes.

46. It will be remembered that two copies of the agreement must be given in a case where the signature of the borrower does not execute the agreement.[50] In the case of a cancellable agreement, the second copy must be sent either by post or agreed form of electronic communication[51] within seven days of making the agreement,[52] except in the case of a credit token agreement where the second copy can be given either with the credit token or at any time beforehand.[53]

47. The wording of the cancellation notices will differ in each of the two copies. The precise terms of each are set out in the Schedule to the

43 Section 82(2).
44 Section 82(5), (6).
45 Section 82(5).
46 Section 82(5A).
47 Section 64(1).
48 SI 1983/1557.
49 Reg 2(1) of the Cancellations Notices Regulations.
50 Section 63(2).
51 In accordance with section 176A.
52 Section 63(3).
53 Section 63(4).

Regulations. The notice in the first copy must contain a general statement of the right of cancellation; the second copy is much more specific specifying the time and manner of cancellation and the person to whom notice may be sent. A cancellation form will also be included in the second copy; this need not be adjacent to the cancellation notice. The former can be filled out by the borrower and sent to the lender to signify the borrower's desire to cancel.

48. If the cancellation notice does not appear on the front page of the agreement (either on the first or second copy), the Regulations provide that the front page of the agreement must have a box containing the words: 'This is a copy of your agreement for you to keep. It includes a notice about your cancellation rights which you should read.'[54]

One copy

49. The borrower need receive only one copy of the agreement where his or her signature executes the agreement (sections 62(2) and 63(1)).

50. In the case of a cancellable agreement, the lender must normally (for the exception, see below) send by post or agreed form of electronic communication a further separate cancellation notice.[55] This notice must be sent by the lender to the borrower within seven days following the making of the agreement[56] (except in the case of a credit token agreement where the notice may be sent by post or approved form of electronic communication either with or at any time before the sending of the credit token).[57] Thus, where an agreement has been executed by the borrower's signature on a Monday, the lender has until the following Monday to send a separate cancellation notice.

51. The first cancellation notice, the one contained in the copy agreement, will explain the borrower's general rights of cancellation; it will follow the same form as the notice contained in the first copy of the agreement given to the borrower in the situation where the borrower is entitled to receive two copies.

52. The second cancellation notice will be sent separately as has already been explained. Its wording and form are dictated by the Regulations.[58] A statutory cancellation form for the borrower to fill in must also be included. The form and notice must all be on a single sheet of paper if sent by post[59] and the form should be detachable. If the cancellation notice is sent by

54 Reg 5(3); Schedule Part V.
55 Section 64(1).
56 Section 64(1)(b).
57 Section 64(2).
58 Schedule Part VI.
59 Reg 6.

agreed form of electronic communication, there is nothing in the Regulations preventing the lender from giving additional guidance on how notice of cancellation is to be given.[60]

Exemption from the second cancellation notice

53. In certain rather rare circumstances the FCA can authorise a lender to dispense with the need to send a second separate cancellation notice.[61] The circumstances in which the Director General will consider such an application are set out in the Schedule to the Consumer Credit (Notice of Cancellation Rights) (Exemptions) Regulations 1983.[62]

54. The requirements that the credit agreement must satisfy are that:

(a) The agreement must be a credit agreement financing the supply of goods (although it need not necessarily be a debtor-creditor-supplier agreement).
(b) The borrower must have been presented with full information in relation to the agreement. This can be presented in the form of circulars or brochures or audio-visual material. The information must be such as would be contained in a full credit advertisement (as to which see Schedules 1 and 2 to the Advertisement Regulations). A notice must furthermore tell the borrower that he or she has a right of access to the source of the information and to study it alone (in the light of this, it is rather unlikely that very many finance companies will be providing audio-visual material, which would inevitably be expensive, for the borrower to remove and perhaps not return).
(c) It must be a term of the agreement that the borrower can return the goods within 14 days without incurring any liability (provided they are returned in good condition).
(d) It must be contemplated that the lender or his or her agents will be keeping in touch with the borrower for the purpose of collecting payments due under the agreement.

55. Even if an agreement actually satisfies these stringent requirements, the lender must still seek clearance from the FCA before being allowed to dispense with the separate cancellation notice. The FCA must be satisfied that dispensation is consistent with the public interest. The FCA will look particularly at the means by which the lender induces the borrower to enter into agreements and the amount of prior information. Dispensation may be conditional.[63]

60 Reg 6B.
61 Section 64(4).
62 SI 1983/1558.
63 Section 64(4)(b).

Contractual cancellation rights

56. Lenders will often be anxious to avoid the cancellation provisions where they possibly can. This can be done by *ensuring* that where a credit agreement is presented to a borrower at a showroom or other business premises, the staff members there are instructed that the borrower must not be allowed to take the agreement away to sign it. If the staff members allow this to happen, the agreement will become cancellable. Furthermore, as will be seen, the form of agreement may also then become inappropriate and there is a risk that the agreement then becomes completely unenforceable. The undesirability of this is obvious.

57. On the other hand, lenders may choose to incorporate cancellation rights in their agreements out of an abundance of caution, even if in some situations the agreement is not cancellable because the requirements of section 67 are not satisfied. In these circumstances, there will be a contractual right to cancel. In these circumstances, the Cancellation Notices Regulations apply.[64]

Failure to comply with cancellation formalities

58. In respect of agreements entered into prior to 6 April 2007,[65] if (a) the cancellation notices were not in the prescribed form as required by section 64(1), or if (b) the separate cancellation notice required by section 64(1)(b) was not sent by post or by agreed electronic means, or was not sent within the seven-day time period, then the agreement became and continues to be completely unenforceable. It is irrelevant that the borrower had not in fact sought to cancel.

59. The above conclusion is reached by the following process of reasoning:

(a) Section 127 provides for application to the court for an enforcement order.
(b) Section 127(4)(b) states that the court shall not make an enforcement order if the requirements of section 64(1) have not been complied with. Section 127(4), although repealed by section 15 of the Consumer Credit Act 2006, remains in force for the purpose of the enforcement of agreements entered into before 6 April 2007.[66] The requirements of section 64(1) are the requirements specified above viz. the incorporation of cancellation notices in the prescribed form and the sending where appropriate of a separate cancellation notice within the seven-day period.

64 Reg 5(4) Cancellation Notices Regulations.
65 The commencement date of section 15 Consumer Credit Act 2006.
66 Paragraph 11 Schedule 3 Consumer Credit Act 2006.

60. Under this strict regime applicable to agreements entered into before April 2007, failure to send a separate cancellation by post or other agreed electronic means in accordance with section 64(1) rendered the agreement totally unenforceable; however, failure to supply a *copy* of the agreement might not be so serious from the lender's point of view since it was still possible potentially to enforce the agreement if the copy, not previously supplied, was given to the borrower before proceedings were commenced against him or her.[67] Thus, the lender may bring enforcement proceedings if the unsupplied copy is provided late, viz. before the date when the lender first sets county court procedures in motion. It will then be a matter for the court, applying principles laid down in section 127 (which are discussed later) to decide whether to make an enforcement order.

61. This strict regime has given rise to expressions of judicial unease. In *Goshawk Dedicated (No 2) Ltd v Bank of Scotland*,[68] Sir Francis Ferris stated: 'If it is thought that the complex and confusing forms represent a thoroughly unsatisfactory mode of legislation, especially when non-compliance produces adverse consequences of the most severe nature, I can only agree.' It also led the provisions to be challenged as being incompatible with the Human Rights Act 1998, a challenge that was rejected by the House of Lords in *Wilson v First County Trust Ltd (No 2)*.[69]

62. It is to be hoped, however, that in circumstances where this strict regime applies, the court will feel able to say that really trivial departures from the prescribed requirements are *de minimis*, thus preventing the borrower from escaping liability simply on a technicality. Authority for this approach can be derived from the approach of the courts to agreements subject to the Moneylenders Acts where the court felt able to ignore errors that were 'too trivial to notice': *Reading Trust Ltd v Spero*.[70] Likewise, where the error could be classified as a clerical error: *Temperance Loan Fund Ltd v Rose*.[71] The court adopted this approach despite the fact that the language of the Moneylenders Acts imposed an equally absolute obligation on lenders to draw up agreements in the correct form (see the Moneylenders Act 1927, section 6). Nevertheless, recently, Mr Justice Field in *Bank of Scotland v Euclidian (No 1)*,[72] not referring to these cases, expressed the view that no *de minimis* exception applies.

63. Fortunately, the strict regime in relation to cancellation notices no longer applies to agreements entered into after 6 April 2007, due to the repeal of section 127(4) by section 15 of the Consumer Credit Act 2006.

67 Section 127(4)(a).
68 2006 2 All ER 610 at [46].
69 2004 1 AC 816.
70 1930 1 KB 492 at page 505 per Scrutton LJ.
71 1932 2 KB 522 at page 526 per Scrutton LJ.
72 2007 EWHC 1732 at [88].

Failure to comply with the cancellation provisions still renders the agreement improperly executed but the court now has the more general discretion to exercise under section 127 as amended.

Method of cancellation

64. The borrower must cancel by serving notice in writing.[73] The borrower need not fill out the cancellation form contained in the second copy of the agreement (where there is a second copy) or in the separate cancellation notice (if there is not),[74] although it will obviously be convenient if he or she does so. The only legal requirement of a cancellation notice is that it should 'indicate the intention of the borrower of hirer to withdraw from the agreement'.[75] It is not necessary that the borrower should refer to cancellation expressly. It may be that the lender agrees to accept notice of cancellation orally; if so, this should be made clear in the notice of cancellation rights provided to the borrower in accordance with the forms set out in the Schedule to the Cancellation Notices Regulations.

65. Notice of cancellation can be served on one of the following:[76]

(a) the lender or owner;
(b) any person specified in the cancellation notices incorporated in the copy agreement as being the person upon whom notice of cancellation should be served;
(c) any agent of the lender or owner, as determined by the principles of the law of agency; and
(d) any deemed agent of the lender (see section 69(6)) who can be either:
   (i) a supplier or credit broker who acted as negotiator (which will include the dealer in a hire purchase, conditional sale or credit sale agreement, or the supplier in a connected lending transaction); or
   (ii) someone who acted on behalf of the borrower or hirer during antecedent negotiations in the course of a business carried on by him (here, the actual agent of the borrower is deemed to be the agent of the lender for the purpose of receiving a cancellation notice).

66. The borrower has five days in which to cancel; time starts from the day after either the second copy of the agreement or the separate notice of cancellation is received.[77] So if a separate cancellation notice is received by

73 The definition of 'notice' in section 189(1) is notice in writing.
74 Section 69(1).
75 Section 69(1).
76 Section 69(1), (6).
77 Section 68(a).

the borrower by post on a Monday morning, the borrower can cancel at any time until Saturday midnight. Cancellation takes place when the notice is actually served on the person to receive it, except that where notice of cancellation is posted or sent by agreed electronic transmission, it is deemed to take effect on *sending, whether or not actually received provided correctly addressed.*[78] The borrower would be wise to use this form of transmission. There is no requirement that the borrower use *first-class* post.

67. These cancellation provisions are capable of working unfairness on lenders in two ways. Because the period of cancellation runs from the time that the second copy agreement or separate cancellation notice was received by the borrower, there will be little to prevent the borrower from extending the cancellation period by falsely claiming that the second copy or separate cancellation notice was 'delayed in the post'. Equally, the lender will be in a difficult position if the borrower claims that his or her notice of cancellation must have been 'lost in the post' even though the lender may never have received it. If this were right, the agreement would have been cancelled on posting. The lender may feel that the borrower is lying about this in order to excuse his or her later non-payment. There is, however, little that the lender will be able to do to combat the lie. The most that can be said is that the burden of proof is on the borrower to prove the initial posting of the notice of cancellation.

68. A difficult situation arises where the lender correctly sends the second copy of the agreement or the separate cancellation notice to the borrower but it gets lost in the post and never arrives. The lender has correctly complied with section 63(2) or section 64(1)(b) as the case may be but the time for cancellation has never arisen. Two possibilities are open in this situation. The borrower either loses his or her right to cancel or it remains indefinitely open to him or her. The latter, however, is correct since section 68 specifies that the borrower may cancel at any time after he or she signs the agreement. The borrower need not wait for the second copy or the separate cancellation notice before cancelling. His or her right of cancellation remains open to him or her at all times.

69. The final situation to be considered is where the Office of Fair Trading, or now the FCA, has exempted a lender from the need to serve a separate cancellation notice pursuant to section 64(4)(a). In such a situation, the borrower has 14 days in which to cancel commencing the day after he or she signed the agreement.[79] So if such an agreement was signed on Monday, first of the month, the borrower would have until midnight Monday 15 in which to cancel.

70. Where there is any dispute about whether a borrower has effectively cancelled, under any of the above provisions, any interested party can apply to the court for a declaration of his or her rights pursuant to section 142(2).

78 Section 69(7).
79 Section 68(b).

The consequences of cancellation and withdrawal under the Consumer Credit Act 1974

71. Sections 69 to 73 of the Act are concerned with the working out of the consequences of cancellation. These provisions apply equally to a withdrawal from a regulated consumer credit agreement prior to conclusion of the agreement by virtue of section 57(1). The legal consequences of withdrawal and cancellation are equated. Furthermore, by virtue of section 57(1), the effects on linked transactions of a withdrawal and cancellation are the same. However, in the case of withdrawal following conclusion of the agreement in accordance with section 66A, there is nothing that directly applies these provisions.

72. The following discussion will consider these situations:

(a) the effect of cancellation on the main credit agreement;
(b) the effect of cancellation on linked transactions;
(c) the legal consequences where the borrower has paid money to the lender or supplier prior to cancellation;
(d) the legal consequences where the borrower has received goods from the lender or supplier prior to cancellation;
(e) the legal consequences where the borrower has received money from the lender prior to cancellation;
(f) the legal consequences where the lender or supplier has received goods given in part exchange by the borrower prior to cancellation; and
(g) the effects on any security taken by the lender to secure compliance with the agreement.

The effect on the main agreement

73. Cancellation (or withdrawal) puts the parties in the position they would have been in as if the agreement never been entered into; neither can enforce it.[80] Any sum payable by the debtor or hirer or a relative,[81] including any item forming part of the total charge for credit, ceases to be payable.[82]

74. The only exceptions to this stark rule are credit agreements:[83]

(a) for the doing of work or the supply of goods to meet an emergency; or
(b) where goods have become incorporated into other goods or land 'by the act of the borrower or relative of his' prior to service of the notice of cancellation.

80 Section 69(4).
81 Defined at section 184(1), (5).
82 Section 70(1)(b).
83 Section 69(2).

75. Under (a), the typical example will be the contract for work and materials to meet a domestic crisis. Very rarely, a contract for private medical care might be included. It would obviously be unfair if a borrower could utilise the goods or services to cope with an emergency and then return them, cancelling the agreement once the crisis had passed.

76. Under (b), an example here will be a domestic installation that is not readily detachable thereafter. It seems that if an appliance can be readily detached, it will not be 'incorporated'. The test will be the same as for attachment of a fixture in real property law. Moreover, only if the process of installation is organised by the borrower or a relative will the agreement not be capable of full cancellation. The rationale for this exemption is doubtless that complete cancellation is unrealistic once goods have become attached to the realty. If the supplier, however, is responsible for the installation, it has only itself to blame and must take the consequences.

77. The exceptions above furthermore only apply where the credit agreements are restricted use debtor-creditor-supplier agreements. In these circumstances, the most common example of such agreements will be: (a) where the supplier of the goods and services itself extends credit; or (b) a connected lending transaction where a supplier is paid directly. Hire agreements are not within the ambit of section 69(2). It is open to a hirer to hire goods under a cancellable agreement to meet an emergency, to utilise them for a short period and then cancel the agreement without incurring any liability.

78. What are the consequences of a cancellation on a credit agreement within section 69(2)? It must not be forgotten that such credit agreements will incorporate cancellation notices and cancellation forms in the usual way. If a borrower cancels such an agreement, it is only the provision of credit that is cancelled; the borrower remains liable to pay the cash price of the goods and services acquired. This, however, is the borrower's only obligation, being relieved of all obligation to pay credit or for items that appear in the total charge for credit or other charges that do not relate to the supply of the goods or the doing of works.[84] The credit element of the transaction is completely excised. The borrower may keep any goods that have been supplied to himor her,[85] title to which will vest in him or her.

The effect on linked transactions

79. Cancellation affects linked transactions in the same way as it affects the main agreement. Cancellation of the main agreement operates to cancel the linked transaction;[86] if the linked transaction has not been concluded

84 Section 69(2).
85 Section 72(9)(c), (d).
86 Section 69(1)(i).

at the time that notice of cancellation is served, the offer to enter into the linked transaction is treated as withdrawn.[87] It is treated as if it had never been entered into.[88] Thus, the contract to supply (e.g. double glazing) will be cancelled along with the credit agreement that was designed to finance it in the case of a connected lending transaction.

80. A limited category of linked transactions will be unaffected by cancellation despite cancellation of the main credit agreement, pursuant to section 69(5). These transactions are those set out in the Consumer Credit (Linked Transactions) (Exemptions) Regulations 1983[89] (discussed earlier). These include contracts of insurance, which will therefore be unaffected by cancellation of the credit agreement.[90] Such transactions will not be cancelled or avoided on cancellation of the credit agreements.

Money paid by the borrower or hirer or relative prior to cancellation

81. The basic principle to be applied is that if a borrower or hirer or relative[91] has paid over money under or in contemplation of the agreement or linked transaction prior to the cancellation of an agreement, following cancellation that money should be repaid to the borrower or hirer or relative.[92] The starting point is that the sum has to be paid by the person that received it,[93] although there is an exception to this as explained below. These principles also apply to agreements that are only partially cancelled in accordance with section 69(2) referred to earlier.[94]

82. Furthermore in the case of a debtor-creditor-supplier agreement falling within section 12(b), if the lender has paid a sum on behalf of the borrower to the supplier prior to cancellation, then the supplier must repay the creditor.[95] An agreement within section 12(b) is one where the agreement is specifically to finance a transaction between the debtor and the supplier and where there either exist arrangements between the lender and supplier or where such arrangements are contemplated by the lender.

83. Section 70 provides a further right of recourse to the borrower or relative, both in the case of a debtor-creditor-supplier credit agreement coming within section 12(b) or in the case of a linked transaction within section 19(1)(b). A linked transaction within section 19(1)(b) is a

87 Section 69(1)(ii).
88 Section 69(4).
89 SI 1983/1560.
90 Illustrated by *Goshawk Dedicated (No 2) Ltd v Bank of Scotland* 2006 2 All ER 610.
91 Defined at section 184(1), (5).
92 Section 70(1).
93 Section 70(3).
94 Section 70(8).
95 Section 70(1)(c).

transaction to be financed by a debtor-creditor-supplier agreement. Both these types of transactions involve a third party supplier who it is assumed has received payment from the borrower or a relative prior to cancellation by the borrower. The supplier will be primarily liable to return the money as the party in receipt but it is provided that the lender is also jointly and severally liable with the supplier for its repayment.[96] The lender is entitled to an indemnity from the supplier in discharging the liability of the supplier under section 70(3)[97] and this indemnity extends to the lender's legal costs. The lender shall be entitled to have the supplier made a party to any proceedings for this purpose.[98]

84. In the case of credit brokerage fees that may have already been paid, on cancellation the borrower is entitled to repayment from the credit broker subject to a retention limited to £5.[99] It may be that the credit broker has sought payment of sums not described as fees or commission. If these sums would enter into the total charge for credit, they are to be treated as fees or commission.[100]

85. Section 70 does not specify a precise time for repayment; presumably, it has to be repaid immediately. However, in the case of a credit card, if there has been a payment made prior to cancellation, the lender is entitled to withhold payment until the credit card is returned.[101]

86. It would seem from section 70(3) and section 70(4) that a supplier is bound to indemnify the lender even in respect of sums paid by the borrower under linked transactions under section 19(1)(b) to which the supplier is not a party. The down payment paid to the installations contractor falls into this category; the supplier will be responsible for this sum, in the first place to the borrower and then to the lender. He or she would, however, have a right of action against the contractor in respect of its ultimate recovery.

Money paid to the borrower by the lender prior to cancellation

87. Section 71 sets out the consequences if money is advanced prior to cancellation. The basic principle is that the borrower cannot keep the money but has to repay it and that in some circumstances the agreement can be kept partially alive for that purpose.[102] This principle does not, however,

96 Section 70(3).
97 Section 70(4).
98 Section 70(3).
99 Section 70(6).
100 Section 70(7).
101 Section 70(5).
102 Section 71(1).

apply to debtor-creditor-supplier agreements for restricted use credit, a matter discussed below.

88. On cancellation, the borrower is given the option of repaying the money interest-free (which will obviously displease the lender). In the type of agreement where the borrower has to make repayments by instalments, the borrower can return all or some of the moneys to the lender prior to the first instalment without charge.[103] With other types of agreement, such as for running account credit, the time period allowed to the borrower to make repayment is one month from the date of cancellation.[104]

89. If the borrower does not take advantage of this opportunity, then 'the agreement shall continue in force so far as relates to repayment of credit and payment of interest'.[105] The borrower in other words cannot be asked to repay the entire lump sum immediately. Repayment terms resembling the original will be imposed upon him or her. The effect of section 71(1), however, is that all charges other than interest charges are cancelled.

90. In the case of an agreement where the repayments by the borrower are to be otherwise than by instalments, the original agreement continues in force after cancellation subject to the exclusion of non-interest charges and subject to the cancellation of any further obligation that the original agreement may have imposed on the lender to make further credit advances. Where the borrower avails him or herself of the opportunity to repay *some* of the credit during the interest-free month, the borrower's continuing obligations are recalculated on a pro rata basis.

91. The position is slightly more complicated in the case of an agreement where the borrower's obligations are to repay by instalments. In such a case, the borrower is under no obligation to make any repayment unless and until he or she is served with a notice signed by the lender requiring him or her to do so (section 71(3)). The form of the notice is prescribed by the Consumer Credit (Repayment of Credit on Cancellation) Regulations 1983.[106] As could be expected, the borrower has to be informed of the amount of the instalments that the borrower will have to pay and the dates when will fall due, without any extension of the period and excluding all sums other than principal or interest. The notice must also refer to the amount repaid by the borrower before the first instalment date; it is obvious therefore that the notice cannot be served until this date has passed.

92. The borrower can repay the money to any person on whom he or she could have served notice of cancellation *except* the repayment cannot be made to any agent engaged by him or herself to act for him or her during the course of antecedent negotiation.[107]

103 Section 71(2)(b).
104 Section 71(2)(a).
105 Section 71(1).
106 SI 1983/1559.
107 Section 71(4).

93. Actually calculating the repayments is problematical. Section 71(1) says that 'the original agreement shall continue in force so far as it related to repayment of credit and payment of interest'; section 71(3) speaks of 'the remaining instalments (recalculated by the lender as nearly as may be in accordance with the original agreement and without extending the repayment period) but excluding any sum other than principal and interest'.

94. The possible approaches to applying these formulae can be illustrated by taking an example. Suppose a credit agreement is concluded on 1 January under which an advance of £2,000 is made and under which the money is paid to the borrower immediately. Suppose further that this is repayable by 10 monthly instalments of £230 a month commencing on 1 February and ending on 1 November. All the charges are interest charges. The APR of the agreement is 36.5 per cent.

95. What are the consequences if the borrower cancels on 4 January? First, the borrower has until 1 February, the first instalment date, to repay any sums lent without incurring any charges. Let us suppose that he repays £1,000 on this basis on 30 January 30; £1,000 only is then outstanding. What repayments thereafter can the lender require of the borrower after service after 1 February of the requisite notice of demand under section 71(3)?

96. There are three possibilities:

(a) The borrower could be required to pay 10 instalments of half the original amount (i.e. £150) monthly on the first of the month for 10 months starting from 1 March. This would almost exactly reproduce the original repayment terms but deferred by one month. This repayments scheme, however, would only be permissible if 'repayment period' (which is not defined in the Act) could be construed to refer to a period of 10 months in *duration* rather than to a period ending on a *fixed date*, in this case 1 November.

(b) The borrower could be required to make nine repayments starting on 1 March and ending on 1 November, the total sum of which would equal the capital and interest charges due under the original agreement (scaled down pro rata). So in the example given, total capital and interest charges of £1,150 would have to be divided over nine instalments, to give an individual instalment amount £127.78. The only difficulty with this approach is that the APR of the revised instalment payments plan differs from that of the original agreement.

(c) The instalments could be recalculated from March to November in such amounts as would give rise to an APR equating to the original agreement. This would give an individual instalment amount of greater than £127.78.

97. Each of these alternatives is attractive for different reasons. Most writers (e.g. Guest, 'Encyclopaedia of Consumer Credit Law', Div. I, para. 617)

favour alternative (b) above. This involves far simpler calculations than alternative (c) and is more favourable to the borrower. Thus, (b) is preferable to (c). Alternative (a), which would be superficially the most sensible, is perhaps unacceptable as being inconsistent with section 71(3). Section 71(3) talks of remaining instalments, which seems to indicate that the number of instalments upon recalculation is not to be the same as that of the original agreement. It is instead to be diminished by one, to take into account the fact that the time of the first repayment has elapsed prior to service of the lender's notice under section 71(3).

98. Finally, it must be noted that section 71 does not apply to restricted use debtor-creditor-supplier agreements. There is, however, no difficulty with this.

99. Such restricted use agreements are:

(a) Agreements within section 12(a) where the lender and supplier are one and the same (e.g. a hire purchase agreement). In this type of transaction, no money is lent to the borrower at all or on his or her behalf; he or she is supplied directly with goods and/or services by the lender. Section 71 cannot therefore apply to this type of agreement.
(b) Agreements within section 12(b). Such agreements are effectively confined to connected lending transactions made under actual or contemplated arrangements with the supplier. Here, money can indeed be advanced prior to cancellation by the lender on the borrower's behalf to the supplier. It is unnecessary, however, for section 71 to provide for this since the situation is met by section 70(1)(c) where it states that such sums shall be repayable by the supplier to the lender. The obligation arises forthwith on cancellation. The fact that this type of situation falls outside section 71 indicates that the lender has, in these circumstances, no right of recourse against the borrower to recover sums paid on the borrower's behalf by the lender to the supplier.

Goods received by the borrower or hirer or relative prior to cancellation

100. The borrower or hirer or relative[108] may receive goods under a debtor-creditor-supplier agreement, hire agreement or linked transaction prior to cancellation. Section 72 governs the parties' rights and obligations in respect of these goods. The basic rule is that the goods have to be made available to the lender/owner following cancellation. Moreover, the debtor or hirer has an obligation to retain possession and take reasonable care of the goods prior to cancellation[109] and can be held liable for breach of statutory duty for failing to do this.[110]

108 Defined at section 184(1), (5).
109 Section 72(3).
110 Section 72(11).

101. On cancellation, the duty of the person with possession of the goods is confined to making them available at his or her own 'premises' (normally the borrower's home).[111] In a case where the possessor's address is given on the credit agreement, this address is the one and only one at which the borrower must make them available.[112] The possessor's duty to hand them over at the premises to 'the other party' being the person from whom the borrower acquired possession.[113]

102. The duty, however, does not arise until the borrower has received a request in writing requiring him or her to return the goods, which must be signed by or on behalf of the person from whom the goods were obtained.[114] There is no prescribed form for such a request. So the lender need not specify a time for collection nor even point out that the borrower has no duty to redeliver them personally. A bare request to the borrower to deliver the goods served at the time when a request is made to collect the goods will suffice to comply with section 72(5).

103. The lender should make the request within 21 days of cancellation. Furthermore, if the borrower does not receive a written request within 21 days of cancellation requiring the borrower to hand over the goods, the borrower has at the end of this time no further obligations in respect of them.[115] However, if the borrower does receive a request, the borrower owes a continuing duty to look after the goods until it is complied with.[116]

104. The borrower need not hand over the goods if sums paid by the borrower under the agreement or linked transaction have not been repaid. The borrower has a lien over the goods to secure repayment.[117] It is not necessary for the lien to operate that the person due to repay money to the borrower should be the self-same person to whom the goods should be restored. They could indeed be completely unconnected. A similar lien also arises where the borrower is entitled to return part exchange goods or the part exchange allowance under section 73.[118]

105. Once the goods are collected, the borrower, hirer or relative[119] is released from any further duty in respect of those goods.[120] Moreover, although the obligation of the borrower or hirer or relative is confined to handing them over at his or her premises, the borrower is not debarred from actively seeking to return the goods. Redelivery can be made to any person

111 Section 72(5).
112 Section 72(10).
113 Section 72(2)(b).
114 Section 72(5).
115 Section 72(8).
116 Section 72(8).
117 Section 70(2).
118 Section 73(5).
119 Defined at section 184(1), (5).
120 Section72(6).

upon whom he or she could have served notice of cancellation[121] or sends them at his or her own expense.[122] If goods are sent, a suitable method of transportation must be used so that it is reasonable to expect that the goods will arrive, and arrive undamaged.[123] Failure in this respect will render the borrower or hirer liable in damages to the lender or owner.[124]

106. Moreover, certain limited categories of goods are excluded from the requirement to make redelivery,[125] namely:

(a) perishables;
(b) consumables that are consumed prior to cancellation;
(c) goods supplied in an emergency;
(d) goods incorporated in any land or thing, not being the subject matter of the main credit agreement or linked transaction.

107. Examples (c) and (d) have been met before. Agreements for the supply of such types of goods will usually not be fully cancellable in any event[126] so the goods are not returnable for this reason. Perishables and consumables, such as food for the freezer and petrol for the car (as in the examples given above), do not need to be returned.

Goods given by the borrower in part exchange

108. In many circumstances, the borrower may transfer goods to the lender or supplier in part exchange. The part exchange operates of course as a part payment by the borrower. The consequences of cancellation on the part exchange transaction are dealt with in section 73. This applies to all types of regulated agreement where the borrower has delivered up goods in part exchange. Central to the understanding of section 73 is the 'part exchange allowance'. This is the amount attributable to the part exchange goods that will have been credited to the borrower. Where a specific sum was agreed upon between borrower and negotiator, this sum is the part exchange allowance. Where no specific figure was arrived at, the allowance is that which it would have been 'reasonable to allow',[127] which may be contentious.

109. The person in receipt of the part exchange goods has 10 days in which to return them starting with the date of cancellation. So if cancellation

121 Section 72(6)(a), but delivery cannot be made to someone who acted as agent for the borrower or hirer on any negotiations for the agreement.
122 Section 72(6)(b).
123 Section 72(7).
124 Section 72(7).
125 Section 72(9).
126 Section 69(2).
127 Section 73(7).

takes place on 1 March, the goods must be returned on or before 10 March. If they are not returned within that time or if their condition on return is not 'substantially as good' as it was when the borrower initially transferred them, then the person in possession, the negotiator, shall be bound to pay to the borrower the part exchange allowance.[128]

110. If the part exchange goods are tendered *after* the 10-day period, the borrower is not bound to accept them and can insist upon the part exchange allowance.[129]

111. In the case of a restricted use debtor-creditor-supplier agreement falling with section 12(b) (i.e. a transaction where there are either present or future contemplated arrangements between the lender and supplier between the lender and the supplier contract separately with the borrower), the lender and supplier (who will actually have taken possession of the part exchange) will be jointly and severally liable for payment of the part exchange allowance to the borrower.[130] By contrast, in the case of a hire purchase transaction,[131] the part exchange allowance must be recovered from the dealer who acted as negotiator in the transaction. The dealer did not act as the lender's agent in taking the goods on part exchange.[132] Section 73(2), which creates the liability to pay the part exchange allowance casts this duty only upon the negotiator (i.e. the dealer in the hire purchase context), to whom the goods were delivered. Nevertheless the lender in the case of a hire purchase transaction may be liable to account to the borrower for the part exchange allowance at common law.[133]

112. Until the borrower receives the return of the part exchange allowance (or, during the first 10 days, the part exchange goods), he or she has a lien pursuant to section 73(5) over any goods he or she in turn may have received prior to cancellation. The purpose of this lien is clearly to ensure that the borrower receives back the part exchange goods or the part exchange allowance.

113. Once the part exchange allowance has been paid, the title to the part exchange goods rests in the negotiator who initially received them.[134]

The effects of cancellation on security provided

114. The effect of either cancellation or withdrawal is to bring the security to an end.[135] In the case of withdrawal, however, the borrower should give

128 Section 73(2).
129 Section 73(2).
130 Section 73(4).
131 Which constitutes a debtor-creditor-supplier agreement within section 12(a).
132 *Branwhite v Worcester Works Finance Ltd* [1969] 1 A.C. 552.
133 *Branwhite v Worcester Works Finance Ltd.*
134 Section 73(6).
135 In the case of cancellation, section 113(3)(a), withdrawal section 113(6), both applying section 106.

written notice to the lender or owner that the security is no longer to take effect. In the case of cancellation, or withdrawal followed by notice, the security is treated as never having had any effect; goods deposited by way of security, such as deeds to land and any security investment, must be returned to the borrower.[136]

115. Where the borrower has cancelled, the borrower cannot be made to repay credit advanced to him or her before cancellation under section 71 or restore goods received by him or her under section 72 unless and until the lender has satisfied the requirements of section 106, such as the return of any security.[137]

116. Any duties placed on the borrower by these sections 'cannot be enforced' while obligations imposed on the lender by section 106 remain unfulfilled. The duties of the borrower, however, seem to survive in limbo even though unenforceable. Thus, the borrower probably remains under a continuing duty to take reasonable care of goods obtained by him or her under the (now cancelled) credit agreement. Once the lender had satisfied his or her obligations under section 106, he or she could sue for any damage done to the goods as a breach of the statutory duty under section 72(11). It would be irrelevant that at the time of the breach, the lender him or herself may have been in breach of his or her obligations under section 106 (for a full discussion of which, see later). Such a breach by the lender does not remove the duties of the borrower, but only suspends their enforcement.

Cancellation rights under the Financial Services (Distance Marketing) Regulations 2004

117. The 2004 Regulations confer cancellation rights. These, however, are of limited effect.

118. But these cancellation rights do not apply to any regulated consumer credit agreement to which the statutory right of withdrawal at section 66A applies;[138] section 66A applies to all regulated consumer credit agreements other than those where the credit exceeds £60,260, or secured on land or for the purchase of land or for a bridging loan in connection with land.[139] However, another exemption removes the cancellation right from agreements secured on land by legal mortgage,[140] from bridging loans for the purchase of land and for the restricted use credit agreements for the purchase of land.[141] This leaves essentially only credit agreements in excess of £60,260 where these cancellation rights may apply.

136 Section 106.
137 Section 113(5).
138 Reg 11(1)(h).
139 Section 66A(14) Consumer Credit Act 1974.
140 Reg 11(1)(d).
141 Reg 11(1)(g).

119. Regulation 9 of the Regulations confers cancellation rights exercisable within the cancellation period of 14 days given in regulation 10. Cancellation can be exercised orally or by post or by email if the supplier has notified an email address available for this purpose. The consequences of cancellation are spelt out at regulation 13.

Cancellation under the Consumer Contracts (Information, Cancellation and Additional Charges) Regulations 2013

120. The Consumer Contracts (Information, Cancellation and Additional Charges) Regulations 2013,[142] implementing EU Directive 2011/83/EU govern pre-contract disclosure of information in the context of on-site, off-site and distance contracts as from 13 June 2014. But they do not apply to agreements of a 'credit nature'.[143] However, they do potentially apply to hire contracts concluded between a trader and a consumer.

121. Distance contracts and off contracts are cancellable.[144] The cancellation period of 14 days[145] starts with the date of the contract.[146] However, if the trader fails to comply with the information requirements, the cancellation period is extended for 14 days until after the requirements are met with a longstop period of one year.[147] This 14-day period is an extension to the seven-day period specified by the earlier Cancellation of Contracts Regulations, SI 2008/1816.

122. In order to cancel a contract, the consumer must inform the trader of the decision to cancel.[148] The consumer may, but need not, use the model cancellation form contained at Part B of Schedule 3. However, any other clear statement setting out the decision to cancel is sufficient. If the consumer posts a cancellation statement to the creditor, it is sufficient that it is sent during the 14-day period.[149] The burden of proof is on the consumer to show cancellation within the required period.[150]

123. Save in the unlikely event that the trader has agreed to collect any goods following cancellation, it is for the customer to send or hand the goods back, unless the goods are of such a nature that they cannot by their nature normally be returned by post, in which event the trader must collect the goods.[151]

142 SI 2013/3134.
143 Reg 6(b).
144 Reg 29(1).
145 Reg 14(1).
146 Reg 29(2).
147 Reg 14(2).
148 Reg 32(1).
149 Reg 32(5).
150 Reg 32(6).
151 Reg 35.

124. Where an off-premises or distance contract is cancelled, any ancillary contract is automatically terminated without cost to the consumer.[152] An ancillary contract is one by which a consumer acquires goods and services 'related' to the main contract where those ancillary goods and services are provided by the trader or by a third party in arrangement with the trader.[153] In this context, an ancillary contract can include a credit agreement.[154] The trader must inform any relevant third party about the cancellation.[155]

125. There is a complication in that both an off-premises hire contract may be cancellable under both the Consumer Credit Act 1974 and these provisions. However, the effect of a cancellation by either route is likely to be the same.

152 Reg 38(1).
153 Reg 38(3).
154 Reg 38(4).
155 Reg 38(2).

10 Rights of the borrower and hirer

The borrower's right to information

1. The borrower (or hirer) has a right to information on his or her financial position throughout the duration of a credit or hire agreement. He or she also has a right to a copy of the agreement. The right extends to all regulated agreements except non-commercial agreements.[1]

2. This right applies to:

(a) fixed sum credit agreements under section 77;
(b) running account credit agreements under section 78; and
(c) hire agreements under section 79.

3. In addition, the borrower or hirer has the right to ask for a copy of any security instrument (such as a guarantee) securing the agreement that was executed *after* the agreement was entered into.[2] For no apparent reason, instruments executed *before* the agreement are excluded from this provision.

4. Under each provision, the borrower must make his or her request in writing accompanying it with a payment of £1 (increased from 50 pence by the Consumer Credit (Further Increase of Monetary Amounts) Order 1998).[3] This fee is payable whether the borrower or hirer asks for: (a) a copy of the agreement; (b) a financial statement; or (c) both. It appears only necessary for the lender (or owner) to supply the information or documentation that the borrower actually seeks in the written request. Thus, if the borrower only requires a financial statement, the lender need not supply a copy of the agreement as well (although the literal wording of the provisions might suggest otherwise). The lender must send the copy and the statement within 12 days of receipt of the borrower (or hirer's) written

1 Section 77(5), 78(7), 79(4).
2 Section 110.
3 SI 1998/997.

request. This time limit is set by the Consumer Credit (Prescribed Periods for Giving Information) Regulations 1983.[4]

5. If there are two or more borrowers and a request comes from one only, it must still be complied with and the information and copy statement must be supplied to each.[5]

6. A lender or owner need not supply a copy of the agreement or financial statement if the borrower or hirer has no further liabilities towards the lender or owner.[6] Nor is it right that the lender or owner be plagued with requests. The lender is accordingly excused if the borrower makes a request within one month of compliance with a previous one.[7]

7. The borrower may make a request through an agent, although because of the requirements of the Data Protection Act 1998, the lender must take reasonable steps that an agent seeking information for a borrower is properly authorised.[8]

The statement of information

8. The financial statement must contain details of the borrower (or hirer's) up-to-date position, particularising the amounts remaining to be paid.[9] On occasions, it may not be possible to give precise figures setting out the borrower's future indebtedness, for instance if the charges element is index-linked (e.g. interest charges tied to bank rate). In such a case, the lender must state the basis of future calculation (e.g. stating that charges are computed in such-and-such a way).[10]

9. The statement must be signed by or on behalf of the lender.[11]

10. The information provided by the lender is binding on the lender.[12] So if the lender understates the amounts of the remaining instalments, the starting point is that the borrower can pay the reduced amount in full discharge of his or her liabilities.

11. There are two possible qualifications to this. The information contained on the statements only has to state information 'to which it is practicable for the lender to refer'. The lender may therefore be able to say in certain circumstances that the information set out was inaccurate or incomplete because of circumstances the occurrence of which could not realistically be reflected in the statement. Such an excuse, however, will more

4 SI 1983/1569.
5 Section 185(1); CONC 13.1.3(2) G.
6 Sections 77(3)(a), 78(3)(a), 79(2)(a), 110(2)(b).
7 Section 77(3)(b), 78(3)(b), 79(2)(b), 110(2)(c).
8 CONC 13.1.3 G.
9 Sections 77(1), 78(1), 79(1).
10 Sections 77(2), 78(2); this provision does not apply to hire agreements.
11 Section 77(1), 78(1), 79(1).
12 Section 172.

usually justify an *overestimate* of the borrower's future liabilities rather than an underestimate. It is the view of the FCA that practicability is to be judged at the time of the request and may entail using information reasonably obtained from third parties.[13]

12. Second, if the lender takes proceedings to enforce an agreement during the course of which the borrower relies upon an erroneous statement of information produced in accordance with sections 77, 78 or section 79, the lender may, in accordance with section 172(3), request the court to give 'such relief (if any) to the lender or owner from the operation of section 172 . . . as may appear to the court to be just'. In other words, the lender may be relieved of its error if it makes application to the court. It is likely, however, that the lender will have to pay all the costs of such an application since the reason for the application was the lender's own initial mistake. The financial cost of such an application, which in many cases will outweigh the advantages to be gained, should act as a warning to lenders to prepare financial statements with care.

The copy agreement

13. The copy agreement supplied need not be an exact replica of the original agreement; it may be a reconstituted copy provided it contains everything that was in the original.[14] But there is no need to reproduce the signature box, the signature or the date of signature on the copy provided, nor any information relating to the personal circumstances of the borrower, hirer or surety.[15] However, where a reconstituted copy is supplied, the lender or owner should explain what has been done.[16]

14. Where an agreement has been varied, the obligation is to supply the latest copy of the varied agreement pursuant to section 82(1) of the Act or a clear statement of the terms of the agreement as varied.[17]

Consequences of failure to comply

15. What are the consequences to the lender or owner who fails to comply with his or her statutory requirements under sections 77, 78, 79 and 110?

16. The lender is 'not entitled while the default continues to enforce the agreement'.[18] Thus, a borrower will be able to rely on a breach of those requirements by way of defence to any proceedings issued but the defence

13 CONC 13.1.2 G.
14 *Carey v HSBC Bank plc* 2009 EWHC 3417.
15 Regulation 3(2) Consumer Credit (Cancellation Notices and Copies of Documents) Regulations 1983; CONC 13.1.4(7) G.
16 CONC 13.1.4(2) G.
17 CONC 13.1.4(6) G.
18 Sections 77(4)(a), 78(6)(a), 79(3)(a), 110(3)(a).

will be circumvented if the lender subsequently supplies the required statement and copy even after the proceedings have been commenced.[19] A continuing breach will also debar the lender from other methods of enforcing the agreement, such as retaking the goods.

17. Nevertheless, it is not enforcement for these purposes, and therefore not a breach of sections 77(4), 78(6) or 79(3), for the lender in breach of these requirements to pass on information about a default in payment by the borrower to a credit reference agency.[20] Nor is it enforcement to issue proceedings (although entering judgment may be).[21]

18. Where an agreement has become unenforceable, the lender or owner must not mislead the borrower or hirer as to the enforceability of the agreement.[22]

The duty to provide statements of account

Running account agreements

19. Section 78(4) stipulates that the lender must provide periodic statements of account to the borrower in the case of a running account credit, save that this duty does not apply in the case of small agreements (as defined in detail earlier but broadly where the credit limit is less than £50) or to non-commercial agreements.[23] The types of statements envisaged are of course such as are now produced on a regular basis by banks, credit card companies and department stores.

Content of statements of account

20. The information to be provided in these statements is specified in the Schedule to the Consumer Credit (Running Account Credit Information) Regulations 1983.[24] Most running account agreements provide for a borrower to make payments in respect of the running account at regular intervals, although this will often be a minimum payment, not necessarily the whole amount required to discharge the full balance owing. The statements must, over the relevant period, show an opening and a closing balance and show all movements in the account in the intervening period. All drawings and repayments by the borrower must be particularised, as must all charges levied.[25]

19 *McGuffick v Royal Bank of Scotland* 2009 EWHC 2386 (Comm) at [14].
20 *McGuffick v Royal Bank of Scotland* 2009 EWHC 2386 (Comm) at [82].
21 *Rankine v American Express Services Europe Ltd* 2009 CCLR 3
22 CONC 13.1.6(2) G.
23 Section 78(7).
24 SI 1983/1570.
25 Schedule, paragraph 5, Running-Account Credit Information Regulations 1983.

21. In the case of an unauthorised business overdraft agreement, the date of the previous statement must also be specified.[26]

22. Broadly, the statement of account will have to have the same information content as the traditional bank statement. There is only one difference. Where the statement shows that interest has been applied to the account, the statement account must provide some information on how the charges are calculated. Either the borrower must be told enough to check the calculation, or the rates of interest applied during the period must be given, or there must be a statement saying that the rates will be supplied on request and explaining how the computation is done.[27] However, in the case of an authorised non-business overdraft agreement (i.e. one determinable in less than three months), the interest rate must be specified and the other alternatives are not available.[28]

23. Where a running account agreement provides for a minimum payment to be made at the end of each month, which is the case with most credit card agreements, there is a need to have a prescribed statement, which must say as follows:[29] '**Minimum Payments**: If you make only the minimum payment each month, it will take you longer and cost you more to clear the balance.' If at the end of a period, a borrower has paid less than this minimum amount, then there is a further prescribed statement setting out the dangers of not making the minimum payment. The statement must also contain a statement of how any repayment will be allocated as between various aspects of the agreement (e.g. capital and interest).

24. All statements, whether providing for a minimum payment or not, must, under the heading '**Dispute Resolution**', contain a statement about the need to contact the lender before referring any dispute to the Financial Services Ombudsman.[30]

When must statements be provided?

25. Statements must be provided within one month after the end of each accounting period in respect of which the borrower is required to make a payment, albeit a minimum payment.[31] Each statement must cover a discrete period and of course one statement must succeed another.[32]

26 Schedule, paragraph 1A, Running-Account Credit Information Regulations 1983.
27 Schedule, paragraph 6, Running-Account Credit Information Regulations 1983.
28 Schedule, paragraph 7, Running-Account Credit Information Regulations 1983.
29 Schedule 2, paragraph 1, Consumer Credit (Information Requirements and Duration of Licences) Regulations 2007, SI 2007/1167.
30 Schedule 2 paragraph 4, Consumer Credit (Information Requirements and Duration of Licenses) Regulations 2007.
31 Reg 3(2) Running-Account Credit Information Regulations 1983.
32 Regulation 2(3).

26. If there is no balance standing in the account at the end of the period and the statement does not include a demand for payment, the lender can wait 12 months after the period covered by a previous statement, before giving the borrower a statement.[33]

27. In all other cases not covered by the above, the period is six months.[34] In the event, however, of there being no credit or debit balance throughout the entire period covered by the statement, the lender can wait for 12 months from that time of first movement in the account taking place.[35] These provisions can be seen to provide a practical answer to the situation where a borrower has decided to close an account but has not formally instructed the lender of this.

Dispensing notices

28. Unless further provision were made, it would be necessary in order to comply with section 78 to send statements to each and every borrower that was party to a joint account. This would obviously be wasteful, particularly since most joint accounts are held by members of the same family. Section 185(2) allows one or more of the borrowers to sign a 'dispensing notice'. The effect of such a notice is to release the lender from its duty to send statements of account to that person.

29. A dispensing notice continues in effect until revoked by written notice addressed to the lender from the borrower.[36] A dispensing notice will be invalid if all the other borrowers to the joint account have previously given such notices since to give effect to such a notice would mean that no statement was served at all.[37] Furthermore, all notices are revoked if any of the borrowers dies.[38]

30. It is specifically provided that there is no need for a fresh dispensing notice if an agreement is modified.[39]

Sanctions with running account agreements

31. There is very little sanction on a lender if he or she fails to comply with the requirements of section 78(4) and send periodic statements of account. The lender is not debarred from enforcing the agreement, in comparison with the position where the lender fails to send a copy of the agreement or

33 Regulation 3(2)(a) Running-Account Credit Information Regulations 1983.
34 Reg 3(3) Running-Account Credit Information Regulations 1983.
35 Regulation 3(2)(b) Running-Account Credit Information Regulations 1983.
36 Section 185(2A).
37 Section 185(2B).
38 Section 185(2C).
39 Section 185(2D).

a statement of information. No criminal penalties attach, nor can the lender be sued for breach of statutory duty.[40]

32. It is possible that a borrower who found him or herself at a severe disadvantage could apply to the court for a mandatory injunction to compel the lender to provide statements.[41] The Competition and Markets Authority could seek also an enforcement order under the Enterprise Act 2002 or complaint could be made to the Financial Conduct Authority.

Statements of account with fixed sum agreements

33. As a result of the Consumer Credit EU Directive and the insertion of section 77A into the Act, there has, from 1 February 2011, been a requirement on a lender to provide successive account statements in respect of fixed sum agreements.[42] These statements must be sent at least annually and must be sent within 30 days of the end of the period to which the statement relates.[43]

34. Unlike the entitlement to statements of information under section 77, these statements must be supplied free of charge.[44] The dispensing notice provisions referred to above apply where there are two or more borrowers.[45]

Content of fixed sum annual statements

35. The information to be included in fixed sum agreement statements is set out in Schedule 1 of the Consumer Credit (Information Requirements and Duration of Licenses and Charges) Regulations 2007.[46]

36. Paragraph 3 of Schedule 1 sets out a variety of information that must be given about the agreement, including the annual interest rate payable, what payments have been made, the charges that have been imposed and the balance at the end of the period. Where a statement contains an error or omission that does not affect the substance of the information or form of wording, then the notice shall not be treated as being in breach of the Information Requirements and Duration of Licences and Charges Regulations on that ground alone.[47]

37. Various guidance has to be included for the edification of the borrower:[48]

40 Section 170(1).
41 Section 170(3).
42 The requirement does not apply to small or non-commercial agreements: section 77A(8).
43 Section 77A(1E).
44 Section 77A(3).
45 Section 185(2).
46 SI 2007/1167.
47 Regulation 41 Information Requirements and Duration of Licences and Charges Regulations.
48 Part 2 of Schedule 1 to the Regulations.

(a) as to the borrower's right to settle the agreement early;
(b) as to dispute resolution, in the same terms as required for running account agreement statements; and
(c) as to the danger of paying less than the agreed sum and the need to contact the lender in the case of financial difficulty.

38. There is also a statement to be inserted into hire purchase and conditional sale agreements as to the hirer's right of termination.[49]

39. Further, in the case of what is referred to as a home credit loan agreement, being an agreement where the repayments are to be collected at the borrower's home, the APR must be specified and the following must be stated: 'You are entitled to one free statement per quarter or one per loan (whichever allows for more requests). We are required to provide you with a statement free of charge within 7 days of receiving your request.'[50]

Consequences of failure to comply

40. Unlike with running account agreements, the sanction for non-compliance is that the agreement becomes unenforceable until the default is remedied. Moreover, it is expressly provided that no interest or default charges are payable over the period of non-compliance.[51] The statement remedying the position must take into account the fact that no interest or default charges are payable over the period of non-compliance. A statement that does not comply with the Regulations is to be left out of account for the purpose of calculating the period of non-compliance since it is not a statement 'under this section' for the purposes of section 77A(7).[52]

Fixed sum instalment statements

41. In addition to the above, there is a specific right granted to a borrower to be provided, free of charge, with a statement setting out details of instalments due under the agreement. This right is available in the case of a fixed sum credit agreement of specific duration where credit is repayable by instalments.[53] But the right is not available in relation to agreements secured on land, pawn agreements, agreements where the credit exceeds £60,260 or agreements entered into predominantly for business purposes.[54]

49 Part 3 of Schedule 1 to the Regulations.
50 Consumer Credit (Information Requirements and Duration of Licenses) Regulations 2007, regulation 12(1).
51 Section 77A(6).
52 *JP Morgan Chase Bank NA v Northern Rock (Asset Management) plc* 2014 1 WLR 2197.
53 Section 77B.
54 Section 77B(9).

There is also no need to comply with a request that follows a request that was complied with made less than a month previously.[55]

42. The statement must be presented in the form of a table giving the amount and the date of all future instalments, together with a breakdown of each instalment as between capital and interest. Where the amount of any instalment may vary in the future, for instance on a change of interest rates, the statement must point out that the table will cease to apply in the event of a variation.[56] An interest variation will have to be notified in accordance with section 78A.

43. Unlike the position with periodic fixed sum statements, section 77B does not provide that the agreement becomes unenforceable if there is a breach of the requirements of the section; instead, the lender is liable for breach of statutory duty.[57]

The right to terminate a hire purchase or conditional sale agreement

44. The Consumer Credit Act 1974 gives the right at section 99 to a borrower to terminate a hire purchase or conditional sale agreement. Section 100 sets out the consequences of termination in this way. These provisions originated with the Hire Purchase Act 1965 (with some alteration). This right cannot be excluded by the terms of the agreement and any attempt to do this will be void.[58]

Exercising the right of termination

45. At any time before the final payment is due, the borrower can terminate the agreement by serving notice of termination of the hire purchase or conditional sale agreement. The notice given can be quite informal, but it must be in writing. A default notice served on a borrower by a lender in respect of a hire purchase or conditional sale agreement must contain a statement drawing attention to the borrower's right of termination under section 99.[59]

46. The notice can be given to anyone entitled or authorised to receive payments under the agreement.[60] Thus, notice can be given to the lender, or to a dealer if payments are made through him or her.

55 Section 77B(6).
56 Section 77B(5).
57 Section 77B(8).
58 Section 173.
59 Paragraph 8A Schedule 2 Consumer Credit (Enforcement Default and Termination Notices) Regulations 1983 SI 1983/1561.
60 Section 99(1).

47. Problems may arise when borrowers send ambiguous letters. For example, the borrower may write to the lender saying he or she is unable to make any further payments under the agreement, or that he or she cannot continue with it. Does such a letter amount to statutory termination of the agreement by the borrower inviting the lender to collect the goods? If the lender receives a letter such as this, the lender should of course clarify that the borrower is intending to terminate the agreement. However, there is a general principle that communications from the borrower should be construed in a manner favourable to the borrower[61] and it will generally be financially advantageous for a borrower to exercise his or her rights under sections 99 and 100.

48. The right of termination does not apply to a conditional sale agreement relating to land (i.e. a contract for the purchase of land on instalments with title passing to the purchase under defined circumstances) once title has passed to the buyer.[62]

49. In fact, the above situations are unlikely to occur very often because most conditional sale agreements are framed so that title passes only when all the payments have been made by the borrower, by which time there is, of course, no agreement left to terminate.

Consequences of termination

50. There are two issues to be considered: what happens to the goods (or land) subject to the terminated agreement and what, if any, financial adjustments have to be made?

Return of the goods

51. Following termination by service of a notice under section 99, title to the goods or land vests irrevocably in the lender even if title has already passed to the borrower under a conditional sale agreement.[63] If the previous owner of the goods has died, then the ownership of goods passes to that person's personal representatives as if the goods had vested in that person the moment before death.[64]

52. Once title to the goods has vested in the lender, the obligation of the debtor is thereafter to make the goods available; there is no positive obligation to make delivery of the goods to the lender.[65] If the borrower

61 *United Dominion Trust Ltd v Ennis* [1968] 1 Q.B. 54.
62 Section 99(3).
63 Section 99(4).
64 Section 99(4).
65 *Capital Finance Lid v Bray* 1964 1 WLR 323.

refuses to comply with a request for redelivery, the borrower will be liable, under standard tortious principals, for wrongful interference with goods.

53. If the borrower refuses to return the goods, the lender will have to apply to the court to seek their return. On application to the court, the court will, unless the justice of the case demands otherwise, order the borrower to deliver up the goods to the lender, rather than giving the borrower the option of paying their value.[66] The reason behind this is to prevent the borrower using the device of termination of the agreement as a means of acquiring the goods more cheaply than would be the case if the agreement continued.

54. If the borrower has failed to comply with an obligation to take reasonable care of the goods (or land), then the borrower will have to compensate the lender in respect of the loss.[67] The obligation will only be relevant if imposed by the contract of hire purchase or conditional sale itself, which it normally will be; the lender will normally provide for this obligation expressly in the relevant contract. If a borrower fails in this duty, the borrower will have to pay the lender a sum equal to the diminution in value of the goods measured against the value of the goods in the state the goods ought to have been in (i.e., assuming reasonable wear and tear).

Financial consequences

55. The borrower must discharge all outstanding liabilities due to the lender prior to the date of termination.[68] This means in practice that the borrower will continue to be liable for arrears after termination. In addition, the borrower will have to make further payments so that the total paid or payable equals half the hire purchase price (or conditional sale price).[69] This is illustrated in the example below. This rule does not apply if the agreement itself provides for the more generous termination provisions, or, as explained further below, in the rare instance of a lender's overall loss as a result of termination being less than the further payments required.[70] There is no entitlement to a rebate under the Early Settlement Regulations when a hire purchase or conditional sale agreement is terminated under section 99.[71]

56. Insofar as the agreement provided for an installation charge, the reference to half the price is to be treated as half the price plus the installation charge (i.e. so that the borrower always has to pay the installation charge in full).[72]

66 Section 100(5).
67 Section 100(4).
68 Section 99(2).
69 Section 100(1).
70 Section 100(3).
71 Reg 2(3) Early Settlement Regulations 2004.
72 Section 100(2).

57. A borrower who terminates having already paid more than half the total hire purchase or conditional sale price is not entitled to any repayment for having paid more than the statutory minimum. Section 100 does not provide for any such repayment.

58. The borrower's liability to the lender may occasionally be reduced by operation of section 100(3), which states that 'if in any action, the court is satisfied that a sum less than the amount specified [by section 100(1)] would be equal to the loss sustained by the lender in consequence of the termination by the borrower, the court may make an order for the payment of that sum in lieu of the amount specified by section 100(1)'.

59. This provision requires an assessment of the 'loss sustained by the lender in consequence of the termination'. An overall figure for the lender's loss must, however, be the total of:

(a) The loss to the lender arising from the fact that he or she will not receive the remainder of the hire purchase (or conditional sale) payments less a discount to take into account the fact that these payments were only due at varying intervals in the future. The Early Settlement Regulations 2004 could be utilised to form the basis for calculating the discount.
(b) The incidental costs of termination such as the costs of collecting the goods.
(c) Deducting the value of the goods returned. The net value to the lender is what is important, so the costs of resale of the goods will be taken into account.

60. If the total of (a) to (c) above comes to less than the amount required to be paid by the borrower to equal half the hire purchase price, then the borrower can ask the court to limit his or her liability to the total of (a) to (c). The court has a discretion in the matter but it can expected that it will normally be exercised in the borrower's favour.

61. But in practice, it seems that section 100(3) will be most unlikely to apply because, in order for it to apply, the value of the goods repossessed by the lender will almost have to equal the value of half the hire purchase (or conditional sale) price.

Worked example

62. *Example*: Assume a washing machine to be acquired on hire purchase. The cash price is £800; the installation charge is a further £80 to be paid for as part of the main agreement; the deposit of £200 is paid by the borrower. Assume that under the agreement, the borrower is required to make payments in 12 monthly instalments of £100 each, with the borrower being given an option to purchase the washing machine at a price of £20, exercisable at the time of payment of the final instalment. The borrower pays the instalments in cash to the local dealer from whom he acquired the

washing machine in the first place. Suppose also that the borrower, having installed the washing machine, then resells and redelivers it to a third party who now cannot be traced. After the time of the fourth instalment, the borrower has fallen behind with his payments by £75. He now informs the washing machine dealer in writing that he wishes to terminate the agreement.

63. *Analysis*: The borrower is entitled to terminate, despite having resold the washing machine and despite being in arrears to the lender. He can also terminate by expressing his desire to do so in writing to the dealer, as the dealer is authorised to accept payments on behalf of the lender under the agreement.[73]

64. The borrower will have to make a financial payment to the lender on termination. The borrower has paid a total of £525 under the agreement (including £200 for the deposit). From this will have to be deducted £80 for the installation charges, leaving £445.The total hire purchase price, excluding the installation charge, is the deposit of £200, 12 instalments of £100 each and a £20 purchase option, less £80 for the installation charge. The total price is therefore £1,380. Half of this total price is £690. The borrower has already, excluding the installation charge, paid £445 and therefore will have *prima facie* a further £245 to pay.

65. In fact, his liability will be greater than this because he has not taken reasonable care of the goods; indeed, he had disposed of them when he had no title to do so. Accordingly, he will additionally have to compensate the lender for the value of the washing machine as at the date of termination.[74]

Comparison with early settlement

66. A borrower is also entitled to bring a hire purchase or conditional sale agreement by early settlement under section 94. In these circumstances, the borrower will have to serve a notice under the lender under section 94 and not section 99. The consequences, however, are different because in relation to termination under section 99, the title to the goods vests in the lender to whom the borrower is obliged to give up delivery.[75] In relation to early settlement, however, the borrower will acquire title to the goods.[76] The financial consequences of each form of termination differ markedly. The amounts due from the borrower are dictated by section 100 in the first instance, and by the Early Settlement Regulations 2004 in the latter. The choice between termination and early settlement will depend on the financial position of the borrower, the number of payments that have already

73 Section 99(1).
74 Section 100(4).
75 Section 99(4).
76 Section 94(2).

been made under the agreement and the desire of the borrower for the goods. If the goods are not of continuing desirability for the borrower, the borrower will probably wish to terminate.

The hirer's right to terminate a hire agreement

67. The policy of the Act is to assist a hirer who finds him or herself subject to a lengthy hire agreement. The Act provides that the hirer may bring the agreement to an end before the time specified under the agreement.[77]

68. Termination must be on written notice given to any person authorised or entitled to receive hire payments under the agreement.[78] The notice must specify a notice period when termination of the hire will take effect. The notice period is the interval between payments or three months, whichever is less.[79] So for an agreement that requires the hirer to make hire payments every month, then the notice period is one month. Should the hire payments be at differing intervals (which would seem unusual), then the notice period is the shortest interval between payments or three months, whichever is less.[80]

69. However, there can be no termination until the agreement has lasted for at least 18 months including the notice period, unless the agreement specifies that termination can take place at an earlier date.[81] Should the agreement be varied in some way, this will not cause any extension to the 18-month period.[82]

70. However, there are a number of types of agreement to which this right of termination does not apply.

71. It does not apply to agreements where the annual hire charge exceeds £1,500 in any one year.[83]

72. It does not apply to 'equipment leases'.[84] Such leases are finance transactions, which are sometimes structured so as to generate tax benefits for the hirer. The essence of an equipment lease is that the owner of the goods buys them solely for the specific purpose of hiring to the hirer. The owner then works out his or her charges over a four- or five-year time span. From the owner's point of view, the transaction is purely financial; the owner has no interest in the goods that the hirer selects and takes responsibility for throughout. Requirements needed to satisfy the exemption are that:

77 Section 101.
78 Section 101(1).
79 Section 101(4).
80 Section 101(5).
81 Section 101(3).
82 Section 101(9).
83 Section 101(7)(a).
84 Section 101(7)(b).

(a) the hirer should select the goods;
(b) the owner should buy them specifically for the purpose of hiring;
(c) the hirer should hire the goods (or purport to be hiring them) for the purposes of the hirer's business (which includes a profession); and
(d) the supplier of the goods must not be 'associated' (as defined in section 184) with the owner.

73. The termination provisions do not apply when the hirer intends, or holds him or herself out as intending, to rehire the goods as part of a business run by the hirer.[85] Such an arrangement is quite common in practice.

74. Moreover, it is possible for the FCA[86] to exempt a particular trader from the provisions of section 101.[87] The trader has to apply and the FCA has to be persuaded that hirers as a whole will benefit from the exclusion of their rights of termination. The trader will presumably only be able to show benefit to hirers when the trader can demonstrate that it will either not hire the goods at all or will hire them on significantly more onerous terms if exemption is not granted. The FCA may make any exemption conditional. As yet, no businesses have been exempted. The FCA is also able to exempt a category of hire agreements from the termination provisions (as opposed to a particular trader).[88]

75. On termination, the hirer will continue to be liable for rental payments that remain outstanding.[89] If the owner tries to attach a financial penalty to the exercise by the hirer of a right of termination or seeks to impose an additional liability consequent thereon, the provision will be void as it would be 'inconsistent with a provision for the protection of the . . . hirer' and void in accordance with section 173(1).

Termination of open-end credit agreements

76. An open-end credit agreement is one of no fixed duration.[90] An agreement that provides for automatic renewal after a fixed period has elapsed is probably to be considered open-ended. Section 98A regulates the termination of such agreements, as well as the circumstances in which, in respect of such agreements, there can be a withdrawal or suspension of credit (which may be permitted by the terms of the agreement but not necessarily involve termination of it).

85 Section 101(7)(c).
86 Previously the Office of Fair Trading.
87 Section 101(8).
88 Section 101(8A).
89 Section 101(2).
90 Section 189.

77. A borrower may terminate an open-end credit agreement free of charge on giving notice of at least one month.[91] The notice need not be in writing unless required in writing by the lender.[92]

78. If the lender is given the right to terminate the agreement, other than for breach of contract, as is likely, the lender must give no less than two months written notice to the borrower (unless the agreement provides for a longer notice period when the longer notice period must be complied with).[93] There is no required form of notice. This two months notice period, however, does not apply in the case of termination for breach of contract; termination in these circumstances can take place after service of a default notice under section 87.[94]

79. The agreement may give the lender the right to terminate or suspend the borrower's right to draw on credit. Before exercising the right, the lender must serve a notice on the borrower and the notice must give reasons for the termination or suspension.[95] However, the two months notice period application to termination of the agreement does not apply to the suspension or withdrawal of credit in these circumstances. Nor is there any need to serve a default notice under section 87 of the Act.[96]

80. Furthermore, the lender is not entitled to act arbitrarily in the withdrawal or suspension of credit; the reasons must be objectively justified, for instance if credit has been misused, or if there is a significantly increased risk of the borrower being unable to repay credit.[97] By contrast, a lender does not have to give reasons for terminating the agreement.

81. This provision does not apply either to an authorised business or non-business overdraft agreement or to an agreement where a borrower overdraws on a current account without pre-arrangement, or to an agreement secured on land.[98]

Liability of the lender for the conduct of the negotiator

82. Section 56 has the effect of making a lender responsible for conduct occurring during antecedent negotiations of a supplier of goods or services. In the circumstances when it applies, the effect of section 56(2) is to make the supplier, labelled by the Act the 'negotiator',[99] the deemed agent of the

91 Section 98A(1).
92 Section 98A(2).
93 Section 98A(3).
94 Section 98A(7).
95 Section 98A(4).
96 Section 87(5).
97 Section 98A(6).
98 Section 98A(7).
99 Section 56(1).

lender. This deemed agency applies only to regulated credit agreements. It cannot be excluded by contrary agreement.[100]

83. Antecedent negotiations are defined for the purposes of the Act at section 56(1). The definition is also relevant in a number of other contexts, for instance in fixing the timetable for the communication of information in respect of credit reference agencies.[101]

84. Antecedent negotiations start from the time of the first communication between the negotiator and the borrower, which may be by advertisement.[102] They extend to representations and 'all other dealings' between lender and borrower. These are wide words. The term 'representation' is itself defined widely by the Act, extending to all conditions and warranties and undertakings and other statements, whether written or oral.[103]

85. The first category[104] is negotiations conducted by the creditor or owner directly. Obviously, the deemed agency has no part to play in this context.

86. The second category,[105] in which a deemed agency does arise, is negotiations conducted by 'the credit-broker in relation to goods sold or proposed to be sold to the creditor before forming the subject-matter of a debtor-creditor-supplier agreement within section 12(a)'.

87. A borrower-lender-supplier agreement within section 12(a) is one where the goods are supplied to the borrower by the lender. Typically, this refers to hire purchase, conditional sale and credit sale agreements. The supplier of goods acts as credit broker who then typically sells the goods to the lender and the lender then supplies the goods to the borrower on credit.[106]

88. At common law, normally a supplier in the context of a hire purchase or conditional sale agreement is not the agent of the lender,[107] although the supplier may become so for some ad hoc purpose.[108] The effect of section 56(2) is therefore, in circumstances where it applies, to reverse the decision in *Branwhite* and to make the supplier the agent of the lender in relation to all antecedent negotiations.

100 Section 56(3).
101 Section 157.
102 Section 56(1).
103 Section 189(1).
104 Section 56(1)(a).
105 Section 56(1)(b).
106 Example 2 Schedule 2.
107 *Branwhite v Worcester Works Finance Ltd* 1969 1 AC 552.
108 *Branwhite* at pages 573 and 578.

The requirements that goods must be sold or proposed to be sold by the credit broker to the creditor

89. Note the limitation in this wording in that the negotiations must relate to *goods sold or proposed to be sold by the credit broker to the creditor.* Only dealings in relation to goods subject to such a sale are within the deemed agency.

90. This limitation was discussed in *Forthright Finance v Ingate.*[109] The facts were that the claimant approached a dealer with a view to taking a new vehicle on hire purchase. The claimant already had an existing vehicle on hire purchase; in order to bring about the new agreement, the dealer agreed to a part exchange allowance on the current vehicle, which equalled the amount needed to pay off the balance due on that hire purchase agreement. The dealer then sold the new vehicle to the lender in the usual way and the lender entered into a hire purchase agreement with the claimant in respect of the new vehicle. However, the dealer broke his promise to the claimant and failed to pay off the hire purchase balance due under the existing vehicle. The claimant took proceedings against the lender, claiming that the lender was responsible for the default of the dealer pursuant to section 56(2). The lender denied the application of section 56(2) on the basis that a promise made in relation to the existing vehicle was not made in relation to the 'goods sold by the credit broker to the creditor' (i.e. the new vehicle).

91. The Court of Appeal rejected this argument. The promises made in relation to the existing vehicle were part and parcel of the transaction relating to the new vehicle – the claimant would not have entered into the new agreement but for the promise made to redeem the hire purchase agreement in relation to the existing vehicle.

92. However, a case on the other side of the line was *Black Horse Ltd v Langford.*[110] That case also concerned a failure by a dealer, in breach of a promise previously made to the customer to pay off a part exchange allowance on an existing car that was subject to an existing hire purchase agreement. In that case, the dealer engaged another credit broker to find a source of hire purchase finance for the customer. The dealer then sold the car to that credit broker who then sold it on to the lender that then entered into a hire purchase agreement with the customer. When the original dealer failed to sell off the hire purchase balance on the previous car, the customer sought to make the lender responsible under section 56(2) for the breach of promise of the dealer. But the customer failed because the person for whom the lender was responsible under section 56(2) was not the original dealer, but the intermediate credit broker that had sold the vehicle to the

109 1997 4 All ER 99.
110 2007 EWHC 907 (QB).

dealer, and it was not that credit broker, but the original dealer, that had made the promise to pay off the existing hire purchase balance. This case would seem to provide a route for a lender to avoid the deemed agency by involving an intermediate credit broker.

Section 56(1)(c)

93. The third category of deemed agency[111] is in respect of negotiations 'conducted by the supplier in relation to a transaction financed or proposed to be financed by a debtor-creditor-supplier agreement within section 12(b) or (c)'.

94. This category includes purchases made using a credit card.[112] The effect of the third category is that statements made by the supplier (e.g. a shop at which an item is purchased using a credit card) will be treated as made on behalf of the credit card company. Section 75 may also apply in this situation and a consumer may have a dual remedy under both sections 75 and 56 in relation to statements made by a deemed agent. Indeed, section 75 does not apply to claims involving an item in respect of which the cash price was less than £100; no such financial ceiling applies to section 56.

No deemed agency with lease agreements

95. The effect of section 56 is to draw a sharp and somewhat arbitrary distinction between hire purchase and conditional sale agreements, on the one hand, and lease agreements, on the other, in circumstances when goods are sourced through a dealer and leased or let on hire purchase through a separate finance company, the goods having been sold by the dealer to the finance company. In the case of a regulated hire purchase or conditional sale agreement, the deemed agency under section 56 will apply and the lender will be responsible for the statements of the dealer. However, in the case of a lease agreement, the lender will not normally be responsible for the statements of the dealer since there will be no deemed agency, section 56(1)(b) not applying to lease agreements. (There may be a collateral contract directly between the hirer and the dealer allowing the customer to enforce any promises made by the dealer against the dealer.)[113]

96. Of course, there may be situations when the owner, in respect of a lease agreement, acts in such a way as to make the dealer the owner's agent. This happened in *Purnell Secretarial Services Ltd v Lease Management Services Ltd*,[114] when the lease agreement was headed with the name of the dealer,

111 Section 56(1)(c).
112 Example 3 Schedule 2.
113 *Brown v Sheen and Richmond Car Sales Ltd* 1950 1 All ER 1102.
114 1994 CCLR 127.

a separate company. Anyone reading the lease agreement would have gained the impression, as the hirer did indeed think, that the lease agreement was being concluded with the dealer. In these circumstances, the owner was bound by the statements of the dealer. But this situation will be unusual and the normal situation will be that there is no agency between the dealer and the owner.

Serving notice of rescission

97. Section 56 made the negotiator the deemed agent of the creditor in respect of all representations and other dealings during the course of antecedent negotiations leading up to conclusion of a regulated credit agreement.

98. Section 102 makes certain persons the deemed agent of the lender or owner for the purpose of service of a notice of rescission by the borrower or hirer.

99. One of the categories of person who are the deemed agent for this purpose include the persons covered by the deemed agency provisions in section 56, namely the negotiator in antecedent negotiations, as defined by section 56.

100. Section 102 of the Act also introduces an additional category of deemed agent, namely someone who acted for the borrower or hirer in the course of antecedent negotiations, typically a credit broker engaged by the borrower or hirer. The borrower or hirer may therefore serve a notice of rescission on such a person and it will count as good service on the lender or owner for the purpose of notification of a desire to rescind the agreement.

101. The deemed agent, having been served with a notice of rescission, has a deemed contractual duty to pass it on immediately to the lender or owner and can be held liable in damages for contract if the deemed agent fails in this respect.[115]

102. The term 'rescission' is not defined in this context. In fact, it has two possible meanings in the law of contract. It can refer to rescission *ab initio*, the remedy available when a contract is set aside in its entirety for fraud, misrepresentation or mistake. It can also refer to the acceptance by the innocent party of a repudiatory breach of contract by the other contracting party, the effect of which is to put an end to further performance of the contract and give rise in addition to a remedy in damages. The legal consequences of the two types of rescission are different. These two different meanings of the word 'rescission' are discussed in the House of Lords decision of *Johnson v Agnew*[116] in connection with a contract for the sale of land. The term 'rescission' in section 102 ought to embrace both meanings.

115 Section 175.
116 1979 1 All ER 883 at p889f.

103. It is not possible for a regulated credit or hire agreement validly to contract out of the deemed agency provision contained in section 102 since this is a provision for the protection of the debtor or hirer.[117]

104. There is one limitation on section 102 and that is that the deemed agency provisions apply only to a notice given in *writing* to the deemed agent.[118] At common law, a notice of rescission does not have to be in writing to be effective, but an oral notice given to one of the categories of deemed agent for the purposes of section 102 will not be effective.

Liability of the lender for breach of the supply contract

105. Section 75 confers upon a borrower a remedy against the lender that would otherwise exist only against the supplier (section 75(1)). No new cause of action is created by section 75. Section 75 confers a remedy against an additional party. There will be many situations where it is easier for a borrower to bring a claim against a lender than against a supplier.

Agreements to which section 75 applies

106. Section 75 applies only to borrower-lender-supplier agreements within subsections 12(b) and 12(c).[119] These agreements include those in which a supplier introduces a borrower to a source of finance to finance the supply contract and a credit card transaction for the purchase of goods or services. The consequences of section 75 can be very serious for a lender in the case of a disreputable supplier; lenders have to be careful about their choice of suppliers.

107. Section 75 does *not* apply to hire purchase, conditional sale and credit sale agreements since these are borrower-lender-supplier agreements within section 12(a). This point has been overlooked in the past, for example by the High Court in *Porter v General Guarantee Corporation Ltd.*[120]

108. Restrictions are imposed by section 75(3) on the types of agreements falling within section 75. First, the section does not apply to non-commercial agreements.[121] Such agreements (discussed earlier) are those where the lender does not provide credit in the course of a business carried on by him or her. Then, very small and very large agreements are also taken out of the ambit of section 75. It does not apply to an agreement that involves the purchase of an item that has a cash price of less than £100 (increased

117 Section 173(1).
118 See the definition of notice in section 189(1).
119 Section 75.
120 1982 RTR 384.
121 Defined at section 189(1).

from the figure of £30 by the Consumer Credit (Increase of Monetary Limits) Order 1983).[122] The idea of this provision is to absolve credit card companies in particular from having to handle a large number of consumer complaints in relation to relatively minor transactions.

109. On the other end of the scale, transactions concluded after 20 May 1985 involving the purchase of an item that has a cash price of over £30,000 are also removed from the ambit of section 75 (for transactions before the above date, the cash price limit is £10,000). The reason behind this exemption is different. With such large transactions, the borrower is highly likely to be entering into the transaction in the course of a business carried on by him or her, or alternatively have access to independent advice. The supplier too is likely to be a reasonably substantial concern to handle such a large transaction. In these circumstances, the protection of section 75 is thought not to be necessary.

110. As from February 2011, there has been a further exclusion from the ambit of section 75; there are excluded running account agreements in which the credit in respect of an agreement not secured on land has to be repaid in its entirety in a period of equal to or less than three months.[123]

111. It is no answer to a claim under section 75 that the borrower may have been acting in breach of the agreement in entering into the transactions, for example by exceeding a credit limit.[124]

112. It is not possible to contract out of the remedy given by section 75.[125]

The statutory indemnity

113. Section 75 operates to provide a remedy against the lender that would otherwise lie solely with the supplier. The liability of the lender is joint and several with that of the supplier.[126]

114. The supplier is, however, the party primarily responsible for any claim that the borrower may have arising out of the supply transaction. It is natural, therefore, that the lender should have a right of recourse against the supplier; this right is conferred by section 75(2), which gives the lender the right to an indemnity from the supplier, the indemnity extending to any costs incurred by the lender in reasonably defending proceedings. However, section 75(2) is expressly made subject to any agreement that may have been concluded between the lender and supplier to the contrary. In a case where a lender is sued by a borrower in reliance upon section 75, the lender is in turn entitled to issue third party proceedings against the borrower,

122 SI 1983/1878.
123 Section 75(3)(c).
124 Section 75(4).
125 Section 173(1).
126 Section 75(1).

subject to rules of court.[127] It is obviously sensible that the respective course rights of borrower, lender and supplier can be determined in single proceedings.

Extent of a lender's liabilities

115. The lender is liable only in respect of a claim arising out of breach of contract or misrepresentation by the supplier.[128] This will cover most situations but it is possible to contemplate some types of claim that would not be covered, for instance mistake.

116. The liability of the lender will be no more than the liability of the supplier; the borrower has a 'like claim' against the lender. The lender therefore can avail itself of any defences open to the supplier such as a right of set-off in a situation where sums are outstanding to the supplier from the borrower. If the lender him or herself has a set-off or counterclaim, this also can be raised on a claim made against him or her under section 75.

117. However, this section has no direct bearing on the credit agreement itself; it is concerned only with conferring additional remedies arising out of the supply transaction. The wording of section 75(1) makes this clear: 'If the debtor under a debtor-creditor-supplier agreement within section 12(b) or (c) has, in relation to a transaction financed by the agreement, any claim against the supplier in respect of a misrepresentation or breach of contract, he shall have a like claim against the lender.' Section 75(1) is concerned therefore with the rights and remedies arising out of the *transaction financed* by the credit agreement (i.e. the contract of supply). The credit agreement itself will be unaffected.

118. In the Scottish decision of *United Dominions Trust Ltd v Taylor*,[129] it was held that the effect of section 75(1) on the facts of that case was to allow rescission of the *credit* agreement. But this involves a misreading of section 75 as held now by the Supreme Court in *Durkin v DSG Retail Ltd*.[130]

119. Nevertheless, although a borrower may not be able to rescind the credit agreement under section 75, it may be able to do so at common law. In the case of *Durkin*, the claimant Mr Durkin bought a personal computer at the same time as entering into a loan agreement to finance the purchase. It was a term of the loan agreement that the loan was to be paid directly to the supplier; accordingly, the credit agreement was an agreement within section 12(b) of the Act.

120. Mr Durkin was entitled to rescind the supply agreement (because the personal computer did not have a characteristic promised by the supplier) and at the same time, he also sought to rescind the credit agree-

127 Section 75(5).
128 Section 75(1).
129 1980 SLT 28.
130 2014 UKSC 21 at [19].

ment as well. His right to rescind was resisted by the finance company and Mr Durkin brought proceedings.

121. The Supreme Court held that section 75 did not give Mr Durkin a direct right to rescind the credit agreement. Nevertheless, it was recognised that Mr Durkin was able to recover as part of his damages *against the supplier* his liability to make payments under the credit agreement. By virtue of section 75, these damages could also be recovered against the lender.[131] In the light of this, the Supreme Court held that it was an *implied term* in the credit agreement that Mr Durkin should be able to rescind the credit agreement if he could also rescind the supply agreement.[132] Accordingly, while Mr Durkin could not rescind the credit agreement directly by virtue of section 75, it could rescind by virtue of the implied term. The creditor would also have a right to rescind in the same circumstances.[133]

122. The Supreme Court held that this analysis applied not only to agreements within section 12(b), but also to agreements within section 12(c).[134]

Rights against goods

123. In a case where goods are rejected by a borrower, they will be returned to the dealer. This can happen either in the event that a borrower rescinds the agreement or accepts the supplier's repudiation of it. Does the lender have any rights over the goods returned? In the vast majority of cases, this right will be unimportant because the lender will have a right of indemnity against the borrower under section 75(2) for all sums paid to the lender. The question will only become important in the event that the supplier is insolvent and the right of indemnity is therefore worthless or almost worthless. It then has to be asked whether the goods rejected are subject to any rights in favour of the lender or whether the liquidator or trustee in bankruptcy of the supplier can claim the full benefit upon their eventual sale.

124. It seems unfair for these circumstances to saddle the lender with the full liability of the supplier and yet give him or her no recourse against the goods. One answer could be to allow the lender an equitable lien over the goods to the extent of his or her indemnity. The lien would arise by operation of law and so would not need to be registered under the Bills of Sale Act 1878 to 1883 to be valid. It must be admitted, however, that no exact parallel exists for the creation of such a lien (although the fact that the goods are not in the possession of the lender is no bar to the creation

131 *Durkin* at [22].
132 *Durkin* at [26].
133 *Durkin* at [26].
134 *Durkin* at [26].

of an equitable lien). It remains to be seen whether the courts would be prepared to extend the law to create one to meet the justice of the case.

Extra-territorial effect

125. Section 75 applies even if the supply contract is entered into wholly overseas or is subject to foreign law, provided the credit agreement is subject to the law of a part of the United Kingdom.[135] It also applies where a bank lends money to acquire a foreign timeshare, notwithstanding that the foreign timeshare may be considered as giving rise to a tenancy agreement on land abroad.[136] The rule of law that accords exclusive jurisdiction to a claim involving land overseas does not apply to claims under section 75.

Cash price in excess of £30,000

126. Section 75 does not apply where the cash price of the goods or services is £30,000 or more. As from 1 February 2011, the borrower can take proceedings against the lender under a linked credit agreement instead of against the supplier in limited circumstances where the cash price is £30,000 or more.[137] A linked credit agreement is one where the lender has used the services of the supplier in connection with the preparation or making of the credit agreement, or where the goods or services are expressly referred to in the credit agreement.[138] Section 75A does not apply if the credit exceeds £60,260, or the agreement has been entered into for business purposes[139] or the credit agreement is secured on land.[140]

127. The borrower can only sue the lender if the supplier cannot be traced, or the borrower has contacted the supplier and the supplier does not respond, or the supplier is insolvent, or the borrower has taken reasonable steps but has not obtained satisfaction for the claim.[141] 'Reasonable steps' in this context does not oblige the borrower to bring proceedings against the supplier.[142]

The interrelation between sections 56 and 75

128. Sections 56 and 75 apply, as has been seen, in different ways. Section 56 creates a deemed agency that may directly affect the contractual

135 *Office of Fair Trading v Lloyds TSB Bank* 2008 1 All ER 205.
136 *Jarrett v Barclays Bank plc* 1999 QB 1.
137 Section 75A.
138 Section 75A(5).
139 Art 60C(5) and (6) RAO applies; see section 75A(7).
140 Section 75A(8).
141 Section 75A(2).
142 Section 75A(3).

relationship between borrower and lender. Section 75 operates by transferring the supplier's liability on to the shoulders of the lender.

129. Section 56 applies to a wider range of agreements than section 75 in that section 56, and not section 75, applies to hire purchase, conditional sale and credit sale agreements.

130. With connected lending and credit card transactions, the protection is comprehensive. The lender can be sued directly for the supplier's breach of the supply agreement under section 75. Where negotiations took place prior to the supply agreement, the lender can be sued in respect of all such negotiations under section 56 (although section 56 cannot be relied upon in respect of a breach of the supply contract itself). Where it is alleged that the negotiator has made false representations, either sections 56 or 75 may be relied upon.

131. Take the example of the car acquired with the aid of a loan described above. The transaction described was a 'connected lending' transaction. Suppose further that the dealer conducting the antecedent negotiations guaranteed all parts of the car for a year after purchase and stated that the vehicle mileage at the time of purchase was 10,000 miles. Suppose further that the mileage represented was false and that the dealer becomes insolvent one month after the car is purchased.

132. Here, the lender will be liable for the consequences of both the failure to provide a continuing guarantee of the parts of the car and for misdescription of the mileage. Moreover, the lender's liability can be established either under section 56 or 75. Section 56 applies because the promises and representations made are deemed to be made on behalf of the lender. Section 75 applies because the liability of the supplier in respect of such statements and representations is transferred to the lender. The end result is the same although the legal reasoning differs.

Challenging unfair contract terms: the unfair terms in Consumer Contracts Regulations 1999

133.The Unfair Terms in Consumer Contracts Regulations 1999,[143] commonly referred to as 'UTCCR', implement the Council Directive (EEC) 93/13 (on unfair terms in consumer contracts), commonly referred to as the Unfair Terms Directive. The wording of the Regulations for the most part follows that of the Directive.

134. The purpose of the Regulations and the Directive is to prevent the use of unfair terms in consumer contracts. These Regulations are applicable to consumer and hire agreements but they also apply in other situations as well.

143 SI 1999/2083, replacing the earlier Regulations SI 1994/3159; these provisions will shortly be reproduced in the forthcoming Consumer Rights Act.

135. The Regulations confer rights on individuals in the context of a claim in which it is sought to enforce the unfair term. There is overlap in the protection afforded to consumers with the protection afforded by the Unfair Contract Terms Act 1977. However, the Regulations apply to a wider range of terms than the Unfair Contract Terms Act 1977, which is restricted to exemption and termination clauses. It will normally only be necessary to rely on the Unfair Contract Terms Act 1977 in circumstances when the borrower or hirer has entered into the loan agreement or hire agreement in the course of business, in which event the borrower or hirer will not be a 'consumer' within the scope of the Regulations.

136. Moreover, the Regulations also confer general enforcement powers on the Competition and Markets Authority, powers that it shares with the FCA. These powers are further extended by the provisions of the Enterprise Act 2002.

When the regulations apply

137. The Regulations apply to terms in contracts between a seller or supplier, on the one hand, and a consumer, on the other.[144] A consumer is defined as a natural person (i.e. not a body corporate) who is acting outside his or her trade, business or profession.[145] So the Regulations do not apply when a natural person is acting in the course of business. A seller or supplier is defined as a natural or legal person (i.e. including a body corporate) acting in the course of a trade, business or profession.[146] A lender lending money is a supplier for the purpose of the Regulations, as is an owner who lets goods out on hire. Most regulated agreements, as defined by the RAO, come within the ambit of the Regulations except when the borrower or hirer is acting in the course of business, or in the case of a non-commercial agreement,[147] when the lender is not acting in the course of business.

When does the unfairness test apply?

138. The unfairness test only applies to terms that are not individually negotiated.[148] The burden of proof is on the seller or supplier to prove that a term is individually negotiated in any particular case.[149] Terms drafted in advance, where the consumer has therefore not been able to influence the substance of the term, are always to be regarded as not having been individually negotiated.[150]

144 Reg 4(1).
145 Reg 3(1).
146 Reg 3(1).
147 As defined in section 189(1) Consumer Credit Act 1974.
148 Reg 5(1).
149 Reg 5(4).
150 Reg 5(2).

139. Even if certain parts or aspects of the contract have been individually negotiated, the Regulations apply to the contract; if viewed overall, it is still to be considered a pre-formulated standard contract.[151] It applies to 'take it or leave it' contracts where the consumer has no choice but to accept the terms and conditions presented by the supplier. Lord Steyn has referred to such contracts as 'contracts of adhesion'.[152]

The core exclusion

140. There is a further important exclusion from the unfairness assessment. Regulation 6(2) provides that: 'In so far as it is in plain, intelligible language, the assessment of fairness shall not relate – (a) to the definition of the main subject of the contract, or (b) to the adequacy of the price or remuneration as against the goods or services supplied in exchange.'

141. The construction of this provision continues to be a source of controversy. However, it is clear that the exclusion only arises in any event insofar as the term in issue is expressed in plain, intelligible language. It is the duty of a seller or supplier to ensure that all written terms are so expressed[153] and insofar as a term is not so expressed, its fairness can be determined even if it relates to the main subject matter of the agreement or the price for the goods or services. It is the view of the FCA that the fact that the meaning of a term is clear to a lawyer does not necessarily mean that it is expressed in plain intelligible language; it is whether it is plain and intelligible to a *consumer* that matters.[154]

142. The requirement that the language is plain and intelligible, moreover, would seem to be one of wide application. In *Prohotovot' s.r.o v Kor Kovska*,[155] a credit agreement had not, when stating the credit charges, stated the APR contrary to a mandatory requirement of the Consumer Credit directive. This was said to render the provision specifying the credit charges not plain and intelligible with the consequence that the amount of charges was open to review under the Regulations on the grounds of fairness.

143. The exclusion should be restrictively interpreted as 'unless that is done [regulation 6] will enable the main purpose of the scheme to be frustrated by endless formalistic arguments as to whether a provision is a definitional or exclusionary provision'.[156] In fact, arguments based on Article 6(2) are likely to continue.

151 Reg 5(3).
152 *Director-General of Fair Trading v First National Bank plc* 2002 1 AC 481 at [31].
153 Reg 7(1).
154 1.3.1(3) UNFCOG G.
155 C76/10, discussed at *Chitty on Contracts, 31st Edition, Volume 1*, para 15.059.
156 *Director-General v First National Bank* per Lord Steyn at [34].

144. Provisions that provide the consequences of what is to happen on a default are not within the exclusion.[157]

145. In *Office of Fair Trading plc v Abbey National Bank plc*,[158] the Supreme Court held that the charges imposed by banks on authorised overdrafts were part of the 'remuneration' of the service of providing a bank account and therefore the adequacy (or amount) of the charges could not be taken into account as part of a fairness assessment of the relevant charging provisions.

146. The Supreme Court rejected a distinction between essential charges and other charges and also rejected the argument that what constitutes the price or remuneration for a particular service is to be viewed from the standpoint of the average consumer. The Supreme Court proceeded [159] on the basis that what Article 6(2) did was not to exclude particular contract *terms* from the fairness assessment, but only certain aspects, namely as to the fundamental contractual purposes, as to the adequacy of the price.[160] The Supreme Court decision remains controversial.[161]

Applying the unfairness test

147. The Regulations proceed on the assumption that the consumer is of weaker bargaining power. The Regulations are not concerned with any potential unfairness to the supplier.

148. Before the question of fairness can be addressed, it is first necessary to establish what a term means. The Regulations provide that in the case of a challenge by a consumer to the fairness of a term, where there is a doubt as to the meaning of a term in a written contract, the meaning most favourable to the consumer must be adopted.[162]

149. A term is unfair if it causes a significant imbalance in the parties' rights and obligations under the contract to the detriment of the consumer in a manner or to an extent that is contrary to the requirement of good faith.[163] The requirement of significant imbalance is met if a term is so weighted in favour of the supplier as to tilt the parties' rights and obligations under the contract significantly in his or her favour.

150. The fairness assessment must take into account the nature of the goods and services supplied and to all the circumstances attending the

157 *Director-General v First National Bank.*

158 2010 1 AC 696.

159 This had been in issue before Mr Justice Andrew Smith but was no longer in contention in the Supreme Court.

160 This was applied by Mr Justice Kitchin in *Office of Fair Trading v Ashbourne Management Services* 2011 EWHC 1237 (Ch).

161 *Chitty on Contracts, 31st Edition, Volume 1*, para 15.064.

162 Reg 7(2).

163 Reg 5(1).

conclusion of the contract at the time it was concluded; the term in question must be considered in the context of all the other terms of the contract or another contract on which it is dependent.[164]

151. In *Director-General of Fair Trading v First National Bank plc*,[165] the Director General challenged the fairness of a provision in the standard terms of the bank loan agreement permitting the bank to continue to charge interest at the contractual rate both before and after any judgment (such a provision had long been recognised as valid at common law). The provision was found by the House of Lords to be reasonable.

The list of illustrative terms

152. Schedule 2 to the Regulations sets out a non-exhaustive list of examples of the types of terms that *may*, not must, be considered unfair. Some of these are relevant in the consumer credit and consumer hire context.

153. An example is: '(c) requiring any consumer who fails to fulfil his obligation to pay a disproportionately his sum in compensation'. Such a clause may be a penalty clause at common law in any event.

154. Another example frequently seen in a consumer credit context is: '(g) enabling the seller or supplier to terminate a contract of indeterminate duration without the reasonable notice except when there are serious grounds for doing so'.

155. The scope of this is qualified by Schedule 2 paragraph 2(a), which says that paragraph 1(g) is without hindrance to terms by which a supplier of financial services reserves the right 'to terminate a contract unilaterally a contract of indeterminate duration without notice where there is a valid reason, provided that the supplier is required to inform the other contracting party or parties thereof immediately'. This surely raises a presumption that such a term in a financial services contract will be considered to be reasonable. In fact, such terms are already subject to regulation in that the right to terminate open-ended credit agreements is subject to control by section 98A of the Consumer Credit Act 1974.

156. Paragraph 1(j) provides that terms may be considered unfair when they enable the seller or supplier to 'alter the terms of the contract unilaterally without a valid reason which is specified in the contract'. This is said, at paragraph 2(b) of Schedule 2, to be without hindrance to terms under which a supplier of financial services 'reserves the right to alter the rate of interest payable by the consumer or due to the latter, or the amount of other charges for financial services without notice where there is a valid reason, provided that the supplier is required to inform the other contracting

164 Reg 6(1).
165 2002 1 AC 481.

party or parties thereof at the earliest opportunity and that the latter are free to dissolve the contract immediately'.

157. This, therefore, is an indication that clauses in loan agreements that allow for a change in interest rates but require the borrower to be informed and allow for a right of termination on the part of the borrower may be reasonable. Terms allowing for a variation of interest rates in credit agreements are already subject to section 78A of the Consumer Credit Act 1974, which provides for interest rate changes to be notified, and also to 6.7.13 R and 6.7.14 R of the CONC Handbook, which provide that interest rate changes can only be made for good reason and, in the case of store cards and credit cards, allow the borrower to pay off the outstanding balance.

158. Paragraph 1 refers to terms by which the supplier of services (e.g. credit or the hire of goods) is able to increase prices without giving the corresponding right in the consumer to cancel the contract if the final price is too high in relation to the price as originally agreed. However, by paragraph 2(d) of Schedule 2, this does not apply to a price indexation clause (i.e. a rate of interest variable in accordance with an index) when this has been explicitly described in the agreement.

An individual challenge to fairness

159. The Regulations allow an individual to challenge a particular term as being unfair in the course of proceedings. The effect of such a successful challenge is that as against the individual the seller or supplier cannot rely on the unfair term as it ceases to be binding on the consumer.[166] Nevertheless, the rest of the contract continues in existence if capable of doing so.[167]

Regulatory challenge

160. However, the Regulations also provide for regulatory action to be taken to challenge unfairness in contract terms. The jurisprudence of the European Court of Justice has made it clear that it regards collective challenges as being the best way of ensuring the necessary consumer protection.

161. Under the Regulations, the Competition and Markets Authority (the 'CMA') or 'other qualifying body' must consider any complaint that is referred to it.[168] The FCA is such other qualifying body within Schedule 1 to the Regulations.

162. The FCA and CMA have decided between themselves that the FCA will investigate the fairness of a term entered into in a contract concluded

166 Reg 8(1).
167 Reg 8(2).
168 Reg 10.

by an authorised person within the RAO.[169] The Regulations provide that if the qualifying body receives a complaint about the fairness of a consumer term, it must investigate it unless it considers the complaint to be frivolous or vexatious.[170] The CMA will investigate complaints of lack of fairness made in respect of unauthorised persons.

163. The investigating body has the power to request documentation or information.[171] If, having investigated the matter, the FCA has concerns about the fairness of a term, the FCA will normally write to the firm in question expressing their concerns. If any concerns of the FCA are not answered to the satisfaction of the FCA, the FCA will then normally ask for an *undertaking* from the firm that the term will no longer be relied upon and no longer included in new contracts.[172] The extent of the cooperation that the FCA has received from the firm is likely to be relevant to the approach of the FCA.[173]

164. Having considered a complaint, the FCA (or CMA) must decide whether or not to seek an injunction preventing continued use of the term and must give reasons for its decision one way or the other.[174] Thereafter, the FCA (or CMA if applicable) may seek injunction proceedings, including an interim injunction, to prevent the general use of the contract term in accordance with regulation 12.

165. An issue arose in *Office of Fair Trading v Foxtons Ltd*,[175] which was whether the court could properly make an injunction restraining at the behest of the OFT (now the FCA) restraining a firm from enforcing what it considered to be an unfair term in *existing* contracts. The Court of Appeal held that this might be an appropriate use of the court's jurisdiction, although the court would be sensitive to the fact that in the particular circumstances of an individual case, a particular term might be fair. Any injunction would be framed with this possibility in mind. The Court of Appeal also held that it may be appropriate for a court to grant a declaration as to the unfairness of a term.

166. The CMA and FCA also have powers to seek an enforcement order under section 212 of the Enterprise Act 2012 in circumstances when the collective interests of consumers are affected. In practice, this will lead to the grant of an injunction.

169 1.1.2 UNFCOG G.
170 Reg 10.
171 Reg 11.
172 1.3.4(1) UNFCOG G.
173 1.3.4(2) UNFCOG G.
174 Reg 10(4).
175 2010 1 WLR 663.

11 Rights and duties of the lender and owner

Collecting arrears

1. A firm must establish clear policies and procedures for dealing with arrears,[1] which must reflect the need to treat the vulnerable with consideration.[2] Debt collection arrangements should be suspended if the lender receives credible evidence that the borrower lacks mental capacity,[3] although this does not prevent a lender from pursuing a debt through a responsible third party acting on behalf of the borrower where the borrower has given prior consent, for instance by way of a power of attorney.[4]

2. A firm must at all times treat someone in arrears with forbearance and due consideration.[5] A firm must never threaten unfairly to disclose information about a person's indebtedness to a third party and indeed should take reasonable steps to ensure that others do not become aware that the borrower is being pursued to repay a debt.[6] Correspondence therefore will need to be tactfully addressed.

3. A firm must not pressurise a customer to act in a way that would have an adverse impact on his or her financial circumstances; specifically, the lender must not push a borrower into selling his or her home or taking on further borrowing.[7]

4. By CONC 7.3.14(1) R, 'a firm must not take disproportionate action against a customer in arrears or default'. Thus, unfair use must not be made of statutory demands or insolvency proceedings and repossession proceedings should be a last resort.

5. By CONC 7.7.5, 'a firm must not impose charges on customers in default or arrears difficulties unless the charges are no higher than necessary

1 CONC 7.2.1 R.
2 CONC 7.2.1(2) R.
3 CONC 7.10.1 R.
4 CONC 7.10.3 G.
5 CONC 7.3.4 R.
6 CONC 7.9.6. 7.9.7.
7 CONC 7.3.10 R.

to cover the reasonable costs of the firm'. This would seem to override any contractual provision in relation to the imposition of charges. Such a provision, if imposing an unreasonable level of charge, will also be a penalty at common law and unenforceable on that basis.

6. In the course of collecting any arrears, the lender may feel the need to contact the borrower. But it is an unfair business practice to contact a customer without the customer's consent unless there is an objective reason for doing so.[8] Such an objective reason might be if the lender reasonably considers that the person appointed by a borrower to act on his or her behalf is not in fact acting in the borrower's best interests.[9]

7. In relation to any contact, the person making the contact must point out who he or she works for, his or her role, and the purpose of the contact.[10] If a visit is made, it must be made on reasonable notice.[11] It is, of course, completely unacceptable for someone to enter a customer's property without that person's consent or to refuse to leave on being asked to do so;[12] it is, in any event, a trespass.

8. Furthermore, it is a criminal offence under section 40 of the Administration of Justice Act 1970 to harass a borrower with demands for payment calculated to cause alarm, distress or humiliation. It is also an offence falsely to claim some official capacity (such as a bailiff) for the purpose of enforcing payment.[13] The offence is to be tried summarily and the penalty is a fine.[14] However, it is a defence to a harassment charge to act reasonably and lawfully to attempt to collect a debt that is due or believed to be due[15] and it also does not apply to anything done in the course of a commercial practice for the purpose of the Consumer Protection from Unfair Trading Regulations 2008.[16]

9. A firm must not operate a policy of refusing to negotiate with someone developing a repayment plan.[17] If a customer informs the lender that he or she is formulating a repayment plan with a debt counsellor or other person, then the lender should suspend active recovery for a reasonable period to allow the repayment plan to be presented.[18] 'Reasonable period' in this context will generally be 30 days with a possibility of a further extension of 30 days.[19]

8 CONC 7.12.2(4) R.
9 CONC 7.12.3(3)(b) G.
10 CONC 7.9.1.
11 CONC 7.9.12(2) R.
12 CONC 7.9.14.
13 Section 40(1)(c).
14 Section 40(5).
15 Section 40(3)(a).
16 Section 40(3A).
17 CONC 7.3.9 R.
18 CONC 7.3.11 R.
19 CONC 7.3.12 G.

10. Indeed, it is an unfair business practice for a lender to refuse to deal with a borrower developing a repayment plan, or with another person acting on behalf of a customer such as a debt counsellor, unless there is an objectively justified reason for this stance.[20] It is also an unfair business practice to refuse to accept or to return a repayment from a debt management firm.[21]

Disputed debts

11. A borrower is entitled to arrears information for the purpose of establishing his or her true position under the credit agreement.[22] The lender has a duty to ensure that it keeps accurate and complete data.[23] If a borrower disputes his or her liability, for instance by denying his or her identity as borrower, or disputing the payments record, that contention must be treated seriously by the lender and the lender must investigate the contentions put forward by the borrower.[24] When the investigations have been concluded, the borrower should be informed of the outcome.[25]

12. A lender should not attempt to recover a debt that is statute barred if the lender has not been in touch with a borrower during the limitation period.[26] Once a customer correctly says that he or she will not be paying a debt because it is statute barred, the lender should cease contacting the borrower.[27]

13. A firm must give proper consideration to any settlement proposal that is put.[28] If a firm rejects a settlement proposal, then it must not try to intimidate a borrower into increasing the proposal.[29]

Collecting payments following assignment

14. If the benefit of a regulated credit agreement is assigned by a lender to a third party, notice of the assignment must be given to the borrower as soon as reasonably possible so that the borrower can know whom to pay; the only basis upon notice can be delayed is if the borrower's repayment arrangements do not change following the assignment in which case notice of the assignment can be postponed until the payment arrangements are altered.[30] Non-compliance with these requirements may affect a firm's authorisation.[31]

20 CONC 7.12.2 R.
21 CONC 7.12.2(6) R.
22 CONC 7.4.1 R.
23 CONC 7.13.1 R.
24 CONC 7.14.3 R.
25 CONC 7.14.5 R.
26 CONC 7.15.4 R.
27 CONC 7.15.8 R.
28 CONC 7.14.8 R.
29 CONC 7.14.10 R.
30 CONC 6.5.2 R.
31 CONC 7.5.1 G.

15. Indeed, whenever a customer's payment arrangements change, prompt notification of the change must be given so that the borrower can know whom to pay.[32]

Sending out arrears notices

16. The Consumer Credit Act 2006 introduced a requirement on lenders to serve an arrears notice supplemented with an arrears information sheet to act as a warning to consumers about the danger of falling into arrears and to encourage consumers to engage with the situation. The requirements apply to both consumer credit and hire agreements but do not apply to small agreements or non-commercial agreements[33] or to green plans.

17. The requirements also presuppose that the relevant agreements stipulate for a number of regular payments by the borrower or hirer (rental payments in the case of the latter). A slightly different regime applies as between fixed sum credit and hire agreements, on the one hand, and as to running account agreements, on the other.

18. The borrower or hirer must not be charged for the cost of serving such notices.[34]

When an arrears notice is needed with a fixed sum credit agreement

19. In the case of fixed sum credit agreements, an arrears notice must be served if a number of requirements are met:[35]

(a) the borrower must already have made two payments under the agreement by the relevant time, although it does not seem to be a requirement that the full amount needs to have been paid on these occasions;
(b) the total sum already paid must be less than the total sum owing by the borrower at the relevant time (i.e. his or her indebtedness must exceed his or her past payments);
(c) the amount of the shortfall must exceed the amount of the last two payments required to be paid before that time;
(d) there must not already be a pre-existing obligation to serve an arrears notice; and
(e) if a judgment has already been obtained against the borrower or hirer, the judgment must have been fully satisfied (the reasoning being that there is no point in serving an arrears notice if there is already a judgment that has not been paid off).

32 CONC 7.5.1 G.
33 Sections 86B(12A), 86C(7).
34 Section 86B(7), 86C(5).
35 Section 86B(1).

20. Where the agreement requires that the borrower or hirer makes payments *weekly*,[36] then before an arrears notice is required to be served, the number of payments outstanding needs to be *four* and not two, and the total in arrears must be more than the total of the last *four* payments.[37]

21. Furthermore, if a *weekly* payments agreement has been running for more than 20 weeks prior to the relevant date when an arrears notice would otherwise fall to be served, then the arrears of four weekly payments must have accrued within the last 20 weeks.[38]

22. The notice must be given to the borrower or hirer 14 days after these conditions are satisfied.[39] If an arrears notice has already been given, and the preconditions for serving a notice recur, then a further arrears notice must be served no less than six months later.

23. Where there are two or more borrowers, each must be served with a notice. The borrower or borrowers may not be charged for the service of a notice.

24. If a debtor becomes subject to a judgment in relation to the agreement or ceases to be in arrears in any respect[40] by the time of serving a notice that is not the first notice, then that notice need not be served. This does not apply to the first such notice, which must be served even if the arrears are discharged prior to the time of serving the first notice, or even if judgment is entered.[41]

An arrears notice with a running account agreement

25. With a running account agreement, the conditions requiring service of an arrears notice are:[42]

(a) the borrower must have made at least two payments before this time (even if it seems that the payments were not of the full amount required);
(b) the last two payments payable under the agreement must be outstanding at least in part (it seems to suffice that the full amount need not be outstanding in relation to each payment);[43]
(c) neither of the payments has formed the basis of a previous arrears notice; and

36 Or at shorter intervals.
37 Section 86B(9).
38 Section 86B(10).
39 Section 86B(2)(a).
40 No payments, interest or charges must be unpaid; section 86B(5).
41 Section 86B(3).
42 Section 86C(1).
43 See Schedule 3 paragraph 17, Information Requirements and Duration of Licences and Charges Regulations 2007.

(d) there is no sum outstanding to be paid under a judgment previously obtained against the borrower or hirer in respect of the agreement.

26. The 14-day time limit applicable to fixed sum credit agreements for serving the arrears notice does not apply to running account credit agreements. The statement can be served either at the same time or before the running account statement is served as required by section 78(4) (which requires statements to be sent within a period of one month following the end of a relevant accounting period). Indeed, it can be incorporated within a running account statement.[44] If the borrower continues to fail to make payments, after another two payments have been completely missed, a further notice will have to be served. With the running account credit agreement, there is no rule allowing arrears notices to be served every six months. This is doubtless because it is not difficult to serve an arrears notice with a running account statement.

The contents of the arrears notices

27. The required contents of the arrears notice are specified by the Consumer Credit (Information Requirements and Duration of Licences and Charges) Regulations 2007.[45]

28. An arrears information sheet must be included with the arrears notice.[46] This information sheet is issued by the FCA pursuant to section 86A of the Act and is available on its website. The form and contents of notice is regulated by the Consumer Credit (Information Requirements and Duration of Licences and Charges) Regulations 2007.[47] An error or omission that does not affect the substance of the information or forms of wording does not invalidate the notice on that ground alone.[48]

29. The notice has to use a form of words that make it clear that the notice has been given in compliance with requirements under the 1974 Act and has been served because the borrower or hirer is behind with sums payable under the agreement. The notice must also invite the borrower to enter into discussions with the lender about the state of his or her account.[49]

30. The notice must also indicate, by way of prescribed wording, if any default sum may become payable and also, again by way of prescribed wording, drawing attention to the possibility of future arrears notices being sent at six-monthly intervals.

44 Section 86C(4).
45 SI 2007/1167.
46 Section 86B(6).
47 2007/1167.
48 Reg 41.
49 Regs 19, 24 Further Information and Duration of Licenses and Charges Regulations 2007.

31. There are differences between the contents of a first and subsequent arrears notices and between fixed sum credit agreement and running account credit agreement notices.

Contents of fixed sum credit agreement arrears notices

32. If the arrears notice is not a demand for payment, wording must be included to show why this is not the case.[50]

33. In addition to the above, there are some differences between what is required with the first arrears notice and later notices.

34. The first notice shall specify the amount of the shortfall at the date when the need to send the arrears notice was triggered.[51]

35. There must also be a statement saying the following: 'If you want more information about which payments you failed to make please get in touch with us. We are required to give this information within 15 working days after your request for it.'

36. The Regulations then go on to impose, by regulation 19(2)(b), an obligation on the lender to supply certain specified information to the borrower within 15 working days after receipt of the borrower's request; however, the legal basis for imposing this requirement on the lender is unclear since the purpose of the Regulations is to stipulate the contents of the arrears notice.

37. With subsequent arrears notices, the information required to be set out is more extensive but, unlike the position with the first arrears notice, there is no requirement to invite the borrower to seek further information from the lender.

38. Special rules apply when the borrower has more than one agreement with a lender when the borrower and lender have agreed to aggregate the payments to allow a single payment to be made combining the payments due under each of the agreements.[52]

Content of a running account arrears notice

39. The notice must give details of all the last two payments that have not been paid in full and state: '*Missed and partly paid payments*: This notice does not give details of missed or partly made payments previously notified whether or not they remain unpaid.' If default sums may become payable as a result of the failure to make payment, this must also be referred to in the arrears notice.[53]

50 Reg 19(4).
51 Reg 19(2)(a).
52 Reg 20.
53 Part 4 Schedule 3.

Failure to serve a required arrears notice

40. So long as an arrears notice is outstanding, the credit or hire agreement cannot be enforced.[54] Moreover, no interest is payable in respect of the period of default and no default sums can be imposed that relate to the period of default.[55]

41. The period of default will come to an end once the required notice is served[56] or, in the case of a fixed sum credit agreement, all the arrears are paid off.[57]

Time order

42. Having been served with a default notice under either a fixed sum credit agreement or running account agreement or hire agreement, the borrower or hirer can apply to the court for a time order seeking time to pay the arrears.[58] However, before making an application for a time order in these circumstances, the borrower or hirer must first serve the lender or owner with a notice making this intention plain.[59] The notice must also state that the borrower or hirer wishes to make a proposal to the lender or owner for the making of payments under the agreement and giving details of the proposal.[60]

43. The borrower or hirer must then wait a further 14 days before making an application for a time order.[61] The purpose of this procedure is to enable the parties to communicate with a view to trying to avoid a time order application.

Default sum notice

44. The Consumer Credit Act 2006 also introduced at section 86E a requirement to serve a default sum notice once a default sum became payable. It applies to both regulated credit and hire agreements but does not apply to a non-commercial agreement or a small agreement.[62] The lender may not make a charge for the preparation of such a notice.[63]

54 Section 86D(3).
55 Section 86D(4).
56 Section 86D(6)(b)(i), 86D(6)(c).
57 Section 86D(6)(b)(ii).
58 Section 129(1)(ba).
59 Section 129A(1).
60 Section 129A(2).
61 Section 129A(1).
62 Section 86E(8).
63 Section 86E(6).

45. What is a default sum? It is a sum payable 'in connection' with a breach of agreement.[64] However, it does not include an interest charge. Nor does a sum become a default sum merely because the time for its payment is advanced by virtue of a breach of the agreement. Therefore, an accelerated payments provision does not attract the need to serve a default sum notice.

46. Where there is more than one borrower or hirer, a default sum notice must be served on each.

Contents of a default sum notice

47. The contents of a default sum notice are set out in the Further Information and Duration of Licences and Charges Regulations 2007. Such a notice has to contain wording that it is given pursuant to the 1974 Act and relates to default sums.[65] It has to give details of each default sum payable not the subject of a previous notice and the date upon which each became payable, the total of all such sums payable covered by the notice and a statement: 'This notice does not take account of default sums which we have already told you about in another default sum notice, whether or not those sums remain unpaid.'[66]

48. No arrears notice needs to be served with a default sum notice.

Consequences of failure to serve a default sum notice

49. The entire agreement, not just the payment of the default sums, is unenforceable until such time as the requisite notice is served.

Interest on a default sum

50. The Act only allows *simple interest* to be charged on a default sum; however, it says nothing about the *rate* of interest.[67] So a provision in an agreement that purports to charge compound interest on a default sum will be void.[68]

51. Moreover, interest can only be charged on the default sum once 29 days have elapsed following service of the default sum notice on the borrower or hirer.[69] This will override any contractual provision to the contrary.

64 Section 187A.
65 Reg 29.
66 Schedule 4.
67 Section 86F.
68 Section 173(1).
69 Section 86E(4).

Using continuous payment authorities

52. A continuous payment authority is given a specific and careful definition in the FCA Handbook Glossary; it is an authority given by a borrower[70] to a lender, directed to a payment service provider (often a bank), entitling the lender to obtain one or more payments from the borrower's payment account (often a bank account). Its most frequent use is by a lender requiring direct payments to be made from a bank account to the lender. However, the definition specifically does not extend to a direct debit; nor does it cover a single payment instruction given at a time following entry into the credit agreement, to operate either on the date of the instruction or on another specified date.

53. The FCA has expressed concerns about reliance by lenders on continuous payment authorities: 'We believe that CPA repayments encourage inadequate affordability assessments and the unfair treatment of customers experiencing difficulties, but we recognise that CPAs also provide some flexibility for customers.'[71]

54. The CONC Handbook contains specific rules about obtaining and thereafter operating continuous payment authorities.

55. Prior to obtaining continuous payments authority from a borrower, the lender or owner must explain a number of important matters to the borrower.[72] The explanation does not have to be in writing. The matters that must be explained include:

(a) the nature of a continuous payments authority and how it works;
(b) how the continuous payments authority will be applied by the lender;
(c) how it can be cancelled;
(d) whether other options are available for making payment;
(e) the consequences to the borrower if insufficient funds are available at a time when the continuous payments authority is operated, and in particular whether and what further attempts may be made to operate the continuous payments authority; and
(f) the policy as to part payments under a continuous payments authority must also be explained (not normally permissible at all in relation to high-cost short-term lending).

56. If a borrower agrees to provide a continuous payments authority, its terms must be included as part of the regulated credit or hire agreement[73] and the scope of the continuous payments authority must be there set out.[74]

70 It also extends to hire agreements.
71 PS 14/3, para 5.21.
72 CONC 4.6.2 R.
73 CONC 4.6.3 R.
74 CONC 4.6.4 R.

Operating the continuous payments authority

57. Having been provided with a continuous payments authority, a lender must not amend its terms without getting the borrower's consent.[75] Moreover, the lender must provide the borrower with an explanation of the reasons for the proposed change and how this will affect its operation.[76]

58. A lender can only operate a continuous payments authority if consistent with the explanation given to the borrower or hirer prior to the continuous payments authority being provided, and if consistent with the terms of the credit or hire agreement.[77] For instance, a lender will only be able to take a part payment in circumstances when the lender has explained to the borrower that this may occur and this is provided for in the contract terms.[78]

59. It is a general principle applicable to all types of agreement that 'a lender must exercise its rights under a continuous payments authority in a manner which is reasonable, proportionate and not excessive and must use appropriate forbearance if it becomes aware that the borrower is or may be experiencing financial difficulty'.[79]

60. It is likely to be a breach of this rule for a lender to operate a continuous payments authority in circumstances when the lender knows or ought to know that this will leave the borrower with insufficient funds for priority payments such as food and utilities.[80] Furthermore, a lender should only make a reasonable number of requests to collect a part payment since this is indicative of the fact that the borrower is likely to be in financial difficulty.[81]

61. Once a lender is provided with evidence from the borrower that the borrower cannot pay and is in financial difficulty, or once the lender becomes aware of this independently, then the lender should no longer operate the continuous payments authority.[82] The view of the FCA is that if a request continues to be unsuccessful at the end of a period of one working day after the request was made, then the lender should be alive to the possibility that the borrower is in financial difficulty and should endeavour to contact the borrower and suspend the operation of the continuous payments authority in the meantime.[83]

75 CONC 6.7.24 R.
76 CONC 7.6.1(2) R.
77 CONC 7.6.1(1) R.
78 CONC 7.6.2(3) G; part payments are normally prohibited entirely with HCSTC agreements.
79 CONC 7.6.3 R.
80 CONC 7.6.5(2) G.
81 CONC 7.6.6 G.
82 CONC 7.6.7 R.
83 CONC 7.6.9 G.

Cancellation

62. A lender or owner must do nothing to inhibit a borrower from cancelling the continuous payment authority.[84]

Requirement for a default notice

63. If the borrower or hirer is in the breach of the terms of the regulated consumer credit or hire agreement, the lender or owner can only take certain types of step by serving a default notice under section 87. When an agreement is concluded with two or more borrowers or hirers jointly, both must be served with a notice.[85]

When a default notice is needed

64. The circumstances requiring such a notice are as follows:[86]

(a) When the lender desires to terminate an agreement, either through exercise of an express right conferred by the agreement or in reliance upon a common law right (i.e. when the lender or owner wishes to accept a repudiation of the agreement by the borrower or hirer).
(b) When the lender demands earlier payment of any sum. This applies, therefore, where the lender or owner wishes to activate an accelerated payments clause that arises on breach.
(c) When the lender seeks to recover possession of any goods or land. This desire may or may not be coupled with a desire to terminate the agreement.
(d) When the lender wishes to treat any right conferred by the agreement as terminated, restricted or deferred. This is a reference to a contractual right vested in the lender or owner that falls short of absolute termination. It would apply, for example, where the owner wishes to reduce the length of a hire agreement without bringing it entirely to an end, or to remove a borrower's option to purchase goods under a hire purchase contract.
(e) When the lender or owner desires to enforce security.

65. However, no default notice is needed if the only action the lender decides to take is to restrict or defer the right to future credit under the agreement;[87] thus, the lender can take immediate action to prevent the borrower from

84 CONC 7.6.16 R.
85 Section 185(1)(a).
86 Section 87.
87 Section 87(2).

obtaining any further credit as well as taking all necessary steps to make the 'restriction or deferment effective'. Thus, the lender can withhold a borrower's chequebook or demand the return of a credit token. Moreover, there is no need to serve a default notice if the lender intends to withhold or suspend the grant of credit under an open-end credit agreement (i.e. one of no fixed duration).[88] There is a separate procedure for the withholding or suspending of credit in these circumstances.[89]

66. There is no need to serve a default notice in order to crystallise a floating charge where the borrower or hirer is in breach.[90] The only individuals that can create a floating charge are farmers,[91] but a corporate surety might conceivably have given such a charge.

67. Nor is there need to serve a default notice prior to issuing proceedings for arrears that have already accrued due under the agreement, as the issue of such proceedings is not within section 87(1); this is sometimes overlooked. It would of course be different if the proceedings sought recovery of an accelerated payment, as a default notice is needed before the acceleration can take effect.

68. Section 87 applies to all regulated agreements (which of course include hire agreements) save that non-commercial agreements are excluded by regulation 2(9) of the Consumer Credit (Enforcement, Default and Termination Notices) Regulations 1983.[92] However, the exemption of non-commercial agreements does not apply to agreements in which security has been given. So those making a domestic loan secured on land will need to serve a default notice before taking possession proceedings against the land in order to realise the loan. This requirement is often not realised.

General form and contents of default notices

69. Notices must be given in the form prescribed by the Consumer Credit (Enforcement, Default and Termination Notices) Regulations 1983.[93] The notice must be on paper[94] and must contain the information specified in Schedule 2 to the Regulations and must also set out certain statements prescribed therein. These statements must be exactly reproduced in accordance with the notes contained in the Schedule; emphasis must be given to those parts of the statement that are given prominence therein.[95]

88 Section 87(5).
89 Section 98A(4).
90 Section 87(3).
91 Agricultural Credits Act 1928.
92 SI 1983/1561.
93 SI 1983/1561.
94 Reg 2(4A).
95 Regulations 2(5), 2(6), 2(7).

It is also provided that the lettering of the notice should be legible and printed in colour readily distinguishable from the colour of the paper.[96]

70. The notice must point out that it is 'Important – you should read this carefully.' There are certain generic statements that have to be set out, such as the right to apply to the court for time to pay and as to the advisability of seeking advice.[97]

Specific information to be included in a default notice

71. Crucially, the term of the agreement breached must be specified.[98]

72. Moreover, the actual breach must then be described, the default notice 'specifying clearly the matters complained of'.[99] Types of breach might be:

(a) a failure to pay money due under the agreement by the dates specified under the agreement;
(b) disposal of goods comprised in a hire purchase, conditional sale or hire agreement; and
(c) failure to look after or insure such goods.

73. Although section 88 of the Act and the Regulations speaks of a default notice being issued in respect of 'a breach', it seems that more than one breach can be specified in a single notice. By Interpretation Act 1978, section 6, in a statute, unless the context indicates the contrary, words in the singular also include the plural and this would seem to permit of a single notice for several breaches.

74. Sometimes a contract term only takes effect consequent on a breach. A common example is a provision providing for the borrower to make accelerated payment following breach. Section 88(3) provides that the relevant breach is the original breach, not the failure to comply with a term that takes effect as a consequence of breach. So in the case of an accelerated payments provision, the breach is not the failure to make the accelerated payment, but the failure to make the original payment. The default notice will refer to the enforcement of the accelerated payment provision under the heading, not of breach, but of what action the lender or owner intends to take.[100]

75. Paragraph 3(c) of Schedule 2 of the Enforcement, Default and Termination Regulations requires the default notice to state: 'If the breach

96 Reg 2(4).
97 Paragraphs 9, 10, Schedule 2.
98 Paragraph 3(a), Schedule 2.
99 Paragraph 3(b), Schedule 2.
100 Schedule 2 paragraph 6(f).

is capable of remedy, what action is required to remedy it and the date not less than 14 days after the date of service, before which action is to be taken.'

76. The distinction between a remediable and irremediable breach is one that is found in several areas of the law, including in the context of breaches of the terms of a lease for the purpose of forfeiture proceedings.[101] Failure to pay a sum of money owing under an accelerated payments clause is plainly a remediable breach and the lender should demand its payment within 14 days or more. There is no requirement that the lender should provide for a reasonable time for payment provided that the period given is 14 days or more. If the breach is remediable, the default notice must go on to contain a statutory statement that no further enforcement action will be taken if the breach is remedied by the date specified.

77. By contrast, paragraph 3(d) of Schedule 2 of the Regulations stipulates what is to happen if the breach is not capable of remedy.[102] Loss of, and in some instances damage to, hired goods may be considered to be a breach not capable of remedy. In these circumstances, the notice must state: 'The sum (if any) required to be paid as compensation for the breach and the date, being a date not less than 14 days after the date of service of the notice before which it is to be paid.'

78. It is for the lender or owner to stipulate the amount of compensation. The default notice does have to state how it has been calculated. The demand for compensation brings with it the possibility that the amount demanded will be paid in due time. If this happens, the lender or owner will be unable to take any further steps; for example, the lender will be unable to terminate. A lender or owner very anxious to terminate would thus be better advised not to ask for compensation in the default notice; section 88(1)(c) makes clear that such a request need not necessarily be made even though the extent of the lender or owner's loss can readily be assessed. If no compensation is demanded, a lender or owner will have an indefeasible right to take the action specified in the notice once at least 14 days has elapsed from its service.[103]

79. A date for payment of the compensation must be given at least 14 days after service of the default notice. A statutory statement must be inserted below the request for compensation saying that if the compensation is paid, no further action will be taken.[104]

80. The lender or owner, having specified the term breached, the circumstances of the borrower or hirer's breach, the remedy required to

101 The distinction is comprehensively discussed in this context in *Savva v Hussein* 1996 2 EGLR 65.

102 Whether a breach is or is not capable of remedy is an objective question. The issue must take into account the time period of 14 days that the lender is entitled to specify.

103 Section 88(2).

104 Paragraph 4 Schedule 2 of the Regulations.

rectify the same or, if appropriate, the compensation to be paid, must finally specify the action that the lender or owner intends to take. This must be one of the types of action discussed earlier. Paragraph 6(f) Schedule 2, in addition, refers to the enforcement of any provision, 'which becomes operative only on a breach of another provision of the agreement as specified in the notice'. This is relevant to the activation of an accelerated payments provision.

Default information sheet

81. The default information sheet produced by the FCA in accordance with section 86A must be served along with the default notice. Indeed, the default notice should itself refer to this.[105]

Service of a default notice

82. Section 87 requires that a default notice must be 'given' to the borrower or hirer. 'Give' means the same as 'serve on' (identical definitions are given in section 189(1)) and notice can be given by either delivering it, or sending it by post, or leaving it addressed at the last known address of the borrower or hirer.[106] In some circumstances, it can be served by electronic communication if the requirements of section 176A are satisfied. It is the time of receipt of the notice by the borrower or hirer that is important for measuring the seven-day period. When a notice is sent by post, there is a presumption that the notice is received in accordance with the ordinary course of post[107] but this presumption can be rebutted in circumstances if the time in which service has to be undertaken is legally important.[108] Here, the time of service is critical because the lender or owner may not take the action described in the default notice until the time stipulated for remedying the breach (or 14 days if no time is stipulated) has elapsed.[109] The lender or owner would be well advised to allow for some delay and to use the facilities of the recorded delivery service so that a record of receipt of the default notice is obtained.

83. The borrower or hirer must be given 14 clear days notice of the action intended to be taken.[110] This means that the date of receipt of the default notice is not to be taken into account in measuring the 14 day period.

105 Paragraph 10A, Schedule 2.

106 Section 176(2), 176(8).

107 Section 7 Interpretation Act 1978.

108 See the analysis of the relevant authorities in *Calladine-Smith v Saveorder* 2011 EWHC 2501 (Ch).

109 Section 88(2).

110 *Re Hector Whaling Ltd* 1936 1 Ch 208; a different rule operates in the field of landlord and tenant, *Schnabel v Allard* 1967 1 QB 627.

84. If a borrower or hirer has died, the notice can be given in just the same way as if he or she was still living, even though the lender or owner may know of the death.[111] Alternatively, the notice can be served on an executor of the estate of the borrower or hirer or upon the administrator once probate has been granted (this follows from the definition of 'borrower' contained in section 189(1)). If the borrower becomes bankrupt, then the borrower can be served provided the lender or owner is unaware of the bankruptcy; otherwise, the trustee in bankruptcy must be served.[112]

85. If the agreement has been guaranteed or secured by a third party surety, then the default notice must also be served on that surety.[113] If this is not done, the breach the subject matter of the default notice will only be enforceable against the surety with permission of the court.[114] The lender or owner will have to apply to the court for an enforcement order under section 127.[115]

Errors in the default notice

86. A default notice that overstates the extent of the arrears is invalid. This was held by the Court of Appeal in *Woodchester Services Ltd v Swain & Co.*[116] In that case concerning a regulated hire agreement of a photocopier, the hirer failed to make payments and the owner, having decided to terminate the agreement, served a default notice. Unfortunately, the amount of the arrears of rental stated in the notice was overstated by over £200. The owner brought proceedings claiming arrears of rental and damages on account of the repudiation of the contract and the borrower raised the invalidity of the notice as a defence.

87. The Court of Appeal said that the Court might overlook an error that was *de minimis*, but on the facts under consideration, the error of over £200 could not be considered *de minimis*, so that the notice was invalid and the defence therefore succeeded. The lender was confined to recovery of the arrears up to the date of the default notice.

88. However, it ought not to invalidate a default notice if the quantum of the arrears is *understated.* It will then be to the advantage of the borrower or hirer to rely upon the notice and the lender or owner will be estopped from denying its invalidity if the borrower or hirer pays the understated sum specified in order to remedy the breach.

89. There is, furthermore, authority in relation to a notice issued in a different but comparable statutory context for the proposition that a notice

111 Section 176(6).
112 Section 176(5).
113 Section 111(1).
114 Section 11(2).
115 Section 127(1)(c).
116 1999 1 WLR 263.

is not invalidated in respect of correctly described breaches by the inclusion in the notice of invalid breaches;[117] however, it is only in respect of breaches accurately stated that the lender or owner can validly act following service of the notice.

90. The notice could also be invalidated by the failure to include one or more of the prescribed statements, or by inaccuracies in those statements. However, it is hoped that the court will feel able to say that really trivial departures from the prescribed form are *de minimis*, thus preventing the borrower or hirer from escaping liability simply on a technicality. Authority for this approach can be derived from the approach of the courts to agreements subject to the Moneylenders Acts, where the court felt able to ignore errors that were 'too trivial to notice'.[118] Likewise where the error could be classified as a clerical error.[119]

Actions of the borrower following service of a default notice

91. If the breach is capable of remedy and the borrower is in a position to remedy the breach within the 14-day period stipulated, the borrower should do this. Once the breach is remedied, it is deemed not to have occurred.[120] Compliance must be full, although in rare cases the borrower or hirer may be able to argue that the respects in which he or she has failed to comply are *de minimis*.[121]

92. A borrower or hirer aggrieved at the length of time afforded to him or her to remedy a breach may apply to the court for a time order under section 129 to have the time extended for the payment of money or for the remedying of another type of breach.[122] The court is likely to grant an extension when the lender or owner has required that the breach be rectified in an unreasonably short time and the borrower or hirer shows that there is at least some prospect of a remedy being possible. If the breach is remedied by the date as extended by the court under a time order, the breach is deemed never to have occurred.[123]

93. If the borrower or hirer does not comply with the notice within the period specified for remedying the breach or if there is no such time, 14 days, the lender or owner can take the action specified in the default notice.[124]

117 *Silvester v Ostrowska* 1959 1 WLR 1060.
118 *Reading Trust Ltd v Spero* 1930 1 KB 492 at page 505 per Scrutton LJ.
119 *Temperance Loan Fund Ltd v Rose* 1932 2 KB 522 at page 526 per Scrutton LJ.
120 Section 89.
121 *Price v Romilly* 1960 1 WLR 1360.
122 Section 129(2).
123 Section 89.
124 Section 88(2).

Effects of an invalid notice

94. More difficult to determine are the rights of the borrower or hirer where no notice is given, or where the action is taken too soon after service of the notice or where the notice is in some way defective.

95. Clearly, failure to comply with the requirements of sections 76, 87 and 98 will provide a defence to any action brought by the lender or owner relying upon an invalid (or non-existent) notice under one of these sections. Sometimes, it will be possible to cure the defect by serving a subsequent valid notice even after proceedings have been issued but this will not always be the case. For instance, for a lender wrongfully to terminate an agreement when not entitled to do this will itself be a repudiatory breach of contract. Goods wrongfully repossessed cannot later meaningfully be returned even if this is a practical proposition.

96. The question remains whether breach of one of these sections can itself give rise to a cause of action in favour of the borrower or hirer. Two situations can be envisaged:

(a) The lender activates an accelerated payments clause without serving a proper notice on the borrower. The lender subsequently demands the money due under the clause from the borrower, who pays it.
(b) The lender terminates an agreement and repossesses goods without serving a valid notice (assuming that the goods are neither protected nor that repossession involved entry on to premises so as to contravene section 92).

97. In the first situation, could the borrower sue, or counterclaim, for the return of the money? In the second situation, would the borrower be able to sue for return of the goods? Would it make any difference if the borrower had in fact consented to the return of the goods by the finance company?

98. First, the borrower or hirer could sue for the return of the money on the basis of money had and received by the creditor. The money was paid over on the basis of a mistake of law since the borrower paid the money not knowing of his or her legal right to refuse payment. A right of recovery for mistake of law arises because the parties are not *in pari delicto*.[125] The lender or owner had a statutory duty to serve the appropriate notice and it was not the responsibility of the borrower or hirer that one was not sent.

99. As well as receiving back the money under the accelerated payments clause, the borrower or hirer will be able to treat the agreement as still on foot and continue making contractual payments thereunder, as it would not have been validly terminated.

125 *Kiriri Cotton Co v Dewani* 1960 AC 192 at 204.

100. The borrower or hirer will also have an action for wrongful repossession of any goods under the second situation referred to above. Such a right of action was recognised in *Eshun v Moorgate Mercantile Co Ltd*,[126] which concerned the requirement to serve a notice of default under the Hire Purchase Act 1965. The lender in a hire purchase transaction did not serve a valid notice of default before retaking the car and purporting to terminate the agreement. The Court of Appeal held that the notice was invalid and that the borrower was entitled to be compensated for the wrongful repossession of the motor car. The borrower received back the sums he had paid under the agreement, although there was no discussion about the true measure of assessment.

101. *Eshun v Moorgate Mercantile*[127] itself seems to have been decided on the basis of the tort of wrongful interference with goods and further authority for this approach comes from the decision of *Brierly v Kendall*,[128] where a lender improperly retook goods under a bill of sale before default had actually arisen. The borrower's consent to the repossession should not affect the cause of action, since consent was given without actual or constructive knowledge of the true legal position.[129]

102. Difficulties arise over the proper measure of damages in these circumstances. In *Brierly v Kendall*,[130] the court said without further elaboration that the borrower should not be compensated for the full value of the article repossessed since his interest in it at the time was only partial. In *Eshun v Moorgate Mercantile*,[131] the Court of Appeal accepted without argument that the borrower should receive back all payments previously made by him. This measure, while fair on the actual facts of that case, could not be applied to a situation where a large number of payments had been made prior to the time of repossession, since this could entail the borrower receiving compensation greater than the value of the goods repossessed.

103. The proper measure of damages, it is submitted, should be the same in these circumstances as in the case of wrongful repossession under section 92. The borrower's suggested entitlement is to the value of the goods at the date of the wrongful repossession, less the future instalments due but excluding from those instalments the element consisting of credit charges. This measure is consistent with *Brierly v Kendall*.[132]

126 1971 1 WLR 722.
127 Ibid.
128 1852 17 QB 937.
129 *Mercantile Credit v Cross* 1965 2 QB 205.
130 Ibid.
131 Ibid.
132 Ibid.

Enforcement and termination notices

104. There is significant overlap between the principles applicable to default notices served under section 87 and enforcement and termination notices under sections 76 and 98 on the other.

105. Section 87 applies to situations when the lender or owner wishes to take certain steps consequent upon breach of a regulated agreement by the borrower or hirer. By contrast, section 76 applies where the lender or owner wishes to take one or more of the following steps pursuant to an entitlement in the regulated agreement consequent upon an event that is not a breach of the agreement:[133]

(a) to demand earlier payment of any sum, for instance by the operation of an accelerated payments clause;
(b) to recover possession of any goods or land; or
(c) to treat any right conferred on the borrower or hirer by the agreement as terminated, restricted or deferred.

106. These steps are the same steps as trigger the requirement to serve a default notice, save that a default notice is also needed to enforce any security that may have been provided,[134] not a requirement in respect of section 76. Moreover, just as with a default notice, these steps do not include action to restrict the borrower's access to credit and to take steps to make that restriction effective, so that where this is the step intended, no enforcement notice is needed.[135]

107. A notice within section 76 is referred to as an 'enforcement notice' by the Enforcement, Default and Termination Notices Regulations 1983[136] and that terminology is adopted here. Section 98 applies to a lender or owner that wishes to terminate an agreement for a reason other than breach.[137] Such notices are referred to as 'termination notices'.

108. The need for notices under sections 76 and 98 typically arises when a borrower or hirer is financially embarrassed, including entering into a voluntary arrangement or bankruptcy or having unpaid judgment debts. These events will not normally constitute breaches of the agreement by the borrower or hirer, but the lender or owner may feel it necessary nevertheless to take steps to protect its position as a result of them. Many agreements make express provision for these types of eventuality, including a right given to the lender or owner to terminate the agreement.

133 Section 76(6).
134 Section 87(1)(e).
135 Section 76(4).
136 SI 1983/1561.
137 Section 98(1), (6).

109. Both sections 76 and 98 permit the required steps to be taken only after giving not less than seven days notice of the termination. (The period is shorter than the comparable 14-day period applicable in respect of a default notice under section 87.)

110. However, neither sections 76 or 98 apply to agreements that are not of fixed duration (an agreement does not cease to be of fixed duration merely because either side is given a right of termination).[138] This has the effect of excluding many running account agreements and casual overdraft agreements from the ambit of these sections. Whether credit token agreements are excluded depends upon whether a fresh agreement is entered into every time a token is renewed (which is the preferred view). Agreements of no fixed duration are what are referred to as 'open-end agreements' within section 98A of the Act and the termination and the withdrawal and suspension of credit in respect of such agreements is subject to the requirements of that section.

111. Nor is there any need to serve a section 76 or 98 notice in the case of a non-commercial agreement *except* in a case where security has been provided.[139]

112. The form and content of such notices is governed by the Consumer Credit (Enforcement, Default and Termination Notices) Regulations 1983.[140] A section 76 and 98 notice may be combined if the lender or owner wishes to combine termination with some other action under the agreement.[141] In *Brandon v American Express Services Europe Ltd*,[142] the Court of Appeal raised the possibility, without deciding, of combining a section 98 notice with a default notice. This, however, is not expressly contemplated by the Regulations.

Form and contents of enforcement and termination notices

113. Schedule 1 sets out the required contents of an enforcement notice and Schedule 3 the required contents of a termination notice.

114. The notice must state under what term of the agreement action is to be taken or termination affected.[143]

115. In the case of a section 76 notice, the nature of the action to be taken to enforce the agreement must be described, as must the 'manner and circumstances' in which the lender or owner intends to take such

138 Section 76(2)(a) and 98(2)(a).
139 Reg 2(9) Enforcement, Default and Termination Notices Regulations 1983.
140 SI.
141 Reg 2(8) Enforcement, Default and Termination Notices Regulation 1983.
142 2011 EWCA Civ 1187.
143 Paragraph 3 Schedule 1, paragraph 3 Schedule 3 Enforcement, Default and Termination Notices Regulations 1983.

action.[144] Thus, the lender or owner must state precisely what it intends to do. For example, if the lender intends to repossess a video on hire purchase, the lender must state the time at which its representative will call to collect it. Further, in a case where the lender or owner demands early payment of a sum due under the agreement, the lender or owner must first of all state what sum would be due in accordance with the agreement, and second the amount of rebate to which the borrower or hirer is entitled under the Early Settlement Regulations 2004.[145] The date, which must be a date not less than seven days after the giving of the notice, when the action (or termination in the case of a section 98 notice) is to be taken must also be specified.[146]

116. The enforcement and termination notices must contain certain generic information in prescribed terms:

(a) as to the right to apply to the court for time to pay (i.e. for a time order);
(b) as to the desirability of getting advice from the citizens advice bureau or the like; and
(c) as to the importance of the notice and the need to read it carefully.

117. This generic information was also required with default notices.

118. For commentary in relation to service of such a notice and the consequences of failure to serve a valid notice, the discussion in relation to default notices should be referred to.

Recovery of goods under hire purchase, conditional sale and hire agreements

119. The Consumer Credit Act 1974 imposes a number of restrictions on the right of a lender or owner to recover goods subject to a regulated hire purchase, conditional sale or hire agreement. A contractual provision may confer a right of entry to recover goods or land from the borrower or hirer but such a right is subject to section 92 and, in the case of hire purchase and conditional sale, section 91 as well. (In the case of a hire agreement, the hirer has a duty to inform the owner of the whereabouts of goods within seven working days of receipt of a request in writing from the owner.[147] Failure for 14 days is a criminal offence.)[148]

144 Regulation 4 Schedule 1 Enforcement, Default and Termination Notices Regulations 1983.

145 Paragraph 5 Schedule 1, paragraph 5 Schedule 3 Enforcement Default and Termination Notices Regulations 1983.

146 Reg 4(c) Schedule 1, reg 4(b) Schedule 3 Enforcement Default and Termination Notices Regulations 1983.

147 Section 80(1).

148 Section 80(2).

120. The restriction imposed by section 92 in relation to goods subject to a regulated hire purchase, conditional sale or hire agreement is that the lender or owner is not entitled to 'enter premises' to take possession of goods without leave of the court.[149] This applies regardless of whether the borrower or hirer has been in breach of the agreement (unlike the position with protected goods) and regardless of whether a default notice under section 87 or an enforcement notice under section 76 has been served. This provision furthermore overrides any contractual provision conferring a right of entry on the lender or owner.

121. The word 'premises' is not defined and a number of meanings are possible. 'Premises' could refer to any land in private ownership, excluding areas to which the public have general access, or it could refer more narrowly to private buildings, outbuildings and their immediate curtilages.

122. So is a car parked on a private driveway parked on premises? Would the same answer apply if the car was left in a private office car park restricted to employees of a particular employer? What if it is open to members of the public paying a parking fee?

123. The term 'premises' is defined in the Oxford English Dictionary. There seems no basis for giving the word a restricted definition.

Contravention of section 92

124. A lender or owner who recovers goods in contravention of section 92 is in breach of statutory duty and can be sued for such breach by the borrower or hirer.[150] No cause of action, however, will arise if the borrower or hirer voluntarily returns the goods.[151] The consent given, however, must be freely given, and probably must be informed consent.[152]

125. What measure of damages will apply if a breach of statutory duty arises? First, the borrower or hirer can recover all consequential losses arising from the wrongful repossession of the goods. Suppose, for example, that the borrower's car is wrongfully repossessed; the borrower will be able to claim for the cost of alternative means of transport until it is returned, as well as for the distress and the inconvenience caused.

126. If goods *are* returned, the borrower or hirer's liability will be confined to these consequential losses. If the borrower is permanently deprived of the goods, the borrower or hirer's rights may be more substantial. The borrower or hirer will be enabled to be placed in the same position as if the breach had not occurred (i.e. the borrower or hirer will be entitled to claim for the additional cost of making alternative hire

149 Section 92(1).
150 Section 92(3).
151 Section 173(3).
152 *Mercantile Credit Ltd v Cross* 1965 QB 205 at 214 per Willmer LJ.

purchase, conditional sale or hire arrangements). With hire agreements, this will be a straightforward exercise; hire purchase and conditional sale agreements involve more complex considerations.

127. There have been three principal cases in which the measure of damages applicable to a hire purchase transaction has been discussed and in all three a different measure was advanced. All cases involved actions for breach of statutory duty in which the lender infringed a requirement not to take possession without leave of the court.

128. In *Can v James Broderick & Co*,[153] the Court of Appeal held that the proper measure was the total hire purchase price less the total amounts remaining outstanding under the agreement (i.e. the borrower was in effect entitled to a refund of all moneys paid). If this measure were to be universally adopted, it would give the borrower a huge windfall if wrongful repossession took place towards the *end* of the agreement as the borrower would have had the benefit of the vehicle without having had to pay for it.

129. In *Fileman v British Railway Traffic and Electric Company Ltd*,[154] the court awarded the borrower the resale value of the goods wrongfully repossessed. This measure heavily favours a borrower who has paid only a few instalments and who could recover the value of almost brand new goods having paid little for it.

130. Finally, in the important New Zealand case of *Harris v Lombard New Zealand Ltd*,[155] where the most detailed consideration to the question was given, it was decided that the proper measure was the value of the goods at the date of repossession less the amount of the remaining instalments. This most nearly puts the borrower in the position he or she would have been in had wrongful repossession not occurred.

131. However, even this final measure is to some extent defective since it imposes upon the borrower a liability for the lender's future credit charges, which the borrower will in any event have to pay again when he takes out alternative credit facilities elsewhere. It is submitted that the proper measure of damages should be the value of the goods at the date of repossession, less the amount of future instalments payable to the lender excluding that element in those instalments consisting of credit charges.

Protected goods

132. Further restrictions are imposed in the case of hire purchase and conditional sale agreements. The Act preserves the notion of 'protected goods' introduced by the Hire Purchase Acts.[156] Goods that are 'protected'

153 1942 2 KB 275.
154 1945 173 [LT] 407.
155 1974 2 NZLR 161.
156 Section 90(7).

are so named because the lender is not entitled to their recovery without an order of the court.[157] Of course, many goods will be covered by the prohibition in section 92(1) in any event but section 92(1) will not apply to vehicles parked in public places. The financial consequences of a breach of section 92 may not be the same as the consequences of wrongful retaking of protected goods.

When goods become protected

133. For goods to be protected, the borrower must have paid at least *one-third* of the total price of the goods.[158] The calculation of the total price will not include interest and other charges that may have fallen due as a result of default.[159] In a case where the lender is obliged under the agreement to carry out installation of the goods, and where the agreement specifies a charge for the work, then the borrower must pay this charge in addition.[160]

134. Sometimes it may be unclear whether and in what amounts a payment made by a borrower should be attributed to the total price or should be divided as between agreements. In *Julian Hodge Bank v Hall*, it was argued on behalf of the lender that one-third had not been paid because part of the payments made by the borrower should be attributed, it was argued, towards interest and other charges that had fallen due rather than to repayment of the total price. On the facts there, the lender was held to have appropriated the payments to the repayment of the total price.

135. Following the general law, section 81 of the Consumer Credit Act 1974 provided that the borrower was entitled to appropriate payments in such manner as he or she sees fit. In the event that the borrower does not make an appropriation and there are a number of secured agreements, which includes hire purchase and conditional sale agreements, then the payment should be divided in proportion with the sum outstanding under each. Section 81 has now been repealed as from 1 April 2014 but CONC 6.4 makes identical provision.

136. The second requirement for goods to be protected is that the borrower must be in breach of the agreement.[161] The goods therefore cannot have this status if their repossession is sought by the lender on account of a event that is not a breach of the agreement (e.g. if the borrower has a bankruptcy petition served on him or her and the agreement provides that this entitles the lender to terminate). This requirement was not one contained in the Hire Purchase Acts,[162] and the Consumer Credit Act,

157 Section 90(1).
158 Section 90(1)(b).
159 *Julian Hodge Bank v Hall* 1998 CCLR 14.
160 Section 90(2).
161 Section 90(1)(a).
162 Section 33(1) Hire-Purchase Act 1965.

therefore, to this extent, grants greater protection to a borrower who is in breach over one who is not.

137. The third requirement is that goods can only be protected if title to them rests in the lender.[163] A lender, however, should be very careful before stipulating for a right of repossession over goods that are *not* his or her property since an agreement containing such a provision could be successfully challenged as an unregistered bill of sale.

138. Goods continue to be protected after the death of the borrower until probate is granted or letters of administration are taken out[164] (section 90(6)).

Addition of goods

139. Special provision is made where goods are subsequently added to an earlier agreement (or where the earlier agreement is modified by the inclusion of additional goods). If the goods included within the earlier agreement become protected, then the protection extends to the goods subsequently added thereafter.[165] For example, a borrower may take out a hire purchase agreement for a computer system; further equipment may subsequently be added, say a printer. If the borrower has paid at least one-third of the payments in respect of the computer system, the printer will likewise be protected. It is, however, essential that one-third of the total hire purchase price of the computer system was paid *before* the printer was added.

140. Another problem arises where several agreements are concluded with the same lender. The problem can be illustrated by an example, which will also illustrate the requirements stated above.

141. Suppose that a hire purchase agreement is concluded for a luxury washing machine in January, the total hire purchase price of which is £1,250, of which £150 is the deposit, £50 is the lender's installation charge and £50 is the amount of the monthly repayment.

142. Suppose further that a subsequent hire purchase agreement is concluded with the same lender for a dishwasher in March, by which time a total of £250 has been paid under the hire purchase agreement for the washing machine. Suppose further that the total hire purchase price of the upmarket dishwasher is £800, including a lender's installation charge of £50, that there is no deposit and that the monthly repayments are £50. The borrower thereafter tenders three lump amounts to the lender of £100 each. These payments are made when both agreements are considerably in arrears. Is either the washing machine or the dishwasher potentially

163 Section 90(1)(c).
164 Section 90(6).
165 Section 90(3), (4).

protected? In order for the washing machine to be protected, a total of £450 needed to be paid under that agreement (including the installation charge). A total of £300 (including the installation charge) needed to be paid before the dishwasher can be protected.

143. The difficulty arises in determining how the three sums of £100 are to be appropriated between the two agreements. This will depend on which or either of the goods are protected. Section 81 of the Act provided guidance on this; section 81 has been replaced in the same terms by CONC 6.4. By CONC 6.4.2(1) R, the borrower or hirer is free to appropriate any sums paid to any agreement as he or she sees fit, and in any proportions, provided that the amount actually appropriated to an agreement is due under that agreement at the time of appropriation. If no appropriation is made, the amount is appropriated in proportion to the arrears due under each agreement.

144. In the example given, both agreements were considerably in arrears at the time that payments were made, so the borrower would have been free to appropriate the sums paid to either agreement as he or she saw fit. If he or she appropriated at least £200 to the washing machine, the washing machine would then become protected since £250 had previously been paid. Or alternatively, if he or she had appropriated the entire amount to the dishwasher, then the dishwasher could have been protected.

145. What is the position if the borrower him or herself says nothing about how payments are to be appropriated? CONC 6.4.2(2) R now provides the answer. The moneys received are to be apportioned between the two agreements in proportion to the amounts due under each of the two agreements at the time that the money is received. However, if no positive appropriation had been made by the borrower, then by virtue of CONC 6.4.2(2) R, neither the washing machine nor the dishwasher would have ended up being appropriated because the arrears under each of the agreements was approximately the same.

Consent by the borrower

146. If goods are protected, it is necessary to apply to the court for an order for their repossession, but this need does not arise if the borrower should actually consent to their repossession.[166] A borrower can, of course, be under no liability if he or she refuses consent.[167]

147. Any consent, however, must be voluntary and with at least constructive knowledge of the relevant legal position; relevant knowledge will, however, come from the wording of the hire purchase or conditional sale agreement with which the borrower should have been provided. In

166 Section 173(3).
167 Section 173(3).

Mercantile Credit Co Ltd v Cross, the goods were protected goods and the lender wrongly asked for their return. The borrower, thinking that he was obliged to return them, voluntarily redelivered the car to the shop from which he had obtained it. This was held to be free and informed consent given without duress so that the borrower could not rely on the protected status of the car; the court relied on the fact that the borrower had been informed of his legal rights in the initial hire purchase agreement, the court finding it irrelevant that he had not read the document. It does not seem to have been argued that the consent of the borrower was vitiated by misrepresentation by the lender as to the legal position.

148. Should the borrower abandon the goods, the lender is free to recover them, even if they are protected, provided that the agreement gives him or her this right. The Act prevents recovery of the goods *from the borrower* and this is not contravened by taking possession of abandoned property.[168] The position is otherwise, however, when the borrower has retained custody or control of goods by depositing them with a third party such as a garage. The lender has then no right to take the goods from such a party without a court order.[169]

Termination by the borrower

149. Goods are not protected if the borrower him or herself exercises his or her statutory right of termination under section 99.[170] Sections 99 and 100 provide that a borrower who terminates has to make the goods available for the lender to collect.

150. Problems may arise when borrowers send ambiguous letters. For example, they may write to the lender saying they are unable to make any further payments under the agreement, or that they cannot continue with it. Does such a letter amount to statutory termination of the agreement by the borrower inviting the lender to collect the goods? Or does it amount to a repudiation, requiring the lender to apply to the court in accordance with section 90 for an order for repossession?

151. The problem does not arise if the borrower actually consents to the lender repossessing the goods; in this type of ambiguous situation, it is always sensible for the lender to seek that consent. Should consent be refused or no answer obtained, the lender will have to construe any written notice to try to determine what the borrower truly intends. In a case of doubt, the lender will be safe in assuming that the notice operates to *terminate* the agreement. Notices given by the borrower are read in the light most

168 *Bentinck Ltd v Cromwell Engineering Ltd* 1971 1 QB 324.
169 *F.C. Finance Ltd v Francis* 1970 114 SJ 568.
170 Section 90(5).

favourable to him or her[171] and the borrower will invariably be in a better financial position on termination than on repudiation. On repudiation, the measure of damages payable is based upon the number of repayments outstanding,[172] which is more onerous than the financial requirements of section 100, which apply on termination. An ambiguous letter is likely to be construed as a letter of termination.

Consequences of wrongful repossession of goods

152. The consequences of wrongful repossession by the lender are drastic. The agreement is automatically terminated and the borrower has no further liabilities thereunder.[173] The borrower can apply for a declaration of his or her rights if the lender claims that the agreement is still on foot.[174] But the borrower is not entitled to a return of the goods wrongfully repossessed.[175] However, he or she is entitled to the return of all his or her money under an action for moneys had and received.[176] This measure of relief afforded to the borrower is generous; the borrower will have had use of the goods comprised in the agreement without charge.

153. Furthermore, the lender will not be entitled to recoup his or her losses against any surety, whether that surety is the borrower him or herself or a third party. The security becomes unenforceable once the lender retakes protected goods.[177]

Procedure on an application to recover goods

154. The application should be made by the lender to the county court. In England and Wales, the claim will be governed by the Consumer Credit Act procedure contained in Practice Direction 7B. In the case of a hire purchase or conditional sale agreement, the claim may only be brought in the county court for the district in which the borrower resides or carries on business.[178] In the case of a leasing agreement, the claim can only be brought where the hirer resides or where the goods are situated.[179] In the case of protected goods, there is a procedure available to a hirer whereby he or she can admit the claim but put forward terms for the suspension of a return order under section 135(1)(b).

171 *United Dominion Trust Ltd v Ennis* [1968] 1 QB 54.
172 *Yeoman Credit Ltd v Waragowski* 1961 1 WLR 1124 and subsequent cases.
173 Section 91(a).
174 Section 142(2).
175 *Carr v James Broderick & Co Ltd* [1942] 2 KB 275.
176 Section 91(b).
177 Section 131(3)(b).
178 Paragraph 4.1 Practice Direction 7B.
179 Paragraph 4.2 Practice Direction 7B.

155. If the lender is concerned about the integrity of the goods pending the hearing, the lender can apply for a protection order safeguarding the goods in the meantime.[180]

Enforcement following the death of the borrower or hirer

156. Section 86 of the Act places restrictions upon the rights of the lender or owner in the event of the death of a borrower or hirer. Without legislative intervention, many credit and hire agreements would provide for termination in the event of death, with all liabilities under the agreement being immediately repayable and with the immediate return of goods subject to hire, hire purchase or conditional sale agreements.

157. The concern of the lender or owner to protect itself on the death of the borrower or hirer is understandable; following death, there is a real prospect that payments will not continue to be made under the agreement. On the other hand, it is clearly socially unacceptable that a household at the point of bereavement should be the subject of snatch-backs from finance companies or faced with demands that items of household furniture or equipment should be immediately returned.

158. The response of the Consumer Credit Act is to prevent the lender or owner from taking certain steps as a result of the death of the borrower or hirer without first obtaining the leave of the court.[181] Section 86 applies to all regulated agreements (including hire agreements) but excluding agreements for indefinite duration.[182] A department store can therefore, on the basis of this exclusion, legitimately ask for the balance outstanding on the account to be immediately discharged when the account holder dies.

159. The steps that may not be taken are those in respect of which service of a default notice is required and include:

(a) termination of the agreement;
(b) demanding early payment of any sums;
(c) recovering possession of goods or land;
(d) treating rights conferred on the borrower or hirer by the agreement as terminated, restricted or deferred; and
(e) enforcement of any security.

160. Section 86 applies whenever termination takes place by virtue of death whether pursuant to an express term allowing termination to take place on

180 Section 131.
181 Section 86(l) and (2).
182 Section 86(3).

death, or whether pursuant to a general power to terminate, which can and is exercised after the death of the borrower or hirer.[183]

161. But the lender *is* permitted to refrain from advancing any further credit after death without needing to obtain permission of the court.[184]

162. If the agreement is fully secured, the steps above may not be taken at all as a result of the death so that any application to the court will be refused.[185] If there is no security or only partial security, the court may, in its discretion, grant permission.[186] Whether security is partial or full must be a question of fact (and often a difficult question in borderline cases) for the court in each case. The extent of the security is to be judged at the date of death; this indicates that it is the true value of the security that has to be considered and not its theoretical scope.

163. Any proceedings brought by the lender or owner to enforce an agreement following death can be served in the same manner as if the borrower were still alive, notwithstanding that the borrower or lender is aware that the debtor or hirer has died.[187]

164. Before applying for an order to take any of the steps listed above, the lender or owner has to satisfy him or herself that there is no likelihood of the terms of the credit or hire agreement being complied with. Unless the lender has made positive enquiries, the court will not make an order.[188] It is not clear precisely what enquiries the lender must make but it must obviously investigate what arrangements the family of the deceased are making for repayments. It is suggested that the lender or owner should prepare a questionnaire to be sent to the deceased's address and addressed to those handling the deceased's affairs asking what arrangements or proposals are put forward to ensure that the deceased's continuing obligations under the agreement are met. The lender or owner can then judge what action to take in the light of the response received. If the lender or owner receives no response to a properly addressed questionnaire, it can then make an application to the court, which will probably find that the lender has satisfied its duty under section 128 to make appropriate enquiries.

Handling complaints

165. No firm operates perfectly and it is inevitable that from time to time, customers will be dissatisfied and wish to complain. It is important that

183 Section 86(6).
184 Section 86(4).
185 Section 86(1).
186 Section 86(2).
187 Section 176(6).
188 Section 128.

firms handle complaints properly and responsibly and use the information gained from complaints to improve their own performance.

166. It is incumbent on all authorised firms to establish a complaints procedure; the relevant requirements are set out in the FCA Handbook DISP. As from 1 April 2014, this is of direct relevance to those in the consumer credit and consumer hire sector. A firm must establish complaints handling rules[189] and publish details of its internal procedures for the reasonable and prompt handling of complaints, details of which must be made available on request.[190]

167. A firm must also put in place procedures for monitoring complaints in order to identify recurring or systemic problems.[191] The firm should appoint a single individual with overall responsibility for the administration of complaints, procedures and complaints publicity.[192]

168. Having received a complaint, it must be acknowledged promptly and thereafter the complainant must be kept informed of progress of its investigation.[193] It must be investigated diligently and impartially.[194] When considering a complaint, the firm has a duty to consider whether redress or remedial action is appropriate.[195] However, the firm can reject the complaint without considering it when it falls outside the time limits for referral to the Financial Ombudsman Service, namely when the complaints referred to events more than six years previously, or, if later, more than three years after the relevant events came to the attention of the complainant.[196] If the complaint is being rejected on this basis, this must be made clear in the final report.

169. The complaint must be resolved within eight weeks[197] by sending a final response to the complainant. The complainant must be informed of the firm's assessment of the complaint in terms that are fair, clear and not misleading.[198] The response must be accompanied by a copy of the explanatory leaflet produced by the Financial Ombudsman Service. The complainant must be separately informed of his or her right to refer the complaint to the Financial Ombudsman Service within a period of six months. If it has not been possible for the firm to produce its final response within the eight-week period, then once the eight-week period has elapsed, the firm must tell the complainant when the final report will be ready. The

189 DISP 1.3.1 R.
190 DISP 1.2.1 R.
191 DISP 1.3.3 R.
192 DISP 1.3.7 R.
193 DISP 1.6.1 R.
194 DISP 1.4.1 R.
195 DISP 1.4.1(3) R.
196 DISP 1.8.1 R.
197 DISP 1.6.2 R.
198 DISP 1.4.1(4).

firm must still send the Financial Ombudsman Service leaflet and say that it is open to the complainant to refer the matter to the Financial Ombudsman Service immediately rather than wait for the final response.[199]

170. If an offer of redress is made, it is up to the complainant whether or not to accept it. If it is accepted, the firm must comply promptly with the offer made.[200]

171. If an offer of redress is made, it is up to the complainant whether or not to accept it. If it is accepted, the firm must comply promptly with the offer made.[201]

172. If, having considered the matter, the firm considers that another firm is solely responsible, then it may forward the complaint to that other firm and explain to the complainant in its final response that it has done this. If the firm considers that it is *jointly* responsible with another firm, then it must respond to that part of the complaint for which it accepts it is responsible, and forward on the complaint for the remainder of the complaint to be addressed.[202] The firm that receives a forwarded complaint must deal with it in the same way as it would a complaint originally made to that firm.[203]

173. The firm must keep a record of every complaint for a period of three years from the date it was received.[204] Moreover, the firm must provide the FCA with a report as to the complaints received twice a year, six months either side of the firm's accounting reference date.[205] However, in connection with a credit-related activity[206] in which annual revenue is £5 million or less, then the firm need only report on complaints received once every year.[207] The report must be by reference to the firm's accounting reference date, submitted within 30 days thereafter.[208] A firm that submits its report late will have to pay an administrative fee of £250 unless it notifies a systems failure.[209] However, a complaint that was resolved by the end of the next business day does not have to be included within a report.[210]

174. However, there is no reporting requirement at all for a firm with limited permission, except that it does apply to not-for-profit debt advisory

199 DISP 1.6.2(2) R.
200 DISP 1.4.1(5) R.
201 DISP 1.4.1(5) R.
202 DISP 1.7.1 R.
203 DISP 1.72 R.
204 DISP 1.9 R.
205 DISP 1.10.4.
206 Defined in this context as including all of the credit and hire activities newly regulated as from 1 April 2014, see the FCA Glossary.
207 DISP 1.10.1(2) R.
208 DISP 1.10.4A R.
209 DISP 1.10.6A R.
210 DISP 1.5.1 R.

firms holding £1 million or more in client moneys.[211] Such a firm with limited permission will still be required to give certain information under the reporting requirement contained in SUP 16.2. A firm with 'limited permission' is one within the categories of business within paragraph 2G of Schedule 6 of the Financial Services and Markets Act 2000[212] (i.e. one subject to light touch regulation). These activities include the supply of goods on interest-free credit, consumer hire, not-for-profit debt counselling and not-for-profit debt adjusting.

175. When a firm receives more than 500 complaints in any one year, it must publish a complaints summary in the format set out at D 1 Annex 1B.[213] The limit rises to 1,000 complaints a year in the case of a credit-related firm in cases when the turnover of that firm is less than £5 million a year.[214] The requirement to produce a summary does not apply at all to firms with what is known as 'limited permission' as discussed above, save when client money in excess of £1 million is held or is likely to be held. It is for the firm to decide how the summary should be published, although the FCA recommends that it be published on the firm's website.[215] The FCA recommends that the summary contain the standard metrics set out at D 1 Annex 1A. The firm must send an email to the FCA confirming the accuracy of the summary.[216]

211 DISP 1.10.4 R.
212 See FCA Glossary.
213 DISP 1.10A.1 R.
214 DISP 1.10A.1(1A) R.
215 DISP 1.10A.7 G.
216 DISP 1.10A.4 R.

12 The provision and regulation of security

Security

1. Security is a phrase widely used in the Consumer Credit Act, and it is as well to know what it means. It is defined in section 189(1) as follows: 'Security in relation to an actual or prospective consumer credit agreement or consumer hire agreement, or any linked transaction, means a mortgage, charge, pledge, bond, debenture, indemnity, guarantee, bill, note or other right provided by the borrower or hirer, or at his request (express or implied), to secure the carrying out of the obligations of the borrower or hirer under the agreement.'

2. Several comments can usefully be made about the definition. The security provided must be provided by the borrower or hirer personally or at *his or her request*. The definition does not, therefore, extend to a recourse agreement entered into between a dealer and finance company whereby the dealer, at the behest of the finance company, guarantees the future contractual performance of hire purchase and conditional sale customers introduced by him or her (for an example of litigation involving such a recourse, agreement see *Unity Finance Ltd v Woodcock*).[1] In *Governor and Company of the Bank of Scotland v Euclidian (No 1) Ltd*, the court rejected a suggestion that a funding arrangement could amount to the provision of security when the facts that it had been provided and that it had been insisted upon by the lender were unknown to the borrower.[2]

3. The question has been debated whether a policy of insurance covering goods comprised in an agreement could be 'security' within the meaning of the Act. It is clear that it could not. The purpose of such a policy is to guard against damage to or destruction of the goods. Such a loss might or might not arise through breach by a borrower or hirer of the agreement. The question of fulfilment of the terms of the agreement is irrelevant to the operation of the insurance policy and the policy could not be said

1 1963 1 WLR 455.
2 2007 EWHC 1732 (Comm) at [56], Mr Justice Field.

to 'secure the carrying out of the obligations of the borrower or hirer' as required by the definition. In any event, several of the Regulations promulgated under the Act such as the Total Charge for Credit Regulations and the Linked Transactions (Exemptions) Regulations make clear that an insurance policy is to be regarded as a linked transaction and therefore cannot rank as security (the definition of linked transaction in section 19(1) of the Act expressly excludes security).

Types of security

4. Some comments may be appropriate about the categories of security that are referred to in the definition:

(a) *Mortgage, charge.* Mortgage and charge, at least in relation to land, are, in the context of this Act, synonymous, since the Act is concerned with security provided by consent. It is possible to create a charge over personal property but this has to be registered as a bill of sale, which is cumbersome.
(b) *Debenture.* This is a reference to the creation of a floating charge. Individuals, other than farmers under the Agricultural Credits Act 1928, cannot create a floating charge; only companies can create such charges and companies cannot normally be party to regulated agreements. Debentures, therefore, are only important as security provided at the request of the borrower or hirer.
(c) *Pledge.* This has a specific meaning and is defined in section 189(1) as an article taken in pawn. Special rules apply to the taking of pledges.
(d) *Indemnity and guarantee.* The distinction between an indemnity and a guarantee is well established and oversubtle. A person giving an indemnity undertakes primary responsibility for the obligations in the agreement that he or she is indemnifying.

5. In the case of a hire agreement, the indemnifying party becomes liable for every instalment of hire as it falls due, a liability that is additional and alternative to that of the hirer. On the other hand, a party entering into a guarantee accepts only secondary liability for the performance of the obligations under the agreement; the liability of the guarantor only arises once the hirer is in default, the guarantor accepting legal responsibility for the financial liabilities arising from that default.

6. Although the distinction between the two types of agreement is logically clear, in practice there are considerable problems in classifying any particular agreement into one or other category (see the difficulties in *Unity Finance Ltd v Woodcock*). The classification is often, however, a matter of great importance, because the legal rule applicable to each differ greatly. A guarantee to be enforceable has to be evidenced by a memorandum in writing in accordance with the Statute of Frauds, but no such formalities

are necessary for an indemnity. A guarantor, furthermore, can avail him or herself of all personal defences open to the borrower or hirer, such as want of capacity, undue influence or misrepresentation; the party liable under an indemnity has no such defences open to him or her since his or her legal liability is independent to that of the borrower.

7. Fortunately, the distinction has now largely disappeared for security governed by the Consumer Credit Act. The distinction will now only be of significance where the borrower or hirer is under the age of 18, and for the purpose of selecting the correct heading to a security instrument.

8. In the past, it has been very common for finance companies to take a promissory note or bill of exchange as collateral security for future payment of sums due under the agreement. Sometimes a series of post-dated promissory notes or bills of exchange would be taken to cover future instalments under the agreement; sometimes a single bill or note might be taken to cover the entire amount. Such security is governed by special restrictions under the Act.

9. The list given of the various types of security in section 189(1) is reasonably comprehensive. Other forms of security are, however, possible (e.g. the deposit of title deeds or share certificates creating an equitable lien over them for the amount either due or to become due).

Surety and security instrument

10. A surety is defined in section 189(1) as the person who furnishes the security. The borrower or hirer him or herself may be the surety or it may be a third party providing security at the request of the borrower or hirer. A surety need not be an individual. Unlike many other provisions in the Consumer Credit Act, the Act, in giving rights and protections to sureties, does not distinguish between individual and corporate sureties. Note that the meaning of surety used in the context of the Consumer Credit Act is wider than the meaning normally attached to the term, which makes surety synonymous with the provider of an indemnity or guarantee.

11. A 'security instrument' is a reference to a deed or written agreement conferring security in favour of the lender or owner entered into by a third party at the request of the borrower or hirer (section 105(2) and (6)). Types of common security instruments are, of course, guarantee, written indemnity, bill of sale, debenture, mortgage and legal charge.

Formalities connected with the security instrument

12. All forms of security provided by a third party must be expressed in writing.[3] This immediately excludes a deposit of title deeds or chattels as

3 Section 105(1).

being proper security. The security instrument has to express fully the terms of the security, omitting only implied terms.[4] It must, of course, be legible and it must be signed by the surety.[5] When presented or sent for signature, a copy of the security instrument must also be presented or sent to the surety.[6]

13. Furthermore, the surety must be given a copy of the credit or hire agreement to be secured, together with copies of any documents referred to therein.[7] The copy of the agreement must be given to the surety within seven days of the credit or hire agreement being executed (excluding the date of execution).[8] Should execution of the agreement take place prior to signature of the security instrument, the copy agreement must be given to the surety at the same time as the security instrument is executed.[9]

14. The copies of the security instrument and of the agreement to be secured have to comply with the Cancellation Notices and Copies of Documents Regulations 1983.[10] These Regulations have been discussed previously and the general points there made in relation to legibility and the truth of the copy apply here. The following specific points can, however, perhaps usefully be made:

(a) there is no need to reproduce the signature box in either the copy security instrument or the copy agreement;[11]
(b) the borrower or hirer's name and address must be inserted into the copy agreement to be secured;[12] and
(c) there is no need to supply copies of documents referred to in the copy agreement excluded by regulation 11 of the Cancellation Notices and Copies of Documents Regulations 1983.

15. These requirements apply to all security instruments. Guarantees and indemnities alone are subject to special rules that prescribe the form they are to take. Such security instruments have to comply with the Consumer Credit (Guarantees and Indemnities) Regulations 1983[13] made under section 105(2). These Regulations provide for the instrument to be appropriately headed (distinguishing between guarantee and indemnity), for

4 Section 105(4)(b).
5 Section 105(4)(a).
6 Section 105(4).
7 Section 105(5).
8 Section 105(5)(b).
9 Section 105(5)(a).
10 SI 1983/1557.
11 Reg 3(2)(b) Cancellation Notices and Copies of Documents Regulations 1983.
12 Reg 3(2)(c) Cancellation Notices and Copies of Documents Regulations 1983.
13 SI 1983/1556.

certain information to be provided and for the precise form of signature box in which the surety or his or her agent must sign.

16. A comprehensive statement of statutory rights must be reproduced.[14] This will tell the surety of any rights to withdraw from provision of the security he or she may have and inform him or her that unless the borrower or hirer is under 18, his or her liability cannot exceed that of the borrower or hirer. The surety's right to receive a copy of any default notice must also be spelt out.

Formalities in connection with security to be provided by the borrower or hirer

17. The Agreements Regulations provide that a description of any security furnished by the borrower or hirer must be given in the Form of Agreement that he or she signs.[15]

The continuing rights of the surety

The right to withdraw

18. A surety can resile from any security provided by him or her until the time that the relevant credit or hire agreement is executed.[16] Clearly, this does not arise if the regulated agreement has already been executed when the security instrument is signed. Withdrawal takes effect by written[17] notice on the lender; the security instrument is treated as if it had never been entered into.

The right to receive further copies of the agreement and further copies of the security instrument: the right to a statement of information

19. The surety is entitled, on payment of a fee, to receive further copies of the regulated agreement and of the security instrument and to a statement of the borrower or hirer's financial position under the agreement. These rights are comparable to those enjoyed by the borrower or hirer under the main agreement. The surety's rights are contained in sections 107, 108 and 109 dealing with fixed, running account and hire agreements, respectively. These provisions are directly analogous to sections 77, 78 and 79 governing

14 Part III, Schedule Guarantee and Indemnities Regulations 1983.

15 Paragraph 20 Schedule 1, paragraph 9 Schedule 3, Agreements Regulations 1983; Paragraph 23 Schedule 1, Agreements Regulations 2010.

16 Section 113(6).

17 The definition of notice in section 189(1) means notice in writing.

the rights of the borrower and hirer. The discussion of these sections earlier should be referred to.

20. The points of similarity between the provisions are as follows:

(a) under both sets of provisions, copies of the relevant agreements have to be provided;
(b) the fee chargeable is £1;
(c) the information that has to be furnished is the same;
(d) the information and copies have to be given by the lender within the same time, 12 working days;[18]
(e) the information given is binding on the lender or owner pursuant to section 172(1); and
(f) none of the provisions apply to non-commercial agreements.

21. The following points of distinction, however, should be noted:

(a) Sections 107, 108 and 109 give a right to a copy of the security instrument while sections 77, 78 and 79 do not. The borrower or hirer, however, has a right to a copy of the security instrument under section 110, again within 12 working days, admittedly on payment of a further £1 fee (sureties therefore get better value for money than borrowers and hirers).
(b) The surety has no right to receive periodic statements of account under a running account agreement. Section 78(4) and (5) does not apply to sureties.
(c) The surety has no right to a copy of an arrears notice served under section 86B or 86C.

22. The obligation to provide a copy of a security instrument does not apply to a non-commercial agreement, to a situation when nothing is or may be due from the surety or if a request has previously been made and complied with less than a month before.[19] If there is non-compliance with section 110(1), the security cannot be enforced so long as the breach continues.[20]

23. If a lender or owner serves a default notice or a notice under sections 76 or 98, the lender or owner must also serve a copy on the surety.[21] The copy must be headed prominently 'Surety's copy of notice served on debtor' or 'Surety's copy served on hirer' as appropriate.[22] So long as the lender or owner fails to do this, the lender or owner is only entitled to enforce the

18 Consumer Credit (Prescribed Periods for Information) Regulations 1983 SI 1983/1569.
19 Section 110(2).
20 Section 110(3).
21 Section 111(1).
22 Regulation 10 Cancellation Notices and Copies of Documents Regulations 1983.

security on an application to the court.[23] There are no criminal sanctions for breaching the section and the section gives no remedy for breach of statutory duty; wrongful enforcement should, however, produce the same civil remedies as were discussed for wrongfully enforcing an invalid default notice. The lender or owner will be permitted to enforce a security if the surety consents to the enforcement,[24] at least if the surety has actual notice of his or her rights.

Extent of liability of a surety

24. An important principle is enshrined in section 113(1). No lender or owner may profit from the taking of security. The liability of the surety is limited in all respects to the liability of the borrower or hirer (although there is nothing to prevent the surety having a lesser liability). Thus, if a borrower terminates a hire purchase agreement in accordance with his or her statutory powers, any liability of the surety will reflect the sums due as a result of the borrower's termination. Section 113(1) applies not only to security to secure performance of the principal credit or hire agreement, but also to security in respect of a linked transaction.[25] Security in respect of a linked transaction is rather unusual, although it may arise where a minor is party to such a transaction.

25. There is only one exception to this general principle. The exception arises because of the difficult legal position of the lender or owner when entering a credit or hire transaction with a minor (someone under the age of 18). The lender or owner may be unable to recover sums due under the agreement through the courts because of the minor's lack of contractual capacity. Section 113(7) preserves the effectiveness of an indemnity entered into to secure an agreement with a minor. The fact of the borrower or hirer's minority is ignored in determining the liability of the person granting the indemnity (although that person could still rely on other personal defences of the borrower or hirer such as misrepresentation or undue influence in an action to enforce the indemnity).

26. The effect of section 113(7) is to ensure that indemnities entered into by parents and adult friends continue to be enforceable and that such indemnities cannot be attacked on the basis of want of capacity on the part of the borrower or hirer. A lender or owner must, however, take very great care to ensure that the agreement signed by the adult in these circumstances is an indemnity and not a guarantee, because if it is the latter, its enforcement may prove very difficult indeed.[26]

23 Section 111(2).
24 Section 173(3).
25 Section 113(8).
26 See *Yeoman Credit Ltd v Latter* 1961 1 WLR 828.

Improper execution of a security instrument and of the regulated credit or hire agreement

27. An improperly executed security is not to be confused with an ineffective security. The effects of an ineffective security are drastic; it is treated as never having had effect.[27] An improperly executed security instrument, however, can be enforced, but only with an order of the court.[28] Improper execution includes both a failure to conclude security in writing and failing to produce a security instrument in the correct form. It will be necessary for the lender wishing to enforce the security to apply to the court for an enforcement order.[29]

28. On such an application, the court shall dismiss the application for an enforcement order only if it considers it just to do so in the light of all its powers.[30]

29. Among the orders a court can make are to:

(a) enforce the security outright; the court might make such an order if culpability was low and no prejudice had been suffered by the improper execution;
(b) enforce it but reduce the amount that the surety has to pay;[31]
(c) give the surety time to pay by instalments, having regard to the means of the surety;[32] and
(d) release the surety from any liability by refusing to make an enforcement and by making a declaration to this effect, thus preventing any further application for enforcement being heard.[33]

30. If an enforcement order is refused and a declaration is made, then the security is treated as ineffective.[34]

31. A similar state of affairs applies when it is the regulated credit or hire agreement that is not properly executed. The agreement can be enforced on an order of the court only pursuant to section 65(1); the court will need to be asked to make an enforcement order.[35] The security will only be enforceable once an enforcement order has been made in relation to the agreement.[36] The surety should be a party to the application by the lender or owner for enforcement of the credit or hire agreement.[37]

27 Section 106(a).
28 Section105(7).
29 Section 127(1)(b).
30 Section 127(1).
31 Section 127(2).
32 Section 129(2)(a).
33 Section 142(1).
34 Section 113(3)(d).
35 Section 127(1)(a).
36 Section 113(1).
37 Section 141(5).

Ineffective security

32. In certain situations, the security is treated as if it was ineffective. These situations are:

(a) where the surety serves a notice on the lender or owner stating that he or she does not wish to provide security for a credit or hire agreement that has not yet been executed;[38]
(b) if the regulated agreement for which the security was provided has been cancelled by the borrower or hirer;[39]
(c) if the lender retakes 'protected goods' under a hire purchase or conditional sale agreement[40] and the agreement is, as a consequence, automatically terminated as a result;[41]
(d) if the court refuses an application to enforce an improperly executed agreement (other than by reason of technicality) or if it refuses an application to enforce an agreement where a negotiable instrument has been improperly taken as security, other than on a technicality (whether or not the court also makes a declaration under section 142 to the effect that no enforcement order has been made, but if a section 142 declaration has been made, that will be conclusive);[42] and
(e) if the court refuses an application to enforce an improperly executed security instrument (except on technical grounds).[43]

33. Security also becomes ineffective if an agreement has been rendered unenforceable by virtue of sections 26, 26A or 27 of the Financial Services and Markets Act 2000 and an application has been made for the FCA to exercise its discretion under section 28A of the Financial Services and Markets Act 2000 to allow enforcement of the agreements and that discretion has been refused (except on technical grounds).[44]

34. If the lender or owner makes an application to the court for an enforcement order, or to the FCA under section 28A, which is dismissed on what the lender considers to be technical grounds, the lender can ask the court or the FCA to certify that this was the basis for the dismissal and such a certificate is conclusive.[45]

35. Conversely, it is open to any interested party to apply to the court under section 142(1) for a declaration that no enforcement order should be made and such a route could be adopted by a surety with a view to having

38 Section 113(6).
39 Section 113(2).
40 Where more than one third of the total price has been paid; sections 90 and 91.
41 Section 113(3).
42 Section 113(3)(c).
43 Section 105(8).
44 Section 113(3((c).
45 Section 189(5).

the security provided by him or her rendered ineffective. The court can make a declaration even if no further sums are due under the agreement (perhaps because of realisation of security by the lender).[46]

36. The consequences of security being ineffective are severe:

(a) an ineffective security is treated as never having had any effect;[47]
(b) property lodged with the lender or owner solely for the purposes of security will have to be returned;[48]
(c) the lender or owner shall take action to remove or cancel any entry in the register so far as the entry relates to the security;[49] and
(d) if the security has been realised, any amount received will have to be returned.[50]

37. 'Realisation' for the purposes of section 106(d) has its conventional meaning of the process by which a lender or hirer releases value from the security so that the proceeds can be applied in discharge of the debt. It does not extend to payments made by the borrower to the lender under the loan agreement.[51]

38. If the agreement is cancelled, the borrower or hirer will become under a duty to return any credit and to restore any goods already received by the borrower.[52] The obligations of the borrower, however, do not arise until the lender or owner has complied with all its requirements under section 106.[53]

Transfer of land charges

39. There is an exception to the effect of section 106 when it comes to the sale of registered charges. This will arise should a lender wish to sell the benefit of a secured loan agreement (or a bundle of secured loan agreements) to an assignee for valuable consideration. The assignee of the benefit of the agreement will need to give notice to the borrower of the assignment and will acquire the status of lender,[54] in theory able to enforce the terms of the loan. In the case of registered land, the assignee will also have the charge registered in its name at the Land Registry, becoming thereby the registered proprietor of the charge.

46 In *re London Scottish Finance Ltd* 2014 Bus LR 424 at [58].
47 Section 106(a).
48 Section 106(b).
49 Section 106(c).
50 Section 106(d).
51 In *re London Scottish Finance Ltd* 2014 Bus LR 424 at [47].
52 Under sections 71 and 72.
53 Section 113(5).
54 *Jones v Link Financial Ltd* 2013 1 WLR 693.

40. Suppose that the loan agreement was improperly executed and an enforcement order is refused so that the security is ineffective. Does this prevent enforcement by the new owner of the registered charge of its security?

41. Guidance is given by section 177(1) of the Act, which is in the following terms: 'Nothing in this Act affects the rights of a proprietor of a registered charge (within the meaning of Land Registration Act 2002) who – (a) becomes the proprietor under a transfer for valuable consideration without notice of any defect in the title arising (apart from this section) by virtue of this Act, or (b) derives title from such a proprietor.'

42. Section 177(3) provides that section 177(1) does not apply to those persons carrying on a consumer credit business, a consumer hire business or the business of debt collecting or debt administration. This is an important qualification to the effect of section 177(1) as many of those acquiring registered charges will be engaged in the business of lending or debt collection.

43. Section 177(1), therefore, draws a distinction between two categories, those within section 177(1) and those without. Those within are those purchasing the charge for valuable consideration without notice of a defect in title and not carrying on a business within the categories specified in section 177(3).

44. Section 177(1) appears to presuppose that those who become registered proprietors of a charge acquire good beneficial title to the charge. This premise is based on section 30 of the Land Registration Act 2002, which provide that if a registrable disposition of a registered charge is made for valuable consideration, completion of the disposition by registration has the effect of 'postponing to the interest under the disposition any interest affecting the charge immediately before the disposition whose priority is not protected at the time of registration'.

45. This operates to confer both legal and beneficial title on the proprietor for valuable consideration in circumstances where there has been a registered disposition for the purposes of the Act. Now a disposition of an ineffective security is probably to be considered a disposition for the purposes of the Act but the contrary is arguable.[55] If it is a disposition, then, subject to any possible remedy of rectification, a registered proprietor of the charge will obtain good title. Section 177(1) seems, however, to assume that those within its protection should not be amenable to a successful attempt to rectify the register pursuant to Schedule 4 of the Land Registration Act 2002.

55 A disposition procured by fraud was held not to be a disposition for the purposes of the Land Registration Act 2002 in *Malory Enterprise Ltd v Cheshire Homes (UK) Ltd* 2002 Ch 216, followed in *Fitzwilliam Richall Holding Services Ltd* 2013 1 P & CR 19. Perhaps similar reasoning could apply to the transfer of an invalid security.

46. What is clear is that those outside the protected categories should not have the benefit of being a proprietor of a registered charge. It must follow that a proprietor of such a charge will hold it on trust for the debtor as there is no other way in which to give effect to the fact that it is ineffective.

47. Difficult questions may arise of whether or not the purchaser of the charge had notice of the defect in title or not. It is plain that section 177(1) is directed to notice at the time of the transfer of the charge. Moreover, the purchaser must have knowledge of facts that would render the charge ineffective within section 106 (it will not, of course, be a requirement that the proprietor should have knowledge of section 106 or its terms). Mere knowledge that an agreement secured by a charge has been improperly executed, or mere knowledge that a charge has been improperly executed, should not be enough because it is only once an enforcement order is refused that a defect in title arises and the charge becomes ineffective under section 106.

48. If a purchaser of an ineffective charge acquires title in this way, the original chargee will be liable to indemnify the borrower or hirer from the loss sustained.[56] It is perhaps surprising that section 177(4) did not confer the benefit of the indemnity on the *surety* as opposed to the borrower or hirer, but given that the borrower or hirer will be bound to indemnity the surety, perhaps this does not matter.

49. Similar provisions apply in Scotland and Northern Ireland.

50. In unregistered land, there is no such protection available to a purchaser of an ineffective mortgage as there is in the case of registered land under section 30 of the Land Registration Act 2002. The purchaser will not acquire title to the mortgage and will not be able to rely upon it.

Exercise of a power of sale in the case of ineffective mortgage security

51. Under the general law, a mortgagee can sell a mortgaged property without recourse to the court in accordance with section 101(1) of the Law of Property Act 1925 in order to realise the value of its security. To act in this way is not permissible, of course, if the mortgage security is ineffective by virtue of section 106.

52. Nevertheless, it is possible that in the case of registered land, a purchaser might acquire registered title on the basis of such a sale. In the case of registered land, the new proprietor, having acquired registered title and assuming that the sale was for valuable consideration, the effect of registration of title will, under the general law, be to confer beneficial title on the registered owner by virtue of section 29 of the Land Registration

56 Section 177(4).

Act 2002; this provides that if a registrable disposition of a registrable estate is made, the effect of registration is to postpone to the interest under the disposition any interest affecting the estate before the disposition. The only remedy that the borrower would have is to seek rectification under Schedule 4 of the Land Registration Act 2002. It is possible, however, that such a remedy may be granted when a purchaser has derived title based on an ineffective security.

53. In unregistered land, the purchaser of a property based on an ineffective mortgage will not acquire good title. Section 104(2) of the Law of Property Act 1925 protects purchasers in some instances from having to make inquiries as to the circumstance in which a power of sale came to be exercisable. While the effect of section 104(2) is expressly preserved in relation to the Consumer Credit Act by section 177(2), the protection afforded by section 104(2) does not extend to a situation in which the mortgage is to be treated as being of no effect whatsoever.[57] Accordingly, the purchaser will not acquire good title when a sale is derived from a power attached to an ineffective security.

Negotiable instruments as security

54. A guiding principle of English Law is that bills of exchange (of which the most common example is a cheque) and promissory notes are to be treated as far as possible as cash. It is desirable for the product conduct of commercial affairs that a person holding a bill of exchange or promissory note should be confident of its eventual payment and should be able to sue on the bill or note as an independent transaction without any need for investigation of the underlying transaction under which the bill was tendered.

55. A 'holder in due course' of a bill or note is in a particularly privileged position. A 'holder in due course' must be someone other than one of the original parties to a bill or note. The bill or note must have been negotiated to him or her by indorsement. Someone who is a 'holder in due course' takes free[58] of what are known as 'defects in title' of the bill. A defect in title arises where there is an irregularity in obtaining the bill, through fraud, duress, illegal consideration or other unlawful means.[59] The holder in due course can sue successfully on a bill or note even if such defects in title exist, nor may the claim be defeated by any personal defences that may be available to the original parties to the bill or note. In order to be a holder in due course, the party in possession of the bill or note and in whose favour it is indorsed must take it for value and in good faith, and must have no

57 By virtue of section 106(a).

58 Section 38 Bills of Exchange Act 1882.

59 Section 29(2) Bills of Exchange Act 1882.

knowledge of any defect in title at the time it is negotiated to him or her.[60] A mere holder of the bill or note, however, who does not derive title from a holder in due course, will take the bill or note subjects to defects in title, as does the original payee of the bill or note. This elaborate legal framework established by the Bills of Exchange Act for protection of bills and notes is not affected by the Consumer Credit Act. The Act does, however, seek to minimise the unfairness that can be wrought on borrowers by the application of these rules.

56. A problem can arise where a lender extracts a bill of exchange or promissory note as security from a borrower for payment of future sums owing under a credit agreement. Two authorities provide illustrations of this, *Modern Light Cars Ltd v Seals*[61] and *United Dominions Trust Ltd v Bycroft*.[62] In each case, the promissory note was expressed to be taken as security to cover future payments of instalments. The unfairness to the borrower can arise, as happened in both these cases, if the bills of exchange or promissory note is subsequently negotiated to a third party. The third party will purchase the negotiated bill or note at a discount, which will represent the third party's profit. The lender will at the same time have the advantage of immediate payment and be relieved of the obligation of having to sue on the bill or note. This right of action will pass to the third party. The third party's position in relation to the borrower in relying on the bill or note will be strong since the third party will be a holder in due course of the bill or note except in the unlikely event that he or she took it with notice of a defect in title. It can normally be safely said that the borrower will be liable for the whole amount of the bill together with statutory interest.

57. What is unsatisfactory about the above situation is that the borrower may be liable for the full amount of the instalments and yet have a legitimate right to withhold payment to the lender. This could arise in a hire purchase, conditional sale or credit sale transaction where the goods comprised in the agreement are defective. Or it could arise in a connected lending transaction where the lender is liable, under section 75, for the liabilities of the supplier arising out of the supply transaction. The effect of the promissory note given by the borrower will be to deprive the borrower of his or her legitimate right of set-off and to put him or her to all the difficulties and uncertainties involved in an action against the lender.

58. It is not to preserve the privileged position of the holder in due course, but to protect the borrower from the possible adverse consequences flowing from the provision of a bill or note as security that sections 123 and 125 were enacted. These sections place three restrictions on a lender.

60 Section 29(1) Bills of Exchange Act 1882.

61 1934 1 KB 32.

62 1954 1 WLR 345.

Taking payment, taking security and negotiating a cheque

59. The three exceptions are as follows:

(a) the lender or owner may not take payment of sums due under a regulated consumer credit or hire agreement or under a security instrument by negotiable instrument other than by cheque or cash;[63]
(b) the lender or owner may not take any negotiable instrument as security in respect of a regulated credit or hire agreement;[64] and
(c) if the lender or owner takes a cheque as payment under a regulated credit or hire agreement or under a security instrument, he or she may not negotiate the cheque other than to a banker.[65]

60. A comment is appropriate on the terms used in section 123. It is submitted that 'cheque' is to be given its everyday meaning and should include a post-dated cheque even though a more restricted definition is given in the Bills of Exchange Act 1882, section 73. Negotiable instrument is a wider term.

61. The standard attributes of a negotiable instrument are that:

(a) it can be transferred on delivery usually be indorsement to the bearer; the instrument transferred is said to be negotiated;
(b) the person taking the instrument can sue upon it; and
(c) the person if in good faith and for value takes good title to it, irrespective of any defect in title of the transferor.

62. The following classes of document are the most common types of negotiable instrument:

(a) cheques;
(b) bills of exchange;
(c) promissory notes;
(d) bankers drafts; and
(e) traveller's cheques.

63. The Act in section 123(1) appears to treat cash as a species of negotiable instrument, which is strange; cash is never normally thought to be 'negotiated'.

64. The effect of section 123 and the meaning of 'negotiable instrument' clearly acts to exclude the former practice of taking bills of exchange and

63 Section 123(1).
64 Section 123(3).
65 Section 123(2).

promissory notes as security. Note, however, that there is nothing in section 123 that prevents a lender or owner from taking a series of post-dated cheques to cover future rental payments or loan instalments. The cheques are not to be treated as security since it is actually intended to present them for payment (see the meaning attached to taking of security in section 123(4)). There is, therefore, no contravention of section 123(3). Nor is there any restriction on taking post-dated cheques arising out of section 123(1).

65. It is perhaps because this situation is permissible that a restriction is placed on the negotiation of cheques. If third parties to whom they were negotiated could sue on a series of cheques made out in this way, there might well be a recurrence of some of the former abuses experienced with promissory notes and bills of exchanges. As it is, a lender who pays the cheque into his or her bank account may make the bank a holder in due course of the cheque (although this may in fact not occur all that frequently – see the requirement for a pre-existing undertaking by the bank to pay on uncleared effects established by *Underwood Ltd v Martins Bank Ltd*).[66] A bank that does become a holder in due course can, of course, sue on the cheque in its own name. Banks, it seems to be presumed, will act responsibly.

Exceptions to section 123

66. Section 123 does not apply to non-commercial agreements (i.e. where the lender or owner is not acting in the course of a business).[67]

67. The Secretary of State may further provide by order that the section is not to apply where the regulated agreement has a connection with a country outside the United Kingdom.[68] Such a provision is needed since much foreign trade takes place on the basis that payment is to be made by way of forward-dated bills of exchange or promissory notes. The special status accorded to bills of exchange and promissory notes is not confined to this jurisdiction; it is internationally recognised that a supplier can be reasonably sure of obtaining payment if he or she supplies goods on the security of a bill of exchange or promissory note rendered beforehand. It could cause considerable uncertainty if exceptions were made to this basic position.

68. Understandably, therefore, the Consumer Credit Act seeks to avoid any disturbance to foreign trade that might arise by inflexible application of section 123. The Consumer Credit (Negotiable Instruments) (Exemption) Order 1984[69] exempts from the effect of section 123 consumer hire

66 1924 1 KB 775.
67 Section 123(5).
68 Section 123(6).
69 SI 1984/435.

agreements made in connection with a trade in goods between the United Kingdom and a person outside the United Kingdom, or between two persons both outside the United Kingdom. The goods must be hired to the hirer in the course of a business carried on by the hirer.

Consequences of non-compliance with section 123

69. If the contravention occurs in relation to the credit or hire agreement, the credit or hire agreement becomes unenforceable except by order of the court.[70] The same principle applies to a contravention in relation to the provision of any security; the security is only enforceable upon an order of the court.[71]

70. In either case, the lender or owner will have to apply for an enforcement order from the courts under section 127(1)(d). The powers of the court on such an application are considered in that context. If an enforcement order is refused either in respect of the credit or hire agreement, or in respect of any security provided thereunder as a result of a contravention of section 123, the security becomes ineffective[72] – it is treated as never having had any effect. Section 106 applies with the consequences previously discussed. The provisions create no criminal penalties attaching to the lender or owner.

71. Leaving aside enforcement of the Agreement, could the lender or owner sue on a negotiable instrument that was improperly obtained as a separate cause of action? Could a lender, for example, sue on a cheque he or she had obtained from a borrower as security for due payment of instalments? Section 125(1) prevents any such independent cause of action arising. A lender or owner taking a negotiable instrument improperly is 'not entitled to enforce it'. Section 125(1) also says for good measure that the lender or owner in these circumstances shall not be a holder in due course. This last stipulation, however, says no more than is the position under the general law in any event.

72. A lender or owner who is the payee of a cheque or other negotiable instrument cannot be the holder in due course because he or she has not obtained the cheque or negotiable instrument by negotiation.[73] Any defects in title to the cheque can therefore be raised by way of defence in an action on the cheque. So also may any irregularity in complying with section 123.

70 Section 124(1).
71 Section 124(2).
72 Section 113(2), 124(3).
73 *Jones (R.E.) Ltd v Waring and Gillow Ltd* [1926] AC 670.

Third party rights in a negotiable instrument

73. A third party to whom a negotiable instrument is negotiated will be a holder in due course in accordance with the Bills of Exchange Act 1882, section 29, if the following conditions are satisfied:

(a) if he or she took the bill because it was overdue and before it had been previously dishonoured if such was the case;
(b) if he or she took the bill in good faith and for value; and
(c) if at the time the bill was negotiated to him or her, he or she had no notice of any defect in the title of the person who negotiated it.

74. Nothing in the Consumer Credit Act alters these requirements or the rights of a holder in due course.[74]

75. When a bill is negotiated to a third party by a lender or owner, the lender or owner is almost certain, in the circumstances discussed earlier, to receive value for the bill, thus satisfying requirement (b) above. It can also be assumed, furthermore, that the bill is not overdue and has not previously been dishonoured. So condition (a) above will also be satisfied.

76. The only question that may throw doubt on the third party's rights to sue on the bill arises if the third party had knowledge of any irregularity affecting the original taking of the bill. The following circumstance may be envisaged:

(a) the third party knew nothing of any contravention of section 123;
(b) the third party knew that a negotiable instrument other than cheque or cash had been taken in payment from borrower, hirer or surety contrary to section 123(1), which is then negotiated to the third party;
(c) the third party to whom a cheque is negotiated knew that the cheque had been originally tendered in payment by a borrower, hirer or surety contravening section 123(2); and
(d) the third party knew that a negotiable instrument, including a cheque, had been taken as security under a credit or hire agreement, which in contravention of section 123(3), which is then negotiated to him or her.

77. The situation posed by (a) is simple. If the third party has no knowledge of any defect in the negotiable instrument, he or she becomes a holder in due course and can successfully sue upon it. The situation posed by (c) is also straightforward. A contravention of section 123(2) constitutes a defect in title to the cheque (section 125(2)) so that a holder of the cheque with knowledge of this irregularity will not become a holder in due course. He or she will not, therefore, be able to sustain an action on the cheque because

74 Section125(4).

the borrower, hirer of surety will be able to raise the contravention of section 123(2) as a valid defence.

78. A consideration of section 125(2) also provides the key to situations (b) and (d). Because the Act specifically states that a contravention of section 123(2) constitutes a defect in title but says nothing of contravention of section 123(1) or section 123(3), it follows that breach of these provisions are not to constitute defect of title. (This commonsense principle of construction can be expressed in Latin as '*expressio unius est exlusio alterius*' – express mention of one excludes the others.)

79. It follows, therefore, that knowledge of contravention of section 123(1) and (3) as referred to in situations (b) and (d) above will not prevent the third party from becoming a holder in due course, because the contraventions do not amount to defects in title. Such knowledge will not prevent the third party from successfully suing on the cheques. This seems the inevitable result of a true construction of section 125 but it leads to anomalous results.

Anomalies

80. It follows from the above that a third party may be placed in a more favourable position as a direct result of a contravention of section 123(1), which is, to say the least, a paradoxical conclusion. If a lender takes a promissory note in payment from a borrower in contravention of section 123(1) and then negotiates it to a knowing third party, that third party can sue on the promissory note because there has been no breach of section 123(2). On the other hand, a lender who takes a cheque in payment complies with section 123(1), but if this cheque is then negotiated to a knowing third party, that third party will not be able to sue upon it because there is then a breach of section 123(2). There seems to be no rhyme or reason for giving the third party a right of action in the former circumstance but not in the latter, especially since the wrongdoing appears greater in the former circumstance.

81. Furthermore, a knowing third party will be able to sue on a cheque taken as a security but not one taken as payments due under the agreement. This is because it is not an infringement of section 123(2) to negotiate a cheque taken as security; the only infringement arises if a cheque has been taken by way of payment. Yet, parliament clearly considers it to be more serious to take a cheque as security since this is expressly prohibited by section 123(3), while taking a cheque by way of payment of sums due is legitimate. It is a strange conclusion that a third party with knowledge of the true position will actually be in a better position as a result of the contravention of section 123(3).

82. This has a further undesirable consequence. In defence to an action on a cheque, the burden of proof rests on the borrower or hirer to prove that the third party knew of the defect in the title. It follows from the above

that the borrower or hirer will have to prove that the third party knew not only that the cheque was obtained in relation to a regulated agreement, but that it was obtained expressly for the purpose of payment of sums due. Since this is an essential ingredient constituting the defect in title, knowledge of this fact by the third party will have to be established. This is likely to remove much of the protection given to the borrower or hirer by section 123(2), since the borrower or hirer may not be able to establish such a specific degree of knowledge.

13 Regulated mortgage contracts

The Mortgages and Home Finance: Conduct of Business Sourcebook

Scope of the Mortgages and Home Finance: Conduct of Business Sourcebook

1. The Mortgages and Home Finance: Conduct of Business Sourcebook section of the Handbook, referred to as 'MCOB', evolved out of the regulation of regulated mortgage contracts by the Financial Services and Markets Act 2000. Entry into and administration of such agreements became regulated activities. The FSA later extended its regulatory reach to include home purchase plans, sale and lease back, and home reversion sales.

2. Regulated mortgage contracts constitute an extremely significant class of loans. They are defined as loans secured by a first charge over land in which at least 40 per cent of the land used as security must be used in connection with a dwelling for use by the borrower.[1] Such loans, of course, include loans for use for the purchase of a home.

3. MCOB applies to any firm that carries on what is referred to as a 'home finance activity', which is defined to include entering into or administering or mediating regulated mortgage contracts, home purchase plans, home reversion plans or sale and rent back agreements. It also to applies to firms that communicate or approve financial promotions of 'qualifying credit', a 'home purchase plan', a 'home reversion plan' or a 'regulated sale and rent back agreement'.[2]

4. The precise and specific meaning of the phrases 'home purchase plan', 'home reversion plan' and 'regulated sale and rent back' have already been discussed since these type of transactions constitute investments for the purpose of the Regulated Activities Order.

5. Not all home finance activities involve the provision of credit. Specifically, credit is provided only in respect of entry into regulated mortgage contracts (whereby the loan is secured by a first mortgage) and home

1 Defined at article 61 RAO; the definition also includes the situation in which a loan is taken out by trustees for the benefit of a beneficiary whose home it is.

2 MCOB 1.2.1(1) R.

purchase plans (in which the seller sells an interest in land but is obliged to repurchase it).

6. The application of MCOB is affected when a regulated mortgage contract is entered into for a business purpose. It does not apply at all in the case of what is referred to as a 'large business customer',[3] being a client carrying on a business with a group annual turnover in excess of £1 million. In other instances, there are a number of 'tailored' provisions applicable to loans for business purposes in respect of which the requirements are less demanding. However, there is no obligation on the lender to comply with these tailored requirements; it is open to the lender to comply with the MCOB requirements in full if it wishes.[4]

7. However, before a lender can treat a regulated mortgage contract as being for business purposes, the lender must see a business plan demonstrating the purpose of the loan[5] and must keep the evidence for three years.[6]

8. There are also tailored provisions when the loan is made to a high net worth mortgage customer,[7] defined as being someone with an income in excess of £300,000 per year or assets in excess of £3 million, or who is guaranteed by such a person. In order to treat someone as a high net worth mortgage customer, a lender must already have knowledge that the customer satisfies this definition from an existing business relationship or must obtain a statement to this effect signed by a suitably qualified business adviser who is not an associate of the customer.[8] The lender must keep the statement for three years.[9]

9. MCOB does not apply to a professional firm in respect of its non-mainstream authorised activities (the professional firm will be exempt in respect of its mainstream activities).[10]

General principles of conduct of business

10. It is axiomatic that all communications with the customer must be 'clear, fair and not misleading'.[11] This does not only extend to written communications.[12] A similar principle applies to financial promotions to be discussed later.

3 MCOB 1.2.3(1) R.
4 MCOB 1.2.3(2)(b) R.
5 MCOB 1.2.9D R.
6 MCOB 1.2.9E R.
7 MCOB 1.2.3A R; where there are two or more borrowers, it is sufficient that at least one is high net worth; MCOB 1.3.3B R.
8 MCOB 1.2.9C R.
9 MCOB 1.2.9E R.
10 MCOB 1.2.10 R.
11 MCOB 2.2.6 R.
12 MCOB 2.2.8 G.

11. A lender must not offer or accept any inducement, or direct business, so as to give rise to a conflict of interest as far as its duties to its customer are concerned.[13] The temptation is for the intermediary to channel business in a way that leads to the receipt of the largest amount of commission even if this is not in the best interests of the customer. Consistent with this, a lender must not offer an inducement, the amount of which is dependent on the level of business exceeding any particular figure[14] because this will tend to induce the intermediary to reach the target set, without regard to the interests of the customer. However, the above rules do not prevent a lender from giving assistance to an intermediary for the purpose of enhancing the quality of the service offered by the intermediary to the customer.[15]

12. MCOB 2.5A.1 says: 'A firm must act honestly, fairly and professionally in accordance with the best interests of its customer.' This is obviously fundamental.

13. MCOB 2.6.2 says: 'A firm must not, in any written or oral communication, seek to exclude or restrict, or to rely on any exclusion or restriction of, any duty or liability it may have to a customer under the regulatory system.' This is equally fundamental; a firm cannot be allowed to contract out of its regulatory obligations. In relation to duties other than those encompassed by MCOB 2.6.2, liability can only be excluded insofar as is reasonable.[16] But the duties envisaged by MCOB 2.6.2 are wide-ranging and include an obligation to act fairly and professionally.

14. MCOB 2.6A.1 relates to mortgage provisions that allow a firm to alter the interest rate from a concessionary rate to a standard variable rate in the event of a breach of contract by the customer. Such a provision can only take effect if the breach of contract is material, and provided it is not arising out of a payment shortfall and provided the standard variable rate has not been especially created for customers that are in breach of contract.

Financial promotion of regulated mortgage contracts

15. MCOB 3 regulates financial promotions by authorised firms. It also governs financial promotions *approved* by authorised persons but communicated by unauthorised persons. In principle, although there is an exception in cases of exempt communications, the Rules in MCOB 3 apply equally whether or not the communication is made directly by an authorised firm or is a communication approved by an authorised firm.[17]

13 MCOB 2.3.2 R.
14 MCOB 2.6.2 R.
15 MCOB 2.3.5 G.
16 MCOB 2.6.3 R.
17 MCOB 3.2.-3 R; MCOB 3.11.1(2) G.

16. The rules in relation to financial promotions, contained in MCOB 3, use the clumsy and ungainly terminology of 'non-real time financial promotion' and 'real time financial promotion'. The distinction is between contact that is interactive, when the firm and customer come together at the same time (even if not in the same place), which is real time, and contact that is more remote, via written communication for instance, or radio or television programme, not involving simultaneous contact, which is non-real-time.[18] A lack of interactivity is the hallmark of non-real time.

17. The rules also distinguish, when it comes to real time financial promotions, between such promotions that are solicited and those that are not. A solicited promotion is one that is expressly requested, or was initiated, by the customer. A promotion is not solicited merely because a customer has agreed to terms and conditions that contain statements in general terms that such visits will take place; there must be a specific targeted consent for such visits to be considered solicited.[19] If a financial promotion has been solicited by one person, and a visit takes place in consequence of it, it is also taken to have been solicited by a relative of that person who may be present at the same time.[20]

Exempt transactions

18. MCOB does not apply to communications made by an authorised person that are in any event exempt by virtue of the FPO.[21] (It will be remembered that the effect of the FPO is to exempt communications that are made by *unauthorised persons* from being treated as unlawful communications in accordance with section 21 of the Financial Services and Markets Act 2000; the FPO does not apply directly to communications made by *authorised persons*.)

19. Thus, the FPO exempts certain *one-off* communications that relate to qualifying credit (i.e. including regulated mortgage contracts) provided certain requirements are met.[22] The first requirement is that the communication must be either non-real time or *solicited* real time. The next requirement is that the communication must be aimed at a single person or a single group of persons and the communication must be tailored for that person or that group. The next requirement is that the communication must not be part of an organised marketing campaign.

20. There is only one situation in which a one-off *unsolicited* real time communication may be exempt and that is under Article 28A of the FPO

18 MCOB 3.5.5 R.
19 MCOB 3.7.1 R.
20 MCOB 3.7.1(4) R.
21 SI 2005/1529; MCOB 3.2.5(3) R.
22 Article 28 FPO.

if the further requirements there set out are satisfied, namely that the communication must be one-off as before, the communicator must in addition reasonably believe that the customer will understand the risks associated with entering into the regulated mortgage contract (or loan or hire agreement), and the communicator must reasonably believe that the recipient of the communication would expect to be contacted.

21. In defined circumstances, an *introduction* to another authorised person engaged in lending money (including on regulated mortgage contracts) may be considered an exempt communication.[23] This is if the introducer is not receiving payment from a person being introduced and if the introducer reveals if there is any connection between the introducer and the lender and provided also that the introducer reveals details of the commission or other advantage, if any, that will be received by the introducer from the lender.

22. There is also a further specific exemption for very simple advertisements that communicate little. A promotion is exempt if it reveals no more than the firm name, a logo, contact details (such as an address or telephone number) and a brief factual statement of the firm's general occupation.[24]

23. These exemptions apply when the communication is made by the authorised firm directly. The exemptions apply only to a qualified extent to a communication *approved* by an authorised firm and made by an unauthorised person. In these circumstances, certain Rules continue to apply for the purposes of the authorised person giving approval, in particular MCOB 3.6.3 R.[25] Specifically, it will be necessary to show that an exempt non-real time financial promotion is fair, clear and not misleading[26] and certain requirements as to content will apply, as explained below.

Non-real time financial promotions

24. A non-real time financial promotion that is not exempt as above must be clear, fair and not misleading.[27] If a non-real time financial promotion includes a comparison with other sources of credit, then the comparison must be fair and truly representative. If a special offer is being promoted, then if it has not already started, the start date of the special offer must be given as well as any date when the special offer comes to an end.[28]

23 Article 28B FPO; an introduction to an appointed representative will also be exempt in the same circumstances.

24 MCOB 3.2.5(2) R.

25 MCOB 3.2.4 R.

26 MCOB 3.6.3(1) R.

27 MCOB 3.6.3(1) R.

28 MCOB 3.6.3(g) R.

25. Certain expressions have to be used with care. 'Overdraft' can only be used to describe an overdraft facility on a current account.[29] 'Interest-free' must only be used if the total amount payable does not exceed the cash price.[30] If there is an early repayment charge or a higher lending charge, these expressions and no other must be used.[31]

26. Non-real time financial promotions must also, in many instances, contain risk statements. When a loan is to be secured on land, it must state: 'Your home may be repossessed if you do not keep up repayments on your mortgage.' Moreover, if the loan being taken out is for the purpose of paying off unsecured debts, the following must be added to the above: 'Think carefully before securing other debts against your home.'[32] Risk statements do not, however, have to be included in transient advertising; this includes radio or television advertising when the primary purpose of the programme, during which the commercial break occurs in which the advertisement is featured, is not to promote lending.[33]

27. An APR must be stated in non-real time promotional material if either it refers to a price of credit or it states or implies that credit is going to be made available to persons who might otherwise consider their access to credit restricted (e.g. perhaps because of a poor credit rating).[34] The APR must be calculated in accordance with MCOB 10 and must be expressed as follows: 'The overall cost for comparison is X% APR.'[35] The APR of the agreement being promoted may be variable; if so, a *representative* APR must be stated that in this context means a rate that will apply to at least 66 per cent of future customers.[36] In assessing this percentage, the firm should look at the history of the last 12 months in which loans of a similar type have been offered, or in the case of a new product, at the relevant business plan.[37] If the APR will be variable depending on the personal circumstances of the borrower, the financial promotion should state: 'The actual rate available will depend upon your circumstances. Ask for a personalised illustration.'[38]

28. When the financial promotion relates to the activities of credit broking, debt counselling and debt administration, in respect of which a fee may be charged, the financial promotion must give a prominent indication of the amount of the fee or, if not known, a representative fee based on the business expected to arise from the financial promotion.[39]

29 MCOB 3.6.8(1) R.
30 MCOB 3.6.8(2) R.
31 MCOB 3.6.9 R.
32 MCOB 3.6.13 R.
33 MCOB 3.6.16 G.
34 MCOB 3.6.17 R.
35 MCOB 3.6.17(3) R.
36 MCOB 3.6.23 R.
37 MCOB 3.6.24 G.
38 MCOB 3.6.25 R.
39 MCOB 2.6.27 R.

29. The firm will have to keep a record of all non-real time financial promotions and the record must be kept for a period of 12 months from the date of the last communication of the financial promotion.[40] A firm should retain a copy of the financial promotion as finally published if practicable.[41]

Real time financial promotions

30. There is a blanket ban on making unsolicited real time financial promotions unless a person making contact has an existing business relationship with the customer such that the customer envisages receiving such financial communications.[42]

31. As has been seen, a solicited real time communication may be exempt under the provisions of the FPO, in which case the provisions of MCOB will not apply in any event insofar as the communication is made by an authorised person. Such a communication will only not be exempt if it is not one-off, which in practice means that it is made as part of a marketing campaign.

32. In the case of a non-exempt solicited real time financial promotion or in the rare case of an unsolicited real time financial promotion that is not prohibited, then the rules in MCOB 3.8 apply. These provide that the communication must be fair, clear and not misleading. Further, any communication must not be made at an unsocial hour or on an unlisted telephone number, and the person making the communication must state the purpose of the communication at the outset and be prepared to end contact on request at any time.[43]

33. Furthermore, under no circumstances must an authorised person approve a real time communication of qualifying credit made by an unauthorised person.[44] This applies even if the communication would otherwise be exempt.[45]

Initial disclosure by the firm to the customer on initial contact

34. There are a number of matters that must be disclosed by the firm to the customer at initial contact. Specifically, a firm must make it clear whether there are any limitations in the range of products that it is able to offer, and

40 MCOB 3.10.1 R.
41 MCOB 3.10.3 G.
42 MCOB 3.7.3 R.
43 MCOB 3.8.2 R.
44 MCOB 3.11.2 R.
45 MCOB 3.2.4(3) R.

the basis of its remuneration.[46] This must be given at the outset when the firm first makes contact with the customer with a view to providing services.[47] If the initial contact is at a meeting or over the telephone, then the initial information must be given orally.[48] If the initial contact is over the telephone, it is also a requirement that the name of the firm is given and the commercial purpose of the call made clear.[49] If the initial contact is made by electronic means, the firm must ensure that the customer cannot proceed to the next stage until the information is given.[50]

35. A firm may give advice about a home finance transaction in relation to either:

(a) the whole market;
(b) a limited number of home finance providers; or
(c) a single provider.

36. Insofar as advice is being tendered in relation to more than one market, then the customer must be informed of any limitation in each market.[51] If an adviser describes its services as unlimited, the adviser need not have access to every product available on the market and may be able to offer a selection of products, but the selection must be sufficiently large so as to be representative of the market as a whole. Moreover, the selection must be updated continually to reflect changes in the market and to reflect new products that come on offer.[52] The firm offering an unlimited range will have to review the market on a regular basis.

37. Insofar as the adviser offers access to only a limited range of mortgage providers, the customer must either be provided with a list of providers on first contact, or must be told that a list can be made available to the customer.[53] If the customer asks for a list, it must be provided as soon as possible and in any event within five days.[54]

38. As far as disclosure of the basis of remuneration is concerned, this should be expressed as far as possible as a single cash sum but insofar as this is not possible, and if the charge is to be computed as a percentage, then the percentage must be disclosed and a representative example given.[55] If other charges may arise, the situation must be fully explained.

46 MCOB 4.4A.1 R.
47 MCOB 4.4A.13 G.
48 MCOB 4.4A.9 R.
49 MCOB 4.4A.17 R.
50 MCOB 4.4A.9 R.
51 MCOB 4.4A.2(1) R.
52 MCOB 4.4A.5G.
53 MCOB 4.4A.4(1) R.
54 MCOB 4.4A.4(2) R.
55 MCOB 4.4A.8 R.

39. In the case of a distance contract, as discussed earlier, certain specific information must be given in good time before the contract is entered into.[56] This information must also be given even if there is doubt as to whether the mortgage product is regulated or not.[57]

Assessing the suitability of the regulated mortgage contract

40. Subject to an important exception in the case of execution-only sales to be discussed later, there is an important requirement that if a firm *gives advice* to a customer contemplating entering into a regulated mortgage contract, then the firm giving that advice must ensure that the regulated mortgage contract is *suitable* for the customer.[58] A mortgage lender can, in some instances, enter into a loan agreement with a customer without giving advice; such loans, when permitted, are 'execution-only' because no advice has been given and the suitability requirement will not apply. If a firm breaches this requirement, it could be become liable in damages as a consequence.

41. For these purposes, the reference to entering a regulated mortgage contract includes a reference to varying the terms of an existing regulated mortgage contract (e.g. by increasing the amount of the borrowing or extending the repayment period).[59] So a firm will also have a duty to assess and advise on the suitability of a variation to a regulated mortgage contract.

42. There is a significant overlap between MCOB 4.7 and MCOB 11 in that MCOB 11 provides that before a regulated mortgage contract is entered into, the firm must assess whether it is affordable and should not, by virtue of MCOB 4.7, advise a customer to enter into a regulated mortgage contract that is not affordable. This is because an unaffordable mortgage will plainly be unsuitable; but MCOB 4.7 is wider than MCOB 11 in that a regulated mortgage contract may be unsuitable for reasons other than unaffordability.

43. A regulated mortgage contract will not be suitable for a customer unless the regulated mortgage contract is appropriate to the needs and circumstances of that customer.[60] MCOB 4.7A.3(2) R provides importantly that: 'A firm must base its determination of whether a regulated mortgage contract is appropriate to a customer's needs and circumstances on the facts disclosed by the customer and other relevant facts about the customer of which the firm is or should be reasonably aware.'

56 MCOB 4.4A.18 R.
57 MCOB 4.4A.21.
58 MCOB 4.7A.2 R.
59 MCOB 4.7A.3 R.
60 MCOB 4.7A5(1) R.

44. This is expanded at MCOB 4.7A.4(1) E, which states: 'A firm should take reasonable steps to obtain from a customer all information likely to be relevant for the purposes of MCOB 4.7A.'

45. MCOB 4.7A.6 R sets out a number of mandatory factors to which a firm must have regard when assessing suitability:

(a) whether the customer falls within the current eligibility criteria laid down by the firm;
(b) whether the customer should have an interest-only mortgage, a repayment mortgage or a combination of the two;
(c) whether the regulated mortgage contract should be for a particular term;
(d) whether it is in the interests of the customer to have stability in the amount of repayments bearing in mind the risk of alteration to the level of interest rates in the future;
(e) whether it is appropriate for the customer to have their payments minimised at the outset;
(f) whether the regulated mortgage contract is appropriate in the light of the credit history of the customer; and
(g) whether fees and charges ought to be paid up front rather than added to the mortgage debt.

46. If the firm considers that an interest-only mortgage is suitable, it must explain to the customer that the customer will have to put in place a clearly understood and credible repayment strategy to put to the mortgage lender in order for the loan to be made.[61] It is not, however, part of the role of a firm to advise on a repayment strategy.[62]

47. There are also suitability criteria for bridging loans.[63] The firm must explain to the customer that a customer must have a repayment strategy in place before being granted a bridging loan.[64] Furthermore, the firm must address with the customer why a bridging loan is necessary at all as opposed to entering into a regulated mortgage contract, which is not a bridging loan.[65]

48. If there is no regulated mortgage contract that meets the needs of the customer from within those falling within the scope of the services offered by the firm, then the firm must make no recommendation.[66]

49. When discussing affordability with the customer, it must be made clear that this is based on the current circumstances of the customer in the light of current interest rates and that both can change.[67]

61 MCOB 4.7A.9 R.
62 MCOB 4.7A.10 G.
63 Defined as loans in which the term is less than or equal to 12 months; a bridging loan normally has the interest rolled up.
64 MCOB 4.7A.12 R.
65 MCOB 4.7A.13 R.
66 MCOB 4.7A.5(3) R.
67 MCOB 4.7A.19 R.

50. The firm is entitled to rely on the accuracy of what it is told by the customer unless taking a common sense view of the matter the firm has reason to doubt the information provided by the customer.[68]

51. Sometimes a customer is concerned to consolidate his or her existing debts into a single regulated mortgage contract, perhaps with an extended repayment period and perhaps giving security when none was previously provided. There are a number of matters to which consideration must be given in assessing suitability; the costs associating with extending the repayment period, the appropriateness of giving security for a previously unsecured loan, the possibility that the creditor with known payment difficulties may be better off by making an arrangement with creditors.[69]

52. The firm must keep a record of the information that the firm has obtained from the customer for the purpose of the suitability assessment; the record must also show the justification as to why any particular regulated mortgage contract was advised to be suitable. The record must also give a record of the customer's decision to roll up fees or charges into the loan.[70] The record must be kept for a minimum of three years from the date of the advice being given.[71] This is an important requirement because if the suitability of any particular loan transaction is later challenged, then the record will have to be produced, and if there is a failure to produce the record, then adverse inferences may be drawn that the loan was not suitable.

Execution-only transactions

53. The essence of an execution-only sale is that the customer receives no advice. This means that a lender that proceeds on this basis is not obliged to carry out the suitability assessment imposed by MCOB 4.7A.[72]

54. A mortgage lender must not encourage a customer to opt out of seeking advice.[73] A firm must still act in the client's best interests and this requirement is not abrogated merely because it is an execution-only sale.[74] Furthermore, if there is an intermediary that is acting without giving advice, someone 'arranging' the mortgage without any advisory role, then the mortgage lender cannot act on an execution-only basis and advice must be

68 MCOB 4.7A.23 G.
69 MCOB 4.7A.15 R.
70 MCOB 4.7A.25 R.
71 MCOB 4.7A.25(2) R.
72 MCOB 4.7A does not apply to a lender per se, it applies to those giving mortgage *advice*; see the table at MCOB 4.1.2 R.
73 MCOB 4.8A.5 R.
74 MCOB 4.8A.4 G.

given.[75] But this prohibition on a mortgage lender acting in an execution-only capacity does not apply if the mortgage arranger is no longer involved in the transaction.[76]

55. An execution-only sale is never permitted if a person is exercising a statutory 'right to buy' from the local authority or if the customer is seeking to raise funds to consolidate debts.[77] In both these cases, it is essential that the customer receives advice and the suitability requirement in MCOB 4.7A automatically applies to these types of transaction.

56. Subject to limited exceptions, an execution-only sale can only arise if there is *no* interactive dialogue at any time during the sale process.[78] Thus, the general principle is that if there has been interactive dialogue, then the sale becomes an 'advised sale' and the principles in MCOB 4.7A become applicable.

57. The exceptions, when a sale can be execution-only even if there has been some interactive dialogue, are if the customer has expressly rejected the advice given by the firm, or if the customer is high net worth, or a professional, or the loan is solely for business purposes and the customer has positively elected to proceed with an execution-only sale.[79]

58. There is a further example where some interaction is permitted and that is when the customer undertakes a rate switch or other variation.[80] But the variation must involve no new borrowing save to finance the switching fee and, in the case of a change in interest rates, the customer must have been provided with the range of all products offered by the lender through a non-interactive channel.[81]

Procedure for an execution-only sale

59. A firm cannot enter into an execution-only sale for a regulated mortgage contract until the borrower has provided certain specified information, namely the name of the mortgage lender, the rate of interest, the interest rate type,[82] the price or value of the property, the length of the term, the sum the customer wishes to borrow and whether the customer wants an interest-only or repayment mortgage.[83] These requirements do not apply if the customer is high net worth or if the loan is being entered into purely for business purposes.[84]

75 MCOB 4.1.2C G.
76 MCOB 4.1.2D G.
77 MCOB 4.8A.7.
78 Interactive dialogue includes emails and text messaging: MCOB 4.8A.3 G.
79 MCOB 4.8A.2 G.
80 For example, a transfer to a different property, MCOB 4.8A.11(1) G.
81 MCOB 4.8A.10 R.
82 E.g. fixed or variable or capped and so on.
83 MCOB 4.8A.14(1) R.
84 MCOB 4.8A.15 R.

60. An execution-only variation can only take place once the customer has specified the following information insofar as it is appropriate to the variation the customer wishes to enter into: the price or value of the property, the length of term required and the amount the customer wishes to borrow.[85]

61. In addition to the above, a regulated mortgage contract or variation can only be entered into on an execution-only basis if, in circumstances when the customer has rejected advice, the firm informs the customer clearly and prominently in a durable medium that the firm had previously advised the customer (if this is the case) that the regulation mortgage contract or variation was considered unsuitable.[86] It must also be pointed out as a separate matter that the customer will not benefit from the protection of the Rules as to suitability.

62. In other cases when advice has not been rejected but the customer wishes to proceed by way of execution-only, the customer must be told clearly and prominently in a durable medium that the firm is not required to assess the suitability of the regulated mortgage contract (or the variation) and also that the customer will lose the benefit of the protection of the Rules insofar as the suitability assessment is concerned. In any case, when there is oral communication between the customer and the firm, this information must also be given orally.[87]

63. Once this information has been given, then if there has been any form of interactive dialogue between the customer and the firm, the customer must be asked to confirm in writing that he or she is aware of the consequences of losing the protection of the Rules and is making a positive election to proceed by execution-only. This written confirmation must be separate from other documents providing information or from other contractual documentation, a requirement clearly intended to underline that this confirmation must be discretely given. This requirement in MCOB 4.8A.14(5) R is part of the tendency in the Rules to limit execution-only sales.

Policy and record keeping

64. The firm must have in place a policy for dealing with execution-only sales that must set out the amount that the firm reasonably expects to transact by way of execution-only sales and what steps will be taken if that limit is exceeded.[88] A record must be kept of this policy.[89]

85 MCOB 4.8A.14(2) R.
86 MCOB 4.8A.14(4)(a) R.
87 MCOB 4.8A.14(4)(b) R.
88 MCOB 4.8A.17 R.
89 MCOB 4.8A.18(3) R.

65. Further, a record must be kept of the execution-only transactions that have been entered into and the information that has been provided to the customer and any advice rejected by the customer.[90] The record must be kept for a minimum of three years from the date when the regulated mortgage contract was arranged.[91]

Providing the customer with an illustration

66. It is a mandatory requirement that a customer must submit a formal application before entering into a regulated mortgage contract.[92] The purpose of this is to ensure that the 'customer has received details of the particular home finance transaction for which he has applied, and has had the opportunity to satisfy himself that it is appropriate for him.'[93] The principal means by which the customer is to be supplied with details of the particular home finance transaction is by way of provision of an illustration. An illustration must be provided to the customer in advance of a customer submitting an application for a loan so that the customer can, when submitting an application, make an informed decision.[94] If the firm formally makes a recommendation of a particular regulated mortgage contract to the customer, the illustration must be provided at the same time as this advice is given.[95] Not only must the illustration be provided, but the customer must be urged to read and understand it.[96]

67. If the customer requests an illustration, it must be provided to the customer without undue delay and the firm is restricted in the information it can seek before the illustration is provided, limited to the information necessary to personalise the illustration.[97] The reason for this is to avoid delay in the production of the illustration.

68. The illustration must be clear, fair and not misleading.[98] The specific content of the illustration is specified at MCOB 5.6 R and MCOB 5 Annex 1 R. The requirements are very detailed; the layout and template of MCOB 5 Annex 1 R must be followed. The information, moreover, must be confined to that laid down in MCOB 5.6.[99] It must be personalised to reflect the specific regulated mortgage contract in which the customer is interested, the amount of the required loan, the price or value of the property, the term

90 MCOB 4.8A.18(1) R.
91 MCOB 4.8A.18(2) R.
92 MCOB 5.3.1 R.
93 MCOB 5.3.2 G.
94 MCOB 5.5.1 R.
95 MCOB 5.5.1(2)(a) R.
96 MCOB 5.4.10 R.
97 MCOB 5.5.15 R.
98 MCOB 5.4.1 R.
99 MCOB 5.6.5 R.

of the regulated mortgage contract and whether it is to be interest-only or a repayment mortgage or a combination of the two.[100] An illustration must be confined to a single mortgage product and it cannot be used as a basis for comparing several different products.[101]

69. In the case of a high net worth customer or a loan for business purposes, an illustration must still be provided but the requirements are somewhat relaxed.[102] But there are still some requirements. So, for example, an early repayment charge and a higher lending charge must still be described as such.[103]

70. An illustration must be provided even if there is uncertainty as to whether a particular mortgage is regulated or not.[104]

The mortgage offer

71. As has already been seen, MCOB 5 requires the firm to provide the customer with an illustration in the prescribed form at a time before the customer submits an application for a regulated mortgage contract. MCOB 6 goes further and requires an illustration also to be incorporated as part of the mortgage offer.

72. MCOB 6.4.1 R states that: 'If a firm offers to enter into a regulated mortgage contract with a customer, it must provide the customer with an offer document containing an illustration.' Obviously, the terms of the offer must reflect that of the illustration.[105] Indeed, the illustration must be included in and form an integral part of the offer document.[106] The offer must be in a durable medium.[107]

73. The illustration must follow the same requirements as that applied to the illustration issued with the application form,[108] but it must be updated as necessary and with some modifications to the wording.

74. Part of the illustration will be headed 'Section 2', setting out details of the service that the firm has provided.[109] The two alternatives, one of which has to be ticked by the customer, are that the firm has recommended the particular mortgage, or that the firm has not recommended a particular mortgage and has left if to the customer whether to accept the mortgage offer. If services have been provided by a different firm, then the other firm

100 MCOB 5.6.6 R.
101 MCOB 5.6.7 G.
102 MCOB 5.7 R.
103 MCOB 5.7.2(6), (7) R.
104 MCOB 5.5.11 R.
105 MCOB 6.4.1(2) R.
106 MCOB 6.4.9 R.
107 MCOB 6.3.2 R.
108 MCOB 6.4.4 R.
109 MCOB 6.4.4(5) R.

must be named and the two alternatives will be addressed by reference to the other firm.[110] When another firm has made a recommendation, the mortgage lender may wish to include a statement to the effect that the mortgage lender is not responsible for the level of service given and that the customer should contact the other firm if he or she has any queries about the level of service provided.[111]

75. A statement in the offer should also invite the customer to compare the terms of the mortgage offer with the key facts illustration given to the customer at the time he or she submitted an application for the offer.[112] The illustration may state the repayment strategy that the customer intends to use.[113] This is of relevance to an interest-only mortgage.

76. Apart from the illustration, the offer document must contain certain other information. Thus, it has to state the duration of the offer (i.e. the length of time it remains open for acceptance).[114] The offer must also state that although no right of withdrawal exists, the customer will have the right of early repayment in accordance with the terms of the regulated mortgage contract.[115] If the illustration does not state the repayment strategy in the case of an interest-only mortgage, this must be stated in the remainder of the offer document.[116] The offer document must also set out how the customer is entitled to complain and details of the Financial Services Ombudsman in the event that the complaint is not satisfactorily addressed.[117]

77. In the case of an offer for a business loan or to a high net worth individual, the offer must contain an illustration tailored in the same way as the illustration was tailored in connection with the mortgage application, updated as appropriate.[118] The firm must keep a record of the offer document for one year after it was issued.[119]

Information to be given following entry into the regulated mortgage contract

78. Once the customer has entered into the agreement but before his or her first payment is made to the firm under the regulated mortgage contract,[120]

110 MCOB 6.4.4(5)(b) R.
111 MCOB 6.4.5 G.
112 MCOB 6.4.4(4)(b) R.
113 MCOB 6.4.4(7A) R.
114 MCOB 6.4.11(1) R.
115 MCOB 6.4.11(6) R.
116 MCOB 6.4.11A R.
117 MCOB 6.4.13 R.
118 MCOB 6.7.1 R.
119 MCOB 6.4.3 R.
120 MCOB 7.4.1 R

the firm must present certain information to that customer, in a durable medium and in a single document.[121] The information that must be provided includes:

(a) the amount of the first payment;
(b) the amount of subsequent payments if different;
(c) the method by which payments must be made; and
(d) confirmation of whether insurance has been purchased through the firm along with the amount of any payments, and whether the payments are to be collected along with the mortgage payments or separately.

79. The information must also set out what the customer should do if he or she fails to make all the due payments and explain the benefit of early contact with the firm and provide a contact point and details of any arrears charges.[122]

80. As is the case with the other categories of information that have to be disclosed, a record must be kept of the information provided to the customer once the regulated mortgage contract has been entered into, which must be kept for a year after the information has been provided.[123]

Annual mortgage statements

81. A firm must supply a mortgage statement to a customer at least once a year (within 13 months in the case of the first statement).[124] The information must cover any linked products purchased through the firm in cases when the payments are combined with payments under the regulated mortgage contract.[125]

82. The statement must specify whether the mortgage is interest-only or a repayment mortgage.[126] There are many specific requirements that attach to interest-only mortgage statements. Thus, if it is the case that the payments of the customer do not include any payments towards a repayment strategy, this must be made clear. The customer should also be advised to check the value of his or her investments that have been put in place in order to make the required capital repayment in due course.[127] There is also prescribed text that has to be inserted into an interest-only mortgage statement.

121 MCOB 7.4.2 R; the information about the purchase of an insurance policy or other linked transaction can be given in a separate document.
122 MCOB 7.4.1(9) R.
123 MCOB 7.4.4 R.
124 MCOB 7.5.1 R.
125 MCOB 7.5.1(2) R.
126 MCOB 7.5.3(1)(a) R.
127 MCOB 7.5.3(1)(b)(ii) R.

83. The statement must contain details of all transactions on the mortgage account that have occurred since the date of the last statement, including the date and amount of each payment made.[128] There must also be shown the rates of interest during the period of the statement and the dates when any interest rate payments changed.[129]

84. Information has also to be given about the state of the mortgage account at the date of the statement.[130] This includes that amount owed by the customer, the length of the remaining term, the date when repayment charges cease to apply and the amount of any charges that are applicable expressed as a monetary amount. There must also be given, if applicable, the date when the obligation to acquire tied products comes to an end.[131]

85. A reminder must be given that the customer should contact the firm if the customer is unable to make regular payments.[132] However, this does not apply if a customer has already changed to an interest-only mortgage with arrears being capitalised so long as payment problems are continuing.[133]

Notification of changes in terms

86. The firm must give reasonable notice in advance of any change in terms or changes in interest rates; in the case of the latter, the revised payment amount must also be specified.[134] If the regulated mortgage contract is sold or assigned by the firm with the result that a different party has the right to set interest rates, the firm must notify the customer of the name of this new party.[135]

87. If a customer takes up a right to borrow further sums in accordance with a right conferred by the existing mortgage terms and conditions, then the customer must be informed of the new amount that is due under the regulated mortgage contract, the new payment amounts and the interest rate charged.

Further advances

88. Certain rules apply to applications for further advances that require the approval of the mortgage lender (i.e. in circumstances when the customer has no existing contractual right to demand a further advance).

128 MCOB 7.5.3(2)(a) R.
129 MCOB 7.5.3(2)(customer) R.
130 MCOB 7.5.3(4) R.
131 MCOB 7.5.3(4)(firm) R.
132 MCOB 7.5.3(3) R.
133 MCOB 7.5.3A R.
134 MCOB 7.6.1 R.
135 MCOB 7.6.2 R.

89. The customer must make a formal application for an advance and must be provided with an illustration for the further advance modelled on the standard pre-application illustration that has to be provided in accordance with MCOB 5.[136] This illustration must relate to the further advance only.[137]

90. The Rules provide that the illustration for a further advance has to be modified in some respects by comparison with the illustration provided in relation to an initial mortgage loan. Thus, the phrase 'additional borrowing' must be used in place of the term 'mortgage' throughout the text of the illustration.[138] The APR must be calculated on the basis of the further advance only.[139] The illustration may depart from the model in MCOB 5 insofar as necessary to reflect the fact that this is a further advance as opposed to an original loan (e.g. removing wording that is of no relevance to the further advance).[140]

Rate switches and removal of a party

91. A customer may, as a result of a right conferred by the regulated mortgage contract, or with the agreement of the firm, be considering an alteration to the interest rate regime to which his or her mortgage is subject. For instance, the customer may contemplate switching from a fixed interest rate regime to a variable rate, or from one fixed rate to another. Before this can take place, the customer must submit a formal application form to change the interest rate regime; prior to this, the customer must be supplied with an illustration referable to the proposed new interest rate regime, which must conform with MCOB 5, subject to such modifications as are appropriate to reflect the limited scope of the change being made.[141]

92. Likewise, an illustration must be provided whenever there is a change in the parties to the mortgage (e.g. if someone assumes sole responsibility for the repayments).[142]

Alteration in payment amounts

93. If a change in terms amounts to a change in the amounts payable by the customer, then the customer must be provided with certain specified information contained in a single document.[143] The firm is entitled, but not

136 MCOB 7.6.7 R.
137 MCOB 7.6.9(1) R.
138 MCOB 7.6.9(2) R.
139 MCOB 7.6.10 G.
140 MCOB 7.6.14 R.
141 MCOB 7.6.18 R.
142 MCOB 7.6.22 R.
143 MCOB 7.6.28 R.

required, to use an illustration under MCOB 5, modified as appropriate, for the purposes of communicating this information.[144] This obligation to communicate further information does not, however, arise if interest arrears are being capitalised due to repayment difficulties.[145] In this latter case, the customer must be given a prominent reminder of the amount outstanding and the implications of deferring the payments must be explained before the change to the regulated mortgage contract takes effect.[146]

Further advances with a business loan, or loan to a high net worth individual

94. The requirement to provide an illustration in relation to a further advance, or in respect of a rate switch, does not apply in respect of a loan to a high net worth individual or in respect of a loan purely for business purposes, as already stated; this, however, is assuming that the tailored provisions for such loans have previously been followed in their entirety. If the tailored provisions have not previously been followed in their entirety, then the tailored provisions set out in MCOB 7 cease to be appropriate.[147]

95. Even in relation to the tailored provisions, there are requirements to be satisfied if the customer wants an immediate increase to the amount of borrowing, or if the customer overdraws on his or her borrowing under the regulated mortgage contract. The customer must, in these circumstances, be provided with either a business illustration or high net worth illustration for the new total borrowing, or must be provided with certain specified information.[148] The information to be provided includes the new amount outstanding under the adjusted regulated mortgage contract, details of any changes to the repayment arrangements and any change to the amount of any repayment charge.[149] This must be done five days in advance of the revised regulated mortgage contract taking effect, in the case of a business loan, or within a reasonable time in advance, in the case of a high net worth customer. When a business or high net worth customer applies for a *further advance*, the customer must be provided with a business illustration or high net worth illustration but it must be based on the total loan and not just the additional borrowing.[150]

144 MCOB 7.6.31 R.
145 MCOB 7.6.28A R.
146 MCOB 7.6.28A(2) R.
147 MCOB 7.7.1A G.
148 MCOB 7.7.2 R.
149 MCOB 7.7.1(2) R.
150 MCOB 7.7.3 R.

Calculation of APR

96. The statement of the APR is an integral element of the rules relating to the financial promotion of qualifying credit and to the disclosure of information prior to the application for a mortgage loan.[151] As is only to be expected, the Rules under MCOB 10 for the calculation of APR in respect of regulated mortgage contracts are the same as the Rules applicable to the calculation of APR in relation to credit agreements secured on land by a *second* charge, as now contained in the FCA Handbook at CONC App 1.1,[152] which in turn originated from the Consumer Credit (Total Charge for Credit) Regulations 1980.[153] The formula and the assumptions to be applied are identical. The FCA considers that fees paid to mortgage intermediaries must enter into the calculation of total charge for credit and hence the APR.[154] The provisions in CONC App 1.1 have been discussed earlier.

Responsible lending

97. MCOB sets out detailed rules and guidance for lenders in relation to the affordability of loans, in force since 26 April 2014.

98. MCOB 11.6.2(1) R enunciates a very important basic principle, subject only to limited exceptions: '(1) before entering into or agreeing to vary, a regulated mortgage contract or home purchase plan, a firm must assess whether the customer (and any guarantor) will be able to pay the sums due: (2) the firm must not enter into the transaction in (a) unless it can demonstrate that the new or varied regulated mortgage contract or home purchase plan is affordable for the customer (and any guarantor).'

99. Thus, the burden is placed on the lender to show that the customer can afford the mortgage and a firm is potentially liable if the customer enters into a regulated mortgage contract (or home purchase plan) that he or she cannot afford. This provides the customer with a defence to a mortgage arrears claim in the case of a regulated mortgage contract if the customer can show that the firm acted in breach of MCOB 11 and if the customer can show that had these Rules been followed, the firm should never have entered into the regulated mortgage contract in these terms with this customer.

100. MCOB 11.6.4 E gives examples of situations that the firm should treat as material to the question of affordability:

151 MCOB 10.2.1 G.
152 MCOB 10.3.2 G; there is some change in terminology that does not alter the substance.
153 SI 1980/51.
154 MCOB 10.4.3 G.

(a) if the term of a regulated mortgage contract or home purchase plan is extended, the fact that the period of extension extends beyond retirement;
(b) if a regulated mortgage contract is changed to interest-only; and
(c) if a customer is removed from the regulated mortgage contract (so that the liabilities become solely those of the remaining borrowers).

Assessment of affordability

101. A firm must not rely on a general declaration of affordability by the customer[155] as satisfying the affordability requirement; the firm must adopt a scientific approach to the question and base its assessment *on evidence*.

102. Affordability is reflected in the surplus of net income over net expenditure. Accordingly, the firm must take full account of the net income of the customer, on the one hand (i.e. net of income tax and national insurance), and outgoings, on the other.[156] Outgoings are divided between committed expenditure, basic essential expenditure and quality of living costs of the customer's household.[157]

103. In approaching affordability, a firm must not base its assessment of affordability on the equity in the property used as security for the purpose of the regulated mortgage contract.[158] The reason for this is that a person should not enter a loan if he or she will need to realise that value of his her home in order to be able to realise the repayments. Likewise, the likelihood of a future increase in property values ought not to be taken into account in assessing affordability.

Income

104. Traditionally, firms have used multiples of a person's income as forming the basis of how much it is prepared to advance. There is nothing inherently wrong with this approach, but a firm must be able to justify each particular loan as being affordable and cannot simply rely on a blanket approach as justifying its decision in a particular case.[159] In particular, this approach cannot obviate the need to look at outgoings.

105. In assessing income, a firm cannot rely on self-certification as has happened at various times in the past,[160] but must instead require independent documentary evidence.[161] Evidence will be considered independent, even if supplied by the customer, provided that it is independently

155 MCOB 11.6.6 R.
156 MCOB 11.6.5(2)(a) R.
157 MCOB 11.6.5(2)(b) R.
158 MCOB 11.6.5(1) R.
159 MCOB 11.6.7 G.
160 MCOB 11.6.8(2) G.
161 MCOB 11.6.8(2) G.

generated; bank statements, payslips and tax returns will all count as independent evidence.[162]

106. Furthermore, the prospect of *future* changes in income must be taken into account (e.g. retirement during the term of the regulated mortgage contract or the prospect of future redundancy if this is known).[163] This may require the firm to obtain evidence of pension provision.

Outgoings

107. The expenditure that has to be taken into account is specified at MCOB 11.6.10 R and is subdivided into committed expenditure, basic essential expenditure and basic quality of living costs.

108. Committed expenditure is that expenditure that the customer is obliged to make and that the customer will continue to have to make after the regulated mortgage contract has been entered into. This includes loan repayments, child maintenance payments and a repayment strategy if an interest-only mortgage is being entered into.[164] While these details can be obtained from the customer, the information should be corroborated by, for instance, checking credit card statements.[165] Future commitments subsequently falling due must also be taken into account, such as a future loan obligation that may become payable thereafter.[166]

109. Basic essential expenditure comprises household necessities, such as expenditure on household bills, specifically including essential travel costs to work and school.[167] A distinction is drawn between basic *essential expenditure* and basic *quality of living costs*. Basic quality of living costs are not the cost of necessities, but of expenditure, which is in practice hard to reduce, as being expenditure needed to maintain a certain quality of life, such as some basic recreation costs.[168]

110. The impact of possible future interest rate changes over a minimum period of five years must be factored in, unless the interest rate is fixed during that period.[169] In assessing what the change in interest rates will be, the firm should look at market expectations and what the prevailing Financial Policy Committee recommendation is and will have to justify its conclusions on these grounds.[170] The calculations must in any event assume a minimum increase in interest rates of 1 per cent.[171]

162 MCOB 11.6.9(6) G.
163 MCOB 11.6.14 R.
164 MCOB 11.6.11(1) G.
165 MCOB 11.6.13(3) G.
166 MCOB 11.6.15(3) G.
167 MCOB 11.6.10(2) R.
168 MCOB 11.6.11 G.
169 MCOB 11.6.18 R.
170 MCOB 11.6.18(2) R.
171 MCOB 11.6.18(3) R.

111. If the purpose of the regulated mortgage contract is to repay outstanding debts (debt consolidation) and if the new loan is only affordable if these existing commitments are repaid, then the firm must take reasonable steps to ensure that these debts are indeed discharged on completion of the transaction.[172] This does not apply, however, if the loan repayments would still be affordable if the outstanding loans remained outstanding after completion.

Policy

112. A firm must put in place a written policy for assessing all these affordability criteria,[173] which must address specifically:

(a) how income is to be assessed and what sources of income may properly be taken into account;
(b) how future variations of income are to be taken into account;
(c) what sort of evidence of income will be required as confirmation of the matters asserted by the customer;
(d) how the calculation of affordability will be carried out;
(e) what actions are to be taken if the method proves to break down in practice; and
(f) what and how records are to be kept.

113. A firm must monitor the effectiveness of its affordability assessments on a periodic basis,[174] which should include putting in place mechanisms capable of triggering more frequent reviews if the level of arrears is higher than expected.[175]

114. Further, a firm must keep records so that it is possible to ascertain the basis of any particular lending decision,[176] which must include a breakdown of all the elements in the calculation.[177]

Loans solely for business purposes and for high net worth individuals

115. The affordability test still applies for loans solely for business purposes and for high net worth individuals[178] but there is no need to examine an application in the same detail as required for an individual application falling

172 MCOB 11.6.16(2) R.
173 MCOB 11.6.20 R, 11.6.18(2) R.
174 MCOB 11.6.22 R; at least once per calendar year; MCOB 11.6.24 R.
175 MCOB 11.6.23 G.
176 MCOB 11.6.60 R.
177 MCOB 11.6.60(2) R.
178 MCOB 11.6.26 R, 11.6.34 R.

outside these categories; there is a need to have a lending policy for these categories of loans but the specific matters set out at MCOB 11.6.20 R need not be addressed,[179] in contrast with a standard application for a loan for domestic purposes.

116. It is still unacceptable to take into account the equity in the house used as security for the purpose of assessing affordability.[180] When repayments are to come from the personal resources of the borrower, the lender must still look at the income and commitments of the prospective borrower,[181] but when repayments are to come from the business, the resources of the business must be examined; the matters that may be considered are cash flow, assets and liabilities.[182] A record must be kept of those aspects of the business relied upon, as well as the customer's personal assets and evidence relied upon.[183]

117. A firm must still formulate a written policy in connection with such loans but it need not contain the same amount of detail as with a loan to a private individual for non-business purposes, or to one who is not of high net worth.[184]

Interest-only mortgages

118. An interest-only mortgage is one where there is no repayment of capital and may include a situation in which some part of the interest is deferred until the end of the term.[185]

119. Before a firm can enter into an interest-only mortgage with a customer, it must be sure that the customer has in place a clearly understood and credible repayment plan to repay the capital in place;[186] such a strategy could include the sale of a property other than that on which the loan is secured, or the making of payments out of an irregular source of income, such as a future bonus payment, or receipt of an inheritance that is assured.[187]

120. An unacceptable repayment plan will be one based on an uncertain inheritance. It is also unacceptable to approve a strategy that involves the sale of a customer's main residence without considering whether, having repaid the capital and any accrued interest, the customer will be left with sufficient funds to purchase a cheaper property or pursue an appropriate alternative strategy.[188]

179 MCOB 11.6.32(1) R, 11.6.39(1) R.
180 MCOB 11.6.26(1), 11.6.34(1) R.
181 MCOB 11.6.26(2), 11.6.34(2) R.
182 MCOB 11.6.30 G.
183 MCOB 11.6.32(3), 11.6.39(3) R.
184 MCOB.11.6.32(1), 11.6.39(1) R.
185 MCOB 11.6.42 G.
186 MCOB 11.6.41 R.
187 MCOB 11.6.45 G.
188 MCOB 11.6.46 E.

121. With an interest-only mortgage, the affordability test is satisfied if the interest-only repayments are affordable, but the affordability calculations must take into account any repayments falling due under any relevant repayment plan insofar as relevant, as part of the committed expenditure that the customer will have to face.[189]

122. The firm must arrange for a review to take place with the customer at some time after the interest-only mortgage has been entered into.[190] The purpose of this is to ensure that the customer is successfully implementing his or her repayment plan and to give an opportunity to the firm to discuss with the customer any other options in the event of any difficulty in meeting the repayment plan. Accordingly, the review must be at a time sufficiently in advance of the date for repayment of capital to enable appropriate steps to be taken if the repayment strategy has run into difficulty.

123. A firm has to adopt a policy in connection with the granting of interest-only mortgages, which will set out the proportion of such business that the firm is prepared to enter into and the criteria that will be considered acceptable for the grant of such a mortgage.[191] The policy will also set out the process that will be followed in relation to the reviews that will be held.

124. A record must be kept of all the interest-only mortgages that have been entered into; in respect of each, this must include the reason that an interest-only mortgage was offered to the customer and the evidence of the repayment strategy put forward by the customer for the repayment of capital, and the outcome of any review.[192]

Interest roll-up mortgages

125. These mortgages add the interest payments to capital to be repaid at the end of the term. Mortgages of this type may not be offered at all save in the following cases: lifetime mortgages, bridging loans, loans to high net worth customers or loans solely for business purposes.[193] There is no requirement to carry out an analysis of income and outgoings in circumstances when the grant of such mortgages is permissible,[194] but it is nevertheless fundamental that a clear repayment strategy must exist before such a mortgage can be granted. The provisions applicable to interest-only mortgages apply to such mortgages as required by MCOB 11.6.40 G to 11.6.52 G.[195]

189 MCOB 11.6.48 R.
190 MCOB 11.6.49 R.
191 MCOB 11.6.50 R.
192 MCOB 11.60(3) R.
193 MCOB 11.6.58 R.
194 MCOB 11.6.57 R.
195 MCOB 11.6.59 G.

Bridging loan

126. A bridging loan is defined as a regulated mortgage contract that has a term of 12 months or less.[196] It is, therefore, fundamentally short term and may often attract a higher interest rate than a longer term loan. It is normally only appropriate when a borrower needs the money for a specific purpose. A bridging loan will invariably be interest-only and will frequently provide for interest payments to be rolled up.

127. A firm must not enter into a bridging loan unless the customer can show a suitable repayment strategy. MCOB 11.6.41 R is applicable to a bridging loan, which says that the repayment strategy must be 'clearly understood and credible'.

128. It is likely to be an unacceptable repayment strategy for the customer to say that he or she will enter into a repayment regulated mortgage contract to replace the bridging loan in due course, without evidence being available that a mainstream lender will be prepared to grant such a mortgage.[197] It is also likely to be unacceptable that a customer should anticipate his or her credit rating being improved as a result of entering into the bridging loan, thereby rendering it possible for the customer to refinance by means of a regulated mortgage contract.[198]

129. A customer may ask to extend the term of a bridging loan, in which case it must be treated as a new loan[199] and all the requirements of MCOB must then be satisfied on the basis that it is a new loan. If a bridging loan is granted on the basis that all the interest is rolled up, which will be frequently the case, then as part of the affordability test, the firm must consider what the impact of rolling up interest will have on the remaining equity in the customer's home.[200]

Regulating the level of charges imposed on the borrower

130. To a limited extent, MCOB 12 regulates the level of charges that a firm can impose in respect of a regulated mortgage contract. The unfair relationship provisions of the Consumer Credit Act 1974 cannot be relied upon to regulate charges since these do not apply to a regulated mortgage contract.[201] A borrower may be able to rely on the Unfair Terms in Consumer Contracts Regulations 1999[202] as these potentially apply to a loan

196 FCA Handbook Glossary.
197 MCOB 11.6.54(2) G.
198 MCOB 11.6.53 E.
199 MCOB 11.6.55(1) R.
200 MCOB 11.6.55(2) R.
201 Section 140A(5).
202 SI 1999/2083.

entered into by an individual other than for business purposes. The Regulations do not apply to a core term of a contract,[203] so the Regulations cannot be relied upon to control interest rates, but the unfairness provisions of the Regulations apply to default provisions. If a term is found to be an unfair term, then it is unenforceable against a consumer.[204]

131. The rules contained in MCOB 12 continue to apply even after a regulated mortgage contract has come to an end.[205]

Excessive charges

132. There is a general rule that charges should not be *excessive*.[206] This leaves open the question of what is 'excessive' for these purposes, as the term is undefined. Some guidance is given in MCOB 12;[207] the amounts charged should be compared with the level of charges imposed generally in the same sector in the market; the extent to which the charges were disclosed in advance of entering into the regulated mortgage contract will be relevant to an assessment of excessiveness; it will also be relevant whether there was an abuse of trust by the firm in relation to the customer, a concept that must be construed in a general rather than technical sense.

Early repayment charges

133. MCOB 12.3.1 provides that an early repayment charge must be expressed in cash (i.e. in purely monetary terms) and must genuinely reflect the cost to the lender of early repayment by the customer. This latter requirement is an important limitation on the amount of repayment charges and gives the borrower a basis for challenging an excessively high charge. It is for the firm to use an appropriate method for calculating the cost to the lender, but the 'rule of 78' should not be used as this is not a fair reflection of the cost to the lender of early repayment.[208] The Consumer Credit (Rebate on Early Settlement) Regulations may provide a starting point for an analysis of what a reasonable charge should be.

134. In equity, an excessive early repayment charge can be challenged on the basis that it constitutes a clog on the equity of redemption and therefore potentially irrecoverable.[209] But the principle is not well developed and is accordingly of uncertain application, but it is clear that in equity, a term can only be challenged if it is morally reprehensible, a high hurdle.[210]

203 Reg 6(2).
204 Reg 8.
205 MCOB 12.1.4 R.
206 MCOB 12.5.1 R.
207 MCOB 12.5.3 G.
208 MCOB 12.3.2 G.
209 *Cityland and Property (Holdings) Ltd v Dabrah* 1968 Ch 166.
210 *Multiservice Bookbinding Ltd v Marden* 1979 Ch 84.

135. The early repayment charge must be disclosed and included as part of any illustration provided to the customer.[211]

Payment shortfall charges

136. MCOB 12.4.1 provides that a firm must be able to demonstrate that a charge imposed on account of a payment shortfall is no more than a reasonable calculation of the cost of the *additional administration* required as a result of the shortfall. However, a firm can standardise its charges provided that the calculation takes into account only appropriate costs to the firm resulting from payment shortfalls.[212] There are some types of cost that must expressly *not* be taken into account, including the cost of capital, unrecovered fees, advertising costs (which, of course, have no connection with payment shortfalls) and regulatory fines.[213] Executive staff costs can only be taken into account in relation to those members of staff that are specifically engaged in managing payment shortfalls.[214] General financial reporting costs should not be included.[215]

137. Specifically, it is prohibited to calculate a payment shortfall charge as a percentage of an outstanding loan as this type of calculation bears no relationship to the costs incurred by the firm in managing a shortfall.[216]

Recovery of arrears

Dealing with customers in arrears

138. An overriding principle is that a firm must deal fairly with a customer that has a payment shortfall.[217] Moreover, a firm must not put pressure on a customer through excessive telephone calls or correspondence, or by contact at an unreasonable hour.[218]

139. This principle of fairness requires that a firm must put a policy in place setting out how it will treat customers that have fallen into arrears.[219] The purpose of this is to ensure that the firm has given thought to the procedures to be adopted to ensure that customers in arrears are treated fairly; the customer is not entitled to see the policy, but nor is the firm prevented from disclosing it.[220]

211 MCOB 12.3.4 R.
212 MCOB 12.4.2 G.
213 MCOB 12.4.4(1).
214 MCOB 12.4.4(3) R.
215 MCOB 12.4.6(3) G.
216 MCOB 12.4.8 R.
217 MCOB 13.3.1 R.
218 MCOB 13.5.3 R; an unreasonable hour is considered to be outside 8 am and 9 pm; MCOB 13.5.4 G.
219 MCOB 13.3.1(2) R.
220 MCOB 13.3.3 G.

140. Many customers arrange with a firm to make payments by way of direct debit. It may happen that in the case of a customer in financial difficulty, the direct debit may be refused. A firm must not process for payment more than two direct debit requests in a single month.[221]

141. A firm must take certain steps if faced with a situation when one or more direct debit requests have been refused in *two consecutive* months; the firm must consider whether the direct debit is the appropriate method of collecting payments, and must make reasonable steps to contact the customer to discuss the matter.[222] In the period when this payment method is under review, if the firm makes a further payment request using a direct debit, and the payment method is once again unsuccessful, the firm must not pass on any charges to the customer of presenting the unsuccessful direct debit request.[223]

142. Faced with a customer in payment difficulties, a firm must make reasonable efforts to reach an agreement with the customer over repaying any payment shortfall.[224] The firm must always have in mind the desirability of not selling the property if an alternative reasonably exists. The firm must be flexible in its approach. It must allow a reasonable time in which any shortfall has to be repaid[225] and it must, if appropriate, agree to a request to change the repayment date or the method by which payments are to be made. If the firm refuses a request for a change in payment method or payment date sought by the customer, the firm must give a *written explanation* to the customer of its reasons for refusal.[226] The customer must be given a reasonable time to consider any repayment plan put forward by the firm.[227]

143. Repossession is a last resort.[228] Some of the options that are to be considered before repossession is sought are extending the term of the mortgage loan, or changing its terms (e.g. to interest-only), or capitalising the shortfall.[229]

144. Capitalisation may not, however, take place automatically when the repayment consequences of capitalisation are significant; for these purposes, the consequences are significant if the interest payable over the whole of the mortgage term will increase by £50 or more, or if the contractual monthly repayments increase by more than £1.[230] The view of the FCA is

221 MCOB 13.3.1A R.
222 MCOB 13.3.1A(2) R.
223 MCOB 13.3.1A(2)(customer) R.
224 MCOB 13.3.2A R.
225 Perhaps over the whole of the remaining term: MCOB 13.3.6 G.
226 MCOB 13.3.2A(4) R.
227 MCOB 13.3.3A R.
228 MCOB 13.3.2A(6) R.
229 MCOB 13.3.4A(1) R.
230 MCOB 13.3.4AA R.

that capitalisation of arrears is also undesirable in principle although preferable to taking repossession proceedings.[231] A firm must also make the customer aware of any government schemes that have been set up to assist borrowers tackle arrears.[232]

145. When no reasonable payment plan can be achieved so that there is no realistic alternative to a sale, the firm must allow the customer to remain in possession for a reasonable period to affect a sale.[233]

Record keeping

146. A firm must keep a record of its dealings with those in arrears, including keeping a recording of all telephone calls with customers when the subject of arrears is discussed.[234] These records must be kept for three years from the date of the dealing.[235] The matters that must be recorded include the date when the first communication with the customer in arrears was made, information relating to any payment arrangement proposed, and the date and time of all telephone calls in respect of which a recording has been kept.[236]

Provision of information in relation to arrears

147. A customer that falls into arrears must be provided with certain information in a durable medium within 15 business days of the arrears having arisen.[237] The required information includes a list of the payments that have been missed in whole or in part, the total amount of the payment shortfall and the charges incurred as a result of the payment shortfall. Furthermore, the Money Advice Service information sheet entitled 'Problems paying your mortgage' must be supplied as well.[238]

148. There is a modification to these requirements if the customer has been in arrears within the last 12 months, was supplied with this information, or has cleared the arrears and has then fallen into arrears again. In these cases, the firm can either supply the information stipulated above again in its entirety or can send the information without serving the Money Advice Service information sheet.[239] In this latter instance, there must also be provided a statement of the consequences of what may happen if the shortfall is not cleared.

231 MCOB 13.3.4D G.
232 MCOB 13.3.4B R.
233 MCOB 13.3.2A(5) R.
234 MCOB 13.3.9(1) R.
235 MCOB 13.3.9(2) R.
236 MCOB 13.3.10 G.
237 MCOB 13.4.1 R.
238 MCOB 13.4.1(1) R.
239 MCOB 13.4.4 R.

149. If the occurrence of the arrears has given rise to a liability to pay charges, then at least every quarter, a customer must be provided with a statement setting out those charges and the amount of the payment shortfall.[240] However, if the arrears do not give rise to separate charges but merely attract interest at the contractual rate on the amount of the arrears, this will not in itself trigger a requirement for a statement; it will be different if the arrears are subject to a differential rate compared with the standard contractual rate.[241]

150. In the case of a high net worth customer or a loan purely for business purposes, there is no need to supply the Money Advice Service information sheet but there is a need to communicate, in a durable medium, details of the consequences if the payment shortfall is not cleared, as well as a description of the options available for clearing the shortfall and (with business borrowers only) detailed sources of free advice services available.[242]

Repossession proceedings

151. MCOB 13.4.5 stipulates certain steps that must be taken before repossession proceedings can be brought. A failure to take these steps will doubtless constitute a defence to any proceedings. The firm must provide the customer with up-to-date information about the arrears, but need not include a Money Advice Service information sheet. In addition, the firm must inform the customer of the need to contact the local authority to see if the customer may be eligible for local authority housing. The firm must unambiguously state that repossession proceedings are intended.

152. If repossession proceedings are taken, the property must be marketed for sale as soon as possible.[243] The mortgagee must obtain the best price that might reasonably be paid, taking account of factors such as market condition as well as the continuing increase in the amount owed by the customer.[244] There may be legitimate reasons for the firm to defer sale other than market conditions (e.g. the need to carry out certain beneficial work to the property).[245] But it is plain that the mortgagee will need to justify any decision taken to defer a sale.

153. The position under MCOB 13.6 is to be contrasted with the position under the general law; there is a duty on a mortgagee in equity to exercise reasonable care in the exercise of a power of sale over mortgaged property in order to obtain the true market value[246] but the mortgagee is not

240 MCOB 13.5.1 R.
241 MCOB 13.5.2 G.
242 MCOB 13.7 R.
243 MCOB 13.6.1(a) R.
244 MCOB 13.6.1(2) R.
245 MCOB 13.6.2 G.
246 *Cuckmere Brick Co v Mutual Finance Ltd* 1971 Ch 949; *Yorkshire Bank plc v Hall* 1999 1 WLR 1713.

constrained by the timing of the exercise of the power[247] and indeed is not obliged to exercise the power at all.[248] The provisions of MCOB 13.6.1 impose additional requirements on a mortgagee in the exercise of a power of sale and are to be welcomed.

154. If, having exercised the power of sale, the proceeds of sale are insufficient to clear the amount due under the mortgage loan, then the customer must be informed of the deficiency and, if the firm intends to try to recover the shortfall, the customer must be informed of this as well. The notification must take place within six years of the date of the sale (which must mean within six years of the date of completion of the sale), or five years in cases when the regulated mortgage contract was subject to Scottish law.[249] This is to be contrasted with the general law, which provides in England and Wales for the limitation period for the recovery of capital (but not interest) to be 12 years.[250]

155. If the proceeds of sale are more than the amount required to discharge the mortgage, then the firm must, of course, account to the customer for the surplus after the interests of other mortgagees are taken into account. The customer must be told of the amount of the surplus *as soon as possible after the sale*, and the surplus must be paid to him or her.[251]

247 *Parker-Tweedale v Dunbar Bank plc* 1991 Ch 12 at 18.
248 *Palk v Mortgage Service Funding plc* 1993 Ch 330 at 337.
249 MCOB 13.6.4(2) G.
250 *West Bromwich Building Society v Wilkinson* 2005 1 WLR 2303.
251 MCOB 13.6.6 R.

14 The conduct of particular types of credit activity

The conduct of credit token agreements

1. A credit token must not be given to a minor who has not asked for it, but this does not apply to a credit token provided in respect of an agreement already made, or to the renewal of a credit token previously accepted by the minor.[1]

2. Prior to entering into the credit token agreement, the lender must explain the terms of the agreement in the usual way. In particular, the lender must point out:[2]

(a) if different interest rates or charges apply to different elements of the agreement (e.g. sometimes different terms apply if a credit card is used to obtain cash as opposed to acquire goods and services);
(b) if interest rates are capable of being increased (they usually are), including in relation to any changes in the status of the borrower;
(c) the implication of making only minimum repayments;
(d) the limitations on any zero percentage introductory offer or the like; and
(e) the conditions attached to any balance transfers.

3. CONC has now introduced a number of welcome rules into the conduct of credit card and store card facilities that were previously only matters of guidance contained in the *Irresponsible Lending Guidance* published by the Office of Fair Trading.

4. Once the credit card or store card agreement has been entered into, then any repayment must be allocated to that element of the agreement attracting the highest rate of interest.[3]

1 CONC 2.9.
2 CONC 4.2.15 R.
3 CONC 6.7.4 R.

5. A credit card or store card invariably sets a minimum monthly repayment. A customer must be given the option of paying more than this even where automated repayments are made.[4]

6. The minimum repayment must be fixed at an amount equal to at least the interest, fees and charges applied to the account for the relevant period, plus 1 per cent of the balance.[5] The purpose of this is to stop the customer falling into increasing debt if the customer pays the minimum payment. Interest in respect of a period prior to the statement may be ignored for the purpose of this calculation.[6]

7. A firm must not increase a customer's credit limit where the customer has indicated that the customer does not want this.[7] Indeed, a customer must be entitled to reduce his or her credit limit and must be given the option of whether or not to accept an increase in limit.[8] Further, 30 days notice must be given before any credit limit increase comes into effect, save where a customer has requested and been granted a temporary increase in limit to cope with an emergency.[9]

8. If, under an agreement, the lender is entitled to increase interest rates, the borrower must be given notice of 30 days before the increase takes effect. This does not apply if the rate tracks an *external* index.[10] The borrower should then be given 60 days in which to decide whether to give notice to the lender closing the account and if the borrower decides to give such notice, the borrower should then have the right to pay off the balance at the *old* rate of interest over a reasonable period of time.[11]

9. Nor should a credit card company increase interest rates to a customer that is in financial risk having missed two or more payments or who has agreed a debt management plan.[12] In fact, the lender can only increase interest rates when it has a *valid* reason to do so.[13] Examples of such valid reason will be where the lender has increased costs (typically increased borrowing costs) or where the borrower genuinely represents an increased risk.[14] However, where the reason for the increase is that the borrower presents an increased risk, the borrower must be informed of this and given an explanation.[15]

4 CONC 6.7.6 R.
5 CONC 6.7.5 R.
6 CONC 6.7.5(2) R.
7 CONC 6.7.7 R.
8 CONC 6.7.8 R.
9 CONC 6.7.9 R.
10 CONC 6.7.12 R.
11 CONC 6.7.13 R.
12 CONC 6.7.10 R.
13 CONC 6.7.14 R.
14 CONC 6.7.15 G.
15 CONC 6.7.16 R.

10. A borrower is only liable under the terms of a credit token if the borrower has accepted it by signing for it, or signing a receipt for it, or used it.[16]

11. Whenever the lender issues a new credit token, a copy of the terms of the agreement must accompany the new credit token.[17] If this is contravened, the agreement cannot be enforced for as long as the position remains unremedied.[18] The burden of proof is on the lender to prove that this requirement has been satisfied.[19]

Misuse of credit tokens

12. Credit facilities can be misused in a number of ways. Traditionally, credit cards have been prone to misuse and special rules have been developed in connection with credit card misuse.

13. In principle, the Act exonerates the borrower from all losses so arising.[20] Section 83(1) provides that 'the debtor shall not be liable to the creditor for any loss arising from the use of the credit facility by another person not acting, or to be treated as acting as the debtor's agent'. The reference to someone treated as acting as the debtor's agent will be to someone having the ostensible authority of the borrower to utilise the credit facility; this requires a holding out by the borrower of that person as having the authority of the borrower to use the facility.

14. If the account balance is increased as a result of the activities of a third party acting in a manner not authorised by the borrower, the lender must restore the level of the account to its proper amount excluding the intervention of the third party.

15. As an exception to the general principle laid down by section 83(1), a borrower can be made liable to a limited extent for the misuse of a credit token by a third party, save one supplied under a distance contract in respect of which no liability can attach at all, whatever the circumstances and where the rule in section 83(1) continues to apply.[21]

16. In order for a borrower to be liable at all under a credit token, the borrower must have accepted it by signing for it, or signing a receipt for it or by using it.[22] Moreover, in every situation, the burden of proof is on the lender to show that the credit token was lawfully supplied and accepted by the debtor.[23]

16 Section 66.
17 Section 85(1).
18 Section 85(2).
19 Section 171(4)(a).
20 Section 83(1).
21 Section 83(3A), (3C).
22 Section 66.
23 Section171(4)(a).

17. Moreover, no liability at all, however, can attach to the borrower unless the credit token agreement must contain details of a person to contact in the event that the credit token is lost, stolen or in any other way liable to misused.[24] The details given have to conform to the Consumer Credit (Credit Tokens Agreements) Regulations 1983,[25] which provides that with credit token agreements entered into after 19 May 1985, the name, address and telephone number of the person to be contacted must be given 'prominently' and 'legibly'.

18. Section 84 makes some rather fine distinctions when specifying the liability of a borrower for misuse of a credit token. In making these distinctions, section 84 refers to misuse by an 'authorised person', namely someone permitted by the borrower to use the token.[26] The lender is also included in this category.

19. The following situations should be considered:

(a) a person using the credit token is not authorised to use it and did not obtain it by consent;
(b) a person is not authorised to use a credit token, but acquired it by consent (e.g. if someone is entrusted with it for safekeeping); and
(c) a person is authorised to use a credit token (and accordingly acquired it by consent).

20. In the first of these situations, the borrower's liability is subject to a limit of £50 (section 84(1); the previous limit of £30 was increased by the Consumer Credit (Increase of Monetary Amounts) Order 1983).[27]

21. In the second situation, there is an apparent conflict between subsections 84(1), which seems to impose a limit of £50, and section 84(2), which seems not to place any restriction on the extent of a borrower's liability. The conflict, however, must be resolved in favour of there being no limit to liability since section 84(2) expressly states that 'section 83 does not prevent the debtor under a credit-token agreement from being made liable *to any extent* for loss to the creditor from use of the credit token by a person who acquired possession of it with the debtor's consent' (emphasis added).

22. In the final situation where the person misusing the token is an authorised person and who acquired possession of the token with consent of the borrower, there is no financial limit to the borrower's liability,[28] section 84(1) not applying. In every situation, the burden of proof will be on the

24 Section 84(1).
25 SI 1983/1555.
26 Section 84(7).
27 SI 1983/1571.
28 Section 84(1).

lender to prove that the person misusing the token was authorised by the borrower to use it.[29] This shifting of the burden of proof does not seem fair since it is the borrower, not the lender, that knows what happened to the credit token.

23. In all of the above situations, the lender must deduct any initial charge imposed by the lender for issue of the credit token from any liability of the borrower, except that this does not apply if the amount has already been repaid to the borrower by the lender.[30] If the agreement was one under which several tokens were issued, such as an agreement concluded with a partnership where several cards are issued thereunder to various partners, the financial ceiling applied by section 84(1) and full liability imposed by section 84(2) apply to each card individually.[31] It is the actions of the individual cardholder that in each case determine the extent of liability.

24. Once the lender has actually *received* notification from the borrower that the token is lost, stolen or otherwise liable to misuse, the borrower's liability for its misuse ceases in any event.[32] Notification can be written or oral; since the borrower must perforce have been supplied with the telephone number of the relevant person in the credit token agreement, the borrower should readily be able to telephone through to report the fact that the card is liable to misuse. The longer the borrower delays communicating, of course, the greater the losses may be (but subject to any financial ceiling that may apply). The burden of proof is on the lender in every situation to show, if he or she can, that a particular act of misuse occurred prior to notification.[33]

25. The credit agreement may require the borrower to confirm any communication of misuse in writing. If so, the borrower must give the required confirmation within seven days or the notification will be invalidated.[34] The seven days will commence the day after oral communication was given. Although it is not expressly stated, it is thought that this confirmation must actually reach the lender within the seven-day period; it is not enough for it to be 'in the post'. The borrower must therefore be sure to see that it arrives within the time limit. Unusually, it is the borrower here who bears the risks of delays in the post.

Overdraft agreements

26. Overdraft agreements are an important category of credit agreements to which increasingly special rules apply, particularly following the imple-

29 Section 171(4)(b).
30 Section 84(6).
31 Section 84(8).
32 Section 84(3).
33 Section 171(4)(b).
34 Section 84(5).

mentation of the EU Credit Directive (although they have been exempted from certain of the formalities relating to entry into the agreements from the outset).

27. An overdraft agreement is a regulated credit running account agreement. The Act distinguishes between various types of overdraft to which different rules apply, namely:

(a) an authorised non-business overdraft;
(b) an authorised business overdraft;
(c) a casual overdraft in which an overdraft is permitted to arise without any prior agreement between borrower and lender; and
(d) other types of overdraft agreement.

28. These distinctions were introduced as a result of the EU Consumer Credit Directive with effect from 30 April 2010. These categories are not all embracing. They do not embrace agreements where no particular purpose for the overdraft is prescribed. They also do not embrace borrower-lender-supplier overdraft agreements, for example, or agreements where the overdraft may continue beyond the period of three months.

29. As far as the legal regime applicable to these agreements is concerned, the starting point is that by virtue of section 74(1)(b) of the Act, Part V of the Consumer Credit Act 1974 does not apply to overdraft agreements. Part V of the Act goes from section 55 to 73 and deals with all the requirements relating to entry into credit and hire agreements, including cancellation and withdrawal. The only exception is that section 56, the deemed agency of the negotiator in the context of antecedent negotiations, applies to all overdraft agreements.[35]

30. However, the exemption from Part V is qualified in relation to authorised business overdraft agreements, authorised non- business overdraft agreements and also to non-business overdraft agreements on a current account where the credit is not repayable within three months. Certain provisions within Part V are applicable to agreements of these types.

Authorised business overdraft

31. This is a borrower-lender agreement where an overdraft has been authorised in advance for the borrower to overdraw on a current account where the credit must be repaid on demand or within three months and it must be entered into wholly or predominantly for the purpose of the borrower's business.[36] An authorised business overdraft may or may not be secured in some way (e.g. on land).

35 Section 74(1E).
36 Section 189(1).

32. In the case of both the authorised non-business overdraft and the authorised business overdraft, the lender is entitled to rely on a declaration by the borrower as to the purpose of the agreement unless the lender has reason to believe that the declaration is untrue.[37]

33. The parts of Part V of the Act that apply to such agreements, often subject to special rules, are as follows:[38]

(a) the deemed agency of a negotiator under section 56 of the Act;
(b) regulations as to form and content of agreements under section 60 of the Act; and
(c) duty to supply a copy of the overdraft agreement under section 61B.

Authorised non-business overdraft

34. This is a borrower-lender agreement where an overdraft has been authorised in advance for the borrower to overdraw on a current account where the credit must be repaid on demand or within three months, and it must be entered into wholly or predominantly for non-business purposes.[39] An authorised non-business overdraft may or may not be secured in some way (e.g. on land).

35. The sections within Part V of the Act that apply to such agreements are the same as with authorised business overdraft agreements, but, in addition, there is an obligation to comply with disclosure of information regulations under section 55 and to supply on request a prospective agreement under section 55C.[40]

Non-business overdraft agreements where the overdraft may be repaid more than three months later

36. These agreements are not authorised for the purpose of the classification introduced by the EU Consumer Credit Directive.

37. The parts of Part V of the Act that apply to such agreements are the same as with authorised non-business overdraft agreements, save that obligations in relation to the signing of agreements and to supply a copy agreement under section 61A, and as to the right to withdraw from such agreements under section 66A also apply.[41]

37 Section 189(2A).
38 Section 74(1B).
39 Section 189(1).
40 Section 74(1C).
41 Section 74(1D).

Disclosure of pre-contract information

38. The Disclosure of Information Regulations 2010 do not apply to authorised business overdraft agreements, but only apply to non-business overdraft agreements on a current account. Moreover, even then, they do not apply to non-business overdraft agreements when the credit exceeds £60,260 or the agreement is secured on land.[42]

39. Regulation 10 sets out the disclosure of information requirements applicable to authorised non-business overdraft agreements. The information set out in regulation 10(3) must be disclosed in good time before the agreement is made.[43] Subject to exceptions, this information must be presented in written form in the manner provided for by regulation 11 and Schedule 3.[44] The prescribed information includes many detailed aspects of the overdraft arrangement and the form must be headed 'European Consumer Credit Information'.

40. The information specified in regulation 10(3) includes, in the case of a distance contract, information about the right of cancellation provided for by the Financial Services (Distance Marketing) Regulations 2004.[45]

41. In the case of a telephone agreement for an authorised non-business overdraft that is not a distance contract, the requirements are somewhat reduced; the creditor must provide, orally or in writing, certain specified information about the terms of the arrangement before the agreement is made; there is no need to provide the full document in the form set out in Schedule 3.[46] In the case of a telephone agreement that is a distance contract, it is permissible to disclose more limited information orally prior to the agreement without using the Schedule 3 form, if the prospective borrower explicitly agrees.[47] If there is no explicit agreement, then the Schedule 3 form must be provided prior to the agreement.[48]

42. If the customer says that he or she wants an overdraft immediately, a Schedule 3 form must be used prior to the agreement but it needs only set out the key terms of the overdraft agreement.[49]

43. In the case of a joint overdraft agreement, the necessary information can be given to only one of them provided both agree to this.[50]

44. The Disclosure of Information Regulations 2004 do not apply to a non-business overdraft agreement on a current account that is not

42 Reg 2(3) Disclosure of Information Regulations 2010.
43 Reg 10(2).
44 Reg 10(2).
45 Reg 10(5)(e).
46 Reg 10(6).
47 Reg 10(5).
48 Reg 10(5A).
49 Reg 10(8).
50 Reg 10(9).

authorised (i.e. where the credit is repayable after more than three months).[51] The Disclosure of Information Regulations 2010 apply to such an agreement provided the credit is less than £60,260 and provided it is not secured on land.[52]

45. If there is a contravention of this provision, the agreement can be enforced on an order of the court only, and a retaking of goods or land to which the agreement relates is enforcement for these purposes.[53]

Pre-contract explanations

46. The requirement to provide pre-contractual explanations only applies to non-business overdraft agreements that would be authorised except for the fact that the credit is not repayable on demand or within three months.[54] There is then a need to provide a pre-contractual explanation of these matters set out in CONC 4.2.5. This, however, does not apply if the credit exceeds £60,260 or is not secured on land.[55]

Creditworthiness assessment

47. This requirement has no application to agreements allowing the borrower to overdraw on a current account.[56] A creditworthiness assessment is, however, needed in the case of an authorised business or non-business overdraft agreement or an agreement that would be a non-business authorised agreement if the credit was repayable on demand or within three months.[57] But even where no creditworthiness assessment is required, it is still necessary for the lender to assess the potential of an agreement to impact on the customer's financial situation so that the exclusions are not of great significance.[58]

Entry into the agreement

48. The Consumer Credit (Agreements) Regulations 2010 apply to authorised and non-business authorised overdraft agreements whether or not they are secured on land.[59] The relevant requirements are contained in

51 Reg 2(3)(c) Disclosure of Information Regulations 2004.
52 Reg 2(4) Disclosure of Information Regulations 2010.
53 Section 55(2).
54 CONC 4.2.1(5) R.
55 CONC 4.2.1(3), (4) R.
56 CONC 5.2.1.
57 CONC 5.2.1 (6).
58 CONC 5.2.2 R.
59 Reg 2(4) Agreements Regulations 2010.

regulation 8 and other provisions in the Regulations do not apply, save as to modifying agreements.[60]

49. Regulation 8 requires that there must be set out in a clear and concise manner a variety of information, including the credit limit, the duration of the agreement, the interest rates and other charges, and the conditions applicable to the interest rate, including if different interest rates. If the overdraft is repayable in full at any time, this must also be indicated. The total charge for credit need not be given in the case of an authorised business non-overdraft agreement or a non-business overdraft agreement secured on land.

50. In the case of overdraft agreements that are non-business overdraft agreements in respect of a current account that are not authorised, the Agreements Regulations 2010 apply in their entirety (including where it is secured on land) and regulation 8 does not apply.[61] The Agreements Regulations 1983 will apply in respect of an overdraft agreement where the overdraft exceeds £60,260, save where the Disclosure of Information Regulations have been voluntarily complied with.[62]

Signature of the agreement

51. The need for the borrower to sign an agreement only applies to non-business overdraft agreements that would be authorised except that credit is not repayable on demand or within three months. The relevant requirements are at regulation 6 of the Agreement Regulations 2010.

Copy of the agreement

52. Where an authorised business overdraft agreement or an authorised non-business overdraft agreement has been entered into, there is an obligation to provide a copy of the agreement before or at the time that the agreement is entered into.[63]

53. However, if the comprehensive information set out at regulation 10(3) has been provided prior to entry into the agreement, then the copy agreement may be provided afterwards.[64]

54. However, if the more limited information provided in advance of the agreement is confined to that required in respect of a telephone agreement or an overdraft agreed in an emergency,[65] being the core financial

60 Reg 2(4).
61 Regulation 2(1) Agreements Regulations 2010.
62 Regulation 2(2), (3) Agreements Regulations 2010.
63 Section 61B(1).
64 Section 61B(2)(a).
65 Disclosure of Information Regulations 2010, reg 10(5), 10(8).

information other than the rate of interest, then the document containing the terms of the agreement must be provided *immediately* following the conclusion of the agreement.[66]

55. If an agreement is made using a means of distance communication other than by telephone other than at the borrower's request, then the copy agreement must be given immediately after the agreement is made.[67]

56. If there is a breach of these requirements, then the agreement is enforceable on order of the court only.[68] It will be necessary to apply to the court for an enforcement order under section 127.[69]

57. In the case of a non-business overdraft agreement that would be authorised but for the fact that the credit is not repayable on demand or within three months, then a copy of the agreement has to be supplied in accordance with section 61A. This does not apply if the amount of credit was in excess of £60,260 or is secured on land, unless the lender has purported to comply with the Disclosure of Information Regulations 2010.[70] Further, such a borrower can seek a copy of the agreement under section 55C, a provision that again does not apply if the amount of credit exceeds £60,260 or is secured on land.[71]

Withdrawal

58. The borrower will have the right to withdraw from a non-business overdraft agreement that would be authorised but for the fact that the credit is repayable on demand or within three months in accordance with section 66A.

Subsequent variation of interest rates

59. Under section 78A of the Act, there is an obligation on a lender to notify a borrower whenever the interest rate changes. There is a lessening of the requirement in the case of authorised business and authorised non-business overdrafts[72] and also in respect of an overdraft that would be a non-business overdraft but for the fact that the credit is not repayable on demand or within three months.[73] In these instances, all that has to be notified is an *increase* in interest rates; the other matters do not have to

66 Section 61B(2)(b).
67 Section 61B(2)(c).
68 Section 61B(3).
69 Section 127(1)(zb).
70 Section 61A(6).
71 Section 55C(4); section 55C also applies to an authorised non-business overdraft agreement.
72 As defined in section 189(1).
73 Section 78A(5).

be notified.[74] Overdraft agreements may, in any event, be entitled to exemption from this requirement as a result section 78A(2), which applies when the agreement provides for the interest rate to vary in accordance with a publicly available reference rate and when information about the reference rate is available from the premises of the lender.

Tacit agreement to allow an overdraft

60. A tacit agreement to allow an overdraft to be exceeded (or to arise) can create a regulated credit agreement. The formalities prescribed by Part V of the Consumer Credit Act 1974 do not apply to such an agreement.[75]

61. If there is a possibility that a customer may be allowed to exceed an overdraft limit, notwithstanding that there has been no prior arrangement to this effect, then the customer must be informed of the rate of interest that will be applicable if this occurs, including how that rate may change, and also the existence of any other charges that will be levied in these circumstances.[76]

62. If this unauthorised overdraft continues at a significant level for more than one month, and the excess is a regulated credit agreement, the customer must be informed of:[77]

(a) the fact and amount of the overdraft excess; and
(b) the rate of interest payable together with any other charges payable.

63. For these purposes, an overdraft is continuing at a significant level if charges start to become payable, or the borrower's credit rating may be affected.[78]

64. The standard requirement on the lender to notify the borrower under section 78A of a change in interest rates does not apply to a tacit overdraft.[79]

Termination of an overdraft agreement

65. If agreements are of fixed duration, they will terminate at the end of the contractual term. But such agreements may be of no fixed duration and therefore open-ended agreements within the definition in section 189(1). Section 98A of the Act lays down rules for the termination of such agreements, or the withdrawal or suspension of credit thereunder. The

74 Section 78A(4).
75 Section 74(1)(b).
76 CONC 4.7.2 R.
77 CONC 6.3.4 R.
78 CONC 6.3.4(3) R.
79 Section 78A(6).

lender can only terminate such an agreement on giving at least two months written notice[80] and whereas no notice has to be given in order for the lender to withdraw or suspend credit under such an agreement, the withdrawal or suspension must be accompanied by a notice that contains objectively justifiable reasons for such action.[81] The borrower can terminate such an agreement at any time.[82]

66. However, these rules do not apply to authorised business or non-business overdraft agreements or to tacit overdraft agreements.[83] But the rules will apply to unauthorised overdraft agreements other than tacit agreements.

High-cost short-term credit

67. High-cost short-term credit, or HCSTC, poses particular threats to consumers and is subject to certain specific regulatory requirements.

68. The definition of HCSTC is to be found in the FCA Handbook Glossary. The term only applies to a borrower-lender agreement or a P2P agreement (i.e. one entered into via an electronic platform) and when the APR of the agreement is in excess of 100 per cent. In the case of a financial promotion, the credit must be described as being for a maximum period of 12 months, or as being provided for a short term. As far as a credit agreement is concerned, it is only classified as HCSTC if credit is provided on terms that it is to be repaid, wholly or substantially, within a maximum 12-month period. Agreements provided by community finance organisations[84] are outside the definition, as are agreements secured on land or by pledge;[85] likewise excluded are agreements enabling borrowers to overdraw on a current account whether by prior agreement or not.

69. Payday lending represents a particular form of HSCTC that has attracted much adverse publicity, including from the Archbishop of Canterbury.

70. The general rules applicable to financial promotions apply with the added requirement that when lending of this type is being promoted, a specific additional warning must be given as follows: 'Warning: Late payment can cause you serious money problems. For help, go to moneyadviceservice.org.uk.'[86] The risk warning must be included in a

80 Section 98A(3); unless the agreement specifies a longer period.
81 Which might include the misuse of credit or an increase in risk to the lender of non-payment.
82 Section 98A(1); if the agreement stipulates a notice period, it must not exceed one month.
83 Section 98A(8).
84 Being registered charities or industrial and provident societies or community interest company limited by guarantee.
85 I.e. so that pawn agreements are outside the definition.
86 CONC 3.4.1 R.

financial promotion contained in an electronic communication unless it is not practicable to include the warning by reason of limited space.[87] The FCA gave consideration to giving a more extensive warning but decided that this would not, in practice, provide any greater consumer protection.[88]

71. In addition to the general obligation to give pre-contractual explanations under CONC 4.2, for this type of credit, the lender is subject to a specific requirement to explain to the prospective borrower that this type of agreement is unsuitable to support long-term borrowing and would be expensive for this purpose.[89]

HCSTC agreements and continuous payment authorities

72. Frequently, a credit company offering this type of borrowing will require the borrower to sign up to a continuous payment authority. A continuous payment authority[90] is a consent provided by a customer to a payment service provider authorising the making of a payment to the lender from a customer's payment account (usually a bank account). Direct debits are excluded from the definition as are instructions given following entry into a credit agreement confined to a single occasion only. Experience shows that use of such an authority can cause serious problems for a borrower.

73. If the lender intends to operate a continuous payment authority, the effect and manner of operation of such an authority must be explained to the borrower.[91] In the case of a prospective HSCTC agreement, the borrower must be specifically told that it can be used only twice to collect the whole sum due under the agreement or if payment under the agreement is to be made by instalments, in respect of each instalment.[92] The lender must also explain to the borrower that the lender will only collect a *part* payment using a continuous payment authority in circumstances when the lender is willing to accept a lesser sum in full payment and provided the borrower thereafter expressly gives consent to the collection of a part payment.[93]

74. Once the lender or owner has been provided with a continuous payment authority, the lender or owner must keep a record of its operation including unsuccessful attempts to operate it.[94]

75. In relation to an HCSTC agreement, the lender must stop operating a continuous payment authority once two unsuccessful requests for payment

87 CONC 3.4.1(2) R.
88 FCA PS14/3 paragraph 5.58.
89 CONC 4.2.8 R.
90 Defined in the FCA Handbook Glossary.
91 CONC 4.6.2(a) R.
92 CONC 4.6.2(b) R.
93 CONC 4.6.2(j) R.
94 CONC 7.6.15(3) G.

have been made of the payment service provider.[95] This is an important limitation on the lender's ability to recover outstanding payments due under such an agreement. The reason for this rule is that the FCA found that there were numerous occasions when customers were losing control of their bank accounts and were unable to make priority payments and were being bombarded with requests for payments even when they had made it clear they were unable to pay.[96]

76. Moreover, if an agreement has been refinanced, this still counts as the same agreement for these purposes so that a continuous payment authority may not be operated after more than two unsuccessful attempts.[97] However, the continuous payment authority may be reset if the lender contacts the borrower and explains that there have already been two unsuccessful attempts to operate the continuous payment authority provided the borrower agrees to a refinancing and agrees to the continuous payment authority being reset.[98] The firm must keep a record of the discussions and of the borrower's consent to the resetting of the continuous payment authority in this way.[99]

77. However, if a lender exercises forbearance, in the sense that the lender extends the repayment period without levying interest or other charges (other than a reasonable administration charge),[100] the continuous payment authority can only be operated twice following forbearance but previous unsuccessful attempts to operate the continuous payment authority prior to forbearance are ignored for this purpose.[101]

78. Where the credit agreement provides for payment in instalments, only two continuous payment authority attempts may be made to collect a particular instalment.[102] Furthermore, the lender or owner must not use a continuous payment authority to attempt to collect a subsequent instalment unless the previous instalment has been paid off by a manner other than operation of a continuous payment authority so that there are no arrears, and provided that during a dialogue with the consumer, the lender has reminded the borrower of the date and amount of the next payment.[103]

79. Even in the case of an instalment agreement when forbearance is exercised, a continuous payment authority should only be operated following dialogue with the customer whereby the customer is notified of

95 CONC 7.6.12(1) R.
96 FCA PS14/3 paragraph 5.49.
97 CONC 7.6.12(2) R.
98 CONC 7.6.12(5) R.
99 CONC 7.6.15(3) G.
100 CONC 6.7. 17 R.
101 CONC 7.6.12(3) R.
102 CONC 7.6.13(1) R.
103 CONC 7.6.13(2) R.

the refusal of the continuous payment authority requests and following that customer's consent to the operation of the continuous payment authority.[104]

80. Furthermore, it is an important rule that a borrower shall not take a part payment using a continuous payment authority; only the full amount may be collected.[105] However, if a lender or owner has agreed, as an indulgence to the borrower, to accept reduced payments under a repayment plan with a borrower or hirer, the lender or owner will be able to collect the lesser amounts payable under the repayment plan using the continuous payment authority.[106]

Rolling over HCSTC agreements

81. It will be often tempting for a borrower in financial difficulty to roll over his or her credit facility (i.e. to refinance). But such a process is dangerous for the borrower because the high charges are compounded. The FCA has pointed out that following a second rollover in respect of an HCSTC agreement, a borrower can find him or herself owing twice as much as he or she had originally borrowed; as the FCA has noted, 'excessive rollovers can hide financial difficulty and can lead to a consumer's debt to spiral out of control'.[107]

82. In relation to all types of agreements, no lender should refinance a debt without the borrower's express request, or when refinancing is considered to be against the borrower's best interests.[108] This applies with particular force to HCSTC lenders, given the high level of borrowing costs imposed and the short-term nature of the credit. It will be against the borrower's best interests if the refinancing will result in borrowing costs that are unsustainable in the sense that the borrower will be unable to afford to make the payments in addition to meeting his or her other commitments on a settled basis. The HCSTC lender can only refinance if satisfied that the refinanced loan is sustainable.[109]

83. Before an HCSTC lender refinances, the lender must provide the borrower with an arrears information sheet contained the wording set out at CONC 6.7.2(4) R. The sheet encourages the borrower to seek free advice.

84. Moreover, it is a strict and important rule that an HCSTC lender may not refinance on more than *two* occasions.[110] This is because of the danger of debts spiralling out of control already referred to.

104 CONC 7.6.13(1) R.
105 CONC 7.6.14(1) R.
106 CONC 7.6.14(2) R.
107 FCA PS14/3, paragraph 5.10.
108 CONC 6.7.20 R.
109 CONC 6.7.22 R.
110 CONC 6.7.23.

APR cap

85. One controversial area is whether this type of lending should be subject to an interest rate cap. In its consultation paper CP13/10 published in December 2013, the FCA considered the question. The FCA wished to undertake further research once credit data had been collected. The Treasury, however, were unhappy with this stance and by section 131 of the Financial Services (Banking Reform) Act 2013, the FCA was required to make further rules in relation to high-cost short-term credit 'with a view to securing an appropriate degree of protection of borrowers against excessive charges'. Such rules have now been made and take effect at least in relation to agreements entered into on or after 2 January 2015.[111] There are the following restrictions. The total charges may not exceed the amount of credit; the charges may not amount to more than 0.8 per cent of the credit per day; the default charges may not exceed £15; no compound interest may be charged. Contravention of these requirements renders the agreement irremediably unenforceable.[112]

Taking a pawn

86. A 'pawn' is defined as an article, subject to a pledge; a 'pledge' is defined as the pawnee's rights over an article in pawn.[113] These definitions do no more than explain the meaning of 'pledge' in relation to 'pawn', leaving the meaning of 'pawn' unexplained, except that it can relate only to chattels.

87. It is clear from its context within the Act that the term is to be given its general meaning. A 'pawn' is an article physically deposited with a lender as security for monies advanced by the lender to the borrower. When a person deposits a pawn with a pawnbroker, he or she represent that he or she is the owner or has authority of the owner to do so.[114] There is also an implied warranty to the same effect.[115] The essence of the pawn transaction is that if the borrower fails to make payment under the agreement at the proper time, the lender may, in accordance with the Act, recoup some or all of the amounts owing to him or her on a realisation of the pawn.

88. The pawn is to be contrasted with the bill of sale in that both constitute security over a chattel. A bill of sale is in the nature of a chattel mortgage and possession of the chattel passes to or remains with the borrower. The formalities required with a bill of sale are quite different.

111 CONC 5A.
112 CONC 5A.5.
113 Section 189(1).
114 *Advanced Industrial Technology Corporation Ltd v Bond Street Jewellers Ltd* 2006 EWCA Civ 923.
115 *The Singer Manufacturing Company v Clark* 1880 61 LTR 591.

89. Sections 117 to 122 of the Act do not apply to documents of title or bearer bonds, but section 116 does.[116] The phrase 'documents of title' is not defined in the Act, but there is a definition contained in section 1(4) of the Factors Act 1889. A document of title must allow the holder for the time being of the document some right to possession, control or ownership of the goods. It is not enough that it merely *evidences* the right of ownership. A car registration document is not a document of title as it in itself confers no rights.[117]

90. Sections 117 to 122 also do not apply to non-commercial agreements, but as from 1 April 2014, section 116 now does. A non-commercial agreement is one entered into by a lender when not acting in the course of a business.[118] This is significant as one can imagine circumstances when a person deposits an article with a friend in exchange for a loan. Section 116, discussed below, will now apply to such a transaction but not other provisions.

91. Note that a pawn may never be taken from a minor (someone under the age of 18).[119] An offence is committed if either the lender knew the person to be a minor or if the person presenting the pawn was and appeared to be a minor. The offence is a serious one. It can be tried on indictment before a jury and the offender imprisoned for up to a year. He or she also faces a fine. A contract concluded with a minor contrary to section 114(2) will be void for illegality and the pawn must be returned to him or her.

Entering into the pawn agreement: the regulatory requirements

92. Lending money on the strength of a pawn is a regulated credit agreement and the normal provisions apply subject to any special modifications that are made in the regulatory regime.

93. The pre-contract information required by Schedule 1 of the Consumer Credit (Disclosure of Information) Regulations 2010 has to be provided to a new customer, defined as a customer with whom the pawnbroker has not dealt within the previous three years.[120]

94. The requirements are lessened where a pawnbroker has dealt with a customer within the previous three years. In the case of such a customer, the pawnbroker is required only to tell the customer of his or her right to receive the pre-contract credit information free of charge on request.[121]

116 Section 114(3)(a).
117 *Joblin v Watkins and Roseveare Motors Ltd* [1949] 1 All ER 47.
118 Section 189(1).
119 Section 114(2).
120 Reg 1(6) Consumer Credit (Disclosure of Information) Regulations 2010.
121 Reg 9(2).

95. A new customer must also receive not only the required information, but the required *explanation* of the transaction in accordance with CONC 4.2. With a customer who is not new, the requirements are lessened; the only explanation that has to be provided is that the customer must be told of the consequences of the failure to make the repayments on the due date (i.e. sale of the pawn) and how the right to withdraw may be exercised.[122]

96. No creditworthiness assessment need be carried out in the case of a pawn transaction[123] and exceptionally the pawnbroker can limit its consideration of the suitability of the transaction to the value of the pawn.[124]

97. A pawn transaction will normally be entered into on the trade premises of the pawnbroker and so not be cancellable under the Consumer Credit Act 1974. The customer must be provided with a copy of the agreement under section 61A of the Act.

98. The form of the agreement must comply with the Agreements Regulations 2010 in the usual way.[125] However, there is an additional requirement. The agreement (and the copy of it) must contain a pawn receipt or a separate pawn receipt must be provided.[126]

99. If the pawn receipt is separate, the form of receipt is governed by the Consumer Credit (Pawn Receipts) Regulations 1983.[127] The Regulations stipulate, in addition to the predictable provisions dealing with legibility, heading, date, etc., that the pawn receipt must be signed by or on behalf of the lender and that it must contain a description of the article taken in pawn. The receipt must also carry on its face a statutory form, as set out in the Schedule to the Regulations, giving a brief statement of the rights of the borrower. The borrower will be told of his or her right to redeem the pawn and what to do should he or she lose the pawn receipt. The borrower will also be told, if such is the case, that the goods are not insured by the lender while in pawn; this puts the borrower on notice so that he or she can arrange his or her own insurance if he or she so wishes.

100. The same statutory form must be reproduced in the copy of the credit agreement provided to the borrower if this incorporates the pawn receipt; the body of the agreement must also contain a description of the article taken in pawn (these requirements are imposed by Agreements Regulations 2010,[128] regulation 6).

101. The borrower will have a right to withdraw from the transaction within 14 days of the date of the agreement in accordance with section 66A of the Consumer Credit Act 1974.

122 CONC 4.2.5(6) R.
123 CONC 5.2.1(4) R.
124 CONC 5.3.4 R.
125 A pawn agreement was found to be non-compliant in *Wilson v First County Trust Ltd* 2001 QB 407.
126 Section 114(1).
127 SI 1983/1566.
128 SI 2010/1014.

Record keeping

102. CONC 6.6 imposes obligations on pawnbrokers to keep certain records. The lender must keep a careful record of all dealings with the pawn, including its redemption or realisation.[129] The required information is detailed.[130] The lender has to keep the records for a considerable time period after the transaction has come to an end; the records have to be preserved for the longer of three years from the date of sale or redemption, or five years from the date of taking the pawn.[131]

Borrower's right to redeem

103. The borrower's principal right under the agreement is to redeem the goods on presentation of the pawn receipt and payment of what is owing under the agreement.[132]

104. The goods may be redeemed as of right at any time during the 'redemption period'. This is the longest of the following periods:[133]

(a) six months from the time the pawn was taken;
(b) the period for which credit is provided; or
(c) such longer period as the borrower or lender may agree (such agreement could be purely verbal; it is not necessary that it be enshrined in the credit agreement).

105. From 1 April 2014, this redemption now also appeals to a non-commercial agreement and to a deposit of documents of title.[134]

106. Additionally, the borrower can redeem the goods at any time before actual realisation[135] (although this does not apply to pawns falling within section 120(1)(a) where title to the pawn passes to the lender at the end of the redemption period). The lender may not attach any penalty to late redemption, whether by levying additional charges or by increasing the rate for storage.[136]

107. A special statutory procedure applies if the borrower loses his or her pawn receipt.[137] The borrower normally has to make out a statutory declaration in the prescribed form under the Statutory Declarations Act

129 CONC 6.6.3 R.
130 CONC 6.6.7 R to CONC 6.6.9 R.
131 CONC 6.6.6 R.
132 Section 117(1).
133 Section 116(1), (2).
134 Section 114(3).
135 Section 116(3).
136 Section 116(4).
137 Section 118.

1835. The form of the statutory declaration is set out in the Schedule to the Consumer Credit (Loss of Pawn Receipt) Regulations 1983.[138] The signature on a statutory declaration has to be witnessed by a Justice of the Peace, notary public or solicitor.[139]

108. If the amount of credit does not exceed £75, then there is no need for a statutory declaration and a statement in the form prescribed by the Loss of Pawn Receipt Regulations will suffice provided the pawn broker agrees (it seems the pawnee has a right to insist on a statutory declaration).[140] The prescribed statement must also be signed by the borrower.

109. The statutory declaration (or, where appropriate, the prescribed statement) takes the place of the pawn receipt so that it ceases to have any validity even if it should later be found.[141] Section 117 will apply to the statutory declaration or prescribed statement so that the lender must still refuse to redeem the pawn if he or she has reasonable cause to suspect that the person presenting the declaration or the statement is not the owner of the pawn or authorised to redeem it.

110. As noted above, there are some circumstances when title to the pawn passes to the pawnee; when this happens, the right to redeem is lost. With very small agreements, the title to the pawn passes automatically to the lender at the end of the redemption period. The amount of credit advanced must not exceed £75 (or with running account credit, the credit limit must not exceed £75) and the redemption period must be six months after the article was taken in pawn. Moreover, the pawn, prior to entry into the current agreement, must not have been the subject of an earlier agreement under which there has been a part redemption under section 94(3). If these conditions are satisfied, property in the pawn passes to the lender once the period has come to an end.[142]

Consequences of a failure to redeem

111. For as long as the lender holds goods in pawn, the lender holds the goods as bailee for the borrower and is bound by the standard obligation of a bailee to take reasonable care of the goods, although the bailee will not be liable to the borrower if the goods are damaged without want of care (as to which the bailee has the burden of proof). The lender is not bound to insure the goods and the lender is permitted to make a charge for their storage.

138 SI 1983/1576.
139 Section 18 Statutory Declarations Act 1835.
140 Section 118(1)(b).
141 Section 118(2).
142 Section 120(1)(a).

112. The lender is only excused from redeeming the pawn when the lender reasonably suspects that the person tending the pawn receipt is neither the owner nor authorised by the owner to redeem the pawn.[143]

113. The lender is given an immunity in tort if:

(a) He delivers the pawn in accordance with section 117(1). The borrower and the owner of the goods will have no cause of action against a lender who delivers a pawn to an unauthorised holder of an appropriate pawn receipt, provided that the lender has no reasonable cause to suspect that the holder of the receipt is not the owner of the goods nor unauthorised by the owner to collect them.
(b) In the converse situation where the lender refuses to deliver a pawn in reliance upon section 117(2) because he or she reasonably suspects that the holder of the pawn receipt is not the true owner of the goods nor authorised to receive them. No cause of action exists in these circumstances even if the holder of the receipt actually *is* the owner or *is* in fact authorised to collect the goods. It is clear from section 117 that it is the *duty* of the lender not to part with the pawn where he or she has reasonable excuse for suspicion about the bona fides of the holder.

114. If the lender unreasonably refuses to redeem the pawn, then the lender is liable in damages to the borrower for the loss of the pawn. This will normally equate to the true value of the pawn. If the pawn has particular sentimental value for the borrower, it may be reasonable for the pawnor to have a replacement made in which event the damages will be the amount of the replacement cost.[144]

115. If the lender without such reasonable suspicion refuses to redeem the pawn, he or she commits a criminal offence. Section 119(1) says that the offence is committed if the lender acts 'without reasonable cause'. This is an objective test and the question of 'reasonable cause' must be considered in the light of the general obligations cast upon the lender by the Act. The burden of proof is on the lender to show that he or she had reasonable cause, a burden that must be satisfied on the balance of probabilities.[145]

116. If a person is convicted of unreasonable refusal to deliver a pawn, the court has a further power, exercisable in accordance with section 119(2), to order restitution of the pawn or of any property (including money) into which the pawn has been converted as if the person had been convicted of theft.

143 Section 117(2).
144 *Wilson v Robertsons (London) Ltd* 2006 EWCA Civ 1088.
145 *R.* v *Carr-Briant* [1943] KB 607.

Realisation of the pawn

117. After the end of the redemption period, the lender may realise the pawn. This must be done by sale.[146] The lender must take reasonable care to ensure a proper sale price. The formalities of sale are governed by the Consumer Credit (Realisation of Pawn) Regulations 1983.[147] In every case where the amount of credit advanced is £100 or over or where the credit limit under a running account agreement is £100 or over,[148] the lender has to give at least 14 clear days notice of the impending sale to the borrower.[149]

118. When giving notice to the borrower, the lender has to provide certain statutory particulars.[150] The borrower has to be told the date of the end of the redemption period, the sale price of the article and where and how it is to be sold (in the case of an auction, it is of course the reserve price that has to be stated). The lender must also point out that the borrower can still redeem the article at any time up until sale if he or she tenders the amount due together with the pawn receipt (or statutory declaration).

119. Can the lender correctly serve a notice of intended sale before the end of the redemption period? It seems so. It is clear from section 121(1) that it is the *sale* of the pawn that is the realisation. Sections 120 and 121 say only that realisation must follow the end of the redemption period and nothing about the timing of the notice of intended sale. There is, in fact, nothing inconsistent in the Act or the Regulations with service of a notice of intended sale prior to the end of the redemption period, even though service at this time would otherwise seem rather premature.

120. After the sale takes place (assuming, therefore, that the borrower has not redeemed the pawn in the meantime), the lender must draw up an account and notify the borrower of the result of the sale.

121. The lender will have to calculate:[151]

(a) the amount owing by the borrower at the date of the sale; and
(b) the net proceeds of the sale, which is the amount received less the expenses of the sale.

122. The difference between (a) and (b) is the amount still outstanding to the lender if (a) exceeds (b), and is recoverable as a debt by the lender from the borrower.[152] If (b) exceeds (a), the lender will have to account to the borrower for the balance.[153]

146 Section 121(1).
147 SI 1983/1568.
148 Reg 3.
149 Section 121(1).
150 Schedule 1 to the Regulations.
151 Section 121(5).
152 Section 121(4).
153 Section 121(3).

123. The borrower may complain about the amount realised for the pawn or about the expenses of sale. The burden then shifts to the lender to show that he or she took reasonable care to realise a true market value and that the expenses incurred were reasonable.[154] If the lender fails to discharge this burden, the balance due to or from the borrower will have to be adjusted with the substitution of the true market value and reasonable sale expenses.

124. Once sale has taken place, the lender must notify the borrower of the result.[155] The borrower must be served with the information within 20 working days (which excludes Saturdays, Sundays and public holidays and excludes the date of sale).[156] The borrower must be given information about the sale in writing and in accordance with Schedule 2. The required information includes a statement of the gross amount realised, an itemised list of the expenses of sale, a statement of the amount that would have been needed to redeem the pawn at the date of sale and finally the consequent account balance.

125. Section 121 provides no express sanctions if the provisions in relation to sale are breached. But it is contended that if the provisions are contravened, the sale becomes wrongful and an improper realisation occurs. It follows from this that the lender has wrongfully converted the borrower's property in selling his or her pawn and an action in conversion will lie.[157] It seems irrelevant that the irregularity may have occurred only after sale. The borrower's measure of damages will be based upon the cost of replacing the goods wrongfully sold.

Default notice?

126. Section 130(3) of the Act provides that: 'A time order under section 129(2)(a) shall not be made where the regulated agreement is secured by a pledge if by virtue of regulations 76(5), 87(4) or 98(5) service of a notice is not necessary for enforcement of a pledge.' This envisages that the Consumer Credit (Enforcement, Termination and Default Notice) Regulations 1983[158] might exempt pawn transactions from the need to serve a default notice before a pawn was realised, but in fact they have not done so; the only category of transaction exempted by the Regulations is non-commercial agreements where no security is taken. The applicability of these sections to the realisation of pawns therefore has to be considered.

127. In fact, only section 87 can be relevant since section 87 is the only one of the three provisions that is concerned with enforcement of security

154 Section 121(6), (7).
155 Section 121(3).
156 Reg 2(2) of SI 1983/1568.
157 *Brierly v Kendall* 1852 17 QB 937.
158 SI 1983/1561.

(compare section 87(1)(c) with section 76(1)). Thus, only section 87 has any bearing on the realisation of a pledge.

128. Moreover, even section 87 would rarely seem to apply. Section 87 requires that a default notice be served where the lender seeks to enforce security 'by reason of any breach by the borrower or hirer'. The right to realise security, however, arises because the redemption period has expired (see section 120(1)(b)), not because of breach; the need for a default notice, therefore, does not normally arise, and one is unnecessary in relation to realisation of the pawn.

129. A default notice, moreover, will never be necessary in a case falling within section 120(1)(a) (i.e. where property in a pawn securing credit of less than £75 automatically vests in the lender at the end of the six-month redemption period). This vesting of the property occurs in accordance with the statute and not by any act of the lender. The vesting cannot, therefore, be considered to be 'enforcement' within section 87(1)(e) and no default notice need be served.

Application for a time order

130. The court can make a time order in the circumstances set out in section 129(1) where (in the present context):

(a) the lender seeks an enforcement order normally because of improper execution of the main credit agreement; and
(b) the lender serves a default notice on the borrower.

131. Since, as has been seen, the lender will not normally need to serve a default notice before realisation of the pledge, it is only in the rare case where the lender seeks an enforcement order to enforce the agreement that a borrower becomes entitled to seek a time order.

132. The effect of the borrower's right to apply for a time order is very limited. The effect is to postpone the end of the redemption period by a mere five days.[159] Thereafter, the lender has a *right* to realise the pawn. The actual making of a time order cannot itself delay the process of realisation (there is nothing in section 129 that gives the court this power). The purpose of the five-day extension granted by section 120(2) is obscure.

159 Section 120(2).

15 Operation of ancillary credit activities

Conduct of credit brokers

1. CONC lays down a number of requirements to be followed by credit brokers. Many of these requirements repeat guidance published by the Office of Fair Trading in November 2011 entitled 'Credit Brokers and Intermediaries Guidance'; this guidance has now been made binding by being made into Rules in the Handbook.[1]

2. When a credit broker takes on responsibility for giving information to a customer or receives information from a customer, it is for the credit broker to demonstrate familiarity with the relevant requirements and have adequate procedures in place to ensure the necessary compliance.[2] If a credit broker has undertaken to research the market, the credit broker must conduct a search to the extent stated.[3]

3. Thus, a credit broker has a duty to explain to the customer the key features of the regulated credit agreement in respect of which the introduction is made.[4]

4. If a credit broker provides a quotation, the quotation must contain a statement if security is required.[5] Moreover, if the prospective agreement may be secured on land, then the quotation must contain warning statements about the risks involved, including, where appropriate, the risk to the home if mortgage repayments are not kept up.[6]

5. The credit broker must encourage the customer to read the terms and conditions of the proposed agreement before the customer enters into it and should allow the customer sufficient time for this to be done.[7] Indeed, it is an unfair business practice for a credit broker to hurry a customer into

1 OFT 1388.
2 CONC 6.8.2 G.
3 CONC 5.4.3 R.
4 CONC 2.5.3(1) R.
5 CONC 4.1.4(1) R.
6 CONC 4.1.4(2) R.
7 CONC 2.5.3(3) R.

entering into an agreement or to offer an incentive to the customer to hurry his or her entry into the agreement.[8]

6. The credit broker must also take reasonable steps to ensure that the proposed agreement is not unsuitable for the needs of the customer.[9] This includes an obligation to consider whether the repayments are affordable by the customer.[10]

7. A creditor must point out if a lender or owner is part of the same group of companies as the credit broker.[11] Obviously, the proposed customer needs to be alerted to the existence of a tie-up, which is likely to compromise the independence of the credit broker.

8. The credit broker should also explain how it proposes to use any personal data with which the credit broker may be provided by the customer;[12] this duty is best satisfied by the presentation to the customer of a privacy notice.[13] The Information Commissioner's Office has prepared a Privacy Notices Code of Practice.

9. CONC 2.5.8 lists a number of unfair practices in which a credit broker should not engage; these are principally concerned with the manner in which a credit broker makes contact with a customer.

10. Thus, it is an unfair business practice for a credit broker to make unsolicited calls to telephone numbers kept on the register kept pursuant to regulations 25 and 26 of the Privacy and Electronic Communications (EC Directive) Regulations 2003,[14] save where the firm has obtained details of a customer in the course of negotiations for the sale of a product to the customer.

11. It is an unfair business practice to send emails or make contact via an automated calling system unless the customer has given consent.[15] Obviously, also a customer's refusal to receive such communications must be respected.

12. It is unfair to make a visit at an inconvenient time or to refuse to bring a visit to an end.[16] It is wrong to ask a customer to use a premium rate telephone number,[17] or having done so to speak for an unreasonable period.

13. It is wrong for a credit broker to pressurise a customer into taking out a payment protection product or to offer incentives to take out such a

8 CONC 2.5.8(9) R.
9 CONC 2.5.3(2) R.
10 CONC 5.4.2(2) R.
11 CONC 2.5.3(5) R.
12 CONC 2.5.3(6) R.
13 CONC 2.5.4 G.
14 CONC 2.5.8 R.
15 CONC 2.5.8(2) R.
16 CONC 2.5.8(6) R.
17 CONC 2.5.8(7) R.

product, regardless of whether the product is required as a condition of the credit agreement or is optional.[18]

Fees and commissions

14. Prior to conclusion of the contract, the credit broker must disclose any fee payable by the customer to the credit broker.[19] The circumstances under which the fee is payable must be explained together with the circumstances in which the customer will be entitled to a refund, including under section 155 of the Consumer Credit Act 1974.[20] The agreement for any such fee must be concluded in writing before any regulated credit agreement is entered into.[21]

15. The credit broker must also disclose its fee to the lender so that the lender can calculate the APR.[22]

16. There are circumstances in which the credit broker is obliged to reveal the commission to be paid to the credit broker by the lender or owner or third party. The commission must be revealed in response to a request (which need not be in writing) from the customer for this information.[23] The level of commission must also be revealed if the amount of commission might affect the impartiality of the credit broker or if it may have a material impact on the customer's decision.[24] Obviously, if the commission is very large, there may be circumstances when to reveal the amount of the commission may induce the customer not to proceed through the credit broker. In these circumstances, the amount of commission should be revealed even though it will not be in the best interests of credit brokers to do so. However, CONC 4.5.3 R leaves a discretion to the credit broker that is likely to be exercised in a way that leads to non-disclosure of the fee.

Return of brokerage fees

17. Where the credit broker successfully introduces a customer to a credit or hire agreement, in most instances the broker will be content to receive fees from the lender or owner and will not look to a customer for the fee. However, if the credit or hire transaction does not proceed, then the credit broker will not be entitled to a fee from the lender or owner, and the credit broker may look to the customer for payment of a fee.

18 CONC 2.5.8(14) R.
19 CONC 4.4.2(1) R.
20 CONC 4.4.4(4) R.
21 CONC 4.4.2(2) R.
22 CONC 4.4.2(3) R.
23 CONC 4.5.4 R.
24 CONC 4.5.3 R.

18. However, in many instances, such recourse to the customer is limited to a sum of £5 by section 155 of the Consumer Credit Act 1974 if the customer does not enter into the relevant credit or hire agreement within six months. Furthermore, if a fee has already been paid, any excess over £5 must be returned.[25] Other payments made to the credit broker in connection with the introduction, even if not referred to as fees or commission, are to be treated as such if they form part of the total charge for credit.[26] Repayment of genuine disbursements is not prohibited by the provision.

19. A firm should respond promptly to a request for a refund;[27] it is not necessary for the customer to refer specifically to his or her rights under section 155.[28] Where it is obvious that no transaction is going to be entered into, the credit broker should not make the customer wait six months for the refund.[29]

20. Section 155 applies to regulated agreements. It also applies to an agreement entered into by an individual for the purchase of a dwelling to be occupied by the individual or a relative to be secured on land regardless of whether it is regulated.[30] This is an important provision.

21. Nevertheless, it does not apply to a fee payable to an authorised person who makes an introduction to an authorised person in respect of a prospective regulated mortgage contract, as defined, or home purchase plan.[31] It will be remembered that a regulated mortgage contract is defined as one where the loan is secured by a first charge in connection with a property, at least 40 per cent of which is a dwelling.[32]

22. It also applies to an exempt agreement as provided for by Chapter 14A of Part 2 of the RAO.[33] This exempts a variety of types of credit agreement such as those with certain specified lenders and for certain specified purposes or at low total charge for credit.

23. The question arises whether section 155 applies when the relevant credit or hire agreement is cancelled under a right conferred by the cancellation provisions of the Consumer Credit Act 1974. On one reading, the final words of disregard in section 155(1) are ambiguous; the final words refer to the fee ceasing to be payable or recoverable in excess of £5 'if the introduction does not result in his entering into a relevant agreement within the six month following the introduction (disregarding any agreement which

25 Section 155(1).
26 Section 155(4).
27 CONC 6.8.4 R.
28 CONC 6.8.5(1) G.
29 CONC 6.8.5(3) G.
30 Section 155(2)(b).
31 Section 155(2A).
32 Article 61 RAO.
33 Section 155(2)(c).

is cancelled under section 69(1) or becomes subject to section 69(2))'. It might be argued that cases of cancellation under section 69(1) or section 69(2) were intended to fall outside section 155 altogether (in which event, the fee would not be repayable) but this would not be correct. A refund is not due if an agreement is entered into within a six-month period, but the concluding words of section 155(1) make it clear that entry into an agreement and then its cancellation does not deprive the customer of a right to the return of a fee. This interpretation is in line within the OFT Guidance issued to brokers in 2011 and repeated at CONC 6.8.3(5) G.[34]

Regulation of credit reference agencies

24. A credit reference agency is an organisation that carries on by way of business the regulated activity specified by Article 89B of the RAO.[35] Put shortly, the activity entails the systematic collection of credit information about members of the public and then furnishing that credit information, often to credit brokers and to prospective lenders.

25. A lender that provides a credit reference agency with information about a member of the public owes a duty of care in tort to that member of the public to ensure that the information is accurate. In *Durkin v DGS Retail Ltd*,[36] the lender was found liable in damages to the claimant for having inaccurately informed a credit reference agency that the claimant was in default under the terms of his loan agreement.[37] This wrong information restricted the claimant in his ability to obtain credit, causing him loss. By contrast, in *Smeaton v Equifax plc*,[38] the Court of Appeal held that a credit reference agency does not owe a duty of care in tort to the subject of an incorrect entry.

Obligations of the lender and credit broker

26. The Act and CONC impose obligations on a lender or owner that consults a credit reference agency in order to decide whether to lend money or hire goods. It also imposes obligations on a credit broker that may have become involved in the potential transaction.

27. A lender deciding to refuse credit to a prospective borrower based on credit information obtained by the lender from a credit reference agency must, at the same time as notification of the refusal of credit, notify the borrower that this is the reason for the refusal, as well as the name and

34 OFT 1388 Guidance, Guidance for Credit Brokers and Intermediaries.
35 Section 145(8) Consumer Credit Act 1974; discussed earlier.
36 2014 UKSC 21.
37 *Durkin supra* at [33].
38 2013 EWCA Civ 108.

address and telephone number of the credit reference agency.[39] This only applies where the prospective borrower is an individual.[40]

28. This compulsory notification requirement does not apply where the prospective agreement is a hire agreement or secured on land.[41] Nor does it apply where a credit broker consults a credit reference agency and decides not to refer the matter to a lender.

29. If a prospective lender does not communicate its decision not to enter into a regulated credit agreement directly with the borrower or hirer but leaves this task to a credit broker that has acted in connection with the transaction, the lender or owner must inform the credit broker of the name and address and email address of the credit reference agency at a time no later than the time that the creditor or owner informs the credit broker of its unwillingness to enter into the agreement.[42] However, in many circumstances, the lender does have a duty to inform the prospective borrower directly under section 157(A1); this requirement to notify the credit borrower will apply principally to prospective regulated agreements secured on land to which section 157(A1) does not apply.

30. In other instances, it is open to the borrower to make a request for information about any credit reference agency consulted by making a request in writing.[43] The request can be made of a creditor, owner or negotiator.[44] (This right is available to an individual hirer or debtor in cases of hire agreements and agreements secured on land.)

31. The information need not be provided if the request is made more than 28 days after the end of antecedent negotiations.[45] The response giving the name and address (but not in this context the telephone number) must be given within seven days of receipt of the request.[46] A negotiator must inform the prospective borrower of any credit reference agency consulted by it[47] but also of any information supplied by the lender to the negotiator about any credit reference agency consulted by the creditor in accordance with the duty placed upon the lender under CONC as referred to above.[48] A similar duty applies to a credit broker that has acted in relation to a transaction even if the credit broker does not fall within the definition of negotiator.[49]

39 Section 157(A1) Consumer Credit Act 1974.
40 See the definition of debtor in section 189(1).
41 Section 157(4).
42 CONC 2.4.2 R.
43 Section 157(1).
44 As defined in section 56.
45 Section 157(2).
46 Reg 3 Consumer Credit (Credit Reference Agency) Regulations 2000 SI 2000/290.
47 Pursuant to section 157(1).
48 CONC 2.5.5 R.
49 CONC 2.5.6 R.

32. The lender or owner or negotiator need not give the information if this would contravene the Data Protection Act 1998, or an EU obligation or would be likely to expose someone to a serious risk of violence or intimidation or would be likely to impede the detection of crime or the prosecution of offenders or the administration of justice.[50] However, none of these outcomes seem likely given that the obligation in question is to provide the details of the credit reference agency consulted.

33. The lender or owner or negotiator that fails to comply with these requirements commits a criminal offence, triable summarily only.[51]

Obligations of the credit reference agency under the Data Protection Act 1998

34. Once an individual has received details of any credit reference agency consulted by the lender or owner, the individual may wish to see what it was that the credit reference agency said about him or her. This request will be made under the Data Protection Act 1998. Prior to this Act, the procedure was that given by section 158 of the Consumer Credit Act 1974. The scope of that section has been much restricted so that while it still remains in force, it has little continuing applicability.

35. Section 7 of the Data Protection Act 1998 gives an individual the right to be informed by a data controller (here, the credit reference agency) whether the data controller holds information about him or her, the purpose for which the information is being held and a description of the information. Further, the individual is entitled to have the information communicated to him or her in intelligible form, along with information as to the source of the information.[52]

36. Nevertheless, it is important to note that the Data Protection Act 1998 only requires *information* to be disclosed to the data subject. There is no obligation on a credit reference agency to disclose copies of documents in its possession, although it may do so if it wishes as a means of complying with its information obligations.[53]

37. The credit reference agency is only obliged to provide the information in response to a request in writing and after having received the prescribed fee,[54] but once this has been complied with, the credit reference agency must provide the information promptly and in any event within 40 days.[55]

50 Section 157(2A).
51 Section 157(3).
52 Section 7(1)(c) Data Protection Act 1998.
53 *Re Southern Pacific Personal Loans Ltd* 2013 EWHC 2485.
54 Section 7(2) Data Protection Act 1998.
55 Section 7(10).

38. Section 7 applies to credit reference agencies, as supplemented by section 9 of the Act. By section 9(2), any request for information directed at a credit reference agency can be limited to a request for personal data related to that person's financial standing and will be assumed to do so.

39. In addition to supplying the information, the credit reference agency must also provide the individual with a statement of his or her rights under section 159 of the Consumer Credit Act 1974 to have this information corrected.[56] The statement must follow the form set out in Schedule 1 to the Consumer Credit (Credit Reference Agency) Regulations 2000.[57] It sets out in some detail the entitlement of the borrower to require false information to be corrected and the procedure for this as set out below.

40. It also refers to the possibility of appealing to the Information Commissioner any correction notice that is not considered acceptable by the credit reference agency.

Obligations of the credit reference agency under section 158 of the Consumer Credit Act 1974

41. There is a very small category of instances where the right to information from a credit reference agency is based on section 158 of the Consumer Credit Act 1974.

42. This applies to requests for information from a partnership comprising two or three partners, at least one of whom is not a limited company, and from an unincorporated association, at least one of whose members is not a limited company.[58] This is a very small category. The reason for this is that this category had rights under the Consumer Credit Act 1974 prior to the Data Protection Act 1998 but have no rights under that Act. So as not to prejudice the position of this small category of persons, section 158 of the Consumer Credit Act 1974 has been preserved for this category.

43. Just as under the Data Protection Act, the partnership or unincorporated association can send a request for the information to the credit reference agency that has been identified. A fee of £2 is payable.[59] The credit reference agency then has seven days to respond with the information in its possession;[60] to be precise, it must 'give the consumer a copy of the file relating to it', which is a more extensive obligation than under the Data Protection Act 1998.[61] The file in this context means all the information kept about an individual by the credit reference agency,

56 Section 9(3) Data Protection Act 1998.
57 SI 2000/290.
58 Section 158(4).
59 Section 158(1)(c).
60 Reg 3 Consumer Credit (Credit Reference Agency) Regulations 1977 SI 2000/290.
61 Section 158(1).

regardless of how the information is stored and if the file is not in plain English (e.g. if it is in electronic code), it means a copy of the file translated into plain English.[62]

44. The response must be accompanied by a statement to the borrower setting out the borrower's rights of correction.[63] The form of the statement is that specified by Schedule 2 of the Consumer Credit (Credit Reference Agency) Regulations 2000.[64] This must set out the rights of the credit reference agency and the borrower to apply to the FCA.

45. Non-compliance with any of the requirements of section 158, where they apply, is a criminal offence, triable summarily only.

46. If the right requirements are satisfied, the FCA may lessen the obligation to comply with section 158. In the case of a business partnership or unincorporated association carrying on a business to which section 158 applies, the FCA may, on application from the credit reference agency, reduce the obligation to disclose the whole file provided the FCA considers that compliance with section 158 would be detrimental to the service provided by the credit reference agency to its customers and provided the FCA considers that it probably will not be detrimental to the interests of the business consumers to make the direction.[65]

47. Where such a direction is made, then the credit reference agency must respond within seven days but may limit the information it discloses to that directed by the FCA,[66] along with a statement of rights in the form set out at Schedule 3 to the Consumer Credit (Credit Reference Agency) Regulations 2000.[67]

The right of the consumer to seek correction of an entry

48. If the borrower considers that the information disclosed to him or her is incorrect, he or she can apply to have it changed.[68] This applies whether the borrower has obtained the information under the Data Protection Act 1998 or under section 158 of the Consumer Credit Act 1974. The individual needs to write to the credit reference agency to explain what is wrong with the information kept about him or her.[69]

49. The credit reference agency has to reply within 28 days saying what action the credit reference agency intends to take as a result of this

62 Section 158(5).
63 Section 158(2).
64 SI 2000/290.
65 Section 160(1).
66 Section 160(3).
67 SI 2000/290.
68 Section 159(1).
69 The reference to notice in section 159(1) is to written notice; see the definition at section 189(1).

notification; if the file has been amended, a copy of the amended file must be included.[70]

50. If the individual is dissatisfied with the reply of the credit reference agency, then the borrower can write his or her own note of the corrections to be added to the file and supplied as part of the information to be furnished on any future occasion.[71] This note must be provided by the borrower within 28 days of receipt of the response from the credit reference agency.[72] Alternatively, if the credit reference agency has failed to reply to the correction request from the borrower, this note must be supplied within eight weeks from the date of the original letter. The correction note must not be more than 200 words long.

51. The credit reference agency then has a choice. It can accept or reject the correction notice. Either way, the credit reference agency must to notify the borrower of its decision within 28 day or it can apply to the relevant authority for directions if it considers that the proposed notice is incorrect or defamatory or for some other reason unsuitable.[73]

52. If the credit reference agency rejects the notice, then under the Data Protection Act, the relevant authority from whom the credit reference agency may seek directions or to whom the borrower may appeal is the Information Commissioner. In the case of section 158, the relevant authority is the FCA.[74]

53. In a case where the FCA has made a direction within section 160 whereby less than the whole of the file has been disclosed, the consumer may challenge this before the FCA seeking further disclosure. The FCA can then direct the credit reference agency to provide the FCA with a copy of the file and the FCA can then take the decision as to how much of the file should properly be disclosed to the consumer.[75]

54. Once the entry held by the credit reference agency has been corrected under section 159, a copy of the corrected information must be supplied to every person that has been supplied by the credit reference agency with the false entry within a period of one month prior to the request being received for the entry to be corrected.[76] If the entry itself was not communicated within the one-month period, but the credit reference agency sent out information that was based on the incorrect entry (e.g. a credit rating), then the credit reference agency must send out corrected information in the form in which it would have been sent out if the entry had been corrected at the time that the information was originally sent.[77]

70 Section 159(2).
71 Section 159(3).
72 Section 159(3).
73 Section 159(5).
74 Section 159(8).
75 Section 160(5).
76 CONC 9.2.3 R.
77 CONC 9.2.2(2) R.

55. The procedure to be followed in an appeal to the Information Commission or the FCA as appropriate, whether the appeal is by the borrower or the credit reference agency, is set out at regulation 5 of the Consumer Credit (Credit Reference Agency) Regulations.[78] Any application to the relevant authority made by the credit reference agency must be accompanied by the file as well as relevant correspondence.

Debt advice and debt management agreement

Requirements prior to contract

56. CONC 8 applies to those firms providing debt counselling, debt adjusting and credit information services. It covers both for-profit and not-for-profit organisations.

57. A debt management firm must point out, on first contact, that free sources of advice are available, in particular from the Money Advice Service.[79]

58. A firm must provide the borrower with pre-contract information on a durable medium about the services that the firm can provide and the terms thereof.[80] In particular, information must be given about the cost of a firm's services as well as other charges that may arise.[81]

59. Before giving any advice or recommendation, the firm must make an assessment of the borrower's financial position and personal circumstances along with any other matters that may be relevant.[82] The firm must point out the various risks and disadvantages associated with each option.[83] Any advice given about a debt solution must be presented in a durable medium.[84] If a firm feels unable to help a person, perhaps because the person will be unable to afford the firm's fees, the firm must refer the borrower to an appropriate not-for-profit body.[85]

60. The firm must disclose any commission arrangement it has with any third party and, if asked by the borrower, disclose the amount of that commission.[86]

78 SI 2000/290.
79 CONC 8.2.4 R.
80 CONC 8.3.1 R.
81 CONC 8.3.1(3) R.
82 CONC 8.3.7(2) R.
83 CONC 8.3.4(2) R.
84 CONC 8.3.4 R.
85 CONC 8.3.7(3) R.
86 CONC 8.7.4(1) R.

The debt management agreement

61. Before any fees are received,[87] a borrower must be provided with a written debt management agreement containing stipulated terms.[88] This must include details of the charges that the customer will have to pay and the circumstances in which the customer may terminate.

62. The fees charged by the debt management company must not undermine the ability of a customer to enter into a debt management plan. So the debt management company must not prioritise the payment of its own fees.[89]

63. It is likely to be viewed as undermining the debt management plan if more than half the monthly payment made by a customer goes towards the fees charged by the debt management firm.[90]

64. Moreover, the agreement must not impose unreasonable cancellation charges in an amount exceeding the actual costs necessarily incurred by the firm in providing the service.[91]

65. There are a number of terms that may *not* be included in such a contract, including a term excluding any liability of the debt management firm, a term that restricts the ability of the borrower to communicate with the lender directly, or one that excludes the right to a refund.[92]

The financial statement

66. As a vital part of attempting to agree a debt management plan with a lender on behalf of the borrower, the debt management company will need to prepare and send out a financial statement on behalf of the borrower to the lender. It will be on the basis of this that a debt repayment plan will be negotiated. It is, of course, a requirement that the statement paints an accurate and complete picture of the borrower's financial position and the availability of any surplus income.[93] The borrower must be asked to approve the statement before it is sent.[94]

67. The financial statement must be kept under review. If circumstances change, for instance due to a change in the charges of the debt management company, then a revised financial statement must be submitted to the lender.[95]

87 CONC 8.7.6(3) R.
88 CONC 8.4.1 R.
89 CONC 8.7.2(1) R.
90 CONC 8.7.3(1) G.
91 CONC 8.7.6(6) R.
92 CONC 8.4.3 R.
93 CONC 8.5.1 R.
94 CONC 8.5.1(3) R.
95 CONC 8.7.4(2) R.

The debt solution proposed

68. Great care should be taken by a debt management company before it recommends to a borrower, prior to a debt solution being agreed, that the borrower should not make one or more contractual repayments to the lender. If this advice is given, the debt management company must be able to demonstrate that this advice was in the best interests of the customer.[96] The FCA considers that it is normally in the best interests of the borrower to make contractual payments, unless the effect of this will be that the borrower will have insufficient money to meet basic expenditure on necessaries.[97] Where the debt management firm has advised that contractual interest payments should not be met in full, the debt management firm must review this advice if it becomes apparent that the effect of not making the payments is not in the best interests of the borrower.[98]

Operating the debt management agreement

69. If it becomes apparent that the debt solution put forward was inappropriate, then the firm must offer a refund of the fees charged for that advice.[99] If the firm feels that it is desirable to change the debt solution by switching options, then this must be fully explained to the borrower.[100]

70. The firm must keep the borrower informed of the state of negotiations with the lender, including if those negotiations are met with hostility by the lender.[101] The customer is entitled to copies of all correspondence passing between the firm and the lender.[102]

71. Moreover, a firm must keep a debt management plan under review, maintaining contact with the borrower.[103] If the borrower's financial circumstances change, so must the debt management plan.[104]

72. The customer must be sent a financial statement at the start of the debt management plan and at least annually thereafter or at his or her reasonable request.[105]

96 CONC 8.6.1 R.
97 CONC 8.6.4 G.
98 CONC 8.6.5 R.
99 CONC 8.7.4(3) R.
100 CONC 8.7.4(2) R.
101 CONC 8.8.1(4),(5) R.
102 CONC 8.8.1(6) R.
103 CONC 8.8.1(2) R.
104 CONC 8.8.1(3) R.
105 CONC 8.8.1(8) R.

Operating an electronic lending platform

73. CONC regulates a firm that is engaged in operating an electronic lending platform within Article 36H; Article 36H makes it a condition that before a regulated activity arises, not only must there be an electronic platform, but the operator must handle the repayments from the borrower and take responsibility for collecting debts due from the borrower. Specifically, CONC imposes requirements on what are known as P2P agreements. P2P are agreements concluded between borrower and lender and to which the firm operating the electronic platform is not a party, but are arranged through and by the operator. Moreover, the borrower must be an individual who must either borrow less than £25,000 or the loan must not be predominantly for business purposes.[106] It is also a P2P agreement if the lender is an individual.

74. It is important to note that the lender in respect of an agreement entered into through an electronic platform may frequently be an individual not acting in the course of business, with the consequence that the agreement will be classified as a non-commercial agreement.[107] The further consequence of this is that many of the requirements imposed by the Consumer Credit Act normally applicable in connection with agreements entered into with a commercial lender will not apply to agreements concluded through an electronic platform. CONC aims to protect borrowers by requiring the operator of the electronic platform in some instances to provide the borrower with equivalent protections.

Pre-contract information and explanations

75. Thus, the firm is required to provide a borrower with an explanation about certain features of the loan agreement, both when the lender is lending as part of a consumer credit business and when the lender is not engaged in business.[108] This does not apply when the credit will exceed £60,260 or when the loan will be secured on land, but even in this instance, CONC suggests that an explanation is given.[109]

76. The matters that must be explained include features in the credit agreement that may make it unsuitable, the amount that the borrower will have to pay periodically and the principle consequences to the borrower if the borrower defaults, including the risk of repossession.[110] The explanation must be given orally or in writing.[111]

106 See the definition of P2P agreement in the FCA Handbook Glossary.
107 As defined by section 189(1) Consumer Credit Act 1974.
108 CONC 4.3.4(1) R.
109 CONC 4.3.3 G.
110 CONC 4.3.2(2) R.
111 CONC 4.3.2(3) R.

77. If the lender is a commercial lender, the lender will have to provide the borrower with the pre-contractual information specified by the Disclosure of Information Regulations 2010 in the normal way. In these circumstances, the firm operating the electronic platform is required to advise the borrower to consider the information and to ensure that when the information is disclosed in person, the borrower can take the information away.[112] The borrower must also be provided with an opportunity to ask questions about the agreement.

78. On top of the requirement to give the borrower *information*, the borrower must also receive the *explanation* of the agreement required by CONC 4.2; the requirements apply as if the firm was the lender.[113]

79. In every case, when a P2P agreement is secured on a person's home is entered into, the firm must give a warning notice to the borrower in the following terms:[114] 'YOUR HOME MAY BE REPOSSESSED IF YOU DO NOT KEEP UP REPAYMENTS ON A MORTGAGE OR ANY OTHER DEBT SECURED ON IT.'

The right of withdrawal from a P2P agreement

80. CONC 11.2 requires the lender, save in a case when the credit exceeds £60,260,[115] to ensure that the borrower is given a right to withdraw from the P2P agreement, without any obligation on the borrower to give reasons for his or her actions.[116] Furthermore, the contract between the lender and borrow must not impose any preconditions or further obligations in connection with the exercise of this right.[117]

81. The right is exercisable, by giving oral or written notice to the firm on behalf of the lender, within 14 days of the P2P agreement (or from 14 days from the date that the firm gave the pre-contract explanation given by CONC 4.3 if later). The pre-contract explanation given by the firm to the borrower should have pointed out the effect of the exercise of the right of withdrawal.[118]

82. If the borrower exercises the right, the borrower will have to return any money that has been lent, together with interest paid at the contractual rate. The borrower must pay this sum within 30 days of withdrawal.[119]

112 CONC 4.3.4(1)(borrower) R.
113 CONC 4.3.5 R.
114 CONC 4.3.6 R.
115 CONC 11.2.2 R.
116 CONC 11.2.3 R.
117 CONC 11.2.4 R.
118 CONC 4.3.4(2)(e) R.
119 CONC 11.2.3(4) R.

Arrears notice obligations

83. The Consumer Credit Act imposes a requirement on a lender to serve a borrower with an arrears notice once a borrower has run up a certain level of arrears, or once the borrower is at risk of having to pay a default sum. In the case of a fixed sum agreement, this arrears notice has to be served initially once the threshold requirements have been reached and thereafter every six months. In the case of a running account agreement, the arrears notice can be incorporated into the relevant running account statements. However, the obligation does not apply to non-commercial agreements.[120]

84. CONC imposes parallel obligations to serve an arrears notice on a borrower, in relation to fixed sum agreements,[121] running account agreements[122] and default sum liabilities[123] but this does not apply if the lender has a pre-existing obligation to serve an arrears notice.[124] Also, the obligation does not apply if the amount of fixed sum credit advanced was less than £50.[125] An arrears information sheet must accompany every arrears notice. This is the same obligation as applied to an arrears notice served by a lender,[126] although there are some minor modifications to be made to the statements made in arrears notice by comparison with that served by a lender.

85. In the case of a fixed sum agreement, the arrears notice must be served initially within 14 days of the threshold conditions arising, and then every six months thereafter.[127] In the case of a running account agreement, the arrears notice must be provided with any statement to be provided by the firm in connection with the agreement.

High-cost short-term credit agreements

86. High cost short term credit agreements arranged through an electronic lending platform are subject to a number of restrictions. The total charges may not exceed the amount of the credit; the charges may not amount to more than 0.8 per cent of the credit per day; compound interest may not be charged.[128] Contravention of these requirements renders the agreement irremediably unenforceable.[129]

120 Sections 86B(12A), 86C(7), 86D(8).
121 CONC 7.17 R.
122 CONC 7.18 R.
123 CONC 7.19 R.
124 CONC 7.17.3(5) R, CONC 7.18.2(4) R.
125 CONC 7.17.2(1) R.
126 CONC 7.17.5(4) R.
127 CONC 7.17.4 R.
128 CONC 5A.4.
129 CONC 5A.5.

16 Powers of the court

The Financial Ombudsman Service

The power of the court to make an enforcement order

1. The Act prescribes a number of circumstances in which a lender or owner needs to apply to the court for an enforcement order in accordance with section 127 in order to be able to take certain types of enforcement action.

When an enforcement order is needed

2. The most important of these circumstances is if the agreement has been improperly executed[1] in some way so that it is enforceable with leave of the court only.[2] Improper execution can take a number of different forms:

(a) a failure of the agreement to comply with the Agreements Regulations in some respect;
(b) a failure to ensure the agreement is signed correctly or at all;
(c) a failure to supply a required copy or copies of the agreement;
(d) a failure to comply with the Cancellation Notices and Copies of Document Regulations.

3. There will also be a need to obtain an enforcement order when there has been a failure to provide the borrower or hirer with the required information to be given in advance of conclusion of the agreement in accordance with the Disclosure of Information Regulations 2004 and 2010 as applicable.[3]

4. Just as an enforcement order is needed to enforce an agreement not properly executed, so likewise an enforcement order is needed to enforce an improperly executed security instrument, whether that enforcement is sought against the borrower or hirer or against a third party.[4]

1 Within the meaning of section 65(1).
2 Section 127(1)(a).
3 Section 127(1)(za).
4 Section 127(1)b).

5. An enforcement order is also needed where there has been a failure to supply a copy of an authorised business or non-business overdraft agreement on a borrower,[5] and when there has been a failure to comply with certain requirements when a negotiable instrument has been taken as security.[6]

Irredeemable unenforceability

6. Prior to the Consumer Credit Act 2006, there were certain sets of circumstances in which the court had no option but to refuse to make an enforcement order. This state of affairs was referred to by Lord Hoffmann as 'irredeemable unenforceability' in *Dimond v Lovell.*[7] Irredeemable unenforceability meant that the lender or owner was left without any recourse under the agreement at all. Plainly, if a borrower or hirer could establish irredeemable unenforceability, this would place the borrower or hirer in a very advantageous position.

7. The circumstances giving rise to irredeemable unenforceability were identified in section 127(3) and (4) and arose when:

(a) the agreement that had been signed did not contain certain core terms (even if other requirements of the Agreements Regulations may not have been satisfied);
(b) there had been a failure by the lender to supply a copy of the agreement prior to the commencement of proceedings;[8] and
(c) when the requirements in respect of the form and service and inclusion of cancellable notices provided for by section 64(1) had not been complied with.[9]

8. These requirements meant that very minor infringements were capable of rendering the agreement entirely unenforceable. This led to a proliferation of technical defences and gave rise to expressions of judicial unease, for instance in *Goshawk Dedicated (No 2) Ltd v Bank of Scotland.*[10]

9. The injustice or perceived injustice caused by irredeemable unenforceability led to it being suggested that irredeemable unenforceability was incompatible with the Human Rights Act 1998. The argument, however, was rejected by the House of Lords in *Wilson v First County Trust ltd (No 2).*[11]

5 Section 127(1)(zb).
6 Section 127(1)(d).
7 2002 1 AC 384 at page 397F.
8 Section 127(4)(a).
9 Section 127(4)(b).
10 2006 2 All ER 610 at [46] per Sir Francis Ferris.
11 2004 1 AC 816.

10. Fortunately, section 127(3) and (4) was repealed by Consumer Credit 2006. However the provisions, although repealed by section 15 of the Consumer Credit Act 2006, remain in force for the purpose of the enforcement of agreements entered into before 6 April 2007[12] so that arguments based on irredeemable unenforceability may occasionally still continue to be raised.

Approach of the court of an application for an enforcement order

11. The approach of the court is spelt out by section 127(2) in the following terms: 'The court shall dismiss the application if, but only if, it considers it just to do so having regard to – (i) prejudice caused to any person by the contravention in question, and the degree of culpability for it; and (ii) the powers conferred on the court by subsection (2) and sections 135 and 136.'

12. Thus, the court is to lean in favour of granting an enforcement order and is to bear in mind its various powers before refusing an order. If the court refuses an application for an enforcement order, it may make a declaration to this effect, and if such a declaration is made then no fresh application can be made.[13] Any interested party can also apply for a declaration.

13. Section 127(2) allows the court, when it considers it just in order to compensate the borrower for any prejudice suffered by any infringement in question, to reduce or discharge any amount payable by the borrower or hirer under the agreement.

14. Section 136 contains a power in the court to amend the terms of any agreement or security consequential upon any such reduction. Section 135 contains a power to suspend the operation of an order or to make it conditional. Although not directly referred to, the court may also make a time order on an application for an enforcement order.[14]

15. The court has a considerable degree of discretion whether or not to make an enforcement order and provided the first instance judge makes a decision on the basis of correct principles, an appellate court will be reluctant to disagree.[15]

12 Paragraph 11 Schedule 3 Consumer Credit Act 2006.
13 Section 142(1).
14 Section 129(1)(a).
15 *Nissan Finance v Lockhart* 1993 CCLR 39.

16. Having exercised its powers under this section, the court may later vary the terms of an enforcement order.[16]

Procedure

17. The application must be brought in England and Wales or in Northern Ireland in the County Court.[17] In Scotland, it should be brought in the Sheriff Court wherever the borrower or hirer resides.[18] If an application is brought in the wrong court, it can be transferred to the correct court,[19] although the court also has a discretion to strike out in circumstances when a lender or owner has deliberately chosen to bring the case in the wrong court. All parties to the agreement, including any surety, should be made parties to the action.[20]

18. In England and Wales, the parties must use the Consumer Credit Act procedure provided for by Practice Direction 7B.[21] The lender or owner must serve its Particulars of Claim with the claim form, which must state that it is a Consumer Credit Act claim, and the Particulars of Claim must set out the circumstances that require the lender or owner to seek an enforcement order.[22]

Power of the court to make a time order

19. A borrower or hirer can apply for a time order entitling the borrower or hirer to pay by instalments in respect of a sum of money in arrears. A time order can also be sought when further time is sought to remedy a non-financial breach.

When a time order can be sought

20. A time order can be sought in a number of discrete situations,[23] namely:

(a) whenever a lender or owner is seeking to recover arrears due under a regulated agreement;
(b) whenever a lender or owner is trying to recover goods or land in relation to a regulated agreement, which for these purposes includes a regulated mortgage contract;[24]

16 Section 135(4).
17 Section 141(1), (4).
18 Section 141(3A).
19 Section 141(2).
20 Section 141(5).
21 Paragraph 6B, Practice Direction 7B.
22 Paragraph 7.4(2), Practice Direction 7B.
23 Section 129(1).
24 Section 126(2).

(c) whenever a lender or owner has served on the borrower or hirer an enforcement notice under section 76, or a default notice under section 87, or a termination notice under section 98;
(d) whenever a borrower or hirer has been served with an arrears notice under section 86B or section 86C, but some special conditions attach to this as will be set out below; and
(e) whenever a lender or owner is applying for an enforcement order under section 127.

21. Having been served with an arrears notice under section 86B or section 86C, the borrower or hirer cannot immediately apply for a time order; the borrower or hirer must first have served a notice under section 129A before applying for a time order. This notice must set out the intention to apply for a time order, proposals for paying the arrears and invite the borrower or hirer to discuss them.[25] Fourteen days must then elapse before the borrower or hirer applies for a time order. The purpose of this procedure is manifestly to try to circumvent the need for a time order application.

22. Section 129(1) does not expressly state that a surety can apply for a time order but this seems to be the implication behind the powers given to the court under section 129(2), which enable the court to make an instalments order in respect of a surety.

The powers of the court on a time order

23. In respect of an application for a time order arising out of arrears, the court can, after taking into account the means of the borrower or hirer and any surety, make an order for the payment of instalments by the borrower or hirer or any surety.[26] In considering whether to make a time order, the court must consider the interests of both the borrower or hirer and the lender or owner.[27]

24. It is clear that the powers of the court in respect of a time order are limited to the sums in arrears. The only power given to the court to reschedule payments falling due in the *future* is given in relation only to hire purchase and conditional sale agreements.[28]

25. Nevertheless, in the case of possession proceedings made in respect of a mortgage debt, the effect of the proceedings is itself to trigger an obligation to repay the entire amount of principal and all arrears without the need to serve a separate demand.[29] The court will frequently suspend a mortgage possession order. So in respect to this category of proceedings,

25 Section 129A(2).
26 Section 129(2)(a).
27 *First National Bank Ltd v Syed* 1990 2 All ER 250.
28 Section 130(2).
29 *Southern and District Finance plc v Barnes* 1996 1 FCR 679.

the court is in a position to make an order in respect of the entire amount outstanding including the principal sum. Importantly, both sections 129 and 135 apply to a regulated mortgage contract despite the fact that such a contract is exempt for the purposes of the Consumer Credit Act 1974.[30]

26. If a court makes an instalment order, it may make a consequential order reducing the rate of interest payment on the arrears so as to reflect this, pursuant to the powers given to the court to vary the terms of an agreement under section 136.[31] The time order jurisdiction therefore has the effect of granting a substantive alleviation of the debt rather than merely rescheduling it. So in the case of *Southern District Finance v Barnes*, by way of example, the court reduced the rate of interest on the arrears from 1.75 per cent per month to 1 per cent per month.

27. In the case of a non-financial claim, the court can extend the time for remedying a breach of the agreement, alternatively increasing the time for payment of any compensation.[32]

28. In the case of a hire agreement, the court cannot extend the contractual period of hire.

The effect of a time order

29. While a time order is in operation, the lender or owner must not take the steps referred to in section 87(1) (i.e. that could have formed the basis of service of a default notice).[33] This means that in relation to the breach in respect of which the time order has been made, the lender or owner cannot terminate the agreement, recover possession of any goods of land, demand earlier payment of any sum (e.g. under an accelerated payments provision), restrict or withdraw any right of the borrower or hirer under the agreement, or enforce any security.

30. Nor can the lender or owner activate any secondary provision that the lender or owner could otherwise have relied upon in respect of the breach that is the subject matter of the time order. This is directed at accelerated payments provisions.[34]

31. Most importantly, if the borrower or hirer complies with the terms of a time order, the breach in respect of which the time order has been made is treated as if it never occurred.[35]

32. Furthermore, in the case of a time order made in relation to a hire purchase, conditional sale or lease agreement, the borrower or hirer

30 Section 127(2).
31 *Southern and District Finance plc v Barnes* 1996 1 FCR 679.
32 Section 129(2)(b).
33 Section 130(5)(a).
34 Section 130(5)(b).
35 Section 130(5)(c).

continues to be the custodian of the goods, and therefore owes duties in relation to them, notwithstanding the agreement may have ended.[36]

33. Given that a time order can bring about a reduction in the interest rates payable under the agreement, it is an advantageous weapon in the hands of the borrower or hirer, particularly since the provisions apply to the important category of regulated mortgage contracts. But of course the court has to be satisfied, based on evidence of the means of the borrower or hirer, that this is a just course for the court to take.

Procedure

34. In England and Wales, proceedings must be started in the County Court, and in Scotland in the Sheriff Court. In England and Wales, when the application is made by the borrower or hirer, it is subject to the Consumer Credit Act procedure contained in CPR Practice Direction 7B. If the claim is brought by the borrower or hirer, it must be in the court of his residence or his place of business, or if it relates to the possession of property, where the property is situated.[37]

35. The Particulars of Claim must be served with the claim form and must state that it is a Consumer Credit Act claim.[38] Where the application is for a time order, the Practice Direction sets out detailed requirements for the Particulars of Claim.[39] In particular, where the application is for an instalments order, the claim must set out the amount of the arrears that are admitted, together with the proposals for payments *and* details of means. In a non-financial case, the Particulars of Claim must set out proposals for remedying any breach.[40]

36. Only if the borrower and lender agree on an instalment arrangement can the court proceed without evidence of means.[41] In other instances, it is clear that evidence of means is a prerequisite before a court has jurisdiction to make a time order. However, a statement of means contained in the Particulars of Claim has the status of evidence and might be sufficient in an appropriate case.

37. In the case of an application for the return of protected goods in the context of a hire purchase or conditional sale agreement, if the borrower admits the claim, the borrower may file an offer of terms setting out the borrower's terms for a time order coupled with a suspended order.[42] If the

36 Section 130(4).
37 Paragraph 4.3, Practice Direction 7B.
38 Paragraph 7.1, Practice Direction 7B.
39 Paragraph 7.3, Practice Direction 7B.
40 Paragraph 7.3(11), Practice Direction 7B.
41 Section 130(1).
42 Paragraph 8.1, Practice Direction 7B.

borrower subsequently does not appear, the court may nevertheless treat these terms as sufficient evidence that the property is in the possession of the hirer.[43]

38. A time order, once made, can be subsequently varied or revoked.[44]

39. If, as will often be the case, the borrower or hirer wishes the court to make a time order having been served with possession proceedings issued under CPR Part 55, then the borrower or hirer can either seek a time order in his or her defence to the proceedings or take out a separate application for a time order.[45] The court has power to suspend a possession order in these cases.[46]

Powers of the court in relation to recovery of goods

40. The court has a number of specific powers in respect of applications by the lender or owner for the recovery of goods; the making of return orders and transfer orders is specific to hire purchase and conditional sale agreements, whereas section 132 contains powers specific to hire agreements. Orders in relation to hire agreements are known as orders for specific delivery.

Return orders

41. Return orders are orders made by the court in respect of regulated hire purchase or conditional sale agreements for the return to the borrower of goods to which the order relates.[47] Section 133 says the court 'may', not 'must', make such an order if 'it appears to the court just to do so'.

42. The court may make a suspended order or conditional order under section 135, for example on condition that the borrower, hirer or guarantor pays the unpaid balance at such times and in such amounts as the court may order (pursuant to a time order) and on such other conditions as the court thinks just (for example, the rectification of a non-financial breach). By section 130(2), the court also has the power to reschedule not only past instalments, but also future instalments not yet fallen due under the hire purchase or conditional sale agreement. The court may combine an order reducing the level of instalments with an order varying the terms of the agreement under section 136. But the court cannot suspend an order if in any doubt about the borrower's continued possession of the goods.[48]

43 Thereby satisfying section 135(2).
44 Section 130(6).
45 Paragraph 7, Part 55A Practice Direction.
46 Section 135.
47 Section 133(1)(b)(i).
48 Section 135(2).

It follows from this that a court cannot suspend an order if the borrower does not appear.

43. Once an order for suspension has been made, either side may return to the court for an order that the period of suspension be varied.[49] This must include a revocation of the order. If the borrower pays off what is owing, and this will include the lender's reasonable costs, the lender's right to seek return of the goods is revoked[50] and title in the goods will pass to the borrower.[51] In fact, section 133(4) and (5) operates even if the return order is not suspended. The borrower is entitled to pay off all that is due up until the time that the goods actually pass into the possession of the lender. If the borrower does this, the borrower will be entitled to keep the goods, and title in them will pass to him or her. Section 133(4) refers to the borrower paying the balance of the 'total price and the fulfillment of any other necessary conditions' but there is no reason why the borrower should not receive a rebate for early settlement if appropriate.

44. If the court feels that a borrower may dispose of or secrete goods during a period of suspension, it may make interim orders for the preservation of those goods (see *Faith Panton Property Ltd. v Hodgetts*[52] for the powers of the court to preserve assets *after* judgment). Section 131 will not, in fact, apply (although parallel orders can be made) since protection orders are orders made pending the determination of proceedings.

45. If the borrower refuses to return the goods, the court can revoke the return order and order the borrower to pay the balance of the hire purchase or conditional sale price referable to the relevant goods.[53] This provision is unusual in that the normal alternative to an order for specific delivery is an order for payment of the *value* of goods. The different formulation in section 133(6) could work either in favour of the borrower or lender (but most likely the lender) depending upon the amounts outstanding under the agreement.

Transfer order

46. When a hire purchase or conditional sale agreement relates to several goods, the court may (it is not required to do so) vest certain of the goods in the borrower and order the return of others to the lender. Under the Hire Purchase Acts, such an order was commonly known as a 'split order'. The term adopted by the Consumer Credit Act for such an order is a

49 Section 135(4).
50 Section 133(4).
51 Section 133(5).
52 1981 1 WLR 927.
53 Section 133(6).

'transfer order'[54] presumably because title to some of the goods is transferred to the borrower pursuant to the order.

47. The court's power to make a transfer order is limited; the court will have to ensure that the requirements of section 133(3) are satisfied. These requirements require the court to ascertain the following:

(a) The total price under the agreement. This (see the definition in section 189) is a reference to the total amount of the deposit and all the instalments plus the option fee in the case of a hire purchase agreement.
(b) The element of the total price attributable to the goods that it is sought to transfer to the borrower. The agreement may itself specify how the total price is to be apportioned but it probably will not. The proper apportionment will then be a matter for the court to decide in line with what is reasonable.[55] The obvious approach for the court to take is to apportion the total price in relation to the cash prices of the goods in question.
(c) The amount already paid under the agreement. If the borrower has failed to pay some amount owing in relation to the goods, other than a sum due under the hire purchase agreement, that amount owing must be deducted from the amount already paid.[56] Thus, a delivery charge would be deducted if the borrower had failed to pay it. However for the purposes of this example, it will be assumed that there are no such charges outstanding.
(d) The unpaid balance of the total price. Having ascertained these amounts, the court can then decide whether or not to make a transfer order. Such an order can be made if section 133(3) is satisfied, which says: 'a transfer order shall be made only where the paid-up sum exceeds the part of the total price referable to the transferred goods by an amount equal to at least one-third of the unpaid balance of the total price'.

48. If a transfer order has been made in respect of some of the goods, and a return order made in respect of the remainder, and the borrower refuses to comply with the return order, the court may not revoke the transfer order. The court can, however, revoke the return order and require that the borrower pay the balance of the hire purchase price in respect of those goods.[57]

54 Section 133(1)(b)(ii).
55 Section 133(7).
56 Section 133(2).
57 Section 133(6).

Example

49. Take the example of a hire purchase agreement for a dining-room table and chairs. Assume that the cash price of the dining-room table is £250 and that of the chairs £750 and that under the hire purchase agreement under which they are hired, the borrower has to pay a deposit of £300 and 12 monthly instalments of £100 (the last instalment includes the option to purchase fee). Suppose further that the borrower pays the deposit and five monthly instalments and then nothing further, causing the lender to serve a default notice under section 87. The default notice requires the borrower to pay off the arrears within 14 days of receipt (or longer) or the lender will terminate the agreement and repossess the goods. The lender then issues proceedings for the recovery of the dining-room table and chairs.

50. The total hire purchase price is £1,500; the total amount paid under the agreement is the deposit of £300 and five instalments, or £800 in all. The unpaid balance is £700 in the example here. The part of the total hire purchase price attributable to the dining room table is 25 per cent (i.e. £375). Can a transfer order be made in respect of the dining-room table?

51. The answer is yes. The paid-up sum (£800) exceeds the part of the price attributable to the transferred goods (£375) by £425. In order for a transfer order to be made, this amount must equal or exceed at least one-third of the unpaid balance of £700 (i.e. £233.33). Accordingly, this condition is satisfied here in relation to the dining-room table and the court then is free to transfer the dining-room table to the borrower.

52. In the example here, assume that the borrower refuses to return the dining-room chairs, a return order having been made in relation thereto. On a lender's application to the court, the court might require that the borrower no longer be obliged to return the chairs but must instead pay the remainder of the total hire purchase price applicable to them. On the facts of the example, 75 per cent of all sums payable are attributable to the chairs so that 75 per cent of the balance outstanding, or £525, will be the amount payable if the borrower refuses to comply with the return order in relation to the chairs.

Procedure

53. The application must, in England and Wales, be made by the lender to the county court[58] and will be governed by the Consumer Credit Act procedure contained in Practice Direction 7B. In the case of a hire purchase or conditional sale agreement, the claim may only be brought in the county court for the district in which the borrower resides or carries on business.[59]

58 Section 141(1).
59 Paragraph 4.1 Practice Direction 7B.

In the case of protected goods, there is a procedure available to a hirer whereby he or she can admit the claim but put forward terms for the suspension of a return order under section 135(1)(b).[60]

54. If the lender is concerned about the integrity of the goods pending the hearing, the lender can apply for a protection order safeguarding the goods in the meantime.[61]

Powers of the court in respect of unfair relationships

55. The CCA 1974 conferred a large number of remedies on the court in circumstances when the court found that a credit agreement was an extortionate credit bargain. The touchstone of such a bargain was that the borrower was required to make payments that were grossly exorbitant or that the bargain otherwise contravened the ordinary principles of fair dealing.[62]

56. The requirements were not easily satisfied and in practice the courts were slow to label a bargain as extortionate. In its White Paper 'Fair, clear and competitive: the consumer credit market in the 21st century',[63] the government expressed the conclusion that existing powers to reopen extortionate credit bargains failed to provide adequate consumer protection.

57. This led to the provisions relating to the reopening of extortionate credit bargains to be repealed by the Consumer Credit Act 2006 to be replaced by the current provisions giving the court extensive powers once the court finds the relationship between a borrower and lender to have been unfair. The 2006 Act inserted new sections, 140A–140D, into the 1974 Act.[64]

The extent of the jurisdiction

58. The jurisdiction exists in relation to a 'credit agreement' entered into by a creditor and an individual in any amount.[65] The jurisdiction exists in relation to exempt as well as regulated agreements, although it does not apply to regulated mortgage contracts or home purchase plans since such credit agreements are subject to regulation by the FCA.[66]

59. The court's powers to regulate an unfair relationship are made retrospective in that the provisions can be applied to an agreement

60 Paragraph 8, Practice Direction 7B.
61 Section 131.
62 Section 138(1).
63 Cmd 6040 at paragraph 3.30.
64 Section 140D has now been repealed.
65 Section 140C(1); the term individual is defined in section 189(1).
66 Section 140A(5).

concluded before the Consumer Credit Act 2006 came into force.[67] The qualification is that an agreement 'completed' before 6 April 2008 cannot now be challenged as having arisen as a result of an unfair relationship. An agreement is completed for these purposes if all payments due or become due under an agreement were made prior to 6 April 2008.[68]

60. However, an agreement completed before 6 April 2008 could still theoretically be attacked on the basis that it is an extortionate credit bargain.[69] The limitation period applicable to claims to reopen an extortionate credit bargain is 12 years from the date of the agreement, unless a claim is made seeking repayment of sums already paid (which would be the case with a completed agreement), in which case the limitation period is six years.[70] Such claims are therefore now likely to be statute barred.

The matters to which the court will have regard

61. A court, in deciding whether the relation between borrower and lender was unfair, is not precluded by the fact that the relationship may have come to an end.[71] The court can consider the following aspects of the relationship in deciding whether or not there is unfairness.

62. The court is directed to consider any of the terms of the agreement or any related agreement.[72] Obviously, the charges payable under the credit agreement in question will be very relevant. There is no definition of the term 'related agreement'. It is obviously not to be confined to linked transactions.

63. The court is also directed to consider the lender's exercise of and enforcement of its rights subsequent to the date of the agreement.[73] In that the court can now consider how the lender has behaved subsequent to entry into the agreement, this marks a change from the approach adopted by the courts previously in relation to alleged extortionate credit bargains, where the focus of the court was on the terms of the agreement at the date of entry. In *Nash v Paragon Finance*,[74] it was submitted that the court should find that a bargain was extortionate because of the way that the lender had subsequently increased interest rates under a variable interest rate clause. The Court of Appeal held that this was irrelevant. Now, however, how the lender operates a variable interest rate clause could, if appropriate, form the basis of a finding of an unfair relationship.

67 Paragraph 14 Schedule 3 Consumer Credit Act 2006.
68 Paragraph 1(2) Schedule 3.
69 Paragraph 15 Schedule 3.
70 *Rahman v Sterling Credit* 2001 1 WLR 496.
71 Section 140A(4).
72 Section 140(1)(a).
73 Scction 140(1)(b).
74 2002 1 WLR 685.

64. An example of an unfair relationship arising out of the subsequent conduct of a lender arose in *Re London Scottish Finance Ltd.*[75] The case concerned certain loan agreements that were irremediably unenforceable because of non-compliance with statutory requirements. Notwithstanding this, the lender sent letters to the relevant borrowers demanding payments and informing them that if payments were not made, their homes would be at risk. This conduct was said to give rise to an unfair relationship and payments made in response to such letters should be returned.[76]

65. Likewise, the court can consider things done by or on behalf of the creditor, before or after the agreement.[77]

66. The construction of the words 'on behalf of' in this context has been considered by the Supreme Court in *Plevin v Paragon Personal Finance Ltd.*[78] The contest was between a narrow and a broad construction, whether unfairness could derive only from the conduct of persons for whom the lender had some legal responsibility, or whether it extended to the conduct of all persons that had provided input into the entry into the credit agreement. On the facts in that case, the question was whether the acts of a broker, not the agent of the lender, could be imputed to the lender for the purpose of a finding of unfair relationship. The Supreme Court has held that the words 'on behalf of' connote agency; it refers to things done or not done for which the lender has responsibility.[79]

67. In *Scotland v British Credit Trust,*[80] the Court of Appeal held that the deemed agency provisions contained in section 56 of the Act also applied when considering whether an unfair relationship existed. In that case, a relationship was rendered unfair because of misstatements made to the borrower by a deemed agent that induced entry into an expensive PPI policy. Nor was it correct to argue that because a misrepresentation might be time barred in the sense that recourse might be unavailable against the perpetrator of the misrepresentation, it should be left out of an unfairness assessment.[81] The Act requires relevant matters to be taken into account without limitation of time.[82]

75 2013 EWHC 4047.
76 *Re London Scottish Finance* at [30].
77 Section 140A(1)(c).
78 2014 UKSC 61 reversing 2013 EWCA Civ 1658.
79 2014 UKSC 61 at [30].
80 2014 EWCA Civ 790.
81 *Scotland* at [82].
82 *Patel v Patel* 2009 EWHC 3264 at [64].

Unfairness

68. The Act gives no guidance on the central question of what constitutes an unfair relationship other than to say that the court may look at all matters it considers relevant.[83] The absence of guidance has been contrasted with the position in relation to other statutes where at least a checklist has been provided.[84]

69. Once unfairness is alleged, the burden of proof is on the lender to disprove unfairness.[85] A finding of unfairness has been characterised as a finding that, provided the first instance judge has taken into account all relevant factors, should be respected and not susceptible to appeal.[86] There is an analogy with a finding of unreasonableness in connection with a contract term where the appellate court will place great weight on the decision of the judge at first instance.[87]

70. In *Deutsche Bank (Suisse) SA v Khan*,[88] Mr Justice Hamblen comprehensively analysed, on the basis of existing authority,[89] the various factors that the court was likely to have regard.[90] The general discussion of what is meant by commercial good faith by Lord Bingham in *Director-General of Fair Trading v First National Bank plc*[91] will also assist. The court will also consider relevant guidance published by the FCA and OFT including OFT 1107, 'Irresponsible lending: OFT guidance for creditors'.[92] Voluntary codes of practice may also be taken into account as establishing appropriate standards of good conduct.[93]

71. The regulatory context is obviously central to any consideration by the court of whether or not an unfair relationship exists; the court will have to pay close attention to whether a lender and any intermediary complied with relevant regulatory requirements in assessing whether a relationship was unfair. The Court of Appeal cases of *Harrison v Black Horse Ltd*,[94] *Conlon v Black Horse Ltd*[95] and *Plevin v Paragon Personal Finance Ltd*[96] were all

83 Section 140A(2).
84 *Harrison v Black Horse Ltd* 2011 EWCA Civ 1128 at [37].
85 Section 140B(9).
86 *Harrison v Black Horse Ltd* 2011 EWCA Civ 1128 at [28].
87 *George Mitchell (Chesterhall) v Finney Lock Seeks Ltd* 1983 2 AC 803 at [816].
88 2013 EWHC 482 (Comm).
89 *Maple Leaf Macro Volatility Master Fund v Rouvroy* 2009 EWHC 257 (Comm), *Paragon Mortgages Ltd v McEwan-Peters* 2011 EWHC 2491, *Rahman v HSBC Bank plc* 2012 EWHC 11.
90 At [345], [346].
91 2002 1 AC 481 at 494F-G.
92 March 2010.
93 *Plevin* at [68].
94 2011 EWCA Civ 1128.
95 2013 EWCA Civ 1658.
96 2013 EWCA Civ 1658.

concerned with the sale of PPI insurance in conjunction with a loan agreement. The sale of such insurance products is subject to mandatory rules, namely the Insurance Conduct of Business Rules ('ICOB'), introduced in 2005 as part of the FSA Handbook. The court considered whether there had been any breach of ICOB in deciding whether the lender's relationship with a borrower was unfair.

72. Indeed, the case of *Harrison v Black Horse Ltd* appears to establish a general principle that a relationship can *only* be considered unfair if there was a breach of a regulatory requirement or other unlawfulness.

73. In that case, the lender, Black Horse Ltd, in addition to the loan, sold the claimant a PPI policy of insurance costing £10,200. The lender charged a commission of 87 per cent of the premium for the insurance policy, which was not disclosed to the claimant. The Court of Appeal considered this level of commission to be 'quite startling and there will be many people who regard it as unacceptable conduct on the part of lending institutions to have profited in this way'.[97] However, there was no requirement in ICOB that the commission should be disclosed absent a request from the borrower.

74. In the circumstances, the Court of Appeal felt unable to make a finding of an unfair relationship. The court said: 'It would be an anomalous result if a lender was obliged to disclose receipt of commission in order to escape a finding of unfairness under section 140A of the Act but not yet obliged to disclose it pursuant to the statutorily imposed framework under which it operates'.[98]

75. Nor did the court consider that the mere size of the charge could lead to a finding of unfairness: 'A seller is not ordinarily obliged to warn his buyer that his product is expensive when compared to other similar products and in my judgment it is telling that in this highly regulated market no such obligation has been imposed'.[99]

76. This decision was followed with reluctance in a later Court of Appeal decision of *Conlon v Black Horse Ltd.*[100] It was not found to be a valid point of distinction that had Mrs Conlon known about the level of commission, she would have tried to obtain a cheaper policy elsewhere.[101] The decision in *Harrison v Black Horse Ltd* has now been overruled by the Supreme Court.[102] Given the high level of commission, fairness demanded that the lender should have revealed the size of the commission. Inequality of financial expertise is capable of rendering a relationship unfair and give rise to a positive duty to explain.

97 *Harrison* supra at [58].
99 *Harrison* supra at [58].
99 *Harrison* supra at [59].
100 2013 EWCA Civ 1658.
101 *Conlon* at [22].
102 *Paragon Personal Finance Ltd v Plevin* UKSC 61.

Procedure

77. The borrower or surety can raise the issue of the existence of an unfair relationship by bringing an application in the county court, or, in Scotland, the sheriff court.[103] The issue can also be raised by a borrower or surety in defence to proceedings to enforce a credit agreement or any related agreement to which the lender and borrower are parties.[104] More widely, the issue can also be raised by the borrower or surety in any claim where the amount payable under the credit agreement or the relevant agreement is in contention.[105]

78. In England and Wales, if the borrower or surety is making the application in accordance with section 140B(2)(a), the borrower or surety should use the Consumer Credit Act procedure set out in Practice Direction 7B.[106] This includes serving the Particulars of Claim with the claim form.[107] It may be necessary for the court to add parties to the proceedings in order to enable the appropriate relief to be ordered, and this will be done at the instigation of a borrower or surety.[108]

79. In the case of a claim brought by a lender or owner to enforce an agreement and the borrower or hirer wishes to allege an unfair relationship by way of defence to the claim, the borrower or hirer should serve a notice of intention in this respect on every other party to the claim within 14 days of service of the claim form.[109] This will be the equivalent to serving a defence for the purposes of the Consumer Credit Act procedure.[110]

80. Once the court has found the existence of an unfair relationship, it has a wide range of options open to it, both in relation to a credit agreement and in relation to a relevant agreement; for instance, the court can order sums to be repaid to the borrower or a surety and it can order that liabilities be discharged. It can order security be returned to a surety.[111] The court can make an order for repayment against a lender even where the party in original receipt of the monies has been a different party to a relevant agreement.[112]

103 Section 140B(4).
104 Section 140B(2)(b).
105 Section 140B(1)(c).
106 Paragraph 3.1(5), Practice Direction 7B.
107 Paragraph 5.2, Practice Direction 7B.
108 Section 140B(8).
109 Paragraph 10.2, Practice Direction 7B.
110 Paragraph 10.3, Practice Direction 7B.
111 Section 140B(1)(d).
112 Section 140B(3).

Financial Ombudsman Service

81. The Consumer Credit Act 2006 conferred a specific consumer credit jurisdiction on the Financial Ombudsman Service even though at that time most lending and hiring were not activities regulated by the RAO.[113] This specific jurisdiction is no longer appropriate now that credit-related activities have become authorised activities pursuant to the amendments made to the RAO as from 1 April 2014.

82. The Financial Ombudsman Service now has jurisdiction to hear complaints in relation to all regulated activities,[114] as well as specifically lending money secured by a charge on land[115] and other types of lending.[116] It will also continue to deal with complaints referred under the previous consumer credit regime and hear new credit-related complaints that arose out of events prior to 1 April 2014 provided that those complaints would have fallen within the previous regime.[117]

Referring a complaint to the Financial Ombudsman Service

83. A complaint should only be referred to the Financial Ombudsman Service once the complaint has first been made to the relevant firm. How the firm should handle that complaint is governed by DISP Chapter 1 of the Handbook and has been discussed earlier. The complainant can then go on to refer the matter to the Financial Ombudsman Service if dissatisfied with the response to the complaint made by the firm, or if the firm fails to give a response within the eight-week period specified for responding to a complaint.

84. The Financial Ombudsman Service will only consider a complaint if, for present purposes, the complainant is a *consumer*[118] (i.e. a natural person acting outside the course of business).[119] Furthermore, the complainant must be *eligible*.[120] In the consumer credit context, for practical purposes, anyone directly affected by the activities of a regulated credit-related activity is almost certain to be eligible within DISP 2.7.3 R. The complaint can be made by an agent, someone acting on behalf of a complainant, for instance

113 Section 226A Financial Services and Markets Act 2000.
114 DISP 2.3.1 R.
115 DISP 2.3.1(3) R.
116 DISP 2.3.1(4) R.
117 DISP 2.3.2-A G.
118 DISP 2.7.3(1) R.
119 FCA Handbook Glossary.
120 DISP 2.7.1 R.

a solicitor, regardless of whether that person would him or herself be an eligible complainant.[121]

85. The Financial Ombudsman Service will only consider a complaint that is referred to the Financial Ombudsman Service in time. This means that it must be brought within *six months* of receipt by the complainant of the final response from the relevant firm against which complaint was made.[122] However, in this context, 'final response' has a precise meaning.[123] Specifically, as well as giving the outcome of the complaint, the final response must, in addition, point out the existence of the six-month time limit for referral to the Financial Ombudsman Service, and a Financial Ombudsman Service leaflet should accompany the final response.[124] If there is no final response (as defined) to a complaint, then the relevant time limit for referral of a matter to the Financial Ombudsman Service is six years from the time that the events in question took place or, if later, three years from the time that the relevant events complained of came to the attention of the complainant.[125]

86. The Financial Ombudsman Service has discretion to consider a complaint that is referred to it outside the time limits if the failure to lodge in time arose out of exceptional circumstances.[126] Such exceptional circumstances may include incapacity.[127] Further, if the firm the subject matter of the complaint does not raise an objection based on late submission of the complaint to the Financial Ombudsman Service, the Financial Ombudsman Service is not bound to take the point itself.[128]

87. Further, the Financial Ombudsman Service will not consider a complaint referred to it too early. At least eight weeks must have elapsed from the time that the complaint was referred to the firm before it can be referred to the Financial Ombudsman Service.[129] If a complaint has not been referred to the relevant firm, or if eight weeks has not elapsed, then the Financial Ombudsman Service will refer the matter to the relevant firm to deal with the complaint and issue a final response.[130]

88. A lender must not institute court proceedings once it appears that the borrower has referred what may be a valid complaint to the Financial Ombudsman Service.[131]

121 DISP 2.7.2 R.
122 DISP 2.8.2(1) R.
123 DISP 2.8.3 G.
124 DISP 1.6.2(1) R.
125 DISP 2.8.2(2) R.
126 DISP 2.8.2(3) R.
127 DISP 2.8.4 G.
128 DISP 2.8.2(5) R.
129 DISP 2.8.1(2) R.
130 DISP 3.2.2 R.
131 Ombudsman NC 7.15.10 R.

Procedure of the Financial Ombudsman Service

89. The Financial Ombudsman Service may dismiss a complaint without considering its merits in a number of different circumstances. These include if the Financial Ombudsman Service considers that the complainant has not suffered any loss, or that the complaint is frivolous or clearly does not have any realistic prospect of success.[132]

90. The Financial Ombudsman Service may also dismiss a complaint without considering the merits if it has already been the subject of court proceedings that have been determined on the merits,[133] or if it is subject to *ongoing* court proceedings (unless the proceedings are stayed, either by agreement or order of the court, for the express purpose of allowing the Financial Ombudsman Service to consider the matter).[134] Furthermore, the Financial Ombudsman Service is entitled to conclude that the dispute, perhaps by the nature of the difficulty of legal issues involved or its complexity, would be better dealt with by way of court proceedings rather than by the Financial Ombudsman Service.[135]

91. The Financial Ombudsman Service has a residual discretion not to hear a complaint where 'there are other compelling reasons why it is inappropriate for the complaint to be dealt with under the Financial Ombudsman Service'.[136] In some instances, the Financial Ombudsman Service may dismiss a claim so it can form the subject of a test case.[137]

92. Assuming that the complaint falls to be determined, the Financial Ombudsman Service must then investigate it by whatever means appear to the Financial Ombudsman Service to be most appropriate.[138] Both sides will be given an opportunity to make representations.[139] The Financial Ombudsman Service may decide that a hearing is appropriate, but a hearing will often not be necessary.[140] A party may request a hearing[141] but this does not mean that the Financial Ombudsman Service will agree. It is for the Financial Ombudsman Service to decide the form of the hearing, which may be by telephone.

93. A firm must cooperate fully with the Financial Ombudsman Service.[142] The Financial Ombudsman Service has the right to call for the production of specific documents or information provided that these are

132 DISP 3.3.4 R.
133 DISP 3.3.4(8) R.
134 DISP 3.3.4(9) R.
135 DISP 3.3.4(10) R.
136 DISP 3.3.3(17) R.
137 DISP 3.3.5 R.
138 DISP 3.5.1 R.
139 DISP 3.5.4(1) R.
140 The decision of the Financial Ombudsman Service not to have a hearing was upheld in *R (Heather Moor & Edgecomb Ltd) v Financial Ombudsman Service* 2008 EWCA Civ 642.
141 DISP 3.5.5 R.
142 DISP 1.4.4 R.

necessary for the determination of the complaint.[143] If a person fails to produce a document, the Financial Ombudsman Service can ask the person to state the whereabouts of the document.[144] Indeed, if a firm fails to cooperate, the Financial Ombudsman Service can refer the matter to the High Court and it can be treated as if it were a contempt of court.[145] In due course, the Financial Ombudsman Service will send a provisional assessment to the parties and both sides will have an opportunity to comment within a defined time frame.[146]

The award of the Ombudsman

94. In reaching a determination, the Ombudsman must act in a manner that is fair and reasonable. That does not necessarily require the Ombudsman to give a ruling that reflects the parties' strict legal position.[147] The matters that the Ombudsman will take into account are the relevant legal principles applicable to the complaint, regulatory guidance, codes of practice and what the Ombudsman considers to have been good industry practice at the time.[148]

95. The Ombudsman will give each party a signed determination, together with reasons.[149] The complainant will be asked whether he or she accepts the determination within a specific time frame. If the complainant accepts the determination within the time specified, it is binding on both parties and can then be enforced against the respondent. If the complainant does not accept the determination, neither side will be bound by it.[150] The complainant may be able to accept the determination out of time if the failure to comply was due, in the view of the Financial Ombudsman Service, to exceptional circumstances, and provided the complainant has not previously positively rejected the determination.[151] If the complainant accepts the award of the Ombudsman, the complainant will not be able to bring a damages claim covering the same subject matter: *Clark v In Focus Asset Management and Tax Solutions Ltd* 2014 1 WLR 2502.

96. The determination of the Ombudsman may include a money award, which can include compensation for financial loss, pain and suffering, damage to reputation, distress and inconvenience, 'whether or not a court would award compensation'.[152] So the amount of the award is not a strict mathematical exercise and the Ombudsman has considerable discretion in the matter.

143 Section 231 Financial Services and Markets Act 2000.
144 Section 231(5).
145 Section 232.
146 DISP 3.5.4(2) R.
147 *R (Heather Moor & Edgecomb Ltd) v Financial Ombudsman Service 2008* EWCA Civ 642.
148 DISP 3.6.4 R.
149 DISP 3.6.6(1) R.
150 DISP 3.6.6 R.
151 DISP 3.6.6(4A) R.
152 DISP 3.7.2 R.

97. The Ombudsman can also make an award of interest[153] and costs, including interest on costs,[154] but a complainant cannot be ordered to pay the costs incurred by a respondent firm.[155] Furthermore, an award of legal costs is unlikely to be made in favour of a complainant as the view of the Financial Ombudsman Service is that normally legal advice is not needed to make a complaint to the Service.[156]

98. The award can also require the respondent firm to take certain steps and this requirement is enforceable in the courts by injunction.[157]

99. Section 299(4) of the Financial Services and Markets Act 2000 allows a financial cap to be imposed on the amount of compensation. It is currently £150,000,[158] having previously been £100,000 up until 1 January 2012. The maximum applies to the sum awarded and does not apply to interest and costs that may be ordered in addition to the maximum amount.[159]

100. The award can be enforced as if it is a county court judgment.[160]

101. Either the complainant or the respondent may be able to challenge the lawfulness of an award in judicial review proceedings, and a number of such applications have been made. However, given the relatively wide discretionary powers given to the Ombudsman in making his or her award, a successful challenge will be unusual.

102. The Financial Ombudsman Service will keep a register of each money award made.[161] The Financial Ombudsman Service must publish a report of the determination but, unless the complainant agrees, it will not identify the complainant.[162]

153 DISP 3.7.8 R; the rate is at the discretion of the Ombudsman.
154 DISP 3.7.9 R.
155 Section 230(3).
156 DISP 3.7.10 E.
157 Section 229(9).
158 DISP 3.7.4 R.
159 DISP 3.7.5 G.
160 Schedule 17 paragraph 16 Financial Services and Markets Act 2000.
161 DISP 3.7.7 R.
162 Section 230A Financial Services and Markets Act 2000.

Index

accounts, statements of *see* statements of account, duty to provide
advertisements 96–104
  controlled investments and activities 109
  credit agreement not secured on land 98–99
  exempt transactions 275
  general provisions 98–99
  information provision requirements 98
  Mortgages and Home Finance: Conduct of Business 275
  statutory provisions 96–97
  telephone calls 98
  see also financial promotions
agreements
  Agreements Regulations
    of 1983 133–134
    of 2010 132–133
    failure to comply with 134
    notice to debtor 132
    operation 130–132
  borrower-lender *see* borrower-lender agreements
  borrower-lender-supplier *see* borrower-lender-supplier agreements
  cancellable 161–164
  see also cancellation
  concluded, withdrawal from 159–160
  conditional sale *see* conditional sale agreement
  consequences 141
  Consumer Credit Act (1974)
    regulated and exempt agreements for purposes of 46–47
    service under 151–154
    variation of agreement 149–150
  continuous payment authorities 317–319
  copy *see* copy agreements
  credit *see* credit agreements
  credit token 304–308
  debt management 340
  entry into
    formalities 143–146
    interest rate variation 148–149
    outside formalities requirements 128–134
    overdraft agreements 128, 312–313
    pawn agreements 321–322
    with unauthorised persons 80
  excluded 137
  executed, duty to supply copy of 134–136
  fixed sum *see* fixed sum agreements
  hire, where payments exceed £25,000 56
  hire purchase *see* hire purchase agreement
  interest rate variation 148–149
  land-related *see* land-related agreements
  lease *see* lease agreements
  modifying 150–151, 161, 164
  multiple 18–20
  open-end credit 198–199
  outside formalities requirements 128–134

overdraft *see* overdraft agreements
with persons insufficiently authorised 80–81
regulated and exempt (CCA 1974 and RAO) 46–47
rent back *see* rent back agreements
running account *see* running account agreements
secured on land, formalities involving 141–146
applicable agreements 141–142
pre-contract requirements 142–143
service
under Consumer Credit Act (1974) 151–154
manner of 152–153
timing of 153–154
small 17–18
supply of copies 137–141
variation 146–150
waiver 130
withdrawal
from concluded agreement 159–160
from a modifying agreement 161
see also withdrawal
ancillary credit activities
credit brokers, conduct 329–333
credit reference agencies, regulation
consumer, right to seek correction of an entry 337–339
obligations of agency 335–337
obligations of lender and credit broker 333–335
debt advice and debt management
debt management agreement 340
debt solution proposed 341
financial statement 340
operating debt management agreement 341
requirements prior to contract 339
electronic lending 342–344
operation 329–344
antecedent negotiations
liability of lender for conduct of negotiator 200
anti-avoidance provisions
small agreements 17
appointed representatives
authorisation 73–75
apportionment and oversight function
authorisation 69–70
approved persons
duties and disciplining of 91–92
APR (annual percentage rate) 29–30
advertisement of regulated credit agreements not secured on land 98–99
Agreements Regulations 133
assumptions to be made when calculating 30–31, 33
calculation 291
high-cost short-term credit 320
Mortgages and Home Finance: Conduct of Business 276
arrangements
borrower-lender agreements versus borrower-lender-supplier agreements 12–13
arrears
collection of 216–219
quantum understated 232
recovery of
dealing with customers in arrears 299–301
information provision 301–302
record keeping 301
repossession proceedings 302–303
repayment plans 217, 218
arrears notices
contents 221–222
electronic lending 344
failure to serve 223
fixed sum credit agreements 219–220, 222
running account agreements 220–221, 222
assignment
collecting payments following 218–219
associated persons
borrower-lender agreements versus borrower-lender-supplier agreements 13

authorisation
appeals 77–78
application for 64–67
appointed representatives 73–75
approved persons, duties and disciplining of 91–92
breach of requirements
agreements made through unauthorised persons 81–82
entry into agreements with persons with insufficient authorisation 80–81
entry into agreements with unauthorised persons 80
civil consequences for breach of requirements 80–85
discretionary enforcement by court 83–84
discretionary enforcement by FCA 84–85
unenforceability 82
consideration of application 64
continuing regulatory powers and obligations following 86–95
controlled functions 68–71
criminal liability for acting without 78–79
discretionary enforcement 83–85
exemption for professionals 75–77
failure to obtain approval 70–71
FCA powers 38, 84–85
insufficient authorisation, entry into agreements with persons with 80–81
interim permission and transitional arrangements 71–73
offences 79
own initiative requirement power 86–87
payment collection following assignment 218
peer to peer lending (P2P) 61, 62
procedure for determining applications 67–68
reference to tribunal 77–78
threshold conditions 65–67
unauthorised persons
agreements made through 81–82
consequences of unenforceability 82
disciplinary action against 89–91
entry into agreements with 80

bailment
consumer hire agreements 15
balance of probabilities
circulars to minors 105–106
timing of service 154
banks/bank accounts
cheques, negotiation 265–266
linked transactions 158
negotiable instruments, as security 263–270
barristers
exemptions relating to 58, 59, 63
bills of exchange
security considerations 263, 264
borrower
actions following service of a default notice 233
consent to recovery of goods 243–244
contacting by lender 217
death, enforcement following 246–247
defined 5–6
entry into agreements, formalities 145–146
goods given by in part exchange 179–180
goods received by, prior to cancellation 177–179
high net worth borrower exemption, RAO 55–56
information, right to 184–187
consequences of failure to comply 186–187
copy agreements 186
statement of information 185–186
money paid by, prior to cancellation 173–174
money paid to, prior to cancellation 174–177
statements of account, duty to provide 187–192
termination by 244–245

borrower-lender agreements
versus borrower-lender-supplier agreement 9, 11–14
canvassing off trade premises 102–104
secured loans 52–53
borrower-lender-supplier agreements
versus borrower-lender agreements 9, 11–14
linked transactions 21
low number of payments exemption 53, 54
secured loans 52
small 17
breach of supply contract, liability of lender for
applicable agreements 204–205
cash price in excess of £30,000 208
extent of liabilities 206–207
extra-territorial effect 208
goods, rights against 207–208
statutory indemnity 205–206
bridging loans
mortgages 280, 297
burden of proof
circulars to minors 105
credit token agreements 307–308
pawn agreements 325
timing of service 154
unfairness 210, 359
business loan
further advances with 290
business model
threshold conditions 67

cancellation
agreements not genuinely cancellable 139–140
Agreements Regulations (2010) 132
consequences
effect on main agreement 171–172
linked transactions, effect on 172–173
money paid prior to cancellation 173–174
continuous payment authorities 227
contractual rights 167
definition of cancellable agreement 161–164
effects on security provided 180–181
exemption from second cancellation notice 166
by FCA 86–88
formalities required with a cancellable agreement 164–166
exemption from second cancellation notice 166
failure to comply with 167–169
one copy 165–166
goods given by borrower in part exchange 179–180
goods received by borrower, hirer or relative prior to 177–179
hire contracts, disclosure of information 123
method 169–170
money paid by borrower, hirer or relative prior to 173–174
money paid to borrower by lender prior to 174–177
negotiator 162, 163
notices 165–166, 169, 170
off-premises contracts 183
oral representations by negotiator 163
redelivery, categories of goods excluded from requirement to make 179
statutory provisions
Consumer Contracts Regulations 182–183
Consumer Credit Act (1974) 161, 171–181
Distance Marketing Regulations 181–182
canvassing
borrower-lender and ancillary credit agreements off trade premises 102–104
regulated activities 59
capitalisation
arrears recovery, mortgages 300–301
capital repayment
total charge for credit 34
ceilings, financial *see* financial ceilings
charges
early repayment 298–299
mortgages

early repayment charges 298–299
payment shortfall charges 299
regulating level 297–299
total charge for credit *see* total charge for credit
chattels
deposit of 253–254
cheque
negotiation of 265–266
circulars
to minors 104–106
clients
protection of money and assets 70
club membership
total charge for credit 29
CMA *see* Competition and Markets Authority (CMA)
Code for Crown Prosecutors
principles set out in 79
Codes of Practice
duties and disciplining of approved persons 91
Competition and Markets Authority (CMA)
complaints referred to 214
enforcement powers 190, 210, 215
regulatory history 38
complaint handling
referring to Financial Ombudsman service 362–363
rights and duties of lender/owner 247–250
compliance oversight function
authorisation 70
CONC *see* Consumer Credit sourcebook (CONC)
conditional sale agreements
liability of lender 209
recovery of goods under 238–246
addition of goods 242–243
consent by borrower 244–245
contraventions of section 92 239–240
procedure on application to recover 245–246
protected goods 240–241
termination by borrower 244–245
when goods become protected 241–242
wrongful repossession, consequences 245
termination
comparison with early settlement 196–197
consequences 193
exercising termination right 192–193
financial consequences 194–195
return of goods 193–194
worked example 195–196
transfer orders 353
conditions and warranties
cancellation 163
connected lending transactions
liability of lender 209
consideration periods
entry into agreements 143
consumer credit
regulatory history 35–38
Consumer Credit Act (1974)
amendment 36–37
cancellation under 161, 171–181
contraventions of section 92 239–240
credit broking 57
disciplinary action against authorised persons 89
enforcement orders 348
interrelation between sections 56 and 75 208–209
lenders acting without consumer credit licence 80
negotiable instruments, as security 268
protected goods 241
regulated and exempt agreements for purposes of 46–47, 51
reporting 92
service of agreement under 151–154
variation of agreement under 146, 149–150
withdrawal under 156–161, 171–181
Consumer Credit Act (2006)
arrears notices 219
regulatory history 37

consumer credit agreements
definitions 3–6
open end, other than overdraft 34
relevant agreements 4
Consumer Credit Appeals Tribunal
licensing appeals, hearing of 37
Consumer Credit Handbook (CONC)
advertisements/financial promotions 96, 97, 99
APR, calculation 291
arrears collection 216–217
arrears notice obligations 344
continuous payment authorities 225
credit broking 330
credit reference agencies, regulation 334
credit token agreements 304
creditworthiness assessment 126, 127
electronic lending 342
high net worth borrower exemption, RAO 55
hire agreements entered into by high net worth individuals 56
hire agreements where payments exceed £25,000 56
pre-contract requirements 142, 143, 312
recovery of goods 243
significance 42
total charge for credit 26–29, 32–33
Consumer Credit Legislation (Goode) 1–2
consumer hire
regulatory history 35–38
consumer hire agreements
defined 14–16
consumers
definitions 5
right to seek correction of an entry 337–339
continuing regulatory powers and obligations
cancellation or variation by FCA 86–88
notification of change in control 94–95
prohibition order 88–89
reporting 92–95
continuous payment authorities (CPAs)
cancellation 227
high-cost short-term credit 317–319
operating 226
using 225–227
control, change in
notification of 94–95
controlled functions
authorisation 68–71
types 68–69
copy agreements
form of copies to be supplied 138–141
Information, right to 186
original requirements 137–141
overdraft agreements 313–314
pre-contract requirements 125
surety, rights of 254, 255–257
County Court, Northern Ireland
enforcement orders 348
Court of Appeal
appeals to 77
courts
discretionary enforcement by 83–84
enforcement orders
application for 347–348
irredeemable unenforceability 346–347
power to make 345–348
procedure 348
when needed 345–346
recovery of goods
example 355
procedure 355–356
return orders 352–353
transfer orders 353–355
time orders
court powers 349–350
effect 350–351
power to make 348–352
procedure 351–352
when can be sought 348–349
unfair relationships
extent of jurisdiction 356–357
matters to which court will have regard 357–358
procedure 361–362
unfairness 359–361

CPAs *see* continuous payment authorities (CPAs)
credit
  amount 30
  concepts 1–3, 45
  for more than £25,000 for business purposes 51
  obtaining for specific purpose 11
  restricted and unrestricted use 9–11, 177
  timing of provision 30
  timing of repayment 30–31
  see also total charge for credit
credit activity, conduct of particular types
  credit token agreements 304–308
  high-cost short-term credit 316–320
  overdraft agreements *see* overdraft agreements
  pawn agreements 320–328
  see also ancillary credit activities
credit agreements
  advertisement 98–99
  ancillary, canvassing off trade premises 103–104
  categories 19
  consequences of cancellation and withdrawal 171–172, 173
  credit sale 209
  defined 1, 16
  and hire agreements 16
  regulated, not secured on land 98–99
  separate 18
  small 17
  unfair relationships 356
credit brokerage
  defined 57
credit broking
  conduct of credit brokers 329–333
    brokerage fees, return of 331–333
    fees and commissions 331
  controlled investments and activities 110
  credit reference agencies, obligations of credit broker in respect of 333–335
  exclusions 58–59
  goods to be sold by broker to creditor 201–202
  promotions by credit brokers 100, 276
  regulated activities 57–59
credit card agreements
  connected lending transactions 209
  monthly repayments 305
  as running account agreements 7, 8
credit limit
  credit token agreements 305
  defined 7
  financial ceilings 8–9, 150
creditor
  defined 4
  goods sold to by credit broker 201–202
credit reference agencies
  consumer, right to seek correction of an entry 337–339
  obligations 335–337
  regulated activities 62–63
credit sale agreements
  liability of lender 209
credit token agreements
  conduct 304–308
  copies 138
  misuse of tokens 306–308
  and running account agreements 7
  small 17
credit unions
  specialist sourcebook 43
creditworthiness assessment
  overdraft agreements 312
  pre-contract requirements 126–127
criminal sanctions
  financial promotions, illegal 112
current accounts
  linked transactions 158

Data Protection Act (1998)
  credit reference agencies 335–336
death of borrower/hirer
  enforcement following 246–247
debentures
  security types 252
debt adjusting
  financial promotion 101
  regulated activities 59, 60

debt administration
financial promotion 276
regulated activities 59, 61
debt advice and management
debt management agreement 340, 341
debt solution proposed 341
financial statement 340
operating debt management agreement 341
requirements prior to contract 339
debt collecting
regulated activities 59, 61
debt counselling
financial promotion 101, 276
regulated activities 59, 60
debt management agreements
requirements in relation to 340
debtor-creditor-supplier agreements
consequences of cancellation and withdrawal 172, 173
extent of a lender's liabilities 206
part-exchange, goods given in 180
restricted use 134
small 129
debts
disputed 218
default notices/default sum notices 223–224
actions of borrower following service of default notice 233
consequences of failure to serve 224
contents of default sum notice 224
default information sheet 231
errors in default notice 232–233
general form and contents of default notices 228–229
interest on default sum 224
invalid, effects of 234–235
pawn agreements 327–328
requirement for default notice 227–235
service of default notice 231–232
specific information to be included in default notices 229–231
types of breach specified 229
when needed 227–228
defects in title
negotiable instruments 263
deferment of payment
credit 1, 2
Department of Enterprise
publications of 101
deposit accounts
linked transactions 158
Director General of Fair Trading
regulatory history 35
disciplinary action
against authorised persons 89–91
disclosure of information
Disclosure of Information Regulations (2004) *see* Disclosure of Information Regulations (2004)
Disclosure of Information Regulations (2010) *see* Disclosure of Information Regulations (2010)
Financial Services (Distance Marketing) Regulations (2004) 121–122
hire contracts 122–123
see also information provision; pre-contract requirements
Disclosure of Information Regulations (2004)
applicability 113–115
hire agreements 113
information to be provided under 114–115
non-compliance, consequences 115
Disclosure of Information Regulations (2010)
applicability 117
authorised non-business overdraft agreement 120–121
distance contracts 120
pawn agreements 120
pre-contract information 118
telephone contracts 118–119
discretionary enforcement
by court 83–84
by FCA 84–85
dispensing notices
statements of account, duty to provide 189

distance contracts/marketing
  hire contracts, disclosure of information 123
  pre-contract requirements 115–116, 120
  telephone contracts 119
  see also off-premises contracts
documents of title
  pawn agreements 321
drawdown
  total charge for credit 33

electronic lending *see* peer to peer lending (P2P), electronic
enforcement
  Competition and Markets Authority, powers of 190, 210, 215
  discretionary 83–85
  enforcement and termination notices 236–238
  following death of borrower or hirer 246–247
enforcement orders
  application for 347–348
  irredeemable unenforceability 346–347
  power to make 345–348
  procedure 348
  when needed 345–346
errors
  default notices 232–233
excluded agreements
  supply of copies 137
execution-only transactions 281–284
  policy and record keeping 283–284
  procedure for sale 282–283
extortionate credit bargains
  court powers 356

fair dealing
  principles of 356
fees and commissions, credit broking
  return of fees 331–333
financial assistance
  appeals 77
  and credit 3
financial ceilings
  defined 8–9
  general abolition 150
Financial Conduct Authority (FCA)
  and authorisation
    application for 64
    controlled functions 68–69
    discretionary enforcement in relation to 84–85
    failure to comply with 70
    interim permission 72, 73
    procedure for determining applications 67, 68
    professionals, exemptions for 77
  and cancellation of agreements 86–88, 166, 170
  on capitalisation of mortgages 300–301
  complaints to 190
  and continuous payment authorities 226
  criminal proceedings brought by 79
  discretionary enforcement by 84–85
  general functions 37–38
  Handbook *see* Handbook, FCA
  on high-cost short-term credit 318, 319
  powers 38–40, 77
  Regulatory Decisions Committee *see* Regulatory Decisions Committee, FCA
  regulatory history 37–38
  Rules, financial limits 16
  unfairness, tackling 215
  warning notices *see* warning notices
financial consequences
  termination of conditional sale or hire purchase agreement 194–195
  withdrawal from agreement 159
financial limit
  defined 16
Financial Ombudsman Service
  award of 365–366
  complaint handling 248
  procedure following referral to 364–365
  referring a complaint to 362–363
Financial Policy Committee
  interest rates 293

financial promotions
advertisement of regulated credit agreements not secured on land 98–99
circulars to minors 104–106
controlled activities and investments 108–110
credit agreements secured on land 99–100
by credit broker 100
exempted communications 110
exempt transactions 274–275
general provisions 98–99
introductions 275
invitation or inducement 107
misleading statements 112
non-real time communication 274, 275–277
not in writing 101
quotations 101–104
real time communication 274–275, 277
regulated mortgage contracts 273–277
solicited real time communication 274
unfair practices by lenders 100
unlawful 106–108, 111–112
unsolicited real time communications 274–275
Financial Services (Distance Marketing) Regulations (2004)
pre-contract requirements 121–122
Financial Services and Markets Act (2000)
acting without authorisation, criminal liability 78
appointed representatives 73
change in control, notification 94
entry into agreements with unauthorised persons 80
and Financial Conduct Authority 36, 38, 39
Financial Ombudsman Service 366
interim permission, authorisation 72
tribunal, reference to 77
unlawful promotions 106
Financial Services and Markets Tribunal
reference to (prior to 2010) 77
Financial Services Authority (FSA)
FCA as successor to 37
regulatory history 36–37
fixed sum agreements
annual statements, content 190–191
arrears notices 222, 219–220
defined 6–9
instalment statements 191–192
statements of account with 190
total charge for credit 33
floating charges
debentures 252
foreign transactions
financing 51

GABRIEL electronic reporting system
reporting requirements 93
general interest test
total charge for credit 55
goods
addition of 242–243
given by borrower in part exchange 179–180
protected 240–242
received by borrower prior to cancellation 177–179
recovery
addition of goods 242–243
consent by borrower 243–244
contraventions of section 92 239–240
court powers 352–356
example 355
under hire purchase, conditional sale and hire agreements 238–246
procedure 245–246, 355–356
protected goods 240–241
return orders 352–353
termination by borrower 244–245
transfer orders 353–355
when goods become protected 241–242
wrongful repossession, consequences 245

return of following termination of agreement 193–194
rights against 207–208
sold/proposed to be sold by credit broker to creditor 201–202

governing function
authorisation 69

green deal consumer credit agreements
and borrowers 5

guarantee contracts
linked transactions 158

guarantees
versus indemnities 252

Handbook, FCA
approved persons (APER) 42, 91
Consumer Credit sourcebook *see* Consumer Credit sourcebook (CONC)
decision procedure and penalties (DEPP) 43, 71, 89, 90
disputes (DISP) 248
enforcement (EG) 43, 79
general (GEN) 41
Glossary 41, 42, 225, 316
manuals 40–41
modules 40–41
Mortgages: Conduct of Business (MCOB) *see* Mortgages and Home Finance: Conduct of Business (MCOB)
perimeter guidance (PERG) 43, 47, 96
principles for businesses (PRIN) 41
sourcebooks 40–41
structure and interpretation 40–43
Block 1 (high level standards) 41–42
Block 2 (prudential standards) 42
Block 3 (business standards) 42
Block 4 (regulatory processes) 42–43
Block 5 (redress) 43
Block 6 (specialist sourcebooks) 43
tailored handbooks 43
SUP (supervision) 42, 74, 93, 94, 95, 250
SYSC (senior management arrangements, systems and controls) 41
threshold conditions (COND) 42, 65
see also approved persons; mortgages; supervision

harassment
by lender 217

high-cost short-term credit (HCSTC) 316–320
agreements and continuous payment authorities 317–319
APR cap 320
rolling over agreements 319

high net worth individuals
exemption, RAO 55–56
hire agreements entered into 56–57
loans to 290, 294–295

hire agreement/hire purchase agreements
cancellation 183
and credit 2–3
definition of hire agreement 16
disclosure of information, hire contracts 113, 122–123
goods received by hirer prior to cancellation 177–179
high net worth hirers 56–57
improper execution 258
liability of lender 209
money paid prior to cancellation 173–174
recovery of goods under 238–246
addition of goods 242–243
consent by borrower 244–245
contraventions of section 92 239–240
procedure on application to recover 245–246
protected goods 240–241
termination by borrower 244–245
when goods become protected 241–242
wrongful repossession, consequences 245
regulated 47
right of hirer to terminate 197–198
security types 252
and small agreements 17

termination
comparison with early settlement 196–197
consequences 193
exercising termination right 192–193
financial consequences 194–195
return of goods 193–194
worked example 195–196
time orders 350
transfer orders 353
hirers
death, enforcement following 246–247
goods received by prior to cancellation 177–179
high net worth 56–57
money paid by, prior to cancellation 173–174
termination right 197–198
holder in due course
security considerations 263, 264, 268
home purchase plans
controlled investments and activities 109
Mortgages and Home Finance: Conduct of Business 271
Regulated Activities Order 49–50
home reversion plans
controlled investments and activities 109
Mortgages and Home Finance: Conduct of Business 271
Regulated Activities Order 49–50

illegality, financial promotions 106–108
consequences 111–112
imprisonable offences
advertisements and financial promotions 103, 104, 112
pawns 321
regulated activities 44
see also penalties
indemnities
versus guarantees 252
individual
borrower as 5
Information Commissioner
Privacy Notices Code of Practice 330
information provision
arrears, recovery of 301–302
borrower's right to information 184–187
consequences of failure to comply 186–187
copy agreements 186
statement of information 185–186
pre-contract requirements, overdraft agreements 311–312
regulated activities 45
regulated contracts, following entry into 286–290
statement of information, right to 185–186, 255–257
see also disclosure of information
Insolvency Service
publications of 101
insurance contracts/policies
linked transactions 158
security 251–252
interest rates
advertisements 98
credit token agreements 305
entry into agreement 146, 148–149
Financial Policy Committee recommendation 293
overdraft agreements 314–315
interest roll-up mortgages
description 296
interim permission
authorisation 72–73
investments
regulated activities 45, 47
Irresponsible Lending Guidance
Office of Fair Trading 304

judicial review
authorisation 77

land charges
transfer 260–262
Land Registry certificates
copies 141
land-related agreements
financial promotions 99–100

formalities involving 141–146
applicable agreements 141–142
following agreement 146
pre-contract requirements 142–143
purchase of land on mortgage for non-residential purposes 52
total charge for credit 32
lease agreements
equipment leases 197
no deemed agency with 202–203
lending
borrow-lender agreement/borrower-lender supplier agreement 11–14
credit reference agencies, obligations of lender in respect of 333–335
electronic system in relation to 61–62
liability of lender
for breach of supply contract 204–209
for conduct of negotiator 199–203
peer-to-peer *see* peer to peer lending (P2P)
responsible 291–297
affordability assessment 292, 294
income assessment 292–293
loans only for business purposes/high net worth individuals 294–295
outgoings, assessing 293–294
policy 294
rights and duties of lender/owner
arrears, collecting 216–219
arrears notices, sending out 219–224
collecting payments following assignment 218–219
disputed debts 218
unfair practices by lenders 100
see also loans
licensing appeals
hearing by Consumer Credit Appeals Tribunal 37
life insurance
low number of payments exemption 54
limitation periods
failure to obtain approval for authorisation 70
linked transactions
cancellation, effect on 172–173
defined 20–22
exceptions 22, 158
purpose 21–22
secured loans 53
and security 21
surety, extent of liability of 257
total charge for credit 27
types 158
withdrawal, effect on 157–158
liquidation of debts
debt counselling 60
loans
borrower-lender agreements 11
bridging 280, 297
execution-only transactions 279
to high net worth individual 290, 294–295
secured 52–53
only for business purposes 294–295
see also lending
location of offices
threshold conditions 66

minors
circulars to 104–106
pawn agreements 321
misleading statements
financial promotions 112
modifying agreements
applicable rules 150–151
definitions 147
effect of Consumer Credit Act 164
withdrawal from 161
Money Advice Service
information sheet 301
pre-contract requirements 339
Mortgage Lending Administration Return
reporting requirements 93
mortgages
administration 48
alteration in payment amounts 289–290
annual statements 287–288
APR, calculation 291

arrears, recovery of
dealing with customers in arrears 299–301
information provision 301–302
record keeping 301
repossession proceedings 302–303
bridging loans 280, 297
business loan, further advances with 290
capitalisation 300–301
charges
early repayment 298–299
excessive 298
payment shortfall 299
regulating level 297–299
charges, regulating level 297–299
direct debt requests, refusal 300
and Financial Services Authority 36
further advances 288–289, 290
ineffective, power of sale in case of 262–263
interest-only 287, 295–296
interest roll-up 296
notification of changes in terms 288
offer 285–286
payment plans, inability to achieve 301
purchase of land for non-residential purposes 52
rate switches and removal of a party 289
regulated contracts 47–49
assessing suitability of 279–281
financial promotions 273–277
information to be given following entry into 286–290
see also Mortgages and Home Finance: Conduct of Business (MCOB)
responsible lending 291–297
security types 252
surplus on sale of property 303
Mortgages and Home Finance: Conduct of Business (MCOB) 271–303
alteration in payment amounts 289–290
annual mortgage statements 287–288
APR, calculation 291
arrears, recovery of
dealing with customers in arrears 299–301
information provision 301–302
record keeping 301
repossession proceedings 302–303
assessing suitability of regulated mortgage contract 279–281
bridging loans 280, 297
business loan, further advances with 290
business standards 42
charges
early repayment 298–299
excessive 298
payment shortfall 299
regulating level 297–299
charges, regulating level 297–299
execution-only transactions 281–284
policy and record keeping 283–284
procedure for sale 282–283
financial promotions of regulated mortgage contracts 273–277
exempt transactions 274–275
non-real time 275–277
real time 277
further advances 288–289, 290
general principles of conduct of business 272–273
home finance activity 271
illustration, providing customer with 284–285
initial disclosure by firm to customer on initial contract 277–279
interest-only mortgages 295–296
interest roll-up mortgages 296
mortgage offer 285–286
notification of changes in terms 288
and powers of FCA 40
rate switches and removal of a party 289
regulated mortgage contracts
assessing suitability of 279–281
financial promotion of 273–277
information to be given following entry into 286–290
responsible lending 291–297
scope 271–273
see also mortgages

multiple agreements
  defined 18–20

negotiable instruments, as security 263–270
  non-compliance, statutory 267
  statutory exceptions 266–267
  taking payment, security and negotiating a cheque 265–266
  third party rights in a negotiable instrument 268–269
  types of instrument 265
negotiator
  cancellable agreements 162, 163
  liability of lender for conduct of 199–203
  oral representations by 163
  role 199–200
non-commercial agreements
  arrears notices 344
  borrowers' rights 184, 190, 210
  cancellation 162
  creditworthiness assessment 126
  defined 22–24
  electronic lending 342
  entry into 142, 149
  formalities requirements 128
  lenders' duties 219, 228, 237
  pawn agreements 321
  pre-contract requirements 113
  running account agreements 187
  security considerations 256, 266
  unfair relationships 24
  withdrawal 156, 157
non-residential purposes
  purchase of land on mortgage for 52
notices
  arrears
    contents 221–222
    fixed sum credit agreements 219–220, 222
    running account agreements 220–221
  cancellation 165–166, 169, 170
  default sum 223–224
  dispensing (statements of account) 189
  rescission 203–204
  termination 236–238
    form and contents 237–238
  withdrawal 156–157, 160
notification requirements
  change in control 94–95

Office of Fair Trading
  and cancellation of agreement 170
  and Consumer Credit Act 2006 37
  interim permission and transitional arrangements 71, 72
  Irresponsible Lending Guidance 304
  regulatory history 36
  residual role 38
off-premises contracts
  cancellation 183
  canvassing 59, 102–104
  disclosure of information 123
  see also distance contracts/marketing
on-premises contracts
  disclosure of information 123
open-end credit agreements
  termination 198–199
overdraft agreements 308–316
  authorised business overdraft 309–310
    copy agreements 313
    entry into 135–136
    interest rate variation 314
    variation 149
  authorised non-business overdraft
    Disclosure of Information Regulations (2010) 117
    entry into 128, 135–136
    interest rate variation 314
    pre-contract requirements 120–121
    repayment more than three months later 310
    variation 149
  copy 313–314
  creditworthiness assessment 312
  emergencies 313–314
  entry into 128, 135–136, 312–313
  interest rate variation 314–315
  non-authorised 313
  pre-contract information, disclosure 311–312
  as running account agreements 7

signature 313
tacit agreement to allow 315
termination of arrangement 315–316
total charge for credit 34
variation 149
withdrawal 314
own initiative requirement power
authorised persons 86–87

P2P *see* peer to peer lending (P2P)
part-exchange
goods given in 179–180
Particulars of Claim
enforcement orders 348
time orders 351
pawn agreements 320–328
borrower's right to redeem 323–324
consequences of failure to redeem 324–325
default notice 327–328
documents of title 321
pre-contract requirements 120
realisation of the pawn 326–327
record keeping 323
regulatory requirements regarding entry 321–322
time order, application for 328
peer to peer lending (P2P), electronic
arrears notice obligations 344
authorisation 61, 62
controlled investments and activities 110
credit broking 58
credit reference agencies 63
debt collecting 61
high-cost short-term credit 316
P2P agreement, withdrawal right 343
pre-contract information and explanations 342–343
regulated activities 61–62
withdrawal right from a P2P agreement 343
penalties
acting without authorisation approval 70, 71
circulars to minors 104–106
financial 89, 90
see also imprisonable offences
plain language requirement
unfair contract terms 211
pledges
security types 252
pre-contract requirements
copy of prospective agreement 125
creditworthiness assessment 126–127
debt advice and debt management 339
Disclosure of Information Regulations (2004)
applicability 113–115
information to be provided under 114–115
non-compliance, consequences 115
Disclosure of Information Regulations (2010) 117–121
authorised non-business overdraft agreement 120–121
distance contracts 120
pawn agreements 120
pre-contract information 118
telephone contracts 118–119
distance contracts/marketing 115–116, 120
electronic lending 342–343
explanations 123–125, 312
Financial Services (Distance Marketing) Regulations (2004) 121–122
hire contracts, disclosure of information 122–123
information, disclosure 113–115
information provision
overdraft agreements 311–312
land-related agreements 142–143
pawn agreements 120, 321
professional firms
specialist sourcebook 43, 75
prohibition orders
continuing regulatory powers and obligations following authorisation 88–89
promissory notes
security considerations 263, 264, 266

Prudential Regulation Authority
regulatory history 37, 38
public censure
disciplinary action 89

quotations 101–104
canvassing borrower-lender ancillary credit agreements off trade premises 102–104
credit broking 329

realisation
ineffective security 260
of pawn 326–327
record keeping
arrears, recovery of 301
execution-only transactions 283–284
pawn agreements 323
redemption rights
borrower 323–324
failure to redeem, consequences 324–325
regulated activities
canvassing exception 59
concepts/requirements 44–46
credit broking 57–59
credit for more than £25,000 for business purposes 51
credit reference agencies 62–63
debt adjusting 59, 60
debt administration 59, 61
debt collecting 59, 61
debt counselling 59, 60
foreign transactions, financing 51
gas, electricity and water meters 56
high net worth borrower exemption 55–56
hire agreement entered into by high net worth hirers 56–57
hire agreement where payments exceed £25,000 56
home purchase plans 49–50
home reversion plans 49–50
investments 45, 47
lending, electronic system in relation to 61–62
low number of payments exemption 53–54
purchase of land on mortgage for non-residential purposes 52
regulated mortgage contracts 47–49
rent back agreements 49–50
total charge for credit exemption 55
Treasury specifications 45
Regulated Activities Order (RAO)
regulated and exempt agreements for purposes of 46–47, 50–57
Regulatory Decisions Committee, FCA
application for authorisation, determining 68
cancellation or variation of authorisation 87, 88
disciplinary action 90, 91
warning notices 90
regulatory framework
regulatory history of consumer credit and consumer hire 35–38
statutory provisions 37
rent back agreements
controlled investments and activities 109
Regulated Activities Order 49–50
repayment plans
arrears collection 217, 218
reporting
continuing regulatory powers and obligations 92–95
repossession proceedings
arrears, recovery of 302–303
credit agreements secured on land, promotion of 99, 100
electronic lending 342, 343
as last resort 300
time orders 349
rescission
service of notice 203–204
resources
threshold conditions 66–67
restricted and unrestricted use credit
defined 9–11, 177
part-exchange, goods given in 180
see also debtor-creditor-supplier agreements
return orders
recovery of goods 352–353

revolving credit
running account agreements as 6, 7
risk statements
financial promotion 276
rule of 78
early repayment charges 298
running account agreement
defined 6–9
running account agreements
arrears notices 220–221, 222
sanctions 189–190
statements of account, duty to provide 187, 189–190
total charge for credit 34

sale, power of
ineffective mortgage security 262–263
sale and lease back
Mortgages and Home Finance: Conduct of Business 271
Secretaries of State
licensing appeals powers transferred to Consumer Credit Appeals Tribunal 37
regulatory framework 35
secured loans
Regulated Activities Order 52–53
security
cancellation, effects on 180–181
continuing rights of surety
further copies of agreement, right to receive 255–257
further copies of security agreement, right to receive 255–257
statement of information, right to 255–257
withdrawal 255
definitions 251
formalities 253–255
ineffective 259–260
instrument *see* security instrument
land, agreements secured on 141–146
applicable agreements 141–142
financial promotions 99–100
pre-contract requirements 142–143
liability of surety, extent of 257
and linked transactions 21
mortgage, ineffective, power of sale in case of 262–263
negotiable instruments as 263–270
provision and regulation 251–270
total charge for credit 27
transfer of land charges 260–262
types 252–253
security instrument
copies, right to receive 255–257
formalities involving 253–255
improper execution 258
and surety 253
Senior Courts Cost Office/Office Guide
appeals 78
service
of agreement
under Consumer Credit Act (1974) 151–154
manner of service 152–153
timing of 153–154
of default notice 231–232, 233
of rescission notice 203–204
services
advance payment for 2
Sheriff Court, Scotland
enforcement orders 348
side agreements
and linked transactions 21
signature
overdraft agreements 313
significant influence
controlled functions 69–70
significant management function
authorisation 70
simple interest
default sum 224
small agreements
debtor-creditor-supplier 129
defined 17–18
solicitors
exemptions relating to 58–60, 63
split orders
hire purchase or conditional sale agreements 353
statement of information, right to
borrower 185–186
surety 255–257

statements of account, duty to provide
  annual statements, fixed sum 190–191
  content of statement 187–188
  dispensing notices 189
  failure to comply, consequences 191
  fixed sum agreements 190
  fixed sum instalment statements 191–192
  running account agreements 187, 189–190
  where compulsory 188–189
store card agreements
  monthly repayments 305
  as running account agreements 7, 8
suitability
  threshold conditions 67
supervision
  supervisory notice 87
  threshold conditions 66
  see also under Handbook, FCA
supplier, identity of
  restricted and unrestricted use credit 10
surety
  continuing rights 255–257
  defined 253
  extent of liability 257
  and security instrument 253
systems and controls function
  authorisation 70

tax relief
  APR calculation 30
telephone contracts
  pre-contract requirements 118–119
termination
  by borrower 244–245
  enforcement and termination notices 236–238
    form and contents 237–238
  hire purchase or conditional sale agreements 192–197
    ambiguous letters sent by borrower 193
    comparison with early settlement 196–197
    consequences of termination 193
    exercising termination right 192–193
    financial consequences 194–195
    hirer's right to terminate 197–198
    return of goods 193–194
    worked example 195–196
  open-end credit agreements 198–199
  overdraft agreements 315–316
third party rights
  negotiable instruments 268–269
threshold conditions
  authorisation 65–67
time orders
  application for 328
  arrears notices 223
  effect 350–351
  power to make 348–352
  procedure 351–352
  when can be sought 348–349
title deeds
  deposit of 253–254
total charge for credit 24–33
  APR 29–31
  assumptions 33–34
  charges to be taken into account 32–33
  Consumer Credit sourcebook (CONC) 26–29, 32
  exempted categories of charge 28–29
  land-related agreements 32
  RAO exemption relating to 55
  TCC Regulations 25, 26–29, 32
trade premises
  canvassing off 59, 102–104
transfer orders
  recovery of goods 353–355

unauthorised persons
  agreements made through 81–82
  consequences of unenforceability 82
  disciplinary action against 89–91
  entry into agreements with 80
uncertain events
  total charge for credit 31
unexecuted agreements
  copies 138
  formalities of entry 145

unfair contract terms
  challenging 209–215
  core exclusion 211–212
  illustrative terms, list of 213–214
  individual challenge to fairness 214
  plain language requirement 211
  regulatory challenge 214–215
  unfairness test
    applying 212–213
    when applicable 210–211
  when regulations apply 210
unfair practices
  advertisements and financial promotions 100
  credit brokers, conduct 329–330
unfair relationships
  extent of court jurisdiction 356–357
  matters to which court will have regard 357–358
  procedure 361–362
  unfairness 359–361
Upper Tribunal
  reference to (from 2010) 77–78

variable rate
  land-related agreements 32
variation
  under Consumer Credit Act (1974) 149–150
  by FCA 86–88

waiver
  agreements outside formalities requirements 130
warning notices
  application for authorisation, determining 67–68
  cancellation of authorisation 87
  disciplinary action 90
  failure to obtain approval for authorisation 70–71
  prohibition orders 89
weights and measures
  and Competition and Markets Authority 38
withdrawal
  common law right 155–156
  from a concluded agreement 159–160
  under Consumer Credit Act (1974) 156–161
  double glazing example 157–158
  and duty to supply copy of executed agreement 135
  effect 160
  financial consequences 159
  linked transaction, effect on 157–158
  notice 156–157, 160
  overdraft agreements 314
  from a P2P agreement 343
  problems 155
  statutory consequences 171–181
    effect on main agreement 171–172
    linked transactions, effect on 172–173
  surety, rights of 255
  upon whom notice served 156–157